THE ARCHAEOLOGY
OF THE ISRAELITE
SETTLEMENT

ISRAEL FINKELSTEIN

THE ARCHAEOLOGY
OF THE ISRAELITE
SETTLEMENT

ISRAEL EXPLORATION SOCIETY
JERUSALEM 1988

Translated by D. Saltz
Layout and cover — A. Pladot
Plates — Tafsar Jerusalem

PRINTED IN ISRAEL
BY BEN-ZVI PRINTING ENTERPRISES, LTD.

ISBN 965-221-007-2

PUBLISHED· WITH THE ASSISTANCE OF
THE DOROT FOUNDATION, NEW YORK

Table of Contents

List of Figures and Plates

10

ACKNOWLEDGEMENTS

A major part of this book was first conceived as a Ph.D. dissertation which I wrote at Tel-Aviv University — *The ʿIzbet Ṣarṭah Excavations and the Israelite Settlement in the Hill Country (1983),* under the supervision of Prof. Moshe Kochavi, whose assistance and encouragement was of great help. This is a revised and updated version of the Hebrew book, which was published in 1986 by Hakibbutz Hameuchad Publishing House and the Israel Exploration Society.

I would like to thank the following individuals and institutions who assisted me in various stages of my field work and in preparation of this book:

To Bar Ilan University, under whose auspices I undertook my field research, especially to Prof. Yehuda Feliks, Chairman of the Department of the Land of Israel Studies, who assisted greatly in initiating the Shiloh excavations and the Land of Ephraim survey, and to Arieh Arzi, Assistant Chairman, who helped with the research in every possible way.

To the Institute for Advanced Studies, the Hebrew University of Jerusalem, where the manuscript was prepared for publication in 1983/4. During that year , I took part in a study group which discussed "Basic Problems of the History of Israel in Biblical Times in view of Historical and Archaeological Research". I would like to express my gratitude to those who participated in the seminars and field trips: The late Prof. Yigael Yadin, Prof. Abraham Malamat, Prof. Pinhas Artzi, Prof. Baruch Halpern, Prof. Siegfried Herrmann, Dr. Amihai Mazar, Dr. Alan Millard, Prof. Lawrence Stager and Prof. Henri Cazelles — all of whom contributed to my views of the Settlement process. The Institute's staff was also extremely helpful in every respect.

To the National Council for Research and Development that aided the Land of Ephraim Regional Project in the years 1983–1986; to the Memorial Foundation for Jewish Culture, New York; to the Archaeological Staff Officer in Judea and Samaria; to Yad Izhak Ben-Zvi and to the Cherna and Dr. Erving Moskovitz Chair for the Study of the Land of Israel, Bar Ilan University, who all supported the research.

To the Dorot Foundation, New York, without whose help this book could not have been published, and to Dr. Daniella Saltz, who translated the manuscript.

To the team who participated in the work in Shiloh and the Land of Ephraim survey, in particular Pnina Ben Hanania, Shlomo Bunimowitz, Amalia Katznelson, Zvi Lederman and Shmuel Yosef. Special thanks are due to Judith Dekel, Bernardina Luttinger and Ora Paran, who prepared many of the illustraitons and to Moshe Weinberg and Yoram Weinberg who took some of the photographs.

To my colleagues Zvi Gal, Adam Zertal, Avi Ofer and Raphael Frankel, who supplied me with valuable information about their surveys and to my friend Benjamin Sass who advised me on many issues.

To my teachers, colleagues and friends, Prof. Gösta W. Ahlström, Dr. Pirhiya Beck, Dr. Diana Edelman, Dr. Zeev Herzog, Prof. Emanuel Marx, Dr. Zeev Meshel, Prof. Nadav Na'aman, Orna Zimhoni and Dr. Baruch Rosen, with whom I discussed many of the views expressed throughout this book.

CHAPTER 1

INTRODUCTION AND HISTORY OF RESEARCH

The Settlement of the Israelites in the 12th and 11th centuries BCE, and their transformation from a society of isolated tribes into an organized kingdom, is one of the most exciting, inspiring, and at the same time controversial chapters in the history of the Land of Israel. For decades, scholars have wrestled with this stormy period[1] from various points of view: the biblical narrative, historical geography, and archaeology. Nonetheless, the subject as a whole has remained problematic, difficult to understand, and, in some cases, utterly obscure. The seeds of scholarly controversy germinated even before archaeology became a primary tool for the study of antiquity, at a time when research focused solely on the biblical source.

As the major excavations of the 1920s and 1930s began to produce finds that were interpreted in the context of the biblical description of the conquest of Canaan, considerable interest was aroused. However, for reasons that will be explained later, not only did the problems that were then of particular interest remain unsolved, the arguments even intensified. The theological implications of this issue further heated up the emotionally charged atmosphere surrounding these debates. Albright, who founded one of the most important "schools" of research into the period, clearly expressed the singularity of this era when he summarized, for the first time, the implications of archaeological findings on "the date of the Hebrew Conquest of Palestine."

> There have been few problems in the field of the historical interpretation of Palestinian archaeological data which have fascinated scholars so much as the one described in our title. At the same time, there have been few problems which have seemed so elusive (1935:10).

---

1 The historical concept "Settlement period" or "period of the Settlement and Judges" is synonymous with the term "Early Israelite period" and with the archaeological definitions "Iron I" and "Early Iron Age." Whatever the label, the period spans the time from the end of the Late Bronze period until the beginning of the Israelite Monarchy. (On the terminology and the chronological framework, see Aharoni 1982:153–158, Kochavi 1984:21–22, and Kempinski 1985.) Throughout this work Settlement with a capital "S" is used to describe the process of the emergence of the Israelites, while settlement with a lower case "s" is used in its regular meaning.

Over 50 years have passed since these words were written. Archaeological activities have expanded and are now at the crux of research on Israelite Settlement (for the use of the term "Israelite" in the book see Chapter 2), yet most of the quandaries that perplexed scholars more than a generation ago have not been resolved. Furthermore, despite the excavation of sites central to the biblical narrative of the Israelite conquest — such as Hazor, Ai, Bethel, Lachish, and Arad — and the many and varied finds they have yielded, no clear-cut answers can be given to the critical questions concerning the nature of the Settlement process, its precise date, the relations between the settlers and the Canaanite population, the origins of the newcomers, etc.

As is well known, interpretations of the biblical narratives concerning the conquest and Settlement of the Land of Israel have been numerous and conflicting. Over the years, many have even given up hope that archaeological evidence could help solve the enigmas of this perplexing period. Not only have the accumulating archaeological data been accepted or rejected by each "school" in accordance with its basic ideology, but the data themselves have, to some extent, increased the confusion and despair.

By the 1930s, two of the three principal approaches to the reconstruction of the process of Israelite Settlement in Canaan had already taken shape. Closely following the first chapters of the Book of Joshua, the Albright school envisioned a uniform military conquest, leaving devastated Canaanite cities in its wake; the destruction layers at the end of the Late Bronze period at sites such as Lachish, Bethel, and Hazor were taken as conclusive evidence of the validity of this scenario. The Alt school, on the other hand, hypothesized the slow and peaceful infiltration of a semi-nomadic population into uninhabited regions, where they subsequently became sedentary; only at a later stage did this infiltration lead to confrontations with the Canaanite strongholds in the valleys. Several important scholars associated with this school, which has gained strength since the 1950s, were even skeptical that archaeology had anything to contribute to the illumination of the period.

The source of this skepticism was, no doubt, the growing perception that the findings heralded by the Albright school as solid evidence in their favor were, in fact, vague and open to more than one interpretation. Noth, the most aggressive proponent of this position, understood the "Gordian Knot" of research into this era: The study of biblical traditions underlay the interpretation of the archaeological finds, and these, in turn, were adduced to explain the biblical narratives (1960:278). According to him,

> We must recognize the fact that even in light of archaeological research, there are fewer certainties about these historical events than we are willing to admit, and that the meaning of the archaeological finds, against a background of written traditions, is much more problematic and complicated than is apparent at first glance... (1938:22; see also 1960:271–282).

Only 15 years ago, Weippert, another scholar of the German school, who knew how to correctly evaluate the new archaeological evidence that was then coming to light in the hill country, nonetheless insisted that:

> The result is largely negative or, at the very best, uncertain.... it seems obvious to me that the archaeological side of the balance, both in general and in individual cases, can have only little weight. The weight of proof falls almost entirely on the literary traditions (1971:135–136).

Indeed, if we take into account the nature of the evidence that was offered in the past, those critics who denied the validity of any archaeological contribution were certainly justified. Practically the only avenue of research open for archaeological investigation of the Settlement period was the excavation of the destruction layers of the large Canaanite tells and their attribution to the activities of the Israelite tribes. However, most of these mounds were located in the Shephelah, the coastal plain, and the northern valleys, regions that, for the most part, lay outside the boundaries of the initial Israelite Settlement. Moreover, it is impossible to determine with certainty that these cities were all devastated at the same time. As for the agents of destruction, the critics rightly observed that during the period of unrest from the mid- 13th to the mid-12th centuries BCE, there were other groups afoot in the land who could have perpetrated these deeds.

This avenue of research — excavating the large Canaanite tells — not only utterly failed to produce the anticipated results, but also amounted to concentrating on the nugatory instead of the significant, which is, of course, the *direct* archaeological investigation of the Settlement period, i.e., the examination of the sites in the central hill country, where most of this historical process took place.

The first landmark in direct archaeological research into the period of Israelite Settlement was Albright's excavation of Tell el-Fūl, just north of Jerusalem, in 1922. Here, for the first time, the remains of a settlement that could be dated to the early Iron period were discovered, and the typical pottery of the Iron I sites of the hill country was defined. The next 15 years witnessed extensive archaeological activities in the central hill country and adjacent areas, as Iron I strata were exposed at Tell en-Naṣbeh (biblical Mizpah) near Ramallah (by Badè, 1926–1935); Tell Beit Mirsim in the southern upper Shephelah (by Albright, 1926–1932); Shiloh (by Kjaer, 1929); Beth-zur north of Hebron (by Sellers, 1931); Bethel (by Albright, 1934); and Khirbet et-Tell (identified with biblical Ai), east of Ramallah (by Marquet-Krause, 1933–1935). Thus within a relatively short span of time, a wealth of information concerning the architecture and pottery of the Iron I inhabitants of the hill country was amassed. A major achievement was the discovery at Shiloh of collared-rim store jars in the destruction layer that Albright attributed to the Philistine attack on the site in the wake of their victory over Israel in the battle of Ebenezer in the mid-11th century BCE, an event alluded to in the Bible. But because most of the results of these excavations were vague, they were overshadowed by the finds from the big Canaanite tells.

The next major developments in field research on the Settlement period came in the 1950s, after two decades during which archaeological research in the Land of Israel was minimal: Yadin excavated Hazor, and Aharoni conducted a survey of Upper Galilee. For the first time, different kinds of information — concerning both a major Canaanite mound and an array of small unwalled Iron I sites — from a single region could be combined. At Hazor, Yadin discovered that the Late Bronze town had been destroyed in a fierce conflagration; later, a small settlement was established at the site, whose sparse material culture reflected, in his opinion, a population in the initial stages of sedentarization. Aharoni's pioneering work in Upper Galilee was the first attempt to understand the history of a specific geographical unit by means of a thoroughgoing survey of its sites. His principal conclusion was that the rough, hilly, and relatively inhospitable terrain of Upper Galilee was almost uninhabited in the Late Bronze period, while during Iron I, a series of small unwalled settlements arose. This image accorded well with Alt's understanding of Israelite Settlement.

Yadin and Aharoni, therefore, gave conflicting interpretations to the same archaeological evidence: Yadin maintained that Israelite occupation began only after the destruction of Canaanite Hazor, which is described in the Bible, while Aharoni insisted that Israelite occupation in the rugged hilly area commenced before the destruction of Hazor.

The sharp debate between these two scholars rekindled the confrontation between the "schools" of Albright and Alt. Once again, attention was turned away from the main issues of the Settlement period, for Upper Galilee is distant from the primary sites of Israelite Settlement in the central hills. Moreover, according to our present interpretation of the evidence, Israelite occupation in Upper Galilee began only during a later phase of the period.

The major research breakthrough occurred in the late 1960s. In the aftermath of the Six Days' War, scholars gained access to the central hill country — the region between the Beersheba and Jezreel Valleys — which was the heartland of Israelite Settlement. At the same time, recognition was growing that the problems of the Settlement period could be resolved only by the long and arduous labor of excavating the actual sites of Israelite Settlement in conjunction with extensive surveys in order to arrive at a comprehensive overview of the occupation in these areas.

The earliest of these endeavors were the excavation of Khirbet Raddana on the western edge of Ramallah (by Callaway and Cooley), the continuation of the Ai excavations (by Callaway), and the 1968 Survey of Judea and Samaria (by Kochavi, Kallai, Gophna, and Porath), all of which gave a strong impetus to further research. The early Iron villages at Ai and Raddana were not covered by subsequent occupations, making it feasible to expose areas broad enough to reconstruct their overall plans, while the 1968 Survey discovered over 100 sites with Iron I occupation. Thus the magnitude of early Iron occupation in the central hills — as opposed to other regions of the country — began to be apparent.

However, the 1968 Survey, for all its importance, was selective: Some areas were combed quite thoroughly, while others were hardly touched, and ecological and environmental aspects were not treated. Attempts to base an understanding of Israelite Settlement in the hill country on the 1968 Survey without being aware of its deficiencies led to evaluations that were both incomplete and incorrect.

In the early 1970s, the focus of research on Israelite Settlement once again moved away from the central hill country to a secondary area — albeit one important in and of itself — the Beersheba Valley. The comprehensive regional study undertaken there by Aharoni included, *inter alia*, the excavation of Tel Masōs, in the center of the valley, by Kempinski and Fritz. The large and prosperous Iron I occupation uncovered at the site was considered by the excavators to be an Israelite Settlement site. The results of these excavations led Aharoni to hypothesize that a large influx of people settled in the Beersheba Valley in the Iron I period. He saw this as further evidence supporting his view that Israelite Settlement began in marginal areas that had been uninhabited during the Late Bronze period. Both Kempinski and Fritz — individually — developed theories about Israelite Settlement based on the finds of the Masōs excavations. However, Kochavi and others subsequently disputed the categorization of Tel Masōs as an Israelite site, and these objections have completely undermined the theories of Kempinski and Fritz.

Since the later 1970s, archaeological research on Israelite Settlement in the hill country has accelerated. Important sites were excavated at Giloh and south of Jenin (by A. Mazar), on Mt. Ebal (by Zertal), and at ʿIzbet Ṣarṭah (by Kochavi and the author). Excavation was renewed (by the author) at Shiloh, a sacred center of the population of the hill country in this period. Giloh was instructive on the process of Settlement in Judah. At ʿIzbet Ṣarṭah we were able to examine the phenomenon of Israelite Settlement on the western fringes of the hill country, facing the Canaanite-Philistine coastal plain, and to trace the development of architecture in Iron I. The excavations of Shiloh, with its rich finds, have naturally shed light on many aspects of early Israelite material culture and on the character of the Settlement process.

At the same time, thanks to the comprehensive surveys conducted in various regions, the general picture of occupation in the country as a whole during the Iron I period is becoming increasingly clear. Surveys in Manasseh (by Zertal), Ephraim (by the author), Judah (by Ofer), Western Galilee (by Frankel), and Lower Galilee (by Gal) have mapped over 250 Iron I sites. These studies have emphasized ecological and environmental conditions, which are crucial to understanding the historical development of occupation in each one of these regions.

Despite the many obstacles confronting scholars studying the period of Israelite Settlement, the six decades following Albright's excavation of Tell el-Fūl have witnessed tremendous progress — a veritable revolution — in research.

The view that archaeology has virtually nothing to contribute to the understanding of the Israelite Settlement, which is the heritage of certain members of the peaceful infiltration school, is no longer tenable. Ironically, certain tenets of this school have been strengthened considerably as a result of the regional surveys integrating ecological aspects. In any case, it is clear that some relatively recent attempts to summarize the period of Settlement solely on the basis of the traditional archaeological evidence, without taking into consideration the new regional studies and the recent excavations, are seriously wanting. Although the reservations expressed in the following quotations are partly justified, their conclusions are essentially erroneous.

> Archaeologists would be totally unaware of any important ethnic changes at the end of the Late Bronze Age were it not for the biblical traditions. (Franken 1975:337)

> Otherwise no clear pattern is discernible in the presently available archaeological remains from the LB and Early Iron I periods which can be identified as artifactual data reflecting a specifically Israelite occupation of the land (Miller 1977a:262).

> So far archaeology has failed to make the Israelites "visible" as a new ethnic group in those hill country settlements (de Geus 1975:70).

Yeivin, after a long and detailed discussion of every shred of information from the large tells, came to the conclusion that

> It is quite true that this so to speak evidence presents bare facts, which in themselves have little to say for or against any historical conclusions drawn from them (1971a:68).

Nonetheless, he composed a "precise" reconstruction of the process of Settlement, including specific dates (!). Yeivin's reconstruction is a perfect illustration of the extent to which research on the Settlement has been rife with speculation and imagination. Such works have quickly become obsolete, and the vacuum left in their wake can now be filled with an up-to-date summary of the new evidence.

An additional failing of quite a few of the scholars who have dealt with the Iron I period in recent years is their strictly superficial acquaintance with the region. This has affected their research adversely, because the process of Settlement was intimately connected with the nature of the land itself — the landscape, climate, and economic potential. While examples of this superficiality abound in fairly current publications, they are especially blatant in the works of members of the "sociological" school of Settlement study, since they, even more than others, are in need of a direct familiarity with environmental data. Gottwald, for example, resorted to distant parallels to shore up his opinions (1979:445), totally ignoring relevant population groups still living in traditional ways in the region under study. Likewise, agrarian technological theories of sedentarization, such as the one positing that Settlement in the hill country was made possible by the increasing use of terraces (see Chapter 8), founder on their estrangement from the land and its finds.

It is impossible to come to grips with the Settlement episode without a thoroughgoing acquaintance with at least one region of the hill country — in which the events took place. This means studying its archaeological and ecological components, as well as the patterns of occupation during the periods immediately preceding and succeeding the time of Israelite Settlement.

In our opinion, it is also extremely important to study in depth the one set of settlements for which complete data are available, viz., the montane villages in this area at the beginning of the present century. Whether inferences can be drawn from the settlement pattern and lifestyle of the local inhabitants of only a few generations ago and applied to the study of the Land of Israel during antiquity is a matter of some controversy. In the 19th century, the validity of such an approach was not even questioned. Later, inferences of this type were increasingly regarded with disfavor on the grounds that the method was not sufficiently "scientific." In recent years, however, there has been a renewed willingness to examine the demographic, economic, and social aspects of life in the land of Israel during the late 19th and early 20th centuries as a means of understanding antiquity — and justly so (c.f. Lemche 1985).

For our part, we attach great importance to two areas of ethnographic research: plotting the settlement pattern of Arab villages of the early 20th century as a key to appreciating the economic potential of the area and as a basis for clarifying the demographic developments of settlements in antiquity; and examining the socio-economic phenomena of contemporary groups in the process of sedentarization, notably the Beduin on the eastern and southern desert fringes of the Land of Israel. Although historical research has lately emphasized the importance of the sociological aspect, little attention has been paid to the very special data about the demographic processes at work in our area in recent generations, processes that have been well documented.

* * * * * * * * * * *

In Part I of this work, we will review the archaeological data concerning the Israelite Settlement sites that have accumulated through excavations and surveys. These data are used in the following chapters.

In Part II, we will reconstruct a comprehensive model of Israelite Settlement in the territory of Ephraim in light of the guiding principles outlined above. As clearly reflected in the archaeological evidence and as expressed in the biblical account, the hill country of Ephraim was an important focus of the Settlement process. This region played a major role in the events of the period of the Judges, and the center of the hill tribes in the early 11th century was located in its midst, at Shiloh. In this context, we will offer a preliminary summary of the comprehensive survey that we have conducted in the region since 1980 and discuss the environmental data underlying the development of Israelite Settlement. We will also describe the results of the four seasons of excavations at Shiloh, the most important site in the central hill country at the time. The combination of these two projects, together with the excavations at ʿIzbet Ṣarṭah on the western edge of this region, makes Ephraim the most extensively investigated area of Israelite Settlement.

In Part III of this work, we will attempt to trace the beginnings of Israelite material culture, while in Part IV, we will explore the historical aspects of the Settlement process.

The present study is primarily concerned with archaeology and settlement history. We will hardly touch upon the biblical evidence at all (except for site identifications etc.). Without in any way minimizing the singular importance of the Bible for the study of the history of Israel, attempts to reconstruct the process of Israelite Settlement by means of traditional biblical archaeology — by seeking direct correspondences between excavated finds and the biblical text — have been notoriously unsuccessful. This was due, *inter alia*, to the fact that the Book of Joshua, the primary biblical source, was redacted centuries after the period it describes and thus reflects, in no small measure, the way that Israelite Settlement was interpreted in Jerusalem at the end of the period of the Monarchy (e.g. Lemche 1985: 357–385). Scholars are therefore divided over the basic issue of understanding the biblical sources themselves.

We believe that archaeological research in our generation must first attempt to reconstruct the process of Settlement on the basis of new work in the field; only later will it be possible to return to the biblical narrative in a fresh attempt to understand it. Thus, despite the present temptation to delve into the implications of our work for biblical studies, we will touch upon these matters only lightly. Similarly, there will be no discussion of the historical geography of the process of Israelite Settlement in the manner of de Vaux (1978:475–680) or Aharoni 1979:200–242). Nor will we rehash such time-worn topics as the identity of the social and/or ethnic groups which, according to historical sources, were present in the Land of Israel at the beginning of the period under discussion.

As for the archaeological material itself, we will deal with it in a selective manner. We have already expressed the opinion that however much the evidence from the large Canaanite mounds may contribute to the understanding of various phenomena at the end of the Late Bronze period, it can do little to advance the study of the process of Israelite Settlement. Our attention will consequently be focused upon direct evidence from the regions of Israelite Settlement. This book makes no pretense of being the last word on the subject. Important regional studies are currently in progress in various parts of Israel; in the near future, they will undoubtedly produce new clues for elucidating the riddle of Israelite Settlement.

PART I:
THE RESULTS OF EXCAVATIONS AND SURVEYS

CHAPTER 2

THE CHARACTERISTICS OF ISRAELITE SETTLEMENT SITES

The main obstacle hindering any attempt to summarize the archaeological data of the period of Israelite Settlement is how to identify an Iron I site as an early occupation of Israelites. During the first half of the 12th century BCE, other ethnic entities were active in the Land of Israel, most notably the Canaanite population, which was still extant in the coastal plain and the northern valleys, as the Bible also indicates; the Philistines, who settled the southern coastal plain and the Shephelah in the 12th century; and assorted groups that were undergoing ethnic consolidation at the same time in Transjordan. Historical sources report the presence of additional groups of Sea Peoples along the coast, Phoenicians in the north, and Amalekites in the arid zones of the south, any of whom may have left behind remains of their existence.

Even before attempting to define the characteristics of Israelite Settlement sites, we must specify what we mean here — and throughout this work — by the term "Israelite"; in other words, who was an Israelite in Iron I? The problem of definition arises because the distinctions between ethnic groups at the beginning of the period were apparently still vague. Moreover, it seems that other groups — such as tribal units in southern Judah, Hivites in Benjamin and Canaanite elements in Manasseh — joined the new and growing entity in the hill country. It is doubtful, for example, that an inhabitant of Giloh in the 12th century BCE would have described himself as an "Israelite"; nonetheless, *we* refer to this site and its material culture as "Israelite." *Merneptah stela Israelites*

The formation of the Israelite identity was a long, intricate, and complex process which, in our opinion, was completed only at the beginning of the Monarchy. An important intermediate phase of this crystallization is connected with the establishment of supratribal sacral centers during the period of the Judges. The most important of these centers was the one at Shiloh, whose special role at the time is elucidated in 1 Samuel — a historical work, as all agree (see Chapter 5).

Accordingly, an Israelite during the Iron I period was anyone whose descendants — as early as the days of Shiloh (first half of the 11th century BCE) or as late as the beginning of the Monarchy — described themselves as Israelites. These were, by and large, the people who resided in the territorial framework of the early Israelite Monarchy, before its expansion began (see different views on the boundaries of Saul's monarchy in Aharoni 1979: 288–290; Vikander-Edelman 1986: 53–130). Thus even a person who may have considered himself a Hivite, Gibeonite, Kenizzite, etc., in the early 12th century, but whose descendants in the same village a few generations later thought of themselves as Israelites will, in like manner, also be considered here as an Israelite. Two areas pose certain difficulties for this definition: Galilee, whose population should be considered Israelite, but which was not initially within the jurisdiction of the Monarchy; and the hills of Manasseh, in the heart of the central hill country, where strong Canaanite groups continued to live in the Iron I period.

"Israelite" sites might also be defined on the basis of their social characteristics, thereby including those Iron I sites where the material culture reflects the initial stages of sedentarization. While such an approach overcomes the problem of determining the identity of the inhabitants of Galilee and the hills of Manasseh, it cannot be applied east of the Jordan River, where other groups settling down at the same time would eventually become the nations of Moab, Edom, and Ammon.

The best solution may then be a combination of both approaches: Israelites in Iron I are those people who were in a process of sedentarization in those parts of the country that were part of Saul's monarchy, and in Galilee. The term "Israelite" is used therefore in this book, when discussing the Iron I period, as no more than a *terminus technicus* for "hill country people in a process of settling down"

In any case, one should not ignore the fact that a group of people living in Canaan of the end of the 13th century BCE was described in the Merneptah Stele as "Israel." The problem, of course, is that we cannot identify their location, nor do we have any clue for the size or socio-political organization of this group. (For recent discussions on Israel in the Merneptah Stele see Stager 1985a; Ahlström and Edelman 1985. For one view on the origin of the name Israel, see Ahlström 1986).

The starting point of a discussion about the characteristics of Israelite Settlement sites is the historical biblical text (the only source available), which specifies the location of the Israelite population at the end of the period of the Judges and at the beginning of the Monarchy. Israelite cultural traits must therefore be deduced from the Iron I sites in the central hill country, especially in the southern sector, where the identity of the population at the time is not disputed.

From written sources and archaeological evidence, we can also determine the areas of Canaanite and Philistine settlement. The characteristics of Canaanite sites are generally easy to define, for their material culture, especially the pottery and small finds, directly continues that of their Late Bronze predecessors. Nor is there any difficulty in identifying the main

Philistine sites. In addition to the geographical aspect, Philistine pottery is most distinctive, with both shape and decoration related to Aegean traditions. This pottery, which cannot be mistaken for anything else, is found in significant quantities at the major Philistine sites.

It is clear, then, that the Iron I sites in the southern and central sectors of the hill country can be defined as "Israelite" even if at that time certain older or foreign elements were present (see, for example, Kempinski 1979: 39, 43; B. Mazar 1981:76–79).

The problem arises when we attempt to determine the identity of the inhabitants of sites in marginal areas such as the Beersheba Valley, the eastern Shephelah at the foot of the hill country, and the eastern fringes of the Sharon. This difficulty also exists, to a certain extent, in the territory of Manasseh in the northern sector of the central hill country, where various considerations — both biblical and archaeological — indicate that a strong canaanite element was present until a late stage of the Iron Age (although, according to the definition we offered above, by the beginning of the Monarchy the area was definitely Israelite).

In all these areas, which are basically transitional zones between the highlands and the plains, the culture was naturally influenced from both directions. Therefore, in attempting to determine the ethnic identity of the inhabitants of sites in these marginal areas on the basis of their material culture, three factors — function, chronology, and quantity — should be considered in addition to location.

The function of certain finds, both ceramic and architectural, is directly related to the geographical areas in which they were used and to the socio-economic conditions of the inhabitants. Their presence or absence at any given site is thus not necessarily a reflection of the ethnic background of its inhabitants, but rather the by-product of the environmental factors that dictated daily life at the site. The importance of chronology lies in the assistance it provides in pinpointing the origin of problematic finds. As for the quantitative factor, it would obviously be a mistake to make definitive determinations of ethnicity on the basis of the presence or absence of certain typical finds, for despite the geo-cultural isolation that characterized this period, there were mutual influences and commercial relations among the various sections of the country. For example, the appearance of a small quantity of Philistine sherds at a settlement whose other features are Israelite does not turn it into a Philistine site. Similarly, every site yielding a limited number of collared-rim store jars is not necessarily Israelite.

Taking these considerations into account, we will now define the characteristics of Israelite sites as evidenced in the principal regions of Settlement (see, most recently, Kochavi 1982:5; A. Mazar 1985a):

A. *Geographical location.* Although we have just dealt with this topic, we again note that the historical biblical text, being the only available source, provides the basis for identifying the principal regions of Israelite Settlement, and that at the Iron I sites in these regions, researchers have indeed discovered a material culture with distinctive features, some of which are appropriate for a poor isolated society in the incipient phases of sedentarization and organization.

B. *Site size.* The Israelite Settlement sites are relatively small, averaging 5–6 dunams or less in area. Only the largest sites, such as Shiloh and Ai, are as big as 10 dunams. In the territory of Manasseh, in the northern reaches of the central hill country, larger Iron I sites were surveyed. Here, however, there was a strong settled element and at some sites, there was continuity of occupation from the previous period.

C. *Settlement pattern.* Any given site should not be considered in isolation, but as part of a larger and more generalized picture. We must attempt to understand its relationship with other sites in the region and its place in the overall pattern of occupation.

D. *Architecture and site layout.* Four factors must be emphasized (and will be expanded upon in Chapter 6):
   1. Most early Israelite sites were not fortified. The few possible exceptions can be explained against the regional background.
   2. On typical Israelite sites, there are no public buildings such as a ruler's quarters or storehouses. As far as is now known, only ordinary dwellings are present.
   3. The appearance of pillared buildings (some of the four-room house type) is characteristic of Settlement sites in the mountainous regions and also typifies Israelite sites during the period of the Monarchy. Structures of this type are also found in non-Israelite areas, such as Philistia and the Negev Highlands. Perhaps their use is connected with topographical conditions. In any case, the evidence accumulating from excavations and surveys indicates that, both chronologically and quantitatively, the source and principal distribution of this architectural type is in the central hill country.
   4. Silos dug into the ground and lined with stones appear by the dozens at Iron I sites in the regions of Israelite Settlement. During all periods, such silos are characteristic of societies in the initial phases of settling down, for the first problem demanding a solution is the storage of grain. On the other hand, such silos are not found in well-organized societies — they are almost unknown in the Canaanite cities or at Israelite sites of the Monarchy period.

E. *Pottery.* The sites of Israelite Settlement are characterized by simple and relatively meager pottery. The repertoire of types is very limited: most vessels are collared-rim store jars and cooking pots (e.g. Mazar 1981a:31). This is undoubtedly connected to the social and economic background of the inhabitants. While the collared-rim store jar (Fig. 91) — the "type fossil" of Israelite sites ever since Albright's excavations at Tell el-Fūl in 1922 — is also found at sites in the Jezreel Valley and the coastal plain, the quantitative factor must be taken into account, as we have already noted (and see Chapter 7).[2]

In any case, the determination of a site as "Israelite" should be based upon the preponderance of all the evidence, and not on any single factor. To illustrate this point, let us examine the case of ʿIzbet Ṣarṭah, a site located on the border between Israel and Philistia, which is "problematic" in terms of the ethnic identity of its inhabitants. The discussion will also bring up additional problematic sites (see also A. Mazar 1985a:61–62).

The site of ʿIzbet Ṣarṭah, which has three occupational strata (Chapter 4), is situated on the edge of the foothills, bordering the coastal plain. It is only 3 km east of Tel Aphek, a Canaanite city that became an important Philistine site. From the standpoint of settlement geography, there are two possibilities for the ethnic identification of its inhabitants: Either it was an Israelite site, whose inhabitants had spread westward from the hills to establish themselves opposite the fertile coastal plain, or it was a Philistine site, a satellite settlement of nearby Aphek.[3] The location of the site is not decisive in this matter, since it was on the border between the Israelites and the Philistines.

As for the settlement pattern, a survey of the area between Jaljulia on the north and Rosh Haʿayin on the south has revealed six additional Iron I sites similarly situated on the fringes of the hills, overlooking the plain (Fig. 1). In other words, this is a regional phenomenon, not just a matter of a single isolated site. (According to the surveys, no such scattered and unfortified Iron I

2 Another factor that may have to be considered in the future is the faunal remains. At ʿIzbet Ṣarṭah and Shiloh, the quantity of pig bones was nil (Hellwing and Adjeman 1986:150–151), which would seem to be a fact that should not be ignored. On the other hand, no pig bones were found in Canaanite Lachish VI either (Drori 1979). Therefore we must await data from other sites before passing judgment.
   The assemblage of animal bones is likely to provide information about the socio-economic background of the population as well. For example, a large proportion of cattle hints at a strong tradition of permanent settlement, while a scarcity of cattle and preponderance of sheep/goat indicate a pastoralist population.

3 In theory, there is a third possibility, namely that Stratum III was a Canaanite site, whose inhabitants might have been refugees from devastated Aphek. However, the phenomenon of an unwalled Canaanite settlement of this type is, in fact, unknown, and it is furthermore hard to imagine the existence of a Canaanite settlement on the border between Israel and Philistia until the beginning of the 11th century BCE. In any case, the material culture of the site is not appropriate for a population that was directly connected with urban Canaanite society of the Late Bronze period.

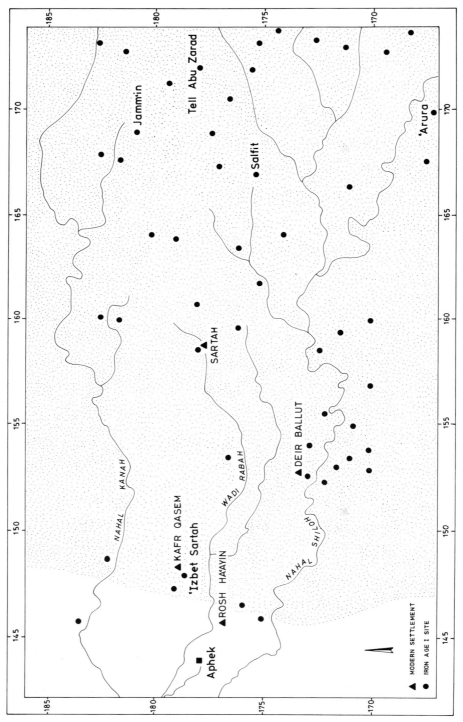

1. ʿIzbet Ṣarṭah and other Iron I sites in the western slopes of the Ephraimite hill country, near Aphek.

settlement is known in the nearby section of the coastal plain.) The excavations at Aphek have shown that the Philistine occupation there was not large, so there is no reason to postulate the development of a network of small satellite sites on its hilly eastern flank, of all places. The surveys indicate that even at its floruit in the Middle Bronze period, Aphek was not linked with any daughter settlements in these hills. On the other hand, from the foothills eastward into the hill country, there was a continuum of Iron I sites. It would thus seem that the sites arrayed along the edge of the hills belonged to the network of settlements in the hill country; they certainly did not fit into the pattern that was prevalent on the coastal plain. The size of ʿIzbet Ṣarṭah, 2–4 dunams (in Strata III and II respectively), also accords with the Israelite Settlement sites in the hill country.

The architecture and layout of the site in Stratum III — a belt of rooms around an open central courtyard — is, in our opinion, typical of a pastoral society at the beginning of the establishment of a permanent settlement, with the plan reflecting the traditions in effect before sedentarization (see Chapter 6). In the Iron I period, the only society answering this description was the Israelite population. Slightly later, in Strata II and I, two of the dominant features of Israelite sites appear: four-room houses and numerous stone-lined silos. Interestingly enough, at nearby Aphek these two features were not present until the 10th century (Kochavi 1981: 82). Thus two unmistakable signs of the material culture of the hill country turned up at Aphek coincident with the waning of ʿIzbet Ṣarṭah and just at the time when, according to the historical evidence, the Israelite population spread into the coastal plain.

Finally, we must consider the ceramic evidence. Philistine pottery does appear at ʿIzbet Ṣarṭah, but in extremely small quantities. At Tell Qasile, for example, painted Philistine material made up 14–24% of the ceramic assemblage of Strata XII–X (A. Mazar 1985b:105); at Gezer, 5%; but at ʿIzbet Ṣarṭah, only 1–2% (Finkelstein 1986:46,91). The quantity of collared-rim store jars found at ʿIzbet Ṣarṭah was relatively large in contrast to the amounts unearthed at other sites in the adjacent coastal plain, such as Aphek, Tell Qasile, and Gezer, which would seem to suit an Israelite rather than a Philistine site. On the other hand, the number of collared-rim store jars was relatively few in comparison to the quantities from settlements in the hill country; this might be explained by the character of the local agriculture. The relatively rich variety of ceramic types found at ʿIzbet Ṣarṭah, as opposed to the hill country, may reflect connections with sites in the coastal plain.

The settlement at ʿIzbet Ṣarṭah was totally unlike the nearby sites in the coastal plain — in nature, location, plan, and finds. These differences cannot be explained as reflecting the disparity between a small village and an urban center. We can thus assert, without hesitation, that the phenomenon of settlement on the western fringes of the hills, facing the coastal plain, had its origins in the hill country.

CHAPTER 3

REGIONAL SURVEY OF THE ARCHAEOLOGICAL DATA

The remainder of Part I will consist of a presentation of the archaeological data relevant to the sites of the Settlement period that have accumulated during the course of some sixty years of research. We will not discuss indirect evidence, such as the destruction layers of Canaanite sites that have, in the past, been attributed to the incoming Israelite tribes; this topic has been so exhaustively treated in the literature (e.g., P. Lapp 1967) that there is almost nothing to add (we will touch upon it in Chapter 8 in our discussion of the Albright school of thought). Here we will treat only direct evidence: the places where remains of early Israelite settlements were uncovered (Fig. 2), and the results of surveys in various regions of the country. The following guidelines determined the contents and arrangement of this chapter.

— The finds are described by region, from north to south. For each region, we begin with the results of excavations and then discuss the material from surveys. The ancient names of sites that have been positively identified will be used; other sites will be referred to by the Arabic or Hebrew names commonly used by scholars.

— For the territories outside the limits of Israelite Settlement that were inhabited by Canaanites and Philistines in Iron I (the coastal plain, the Shephelah and the northern valleys) we will refer, briefly, only to occupation in the northern valleys, and we do this only because in the past there have been debates over the question of when Israelite activity began in these areas. Problematic regions and sites, i.e., places that were on the margins of Israelite Settlement, will be discussed in this chapter because the identity of their inhabitants is uncertain.

— In discussing both the excavations and the surveys, we will attempt, in some cases, to note briefly the situation before and after Iron I. The before-and-after data are naturally very important for understanding the process of Settlement. While we will cite only the finds of the Late Bronze (and occasionally Middle Bronze) and Iron II periods, this is not to say that the remains of other periods were not found at these sites.

— At the time of this writing, intensive archaeological surveys underway in

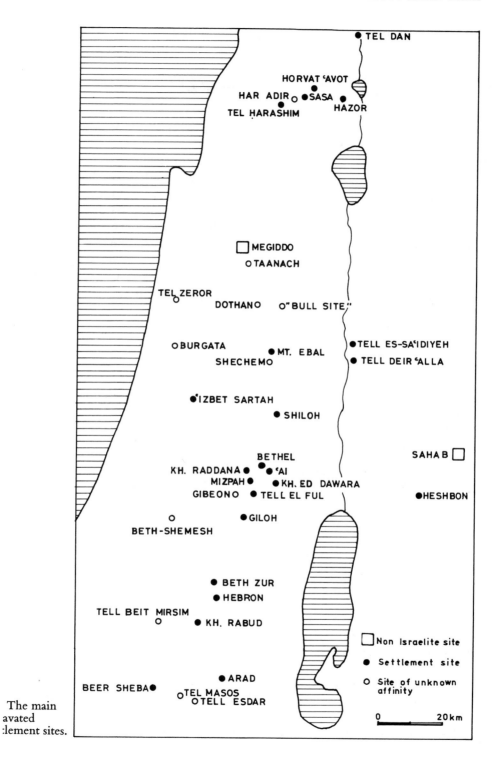

TEL DAN

HORVAT ʿAVOT

HAR ADIR ○ ● SASA
TEL HARASHIM ● HAZOR

☐ MEGIDDO
○ TAANACH

TEL ZEROR ○
DOTHAN ○ ○ "BULL SITE"

○ BURGATA ● TELL ES-SAʿIDIYEH
● MT. EBAL ● TELL DEIR ʿALLA
SHECHEM ○

● IZBET SARTAH
● SHILOH

BETHEL
KH. RADDANA ● ● ʿAI SAHAB ☐
MIZPAH ● ○ KH. ED DAWARA
GIBEON ○ ● TELL EL FUL ● HESHBON
○ ● GILOH
BETH-SHEMESH

● BETH ZUR
● HEBRON
TELL BEIT MIRSIM
○ ● KH. RABUD

☐ Non Israelite site
● Settlement site
○ Site of unknown affinity

● ARAD
BEER SHEBA ● ○ TEL MASOS
○ TELL ESDAR

0   20km

The main
:avated
:lement sites.

35

many parts of the country are producing numerous finds that are important for the picture of Iron I occupation. Although interim reports of some of these surveys have yet to be published, our colleagues have kindly made preliminary information available to us (updated to 1985–1986).

— In general, we have refrained from using the data gathered in old field trips. The methods of surveying and the techniques of collecting sherds and dating them were, until recent years, in their infancy. The utilization of imprecise or unclear data would be more harmful than beneficial. The results of older surveys will be described, therefore, only when we are certain that their classifications are reliable or, *faute de mieux* , when other data are lacking. The extent of our knowledge about the various regions is not uniform. In most regions, research has been comprehensive, but for a few areas, we do not have much information. This inconsistency must be taken into account in any attempt to summarize the field data concerning the Iron I period (see the chart in Chapter 10). While the full publication of surveys will, in the future, undoubtedly add new dimensions to our understanding of the process of Settlement, the data presently at our disposal seem to be sufficient to appreciate the overall Iron I settlement pattern.

— As far as possible, we will attempt to shed light on the pattern of occupation in the secondary areas of the various regions. This is of great importance for understanding the historical process of Settlement and it will be tackled in detail in Chapter 4.

— It has been practically impossible to make fine chronological distinctions in the pottery from Settlement sites. This problem will naturally crop up at various points in this work, since it is crucial for understanding the processes of occupation and the development of material culture at early Israelite Settlement sites. To discuss sites from the beginning of the 12th century in the same breath, so to speak, as sites from *ca.* 1000 BCE (and the sherds collected from all of them would generally be classified "Iron I") is obviously undesirable. In other words, even the ability just to distinguish between the situation at the beginning of the Iron I period and that prevalent at a later stage would be highly instructive. In some instances, we will thus try to make the distinction between early and late pottery of the Iron I period, despite the risks inherent in this attempt; to refrain from doing so would obviously impede our attempts to advance the analysis of the process of Settlement.

— The findings of the regional study we have conducted in the territory of Ephraim for the last seven years will be dealt with in a separate chapter. Our work in that region, located at the heart of the area of Israelite Settlement, includes the excavation of Shiloh and an intensive survey throughout the territory of Ephraim. The interim results of these labors provide a basis for comparison with other regions of Settlement.

BEERSHEBA VALLEY

The last twenty years have witnessed an acceleration in archaeological activity in the Beersheba Valley, during the course of which seven major sites have been excavated. The great amount of information that had already accumulated some years ago enabled Y. Aharoni, who was connected with most of these projects, to attempt to summarize the history of occupation in the region. Aharoni described Israelite Settlement in the Beersheba Valley as an "intensive wave of settlement manifest in all of the earliest sites, and in places that had never been inhabited ... there was now a chain of established settlements that inaugurated a period of flourishing occupation ..." (1979a:211). As for the date of Israelite Settlement, he observed that "at every place in the Negev where archaeological excavations have been conducted, the beginning of Israelite occupation has been fixed at the end of the 13th or during the 12th century BCE" (1982:202; see also 1976a:74; Aharoni, Fritz and Kempinski 1975:118).

Aharoni's appreciation of the intensity of Israelite Settlement in the valley seems to have been influenced by the overwhelming impression created by the large and well-developed settlement uncovered at Tel Masōs. His chronological determination was based on the relatively early ceramic material found there in Stratum III (Fig. 5), and especially on a scarab (Fig. 104) that was first dated to the time of Seti II (Giveon 1974). No doubt, Aharoni's interpretation was also influenced by his general understanding of the character and date of Israelite Settlement.

The time has now come for a reevaluation of the Israelite Settlement in the Beersheba Valley in regard to both the intensity of the process and its date. A review of the situation in this region (see also Herzog's summary, 1984:70–75) is particularly important, because the findings of excavations here have served, for many, as a model for understanding the process of Settlement. Our new approach stems primarily from a different interpretation of the finds from Tel Masōs, the largest and most important Iron I site in the valley. As we already noted in Chapter 2, The Beersheba Valley is one of those areas where the identity of the inhabitants of some of the sites is difficult to determine. We will first examine four sites where remains of the period have been discovered[4] and will then attempt to clarify their ethnic affiliation.

4   At three other sites in the valley — Aroer, Tel Malḥata and Tel ʿIra — no remains of the Iron I period were found (*contra* Fritz 1975:33). For Tel Malḥata, there is one reference (*Had. Arch.* 40, 1971:35) to the finding of unstratified sherds of the 11th century BCE, and Aharoni frequently referred to this evidence (e.g., Aharoni, Fritz and Kempinski 1975:118). However, it was subsequently determined that no settlement existed at this site before the 10th century BCE (oral communication from the excavator, Kochavi).

Excavations

Tel Esdar

The site is located on a moderate hill on the southern margin of the Beersheba Valley, adjacent to the Beersheba-Dimona road (map ref. 1475 0645). It was excavated in 1963–1964 by M. Kochavi under the aegis of the Department of Antiquities and Museums (Kochavi 1969a).

Stratum III, the important one for our purposes, was dated to the 11th century BCE. The eight units excavated (and two more were discernible on the surface) created a kind of oval band around a large and open courtyard (Fig. 3). Aharoni reconstructed a total of 20 such units (1976a:69). The site covers about 3.75 dunams (measuring roughly 85 x 55 m). The houses were close to one another for protection, but there is no evidence that they created a continuous line of defense on the outer side. Since the long sides of the houses were on the line of the perimeter and the entrances faced the courtyard, these structures can be classified as broad-rooms. The buildings featured pillars and beaten-earth floors. Kochavi hypothesized that the layout of the site reflected "an attempt by a nomadic or semi-nomadic tribe to settle and adopt a sedentary way of life" (1969a:45), and he associated it with Israelite Settlement in the south. In his opinion, the site was damaged by the Amalekites and then revived, in the 10th century, as a small agricultural settlement (Stratum II).

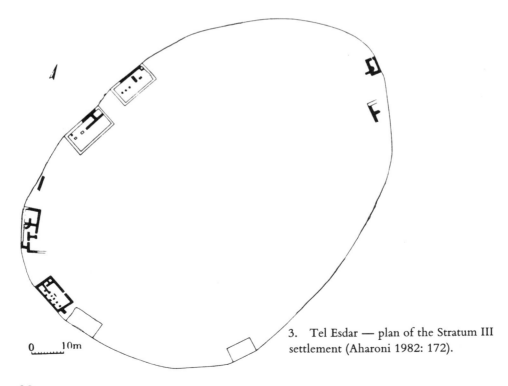

0 ____ 10m

3. Tel Esdar — plan of the Stratum III settlement (Aharoni 1982: 172).

The date of Stratum III can now be narrowed to the second half of the 11th century BCE. It is difficult to determine whether the site was part of the Israelite framework in the Beersheba Valley or whether it belonged to the network of sites established by desert dwellers in the Negev Highlands at that time. Its position on the southern side of the valley, its date, and various elements of its plan (which are quite similar to the sites of the Negev Highlands; Chapter 6) would seem to favor the second possibility. On the other hand, it is quite tempting to follow the suggestion of Biran and Cohen (1981:273 n. 65) that the site should be identified as Aroer of the time of David.

Tel Arad

Iron Age Arad was excavated from 1962–1967 by Y. Aharoni on behalf of the Department of Antiquities, the Hebrew University and the Israel Exploration Society. There was a long hiatus in occupation at the site between the abandonment of the EB II city and the Iron I period. This was therefore one of the places mentioned in the narrative of the conquest at which no remains of the Late Bronze period were found. The first Iron Age level was Stratum 12, of which only sparse remnants of few structures were exposed because a fortress of the period of the United Monarchy was erected over it. Stratum 12 comprised several phases: 12A and 12B were dated to the 11th century, while the upper phase of this stratum belonged to the first half of the 10th century BCE (M. Aharoni 1981. But see recently Zimhoni 1985:87 who dates Strata 12–11 to the 10–9 centuries respectively).

Evidence that has accumulated in recent years again makes it possible to limit the date of the early settlement, which was small in size, to the second half of the 11th century or to the beginning of the 10th century BCE. There is no problem in identifying this site as Israelite for two reasons: the occupational continuity to Stratum 11, with its Israelite fortress of the United Monarchy period; and the possibility that the small unfortified site should be connected with the biblical tradition that descendants of the Kenites, Moses' in-laws, went up "from the city of palms into the wilderness of Judah, which lies in the Negeb near Arad" (Judges 1:16).

Beersheba

Eight seasons of excavations were conducted at Tel Beersheba from 1969–1976 by an expedition from the Institute of Archaeology of Tel Aviv University under the direction of Y. Aharoni. Three strata of Iron I date were uncovered (Herzog 1984). These remains were preserved primarily on the southern slope of the tell, since this level had been damaged on the summit during the preparation of the foundations for the first fortified city. Stratum IX spanned the mid-12th to mid-11th centuries BCE. Seven large pits, about 7–8 m in diameter, were found. The deepest were used for storing grain, while the shallower ones functioned (according to Herzog) as dwellings roofed with branches. Herzog reconstructed a total of 20 pit-dwellings and 10 silos within an area of slightly over 2 dunams. He viewed the site as the winter residence of people who went north into the hill country in the summer.

Stratum IX was abandoned. The pits were re-used in Stratum VIII, dated to the second half of the 11th century. At this time, the first structures on the tell were erected, but only a few remains of them were unearthed. This settlement was also abandoned. At the end of the 11th century, Stratum VII — the first protected settlement — arose. In the process of preparing to build, the ground was leveled, thereby sealing the earlier pits. On the southeast slope, the remains of five adjoining four-room houses were uncovered; their rear broad-rooms created a kind of belt of casemates. Since no remains of this stratum were discovered in one sounding made in the middle of the site, Herzog

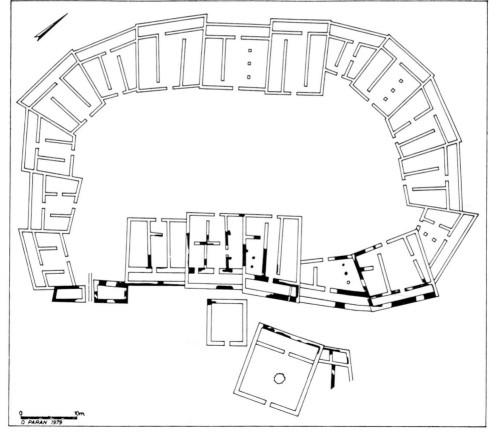

0 PARAN 1979

4. Beersheba — plan of the Stratum VII settlement (Herzog 1984: 79).

reconstructed the site-plan as an elliptical belt of 18 structures surrounding an open central courtyard (Figs. 4, 79). Access to the buildings was from the courtyard. The site itself was entered through a gate flanked on each side by a tower- chamber. A few other structures belonging to Stratum VII were found beyond the peripheral belt, near the well on the slope.

Because only part of Stratum VII was excavated — and the remains were relatively few — the reconstruction is hypothetical. What is certain is that along the southern edge of the site, there was a series of broad casemate-like rooms, at least some of which served as the rear rooms of houses. The outer walls of these broad-rooms did not form a straight line, but leaned one against the next. If Herzog's reconstruction is accurate, then the size of the site at this period was just over 3 dunams. There is no problem in defining the inhabitants of Beersheba as Israelites primarily on the basis of the continuity from the earliest strata to the fortified stronghold of the Monarchy period.

Tel Masōs

As already noted, Tel Masōs was the most important Iron I site in the region. From 1972–1979, four seasons of excavations took place here under the aegis of the Institute of Archaeology of Tel Aviv University in cooperation with German institutions. The campaigns were directed by Y. Aharoni, A. Kempinski and V. Fritz (Fritz and Kempinski 1983:7–113, 227–234). The remains of the ancient settlement are scattered on both sides of Naḥal Beersheba, adjacent to a concentration of wells. On the southern side of the wadi, a fortified enclosure of about 17 dunams was established in MB IIB. Neither here nor at any of the other sites in the valley were any Late Bronze remains found. The Iron I occupation, which was uncovered on the northern side of the wadi, in the main part of the site, comprised three levels.

The earliest phase of Stratum III (IIIB) was characterized by ash-pits, a few silos, ovens, and beaten earth floors that might have belonged to tents or huts. According to the excavators, this stratum marked the first phase of sedentarization by a group of semi-nomads. The pottery (Fig. 5) was related to the Canaanite ceramic tradition of the south; Philistine types are completely lacking. During the next phase, Stratum IIIA, several structures were built, including the prototype of the four-room house with pillars. At that time, in the opinion of the excavators, a governmental structure was erected in the southern part of the site. Stratum III was dated from the end of the 13th to the middle of the 12th centuries BCE.

Stratum II represented the period when Tel Masōs reached its largest size and achieved its greatest prosperity. According to the excavators, there was no cultural or ethnic gap between Strata III and II because there was continuity in both architecture and pottery. Stratum II, which had two phases, was dated

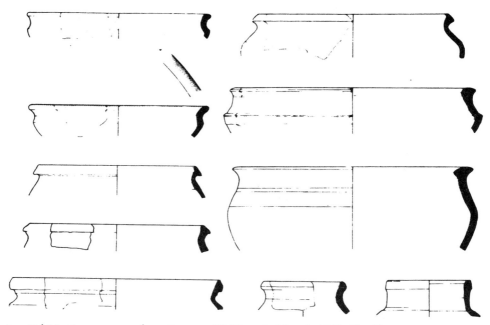

5. Tel Masōs — pottery from Stratum III (Kempinski *et al.* 1981: Fig. 9).

from the mid-12th to the mid-11th centuries BCE.[5] It was destroyed by an enemy or an earthquake. For the first time, public buildings and four-room houses appeared. The excavators were of the opinion that the basic idea underlying the layout was the enclosure of the center by means of a belt of houses along the outer edge of the site. These peripheral structures, attached to each other and alternately recessed and projecting, created a kind of defense (Fig. 6). A few structures were exposed in the center of the site, and there were also buildings outside the line of defense. In several structures, the influence of Egyptian and Canaanite architecture of the southern coastal plain was perceptible.

Kempinski suggested that certain buildings (perhaps already as early as Stratum III) were associated with the Egyptian, and then Philistine, domination of the south; they served to control the important trade route that crossed the Beersheba Valley. The rich and varied finds of Stratum II included, *inter alia*, Midianite and Philistine pottery, vessels of coastal types (Fig. 7), an ivory lion's head executed in the Canaanite tradition, and evidence of local copper-working. These attest to lively trade activities and strong connections with the southern Arabah and the coastal plain.

5   Fritz's dating (1980:121) is slightly later than Kempinski's. He placed Stratum IIIB during the first half of the 12th century; IIIA at the middle of the 12th century; and II from the end of the 12th to the second half of the 11th centuries BCE.

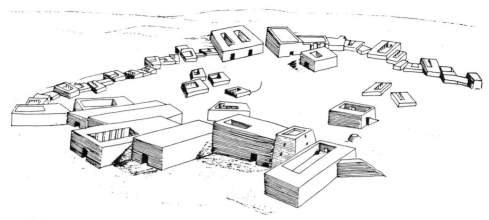

6.   Tel Masōs — reconstruction of the Stratum II settlement (Kempinski *et al.* 1981: 177).

In Stratum I, dated to the end of the 11th and beginning of the 10th centuries BCE, the site-plan was changed. In one place, near the wells, a kind of citadel was erected. There is no evidence of a peripheral belt of buildings as in the previous stratum. While several of the Stratum II buildings continued to exist in Stratum I with only minor changes, others were replaced by silos and stone pavements. Following Stratum I, there was a gap in occupation at Tel Masōs until the end of Iron II.

The excavators saw Tel Masōs as an Israelite Settlement site and identified it with Hormah, one of the most important cities in the south (Kempinski *et al.* 1981:155; Fritz and Kempinski 1983:234–238; for another opinion, see Na'aman 1980). The findings from this site served as the basis for their views on the entire Settlement process.

Aharoni emphasized the penetration into a region that had not been inhabited in the previous period (LB) and described, as noted, a large and early wave of Settlement in the Beersheba Valley. Fritz (1981) noted the connections to the material culture of the Late Bronze period and developed a theory of a symbiotic relationship between the Israelites and the Canaanites in the early stages of Settlement.

Kempinski explained the arrival of Israelite settlers in the Beersheba Valley as the result of overpopulation in the Hebron Hills, causing Simeonite clans to move southward into a valley whose climate was, in his opinion, less arid than it is today. While Kempinski admitted that the assemblage from Tel Masōs was not typical of other Israelite Settlement sites (1981:176), he nonetheless clung to his view that the site was Israelite and was thus caught in a contradiction. In his description of the public buildings of Stratum II, he claimed that "they seem out of place in such a rural settlement" (1978:36). Kempinski tried to explain away this contradiction by hypothesizing that the

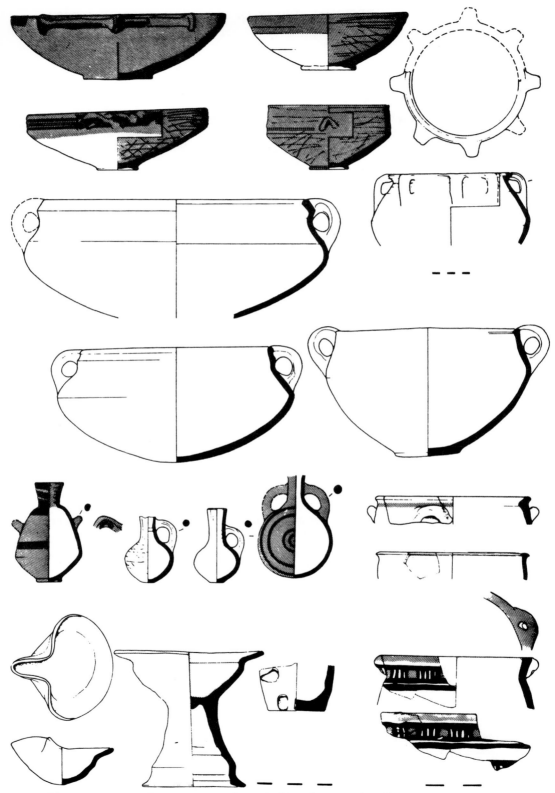

7.   Tel Masōs — pottery from Stratum II (Kempinski *et al.* 1981: Fig. 10).

site comprised elements of both urban Canaanite culture and tribal Israelite society (Kempinski *et.al.* 1981:176).

Kochavi (1982:5) was the first to object to the classification of Tel Masōs as an Israelite Settlement site, identifying it instead as the "city of Amalek" mentioned in the Bible (1 Samuel 15:5). More recently, B. Mazar proposed connecting the phenomenon of Tel Masōs to the floruit of the Philistine coast (lecture at the 10th Archaeological Congress, Jerusalem, 1983).

The finds from Tel Masōs and the settlement pattern of the Beersheba Valley and the southern hill country support, in our opinion, the rejection of Tel Masōs as an Israelite Settlement site. The reasons are as follows (see also Herzog 1984: 72; Ahlström 1984a):

A. *Site size.* The Stratum II occupation covered an area of at least 30 dunams, which is three times as large as the very largest Israelite Settlement site in the hill country and more than ten times larger than the other sites in the Beersheba Valley. Had this been the only problem with the excavators' interpretation, the size might have been explained away as reflecting the economic success of the desert routes; however, it was but one of the difficulties.

B. *Settlement pattern.* First of all, Tel Masōs was acknowledged as exceptional in the Beersheba Valley, totally unlike the few small sites founded there at the end of the 11th century BCE. In the 12th century, it was, in fact, the *only* permanent settlement in the region. It is thus necessary to reject Aharoni's view that "Tell Masos, although the largest of the Negev towns of the period, was typical of the entire region" (1976b:13). Second, as we shall see, the Judean Hills were relatively sparsely settled in Iron I, so that there are no grounds for the theory that overpopulation in the hills led to settlement in the valley.

C. *Continuity of occupation.* Tel Masōs differed from the two Israelite Settlement sites in the valley — Arad and Beersheba — in an yet another way. Whereas the occupation of Arad and Beersheba in the 11th century heralded their transformation into prosperous Israelite centers in the period of the Monarchy, Tel Masōs was abandoned precisely at this time and not resettled for several centuries.

D. *Material culture.* The large public buildings, the Egypto- Canaanite influences in architecture, and the varied pottery are completely foreign to Israelite Settlement sites and, indeed, were utterly unknown at Arad and Beersheba in this period. The only "Israelite" feature at Tel Masōs was, in fact, the presence of four-room houses; however, such structures also appeared in Iron I in other regions on the fringes of Israelite occupation (Chapter 6).

Practically every feature of Tel Masōs thus stood in complete contrast to the characteristics of Israelite Settlement sites in the hill country, from whence Kempinski would have the inhabitants of Tel Masōs originate. The site was also completely unlike the Israelite settlements in the valley itself. The growth of Tel Masōs in the heart of the Beersheba Valley in the 12th- 11th centuries BCE was a unique phenomenon that cannot be forced into the framework of Israelite Settlement (see more in Finkelstein, forthcoming a). On the other hand, the possibility that the mixed population of the site may have included a few "Israelite" families cannot be ruled out completely either.

Surveys

In the field trips and local surveys accompanying the excavations in the valley, and also in the more recent survey conducted in the region by Beit-Arieh, Eitam and Lederman (Eitam 1980b:57), not even one additional Iron I site was found.

* * * * * * * * * * *

The data that have accumulated from excavations and surveys in the Beersheba Valley present a picture differing from earlier descriptions. The region was indeed uninhabited in the Late Bronze period, but even in Iron I, occupation was surprisingly sparse. In the 12th century, there was only the large site of Tel Masōs and perhaps a little activity at Tel Beersheba as well. Not until the 11th century, actually toward its end, did any significant changes take place: The occupation of Tel Masōs waned while that at Beersheba intensified and Esdar and Arad made their debuts.

An analysis of the finds uncovered at sites in the valley against the background of what we know of the settlement patterns and material remains in the adjacent regions to the north and south shows that only Beersheba and Arad can be characterized with certainty as Israelite sites. (Interestingly enough, the sites of the Beersheba Valley did not yield any of the collared- rim store jars so typical of Israelite Settlement sites in the hill country; discussion in Chapter 7.) Tel Masōs did not belong to the phenomenon of Israelite Settlement (except, perhaps, for Stratum I), and Tel Esdar may have been a site of desert dwellers, like those known from the Negev Highlands.

In summary, then, extremely sparse Israelite Settlement began in the Beersheba Valley only in the 11th century, with the establishment of two small sites. The turning point did not come until the 10th century, when the large fortifications of Arad, Beersheba and Tel Malḥata were constructed and the Beersheba Valley became the southern fortified boundary of the Monarchy as well as the center for activities in the desert regions to the south.

JUDEAN HILLS

The importance of the Judean Hills for understanding the process of Israelite Settlement stems from both geographical and historical considerations. First, as an isolated mountainous bloc, bounded on two sides by arid regions, it was singularly suitable for occupation. Second, most of the biblical traditions describing the conquests of Canaanite cities that were not part of the unified conquest narrative are connected with this region, indicating its importance for understanding certain issues of the Settlement of the entire Land of Israel. The historical biblical literature makes hardly any reference to the Judean Hills prior to the establishment of the Monarchy, but it then became one of the most important regions in the kingdom. The results of archaeological research shed light on the processes of settlement that took place not only in the region itself, but also in the adjacent areas to the south and west, from the end of the Late Bronze period until the beginning of Iron II.

Excavations

Khirbet Rabūd (Debir)

Located between edh-Dhaheriyeh and es-Samuᶜ, Khirbet Rabūd (map ref. 1515 0933) is identified with biblical Debir. Kochavi conducted two short excavation campaigns at the site in 1968 and 1969 on behalf of the Institute of Archaeology of Tel Aviv University and other institutions (Kochavi 1974). The site was inhabited in the Late Bronze period, in the 14th and 13th centuries BCE. Four occupational strata and the city wall were uncovered, as well as the necropolis of this period, whose rich finds included many imported vessels. An Iron I stratum overlay the Late Bronze remains. The limited area excavated prevents drawing conclusions about the character of the site in that period. During Iron II, a fortified town was located here.

Hebron

Biblical Hebron is located at Jebel Rumeideh, south of the center of the present city. Hammond undertook three seasons of excavations here in 1964–1966 under the aegis of the University of Vermont, the University of Southern California and Princeton Seminary. The excavations were recently renewed by the Institute of Archaeology of Tel Aviv University under the direction of A. Ofer. The principal find of the American team was a massive MB IIC fortification wall. Some remains of the Late Bronze (only burials) and Iron I periods were discovered, but they had been disturbed by the activities of the Iron II and later inhabitants (Hammond 1965; for the first news on the recent excavations, see *Had. Arch.* 85, 1984:43–44; 88, 1986: 28).

Beth-zur

Beth-zur has been identified with Khirbet et-Ṭubeiqah, north of Hebron (map ref. 1589 1108). The site was excavated twice, in 1931 and 1957, under the aegis of the Presbyterian (McCormick) Theological Seminary of Chicago and the American Schools of Oriental Research. On both occasions, the director was O.R. Sellers (Sellers 1933; Sellers *et al.* 1968).

Beth-zur was a fortified site of medium size in the MB IIC period. Funk, who studied the pottery from the excavations, claimed that there had been some kind of activity at the site at the beginning of the Late Bronze period (Sellers *et al.* 1968:1,37). Indeed, in the first report, a few sherds of Cypriote milk-bowls, the handle of a Base-Ring vessel and a Dynasty XIX scarab were published (Sellers 1933:Figs. 26 and 50:6). The published pottery plates include other finds that might belong to the Late Bronze period, such as several cooking pots and the bases of "Canaanite" jars (Sellers 1933: Pl. VIII; Sellers *et al.* 1968:Figs. 4,10). While it is true that these jars could also appear in the 12th century, they were rarely that late in the hill country. In short, it is likely that there was some kind of activity at the site during the Late Bronze period.

Beth-zur was inhabited in Iron I, but the areas where early material was found were so limited in size that no conclusions could be drawn about the character of the site. Funk dated this occupation, which was apparently destroyed by fire, to the 11th century BCE ("with some lapping into the 12th and 10th" centuries — Sellers *et al.* 1968:44, see also *ibid;* 6,7), which is later than the original date determined by Sellers and Albright (1931:7). An examination of the published pottery suggests that the site was already inhabited in the 12th century (see also T. Dothan 1982:48). The settlement slowly revived in Iron II, but reached its zenith only toward the end of the period.

Giloh

This site, which is located in southwestern Jerusalem (map ref. 1655 1254), was discovered in the 1968 Survey. Three seasons of excavations were carried out in 1978–1979 by A. Mazar on behalf of the Department of Antiquities and Museums and the Institute of Archaeology of the Hebrew University of Jerusalem (A. Mazar 1980a; 1981a). Situated on the top of a ridge, Giloh enjoys a panoramic view. Because the site was occupied during only a single period (except for an Iron II tower erected north of the site), a large proportion of it could be excavated. Mazar noted that the site was located in a place that was difficult to inhabit: a rocky area lacking soil for agriculture, far from any permanent water source, exposed to strong winds, and distant from the main route of the central ridge.

The principal remains, which were excavated on the southern end of the site (Fig. 8), comprised a house on the northern side of a large courtyard with long walls built of large field stones, which might have been a sheepfold. The plan of the house was not unlike the four-room house type and stone pillars were utilized. The masonry was crude and poor in quality, and the floor consisted of beaten earth. As there was no evidence of reflooring or any other internal changes or repairs, the excavator concluded that the house was abandoned shortly after it was built.

Remains in two areas excavated on the periphery of the site were interpreted as part of a defense system. In Area E in the northeast, two well-built parallel walls, 2.5 m apart, were discovered; the outer one was 1 m thick while the inner one was 1.8 m thick. Their course was followed in the surface survey

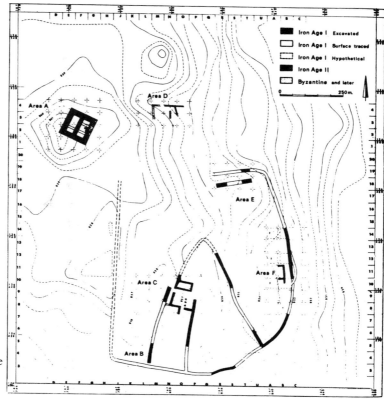

8. Giloh — general plan of the site (A. Mazar 1981a: Fig. 2).

(Fig. 8). In Area F in the east, another section of the "fortification" was exposed; here it was a single wall 1.5 m wide. Parallel to it on the inside was the outer wall of a house. Because of the variations in the character of the masonry of this defense wall at different parts of the site, the excavator concluded that it was constructed in sections by various groups of inhabitants. Long massive walls seem to have divided the interior of the settlement into a number of large units; each family apparently had its own area with a house and courtyard for the flocks. Mazar categorized the site as a "fortified herdsmen's village" for there is no arable soil in the vicinity, and the plan of the site hinted at animal husbandry.

The ceramic finds were sparse (Fig. 9), but since the sherds from the southern building were examined statistically, they are important for comparing with other early Israelite sites. Cooking pots made up 27% of the assemblage, collared-rim store jars 34%, and other jars 17%. Bowls, kraters, jugs and juglets comprised 21% of the collection. Among the cooking pots and jars were types belonging to the LB Canaanite ceramic tradition. This led the excavator to date the site to an early phase of the Iron I period: established about 1200 BCE and abandoned during the course of the 12th century.

Mazar saw Giloh as an example of occupation by a previously nomadic tribal group that had become sedentary. The meager material finds suggested that the inhabitants lacked a ceramic tradition and acquired their pottery from one of the urban centers remaining in the hill country and the Shephelah. In his opinion, the settlement was established on the outskirts of Jebusite Jerusalem (where Iron I remains have only recently been discovered — *Had. Arch.* 82, 1983:47); or else, if the tradition of the conquest of Jerusalem early in the period of Israelite Settlement (Judges 1:8) is accepted, it was founded in the wake of this event and abandoned when the Jebusite city regained strength. In either case, the fortification wall, which is anomalous among Israelite Settlement sites in the hill country, was connected with the proximity of the foreign enclave that remained in Jerusalem until David's time.

Mazar accorded the Giloh finds a place of particular importance in the debate over the character of the process of Israelite Settlement (1980a:38; 1981a:33–36; see also Kempinski 1981 and A. Mazar 1981c); we will return to this matter later on. Ahlström (1984b) claimed that the inhabitants of Giloh were Canaanites, perhaps even Jebusites who attempted to defend the territory to the south of their city; however, according to our definition of "who is an Israelite" in Iron I his discussion is moot (Chapters 6–8).

Surveys

The 1968 Survey (Kochavi's group) showed that three of the sites occupied in the Iron I period did not continue to be inhabited in Iron II. Each of these sites

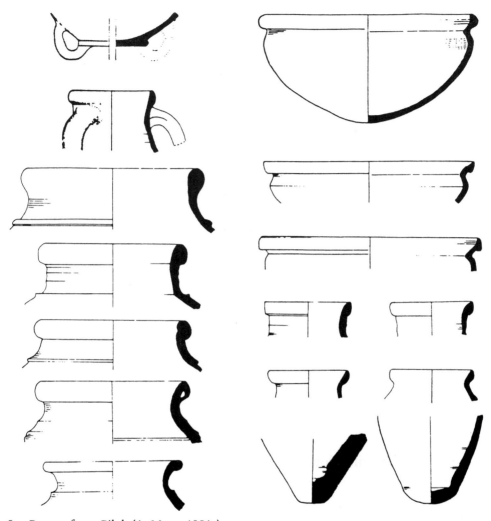

9. Pottery from Giloh (A. Mazar 1981a).

was 6–8 dunams in area. In addition, 22 sites were attributed to the "Israelite period," but there is no mention of whether they yielded pottery specifically indicative of Iron I (Kochavi 1972b:20–21, 83). A. Mazar, who participated in the survey, noted that such sherds were collected at only a minority of these sites (1980a:34). More recent surveys of the area conducted by A. Mazar and Ofer have not revealed any new sites of the period in question (oral communication). Nor has even one single early Iron Age site been picked up in the hills of Jerusalem to the west of the city. Ofer estimated the number of Iron I sites in the Judean Hills to be 10–12, most of them located north of Hebron (lecture, Tel Aviv University, December, 1985).

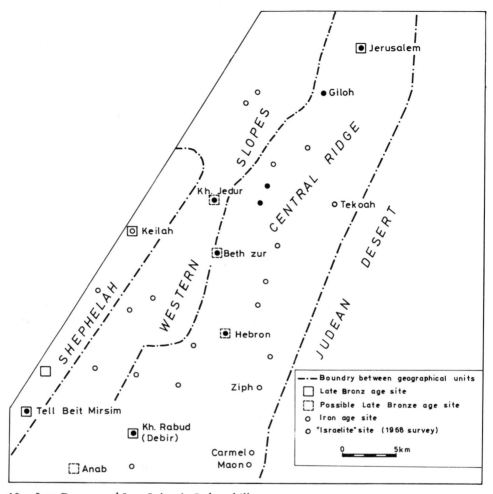

10.   Late Bronze and Iron I sites in Judean hill country.

The distribution of the sites in the area is noteworthy (Fig. 10): 10 of the 25 mapped in the 1968 Survey (as noted, definite finds of the period have not been found at all of them) — 40% — are located on the eastern and southern margins of the mountainous plateau, near the edge of the desert. Only four are situated on the western slopes of the hills and 11 on the ridge proper.

*   *   *   *   *   *   *   *   *   *

In summarizing the data from the Judean Hills, we must reiterate that for the Late Bronze period, we know of only two certain sites (Jerusalem and Khirbet Rabūd), one dubious settlement (Beth-zur) and three burial grounds with no corresponding occupation (Kh. Jedur, Hebron, and Kh. ʿAnab el-Kabir; for the latter, oral communication from Ofer). The general picture of the Iron I period arising from the excavations and surveys in this large area (c. 900 km²) is one of relatively few sites. This is certainly surprising, especially in contrast to what we now know of the central hill country to the north of Jerusalem. As far as chronology is concerned, we simply note that the published pottery from Beth-zur and Giloh (Sellers 1933:Pl. VIII; A. Mazar 1981a:22) seems to belong, at least in part, to the early phase of the period. During the course of Iron II, the region filled up with dozens upon dozens of sites of every size.

JUDEAN DESERT

In the 1968 Survey, 20 Iron I sites were reported, most of them isolated structures and round or elliptical enclosures (Bar Adon 1972). However, an examination of the boxes of pottery collected from more than half of these sites yielded not one single sherd indicative of the Iron I period. Chronological assignation was apparently based strictly on body sherds. More recent surveys in the northern Judean Desert, conducted by Hirschfeld and Patrich, did not reveal any Iron I sites (oral communication). The general picture seems to indicate that there were virtually no sites with permanent occupation in this region in Iron I.

SHEPHELAH

The dense Canaanite occupation in the Shephelah during the Late Bronze period apparently continued into the 12th century at quite a number of sites (on the date of the destruction of the last Canaanite city at Lachish, Stratum VI, see Ussishkin 1983:168–170). During the second quarter of the 12th century BCE, Philistines began to inhabit the region. It is thus difficult to imagine that Israelites settled in the Shephelah, and, indeed, there is no hint of their presence in the archaeological record. Only at two sites on the eastern edge of the Shephelah, at the foot of the hill country, did archaeological finds offer any indication of a possible brief occupation by Israelites following the destruction of the Canaanite cities, but prior to the advent of the Philistines.

Excavations

Tell Beit Mirsim

The site is located in the longitudinal valley at the base of the slope of the Judean hills. Between 1926–1932, Albright undertook four seasons of excavations here, sponsored by Xenia Theological Seminary of Pittsburgh and the American School of Oriental Research in Jerusalem. Albright incorrectly identified the site with biblical Debir (see Kochavi 1974).

Stratum C, the last Canaanite city, was destroyed in a conflagration that the excavator dated to the third quarter of the 13th century BCE. Albright divided Stratum B into three sub-phases (1932:53ff; 1943:4,37). Of the earliest phase, B1, only silos were excavated. Their ceramic contents, described as extremely meager, included degenerate Late Bronze types together with forms heralding the pottery of Iron I — but no Philistine material. In the succeeding phase, B2, there were already some structures and Philistine pottery appeared. This phase was destroyed by fire. The settlement of phase B3, dated to the 10th century, was surrounded by a casemate wall. The silos attributed to B1 cut through the destruction debris of Stratum C and were either cut in turn by the silos of B2 and B3 or cancelled by the walls of these later phases that passed over them.

Albright attributed phase B1, which lacked Philistine pottery, to the period immediately following Merneptah but before the advent of the Philistines, i.e., to the end of the 13th and beginning of the 12th centuries BCE. Phase B2, in turn, was dated to the time when Philistine material culture was already present in the Shephelah.

Greenberg (1987) has recently presented unpublished material from the Iron I silos as part of his reevaluation of the finds of Strata C, B1-2. He indicates that features of continuity between strata C and B, are particulary evident in the layout of the site and in its pottery assemblage, and concludes that the material culture of Stratum B is different from that of both Philistine and Israelite Settlement sites. Greenberg argues that stratum B represents a continuation of Canaanite occupation (as is the situation in Gezer) and, on the basis of ceramic similarities, suggests that the inhabitants came from nearby Lachish, after the destruction of its Stratum VI.

Because great importance has been attached to the finds from Tell Beit Mirsim for understanding Israelite Settlement in the hill country and adjoining areas, the evidence must be examined very carefully. Our experience at ⁽Izbet Ṣarṭah made us aware of the difficulties in associating silos stratigraphically and in dating their finds. The pottery found in a silo need not reflect the time of its use unless whole vessels are found. Nor is it easy to determine the relationship between silos. It is entirely possible that where one silo is said to cut another (e.g., Silos 21 and 24 at Tell Beit Mirsim), in fact one silo merely leans against the other. Finally, where it appears that a wall cuts a silo, leaving only half of it (e.g., Silo 21 at Tell Beit Mirsim), it is also possible to interpret it as a silo that was originally intended to be semi-circular and built against the base of the wall. That, in any case, was the situation at ⁽Izbet Ṣarṭah. From all this, we conclude that it is difficult to determine whether or not there had been at Tell Beit Mirsim a phase of silos that preceded the structures with Philistine pottery. As for Stratum B2, it is hard to decide the ethnic affiliation of the populace, in part because the excavation report provides no quantitative data about the Philistine pottery of that level.

In regard to the new data, the pottery published by Greenberg must be dated to the very end of the 13th century or the very beginning of the 12th century BCE, and is, admittedly, in the Canaanite Late Bronze tradition. Nevertheless, it is still difficult to identify the origin of the inhabitants of Stratum B1–2.

Beth-shemesh

At Beth-shemesh, excavated from 1928–1931 by the Haverford College Expedition, under the direction of Grant, a situation similar to that described for Tell Beit Mirsim was discerned: Silos 515 and 530 were found under the walls of Stratum III, which was the Philistine level at the site. In the excavation report, the silos were attributed to the end of Stratum IVb, the last Canaanite city, which had been destroyed by fire (Grant and Wright 1939:10, 41). But elsewhere, Wright, who prepared the finds for publication, noted that the silos were later than Stratum IVb (Wright 1975:251). The pottery found in them resembled that from the silos of Stratum B1 at Tell Beit Mirsim. At first glance, this would appear to be evidence of a pre-Philistine Israelite occupation at Beth-shemesh; the finds, however, are too few and too indecisive to permit a resolution of this sensitive and important issue.

Surveys

During the survey of the Shephelah that Dagan has been conducting for the last few years, no Iron I site with clear evidence of Israelite Settlement has been discovered (oral communication).

*　*　*　*　*　*　*　*　*　*　*

Although the ethno-demographic settlement pattern of the Shephelah in Iron I is not yet sufficiently clear, it is already certain that in most of the region, Israelite Settlement was simply not possible. Kempinski proposed attributing Tel Ṣippor in the Shephelah to the wave of Israelite Settlement at the end of the 13th century BCE (1981:64; also Kempinski and Fritz 1977:144 n.7, 147), but this peculiar suggestion cannot be accepted. The site is located in the western part of the Shephelah, there are no Israelite Settlement sites in the vicinity, and the finds furnish not the slightest hint of Israelite occupation. Nor is there any historical biblical evidence for Israelite activity in the Shephelah before the time of David. Only in the eastern Shephelah, near the foothills, was it conceivable that a brief and limited pre-Philistine Israelite occupation took place; however, the present archaeological evidence is too vague to permit a decisive determination.

Benjamin

For the Iron I period, the plateau of Benjamin, delimited by Jerusalem on the south and Bethel on the north, is one of the best known areas in the country. Assemblages of this period have been excavated at Tell el-Fūl, Tell en-Naṣbeh, Khirbet ed-Dawara and Gibeon, and other sites have been surveyed.

Besides the archaeological evidence, there is a considerable amount of important historical data. Most of the events of the time of Samuel and Saul took place in this region and are described in relatively great detail in the Bible. The population centers of the hill country at that time were Bethel, Mizpah, Gibeah and Gilgal — all in Benjamin — and other sites in the territory, e.g., Gibeon, Ramah, Geba and Michmash, were also very important in those days. The identifications of all these places are absolutely certain. The Bible relates that in the central and western parts of the hills of Benjamin, there were four Gibeonite cities, while to the south, Jerusalem remained a Jebusite city until the time of David. The principal questions are whether or not it is possible to distinguish archaeologically the non-Israelite elements of the area, and to what extent the Gibeonite cities and Jebusite Jerusalem influenced the regional settlement pattern at the beginning of the period of Israelite Settlement.

Excavations

Tell el-Fūl

At Tell el-Fūl, generally identified as biblical Gibeah (sometimes also as Gibeah of Saul and Gibeah of Benjamin; on the problems of the identification, see Demsky 1973, Miller 1975), three seasons of excavations were conducted in 1922, 1933, and 1964. The first two seasons were directed by Albright for the American Schools of Oriental Research, while P. Lapp headed the last campaign under the aegis of ASOR and the Pittsburgh Theological Seminary (Albright 1924; Sinclair 1960; N. Lapp 1978).

Albright and Sinclair (who prepared the material for publication) interpreted the results of the first two seasons as follows: There was some activity at the site in the Middle Bronze period, though no architectural remains were found. During the Late Bronze period, the site was abandoned. The Iron Age remains were divided into three "periods." The meager architectural remains attributed to Period I, preceding the erection of the fortress, were dated (in 1933) to *ca.* 1100 BCE; they were destroyed by a fire (traces of which were discovered beneath the foundations of the fortress), which was associated with the destruction of Gibeah described in Judges 20:37–38.

Period II was divided into two sub-phases, Fortress I and Fortress II. The first fortress was dated to the end of the 11th century BCE and attributed to Saul. The conflagration that destroyed it was connected with the expansion of the Philistines in the wake of their victory at the battle of Gilboa (1 Samuel 31). The second fortress, which was a repaired version of the first, belonged to the beginning of the 10th century BCE. It was abandoned in an orderly manner, for there was no evidence of destruction. Period III was also divided into two: Fortress IIIA was dated to the 8th century, while Fortress IIIB was assigned to the 7th and 6th centuries BCE, at the end of the kingdom of Judah.

Of Fortress I, only a corner portion of a casemate wall with a large projecting rectangular tower was excavated. Albright saw this as the southwest corner of a casemate fortress with four corner towers whose overall dimensions were estimated as about 35–52 x 62–65 m (Fig. 11). These were believed to be the earliest casemates ever discovered in the Land of Israel. He also assumed that Fortress II was a restoration of Fortress I on the same plan. Fortress III was described as a fortified watchtower, with sloping stone buttresses, which had been constructed on top of the southwest corner of the earlier fortress.

After those first two seasons — and especially in the wake of the publication of the casemate wall — various criticisms were voiced over the interpretation of the finds. The main objection was directed at the reconstruction of Fortress I as a large rectangular fortress, since only a single corner had been exposed (e.g., Franken 1961a:472). Others proposed a somewhat different historical interpretation of the finds. Alt and B. Mazar, for instance, connected Fortress I with the Philistines and attributed only Fortress II to the time of Saul (B. Mazar 1954:415; Alt 1964:30–31).

The 1964 season aimed at clarifying the vague spots in the history of the site and in the results of the earlier excavations. The stratigraphic and chronological corrections arrived at were as follows (N. Lapp 1978:xvii): Period I, preceding the first fortress, was now dated to the first half of the 12th century BCE. Period II, with Fortresses I and II, was dated 1025–950 BCE (Fortress I was again associated with Saul). Period III was divided into two phases. The first was further refined into two stages, one dating from about 700 BCE (=Fortress IIIA) and the second dating from about 650–587 BCE (=Fortress IIIB). Lapp changed the reconstruction of Fortress I, proposing instead that it was square in plan and that the wall was of solid rather than casemate construction. On both sides of the hill, casemate-like units were found and attributed to Period III.

Despite the fact that this relatively small site has been intensively investigated over a period of years, it is practically impossible to place the architectural remains into a clear historical and chronological framework. All we can do is study the ceramic finds to learn at what periods the site was inhabited. This minimalistic approach has two causes: The massive architecture of later periods damaged the earliest structures, and the excavations were conducted and published in a manner that frustrates attempts to understand the findings.

A close examination of the results of the first two seasons reveals that no assemblages of pottery were discovered in any of the fortresses; indeed, for all

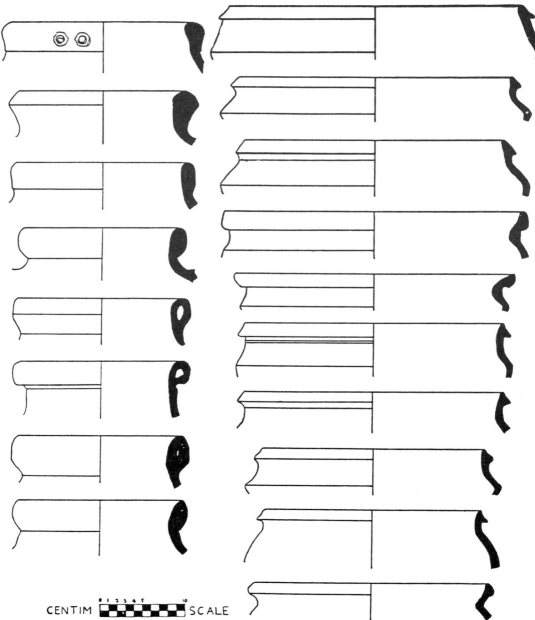

11. Iron I pottery from Tell el-Fūl (Sinclair 1960: Pls. 20–21).

intents and purposes, no floors were found in them either. The stratigraphic divisions were apparently made on the basis of architectural distinctions, with the finds then divided among the various strata! The separations by masonry styles and connections between walls, especially between Fortresses I and II, are not convincing, and it is possible that these distinctions represent constructional rather than chronological phases.

The findings are published in a deficient manner — neither elevations nor sections are provided. The ceramic material presented in the report came largely from accumulations outside the fortress and from the structures to the east of the summit, where the material was mixed. With regards to Sinclair's publication of the pottery (Fig. 11), we will comment on just one matter. The distinctions he drew among the collared-rim store jars (Sinclair 1960:16–17,26) collapse in the face of critical examination (see also R. Amiran 1962:263); a perusal of the published plates shows that they are merely variants of the same vessel, devoid of any chronological significance.

The 1964 excavations not only failed to shed light on the problems that arose from the first two seasons, but raised new difficulties. This is not the place to delve into all the archaeological issues touched on by the most recent archaeological report published, but a few comments are called for.

— Once again, no assemblages were actually found on floors, and no new evidence for dating the earliest fortress was discovered. The section cut to the west of the corner of the fortress made no real contribution to the resolution of this issue.

— The new reconstruction of the early fortress is even less convincing than the original proposal. It is highly unlikely that the wall Lapp considered to be the western continuation of the fortification even belonged to the fortress. The casemate- less reconstruction is strange, since the inner walls of the sections of the casemates uncovered by Albright were left on the plan as stumps!

— The "casemates" of Period III cannot be passed over without comment. They are certainly scrappy in comparison to what is known from other sites. Generally, the outer wall of a casemate was about 1.6 m wide and the inner wall about 1.1 m thick (e.g., Aharoni 1982:198). But at Tell el-Fūl, the outer and inner walls of the western casemates were only 0.8 and 0.5 m wide, respectively. The plan also shows that the casemates on the east were completely different in width; their inner wall was about twice as thick as the outer wall of the western casemates. And finally, the connection between the western casemates and the "watchtower" built over the corner of the early fortress is not at all clear. Nor was any serious attempt made to clarify the relationship between these "casemates" and the early fortress.

— Once again, the findings were published in an obfuscating manner. The plans are insufficiently detailed, there are no clear locus numbers, and a list of walls is lacking. The value of the published north-south section is limited, and there is not a single good east-west section through the casemates.

Can anything nonetheless be said about the history of the site? It seems that the narrowing of the date of Period I to the first half of the 12th century (in the latest report) reflects the absence of Philistine material at the site. However, the fact that the rich and well-dated assemblage at Shiloh (which was destroyed only in the mid-11th century BCE) also included not one single Philistine sherd suggests that Philistine pottery reached the hill country only in the second half of the 11th century, with the military penetration of the Philistines into the region. Thus there is no obstacle to dating Period I to the entire 12th century and the first half of the 11th century.

The absence of Philistine material does raise the question of whether the site was inhabited in the second half of the 11th century BCE (see Chapter 9). The Philistine garrison (1 Samuel 13:3) may have been located at Geba (the Arab village of Jabaᶜ), northwest of Tell el-Fūl. (This is actually also the straight-forward reading of the text: Jonathan defeated the Philistine garrison at Geba, and then prepared himself there for battle.) The reason why the Philistines chose Geba, on the eastern slope of the central ridge, as the seat of their garrison becomes clearer in light of what we now know of the settlement pattern in the territory of Benjamin: Most of the Israelite sites of the period of Settlement and Judges were located in the desert fringe, east of the watershed (see below).

As for the large fortress, there is, in fact, no certainty about its date, since the few sherds found in it seem to have come from fill. It is doubtful whether a large fortress — square or rectangular — can be reconstructed at the site, since all the excavations across the summit have failed to produce any evidence of its existence. If, indeed, there had been a fortress here, it might have belonged — on the basis of comparisons to fortresses in the south of the country, such as Kadesh Barnea, Arad and Khirbet ᶜUza — to a later phase of the Iron Age.

The tantalizing questions of history and historical geography connected with this site, which have repercussions for the study of the entire region, still remain unanswered.

Gibeon

During the years 1956–1962, five seasons of excavations were undertaken at Gibeon on behalf of the University Museum of the University of Pennsylvania under the direction of Pritchard. The stratigraphy of the tell is so muddled that it is practically impossible to date with certainty the fortifications, houses, rock-hewn installations — or any other feature found there (for a harsh critique of the excavation report, see P. Lapp 1968). However, the ceramic assemblage from the tell (even if not from clean levels) and the evidence from the cemetery discovered at the site make it possible to outline the history of Gibeon. The site was inhabited during MB II,[6] LB (as the finds came

---

6   The possibility that the large wall, what Pritchard calls the "later city wall," belonged to this period cannot be ruled out. Pritchard dated it to the 10th century, but its stratigraphic position is not at all clear. Its width and, to a great degree, its construction method, recall the Middle Bronze fortifications found at Hebron, Beth-zur, Bethel and Shiloh, all in the hill country. For a description of the wall, see Pritchard 1962:101–104.

exclusively from the necropolis, it is doubtful whether there was permanent occupation on the mound), Iron I and Iron II. Pritchard dated the "earlier wall," which was 1.6–1.8 m wide, to Iron I. Indeed, evidence of this period was also found inside this wall, according to the published section (Pritchard 1964:34–39), but the area excavated was too small to permit any unequivocal conclusions to be drawn.

Since Gibeon is the only one of the "Gibeonite cities" to have been excavated, it is particularly distressing that, contrary to expectations, the work there made no contribution to clarifying the historical and archaeological background of the Hivite population which, according to the Bible (Joshua 9), lived in the hills of Benjamin at the time.

Tell en-Naṣbeh (Mizpah)

Tell en-Naṣbeh, located south of Ramallah, was excavated during five seasons between 1926–1935 by Badè on behalf of the Pacific School of Religion (McCown 1947a; Wampler 1947). No occupation of either the Middle or Late Bronze period was found here (in one place — McCown 1947a:180 — Wampler noted that fragments of a wishbone-handle bowl and several *bilbils* were found, but it is hard to know what he meant; in any case, such items — as they are understood today — do not appear on the pottery plates of the excavation report). On the basis of a few vessels where the Canaanite ceramic tradition is perceptible, Aharoni estimated that Israelite Settlement at the site had already begun in the 13th or even 14th (!) century BCE (1982:174; Aharoni, Fritz and Kempinski 1975:121). However, these vessels could just as easily appear in the 12th century, especially at its beginning (Chapter 9).

Almost the entire Iron Age city — its fortifications, houses, streets — was uncovered; only the highest part was eroded down to bedrock (Fig. 12). The excavators had difficulty distinguishing the various construction phases and thus divided the remains into only two strata of long duration.

The excavators characterized the Iron I settlement as a village or small poor provincial town. To this stage, which they dated to the 11th century, they assigned the "inner wall," two towers, and several houses. The width of the inner wall, which was discerned primarily on the southern and northwestern sides of the mound, was a meter and sometimes a little more. The excavators hesitated over the question of whether or not it was part of a casemate wall, especially since it was hard to distinguish the wall from the buildings adjoining it.

Later on, in Iron II, a massive solid wall was constructed (it was asociated with Asa, based on 1 Kings 15:22). Three of the buildings attributed to this stage were exceptional. They were large four-room houses adjacent to the fortification wall and may have had a public function of some kind (Branigan 1966). At least one of them was erected on top of earlier buildings. (For a new

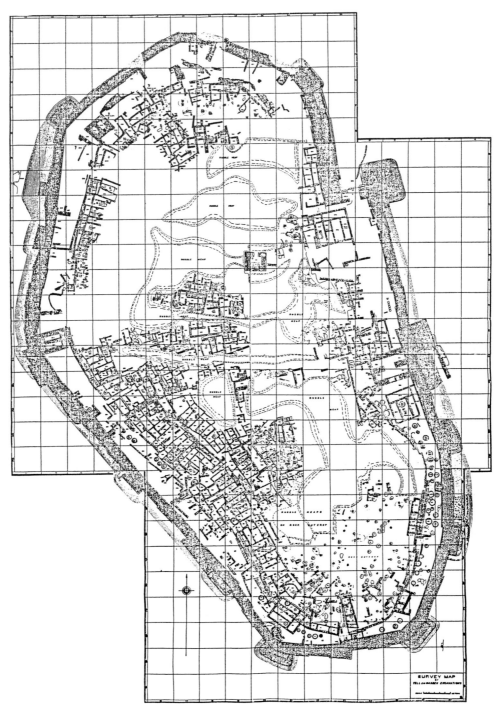

12. Tell en-Naṣbeh — general plan (McCown 1947a).

attempt at an architectural-stratigraphic analysis of the buildings at the site, see McClellan 1984.) The settlement unearthed at Tell en-Naṣbeh has two prominent features — pillared houses and stone-lined silos; most of the latter were found in the area between the outer row of houses and the large (outer) fortification wall.

The plan published in the excavation report included all the architectural remains that were found on the site, spanning the Iron I to Persian periods. Given this, it is rather surprising that the plan looks very uniform, with few modifications. The almost unavoidable explanation is that these buildings, with only minor changes, remained in use from their foundation until the site was abandoned. Bearing this in mind, and in light of the amazing resemblance, in many details, between the layout of Tell en-Naṣbeh and that of the Iron I village uncovered at Ai (Chapter 6), one might suggest that Tell en-Naṣbeh really was a village founded in Iron I that underwent almost no subsequent alterations.

All that was added to the core of the settlement in Iron II was the large fortification wall and the three four-room houses noted above. (The available historical evidence also supports this proposal: The Bible breathes not a hint of any destruction of Mizpah, neither in the wars between Israel and Judah after the kingdom split nor, apparently, during Sennacherib's campaign — the site is not mentioned in the famous itinerary of Isaiah 10:28–32). If this hypothesis is correct, then Tell en-Naṣbeh presents a unique example of the plan of a large Israelite village from the period of the Judges.

Elliptical in outline and covering an area of over 15 dunams, the site was well-adapted to the topography. The houses along the outer edge of the village, some of which were pillared buildings of the three- and four-room types, were contiguous and rested against a thickened wall to form a line of defense toward the slope. In some places, a chain of their broad rear rooms formed what look like casemates. The uppermost part of the site has unfortunately been eroded, so there is no way of knowing its full layout. Most of the grain silos, which are more characteristic of Iron I than Iron II (as noted in Chapter 2), were found in a peripheral belt surrounding the village; there may be examples of this phenomenon from other sites as well (Chapter 6). The builders of the massive wall took this belt of silos into consideration, as is evident from the unusual space separating the houses from the fortification wall. This wall, which may well have been built by Asa, thus "wrapped up" the existing village of houses and silos. The three large houses were constructed later on, apparently for administrative purposes. (Two of them were erected in the relatively empty area between the walls.)

It is difficult to determine when the settlement was founded—perhaps it developed slowly during the Iron I and 10th century until it achieved its final form. However, there is nothing in the published material to prevent dating the beginning of activity to the 12th century BCE (see already Albright 1948:204).

Khirbet ed-Dawara

The site is located in the desert fringe, adjacent to the village of Mukhmas (map. ref. 17775 14150). The author conducted two seasons of excavations there in 1985–86, on behalf of the Department of Land of Israel Studies at Bar-Ilan University (Finkelstein, forthcoming b). The surface area of the site is about 5 dunams, and its outline is circular (hence the Arabic name, which means "round"). Even before the excavation began, a collapsed peripheral wall and rows of monolithic pillars (Fig. 13) were visible on the surface.

Khirbet ed-Dawara turned out to be a one-period site, founded in the second half of the 11th century BCE and abandoned at the end of the 10th century. All of the remains belonged to a single architectural phase. The settlement was surrounded by a solid wall, 2–3 m in width, built of large field stones. Within the fortification, on the western side of the site, we exposed three four-room houses in which monolithic pillars were used. Two of the houses were perpendicular to the outer wall, while the third (which was between them) was parallel to the wall (Fig. 86). The broad-rooms of the two perpendicular houses and a parallel unit to the side aisles of the middle house formed a series of "casemates" adjacent to the outer wall. Another four-room house, perpendicular to the wall, was unearthed on the north-eastern side of the site. Because bedrock was already exposed in the entire center of the site, we cannot determine the plan of the core of the settlement.

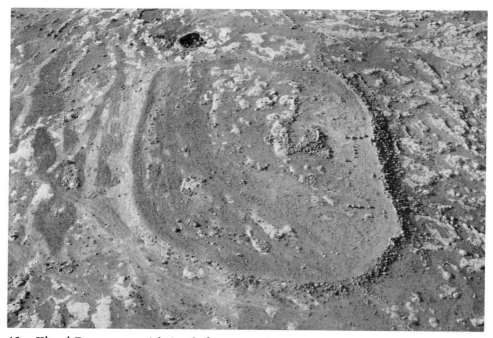

13. Kh. ed-Dawara — aerial view before excavation.

Surveys

Eight Iron I sites discovered in the territory of Benjamin during the 1968 Survey supplement the excavated sites (Kallai 1972). The distribution of these sites is most interesting. Seven of them (87.5%) are in the eastern part of the region, in the desert fringe, where they represent 28% of all the sites of all periods investigated. The single Iron I site up on the ridge — Khirbet el-Burj, biblical Beeroth (Yeivin 1971b:140–144) — constitutes only 3% of all the sites examined in that topographical unit. In Iron II, the balance of settlement changed, and the desert fringe sites then constituted only 53% of all the sites in Benjamin in that period. Although the survey was incomplete (the western slopes of Benjamin were hardly surveyed), the above percentages do suffice to show a trend toward a concentration of sites in the eastern part of the territory of Benjamin — even taking into account the excavated sites, which are all located in the central ridge. As for the chronological aspect, the finds from Tell el-Fūl and Tell en-Naṣbeh attest that Israelite Settlement in Benjamin began early in Iron I.

* * * * * * * * * *

The accumulated archaeological data from Benjamin, combined with the biblical descriptions of the days of Samuel and Saul, indicate that the main Israelite activity in Benjamin in Iron I was concentrated in the eastern part of the ridge and in the desert fringe (Fig. 14). It is probable that the reason for this was the presence of the Gibeonite cities in the western part of the ridge (Gibeon and Beeroth) and slopes (Kiriath-yearim near Abu Ghosh and Chephirah near the small village of Qatanna, north of Maᶜale ha-Ḥamisha). Incidentally, neither the Gibeonite cities nor Jebusite Jerusalem had any "daughter" villages.

The territory of Benjamin was thus divided along ethnic lines: The Hivites settled in the west and the Israelites in the east. In any case, we are unable to single out differences in the material culture between these two ethnic entities living in the territory of Benjamin at the beginning of Iron I. Nor do we presently know when the Hivites came to the region or how their cities, headed by Gibeon, later became Israelite settlements (see Yeivin 1971b; on the possibility that Saul's family originally came from Gibeon, see Demsky 1973).

EPHRAIM

In this important territory, in the heartland of Israelite Settlement, we have undertaken an intensive regional project with the Iron I period as a central

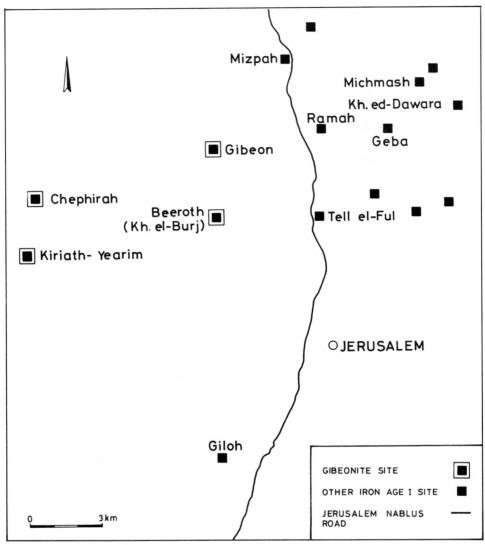

14. Iron I sites in Benjamin.

focus. The interim results of our excavations at Shiloh and of our survey in Ephraim will be described in depth in Chapters 4 and 5; there we will also discuss the conclusions arising from our study of the pattern of settlement in Ephraim during the period of Israelite Settlement. Here we will confine ourselves to summarizing the results of four excavations on the margins of this region, Khirbet Raddana, Ai and Bethel on the south and ʿIzbet Ṣarṭah on the west.

Excavations

Khirbet Raddana

Four campaigns of salvage excavations were conducted at this site, located on the western edge of the city of el-Bireh (map ref. 1693 1466) by Callaway and Cooley (1971; Cooley 1975). Khirbet Raddana is situated on an extension of a ridge surrounded on three sides by deep wadis with springs. Although there was some activity here in the EB I and Byzantine periods, for all intents and purposes, this is a one-period site. The Iron I settlement covered — according to the excavators — an area of 8–10 dunams (but it might have been smaller) and comprised five or six groups of structures, each featuring two or three pillared houses around a central courtyard. Alterations in the buildings indicated two phases. The earlier one was dated to the end of the 13th century BCE and the later to the span 1125–1050 BCE. Khirbet Raddana was destroyed by fire. (Y. Aharoni 1971a:133–135 proposed to identify the site with biblical Ataroth.)

A relatively large number of metal implements were found (Waldbaum 1978:25). Although most were made of bronze, three were of iron (one was the tip of a plowshare). Additional finds included three bases of incense burners and a conical seal of black steatite. Two other ceramic artifacts are of particular importance: a jar handle inscribed with three letters in proto-Canaanite script (Y. Aharoni 1971a: Cross and Freedman 1971; Cross 1979; our Fig. 103) and a multihandled krater with a kind of tube which almost encircled the inner circumference just below the rim and which opened inward by means of two bovine heads (Fig. 15).

Aharoni saw the Raddana inscription as supporting his elevation of the beginning of Israelite Settlement to the 14th century BCE, while Cross and Freedman dated it to the end of the 13th century or *ca.* 1200 BCE (Chapter 9). The krater, which was probably used for libations, has parallels from the period of the Old Hittite Kingdom. Kempinski (1973:39,43) took this as evidence of Hittite influence in the Land of Israel and related this to B. Mazar's view (1981:76–79) that at the end of the 13th century and beginning of the 12th, when the Hittite empire was devastated, some groups emigrated from Anatolia into the Land of Israel.

The village of Khirbet Raddana is of unquestionable importance for the study of Israelite Settlement in the hill country both because it is a well-preserved single-period site and because of its relatively well-developed material culture. When the final excavation report is published, it will certainly enrich our knowledge of the culture of the inhabitants of the hill country in the Iron I period. But even now, it is worth commenting on the issue of chronology (and these remarks also hold true for the dates assigned in the past to other sites in the hill country).

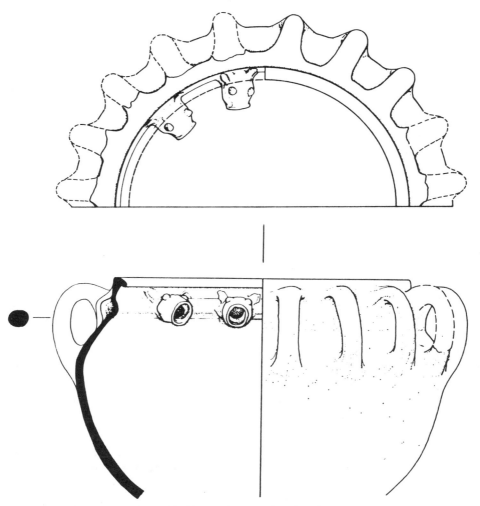

15. Kh. Raddana — multihandled krater decorated with bulls' heads (Callaway and Cooley 1971: 17).

In their preliminary reports, the excavators of Raddana did not specify the reasoning behind their dates for the beginning and end of activity at the site, but it seems that at least some of the considerations were not archaeological (archaeology still cannot provide absolutely precise dates in the Iron Age), but rather general historical ones that are not necessarily valid for every single site in the hill country (Chapter 9). Their initial date was obviously based on the mention of Israel in the Merneptah stele. Their closing date apparently derived from the biblical allusion to the destruction of Shiloh by the Philistines in the mid-11th century BCE (Jeremiah 7:12 etc.), in the wake of their defeat of Israel in the battle of Ebenezer (1 Samuel 4).

The preliminary excavation reports present no hard evidence for raising the date of the founding of Khirbet Raddana to the end of the 13th century — except for the inscription, whose date is largely and tautologically based on the date of the site. Quite the contrary, the well-developed pillared buildings uncovered there strongly suggest that this one-period site was not established during a very early stage of Iron I. A date in the mid-12th century — or even a bit later — best fits all the evidence. Because the preliminary reports made no mention of finding any red-slipped and burnished sherds or any Philistine material, the excavators' dating of the destruction of the site to the mid-11th century BCE seems reasonable.

Ai

Two expeditions worked at Ai (Khirbet et-Tell east of Ramallah). From 1933–1935, J. Marquet-Krause undertook three seasons of excavations on behalf of the Rothschild Expedition. During the years 1964–1972, J. Callaway directed seven campaigns under the aegis of the American Schools of Oriental Research and other American institutions. Ai was uninhabited from the end of EB III (*ca.* 2400 BCE) until the beginning of the Iron Age, a fact which naturally has far-reaching implications for evaluating the biblical conquest traditions (on the problems of the identification and conquest of Ai, see Yeivin 1971c:179–181; more recently, Zevit 1983; and Chapter 8 below). The remains of the early Iron Age village are very important for the study of early Israelite architecture because, as in the case of nearby Khirbet Raddana, the absence of later occupation made it possible to expose a considerable portion of the settlement.

Marquet-Krause uncovered a group of buildings along the northern edge of this village (1949:22–24; our Figs. 16, 85). They were typical pillared buildings of the three- and four-room types, adjoining one another so that the broad rear rooms created a kind of casemate wall that served as a line of defense. Access to the buildings was, of course, from inside the settlement. The broad rear rooms did not create a straight line, but were alternately offset and inset. This special manner of building, which was apparently paralleled at other Iron I sites in the hill country, heralded the construction techniques of the Monarchy period (Shiloh 1978:45–46; Chapter 6 below).

Callaway continued to expose the early Iron Age village (1965:22–27; 1969a; 1975:49–52; 1976:29–30), which covered an area of 10–12 dunams (as opposed to the *c.* 110 dunams of the Early Bronze city) and comprised, according to the excavator, some 20 groups of pillared buildings. This settlement, too, was dated to the span 1220–1050 BCE, with two phases discerned. The first, in which there were paved streets, was described as an unfortified rural village and dated 1220–1125 BCE. In the second phase, dated 1125–1050 BCE, the population — according to the excavator — was greater,

16. Ai — Iron I remains, Marquet-Krause excavation (courtesy of the Department of Antiquities).

houses underwent minor renovations, silos were dug next to the houses, and some of the alleys were blocked. The abandonment of the site was placed in the mid-11th century BCE because no burnished vessels were found.

Callaway claimed that the archaeological evidence suggested that the inhabitants of the first phase came from a background of village life, while the occupants of the second phase brought with them new traditions that hinted at a nomadic background. He based his argument that the latter lacked a sedentary tradition on the fact that they blocked the paths between the buildings with silos. In this manner, Callaway (1968; 1969a) "solved" the problem of the contradiction between the biblical narrative (the conquest of Ai) and the archaeological evidence (the absence of Late Bronze remains): The inhabitants of the first phase were not Israelites, but perhaps Hivites, and the "conquest" of Ai was simply the takeover of this village by Israelites who then became the occupants of the site in the second phase.

Callaway also attempted to make chronological distinctions among the collared-rim store jars from the excavation: Those of the first phase had long collars and high rims, while those of the second phase had short collars and folded rims (1969a:8–9; our Fig. 92).

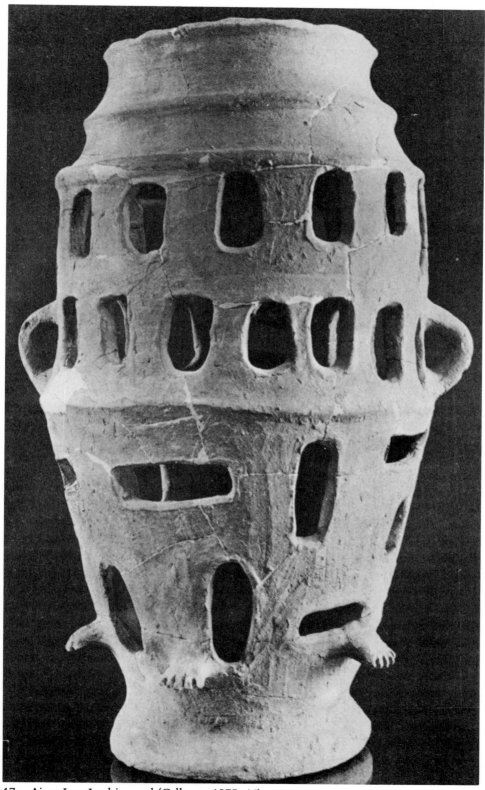

17.   Ai — Iron I cultic stand (Callaway 1975: 46).

Although in the case of Ai as well, the final excavation report has yet to be published, we must take issue with several important points. First, it is extremely doubtful that there are sufficient archaeological data for building a theory about the conquest of Ai as far-reaching as Callaway's. He obviously arrived at this strange solution in a desperate attempt to find some way to accommodate the biblical narrative with the archaeological evidence.

Even if there were two Iron I phases at Ai, it is highly unlikely that the difference between them could be attributed to populations coming from different social and economic backgrounds. At other sites in the hill country, there is no evidence for such a phenomenon; on the contrary, all the features of Ai, including those of the first phase, also appeared at other Israelite sites in the region throughout Iron I.

Callaway's fixing of 1220 BCE as the foundation date of the settlement clearly derived from a historical conception for which there is no archaeological support (Chapter 9). As far as can be determined from the preliminary reports, there is no reason — ceramically speaking — why the establishment of the settlement cannot be dated to, say, 1150 BCE, a date that would suit the architectural evidence of the relatively well-developed pillared buildings found at the site. Finally, the notion that chronological distinctions can be drawn among types of collared- rim store jars is successfully challenged by the data from the other excavations in the hill country (Chapter 7).

Bethel

The mound of Bethel, one of the most important sites in the central hill country, was excavated in the years 1934, 1954, 1957 and 1960 by the American Schools of Oriental Research and the Pittsburgh Theological Seminary. The first season was directed by Albright and the others by Kelso with Albright's assistance (Kelso 1968:32–35, 63–66).

Bethel was a fortified city in the Middle Bronze period. During LB I, there may have been a gap in settlement. The site then made a rapid comeback, but the flourishing LB II city was eventually destroyed in a massive conflagration that was dated *ca.* 1240–1235 BCE.

The Iron I occupation was poor and entirely different in material culture from its predecessor. On the basis of architecture and pottery, four phases were discerned. The first two were apparently destroyed by fire. The end of the first phase was dated to no later than the beginning of the 12th century BCE; the second phase spanned most of the 12th century. Phase 3, in which hand-burnished pottery made its debut, was dated to the first half of the 11th century or even down to 1025 BCE or later. Phase 4 was further divided into two sub-phases, with the earlier one dated to the end of the 11th and beginning of the 10th centuries BCE and the second to the late 10th century. The meager pottery of the first three phases was compared to the material from Stratum B1 at Tell

Beit Mirsim and that of Phase 4 was compared to Strata B2 and B3 of the same site. The feature that characterized the architecture of the Iron I buildings was the use of rows of pillars.

The stratigraphic situation at Bethel was classic in that it seemingly fit the biblical description of the conquest of the Canaanite cities in general and Luz in particular: A prosperous Canaanite city of the Late Bronze period was set ablaze and replaced by Israelites whose material culture was very sparse. However, Bethel turns out to be the only site in the entire Land of Israel with just this succession (Chapter 8). Here, too, the date of the destruction of the Late Bronze city was obviously determined by recourse to historical, non-archaeological considerations; none of the actual finds prevents a later date (Chapter 9).

The layout of the Iron I settlement is not sufficiently clear because the village of Beitin, located on the tell, prevented large areas from being excavated. The data presented in the excavation report are insufficient for determining the significance of the four phases, so it is hard to decide whether they represent genuine occupation stages or simply minor changes in the buildings over the course of time. Bethel became an important city during the period of the Monarchy.

ʿIzbet Ṣarṭah

The site is situated on a low hill (map ref. 1467 1679) northeast of Rosh Haʿayin and southwest of Kafr Qasem, close to the place known as ʿIzbet Ṣarṭah. The name stems from the fact that in recent generations, the inhabitants of the village of Ṣarṭa, which is about 12 km to the east, cultivated the area seasonally (ʿizbah = seasonal farm or rural settlement in Egyptian Arabic). The hill on which the site is located overlooks a broad expanse of the coastal plain. On the other side of the Aphek pass, Tell Aphek is situated about 3 km to the west, at the headwaters of the Yarkon River (Fig. 1).

The site was discovered in 1973 by the archaeological survey team of Tel Aviv University. Kochavi, who headed the survey, proposed identifying the site with Ebenezer (e.g. 1977:3,12), the place where the Israelites encamped before their battle with the Philistines (1 Samuel 4:1). However, it is uncertain whether this was the name of a settlement rather than a topographical landmark (Garsiel and Finkelstein 1978; on the identification of the site, see also Miller 1983:125–128).

Between 1976–1978, four short excavation campaigns were undertaken at ʿIzbet Ṣarṭah under the joint sponsorship of the Institute of Archaeology of Tel Aviv University and the Department of the Land of Israel Studies of Bar-Ilan University. The expedition was headed by Kochavi, and the author was field director (Finkelstein 1986). Three strata were uncovered. The earliest (Stratum III) was dated to the span between the end of the 13th or beginning of the

12th century BCE and the beginning of the 11th century. Stratum II had a shorter existence at the end of the 11th century, while Stratum I, also short-lived, was dated to the beginning of the 10th century BCE.

In the vicinity of the site, and in a similar topographical position on the border of the foothills and the coastal plain, the survey discovered six additional sites of this period in an 8-km long stretch between Jaljuliya on the north and Rosh Haᶜayin on the south. Considerations that were fully described in Chapter 2 led us to the conclusion that these represented an influx of hill-country people.

The site is of great importance for the study of the period of Israelite Settlement for three reasons. First, the absence of later occupation at the site enabled a large area to be exposed with relative ease, and the site-plan of each stratum could be recovered. The results of the excavations thus have direct implications for understanding the development of Israelite architecture in the Iron I period (Chapter 6). Second, the proximity of the site to Aphek, which was intensively excavated, makes it possible, for the first time, to examine the relationship between a Canaanite city that subsequently became an important Philistine center and a small Israelite Settlement site nearby. Finally, the location of ᶜIzbet Ṣarṭah on the geographical border between the foothills and the coastal plain — which was, at that time, also the ethnic boundary between the Israelites in the hill country and the Canaanites and (later) Philistines in the coastal plain — meant that events occurring both in the immediate vicinity and in more distant regions were felt at once. The history of ᶜIzbet Ṣarṭah was thus a reflection of the historical and demographic development in this sensitive and intriguing region.

Stratum III was elliptical in outline and covered an area of 2.2 dunams (Fig. 76). Access to the site was on the northeastern side through a narrow opening between two monolithic jambs, leading to a vestibule paved with stone slabs. The broad central courtyard was enclosed by a wall composed of large field stones. From this wall, other walls projected outward at right angles to separate the adjoining rooms from one another. The outer wall of these rooms — unlike the inner wall — was not a smooth line; in other words, the width of the rooms varied. Bedrock generally served as flooring. The rooms opened onto the courtyard but there were no doors between them. There were a number of stone-lined silos in the courtyard. Two segments of the inner wall (around the courtyard) and the adjoining rooms were excavated, for a total length of 55 m (Fig. 18). Light bricky material of Stratum III was found between the rock surface and the floors of the next stratum; it had been leveled to serve as makeup for the Stratum II buildings.

Stratum III was abandoned in an orderly manner, so only a few whole vessels were found. These include three collared-rim store jars (Fig. 19). Because this was the first occupation at the site, the sherds reflect the accumulation from throughout the existence of that stratum. Among the

18. ʿIzbet Ṣarṭah — aerial view. Note Stratum III peripheral wall on left and right and Stratum II four-room house in center.

earliest finds are a small fragment of an imported stirrup jar, apparently executed in the Simple Style of Late Mycenaean IIIB (Fig. 105; Chapter 9); a large fragment of a big krater decorated in the palm-and-ibex style; part of a krater with an applied plastic ornamentation of a head of an ibex (Fig. 102); bases of "Canaanite" store jars; and rims of bowls and cooking pots manufactured in the ceramic traditions of the Late Bronze period (Fig. 20). This pottery pegs the beginning of activity at the site to the end of the 13th or beginning of the 12th century BCE. A few rims of rounded red- slipped bowls and fragments of jars with straight, unprofiled rims also came from this stratum, indicating that it lasted until the first half of the 11th century. The entire ceramic assemblage, which included a few Philistine sherds, demonstrates that the inhabitants were in contact with the nearby coastal plain.

Following a brief gap, there was renewed activity at the site. Stratum II was totally different in plan from Stratum III and gave evidence of a certain amount of planning (Fig. 21). In the center of the site, which now covered an area of about 4 dunams, a large four-room house was erected. It was surrounded by dozens of silos (Fig. 22), crowded together, which had been dug into the bricky make-up and the building remains of Stratum III. The periphery of the

19. ʿIzbet Ṣarṭah — Stratum III storage jars.

settlement was delineated by a series of small houses. The plans of two of them could be reconstructed and they, too, belonged to the four-room house type. These houses were not contiguous, so that unlike the Stratum III settlement, there was now no line of defense facing the slope.

The dimensions of the central house were about 12 x 16 m, and it was preserved to a height of two to three courses. Its outer walls were up to 1.4 m thick; both faces were constructed of large field stones. Parts of these outer walls were robbed at a later date and reused in an agricultural terrace. Two rows of stone-built pillars divided the house into three long rooms. The side rooms were paved with stone slabs, while the rest of the area used the native bedrock and beaten earth as flooring. The entrance to the building was at the end of the western wall and led into a side room. A small room was attached to the northern side of the building.

Altogether 43 silos were uncovered around the central building (Fig. 89). Their sides were lined with stone and their floors consisted of either bedrock or a pavement of small stones. A few of the silos leaned against the walls of the

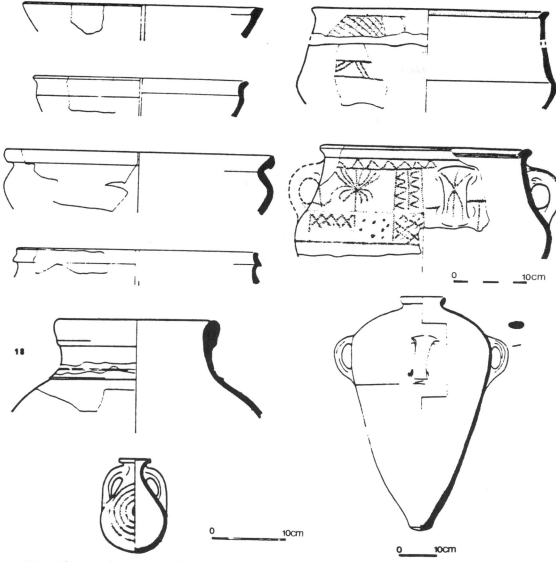

20. ʿIzbet Ṣarṭah — pottery from Stratum III.

building; in some parts of the site, they were contiguous. In several places, a hard surface of beaten earth was found between the silos.

One of the most important finds was an ostracon in proto- Canaanite script discovered in Silo 605 (but it did not necessarily belong to Stratum II). Some 80 characters were inscribed in five rows. The upper four rows seem to be some kind of student exercise, while the entire alphabet appears in the fifth row, written from left to right (Kochavi 1977; Demsky 1977; see also Naveh 1978;

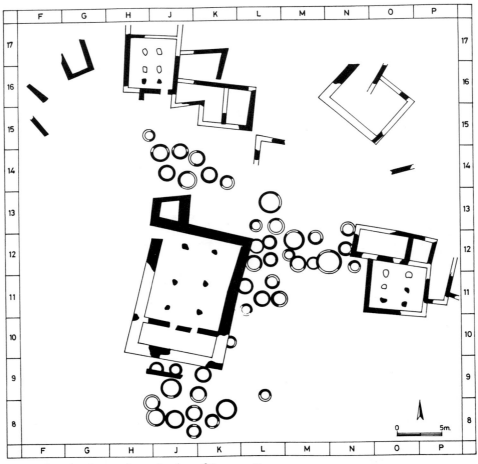

21. ʿIzbet Ṣarṭah — schematic plan of Stratum II.

Cross 1980:8–15; Dotan 1981). This find provides important evidence of literacy among the inhabitants of the hill country during the period of Israelite Settlement and the Judges.

Stratum II had a brief existence at the end of the 11th century and was then abandoned, also in an orderly manner. Shortly afterward, the site came to life again for a decade or two at the beginning of the 10th century BCE. The Stratum I settlement was even smaller. The central four-room house was restored with several changes: low partition walls were built between the pillars in each row; two rooms were added on the north side; and several installations were built inside the building. A few new silos were dug to replace those that had gone out of use. During the cutting of these silos, now numbering about 10, the Stratum II buildings at the edge of the site were damaged. The ceramic types present in the Stratum I assemblage were virtually

22. ʿIzbet Ṣarṭah — four-room house after reconstruction. On left, silos of Stratum II.

23. ʿIzbet Ṣarṭah — Proto-Canaanite ostracon.

identical to those from Stratum II; however, statistical analysis revealed differences in the relative quantities of the various types from one stratum to the next.

The history of occupation at ʿIzbet Ṣarṭah faithfully reflected the historical development of settlement in the border area between the coastal plain and the foothills during the Iron I period. At certain times, Israelites reached the margins of the coastal plain; at other times, the inhabitants were driven back into the heart of the hill country.

There are two alternatives for the date of the first occupation at ʿIzbet Ṣarṭah: shortly before the destruction of nearby Egypto-Canaanite Aphek or during the brief period after its destruction, but before the Philistines became established there (on the history of Aphek in this period, see Kochavi 1981:80-82). It is possible that some of the other sites found during the survey along the edge of the foothills were also first settled at this time. Their concentration opposite Aphek — while at the same time and in a similar geographic setting, practically no sites of this period were found further south — demands an explanation, and the matter will be discussed in Chapter 11.

The abandonment of Stratum III was apparently related to the rising tensions between Israel and the Philistines in this region at the beginning of the 11th century, tensions that would eventually culminate in the decisive battle at Ebenezer. In the wake of the Israelite defeat, it was not possible to resettle ʿIzbet Ṣarṭah until the time of Saul, at the end of the 11th century (=Stratum II). After a while, however, the Philistines regained the upper hand and once again repulsed the Israelites eastward. The renewed westward expansion at the beginning of the 10th century (=Stratum I) must be associated with the reign of David. Soon after, when the fertile plain of the Yarkon basin became available for Israelite settlers, ʿIzbet Ṣarṭah was abandoned forever. It is precisely at this time that we find the first evidence of Israelite occupation at nearby Aphek (Kochavi 1981:82).

MANASSEH

The geography of the northern part of the central hill country, the territory of Manasseh, is completely different from the regions to the south. In Manasseh, wide valleys and broad areas composed of soft limestone produce a relatively moderate landscape. On either side of the Shechem Basin, there are two rows of relatively large springs. For these reasons, Manasseh was easier to settle than the hillier areas to the south. Certain locales, such as the Dothan Valley, are actually more like the northern valleys than the central hills in their suitability for settlement. As a result, the mounds of large cities — Shechem, Tirzah, Samaria and Dothan — are found in this region, as well as the densest array of settlements of any of the mountainous areas of the Land of Israel.

The importance of the territory of Manasseh during the period of Israelite Settlement is evident from both the Bible and archaeology. The Bible gives pride of place to the traditions of the sanctity of Shechem and Mt. Ebal, while archaeological surveys have revealed an almost unparalleled site density. However, the population in the region during Iron I was not homogeneous, and this complicates efforts to understand the historical and demographic processes that operated in this part of the country.

Excavations

Shechem

"The uncrowned queen of Palestine," as Wright (1965:9) described Shechem, was the most important city in the northern part of the central hill country from the Middle Bronze to Iron I periods. Mentioned frequently in the historical sources, Shechem was an important cult place throughout this time span. From the Bible, it is difficult to comprehend the character and date of the process of Israelite infiltration into Shechem; the Iron I inhabitants there were apparently mixed, that is, composed of different ethnic elements (Chapter 5).

The abundance of historical information makes Shechem one of the most tantalizing sites in the country. Indeed, Tell Balaṭa, the mound of biblical Shechem, has been excavated by various expeditions since the beginning of the century. Sellin dug here as early as 1913–1914, and then returned for four more campaigns in 1926 and 1927. Under the direction of Wright, an expedition sponsored by Drew University, McCormick Theological Seminary, and the American Schools of Oriental Research conducted eight campaigns at Shechem from 1956–1969 (Wright 1965; for the last two seasons, see Dever 1974).

Despite the great effort expended by the American expedition in excavating the site, their final reports have yet to be published, and it is hard to understand the character of Shechem in our period from the preliminary reports. Toombs, one of the excavators, recently (1979) attempted to summarize the history of the site during the Late Bronze and Iron I periods. The prosperous Late Bronze city was destroyed even before the end of that period, some time at the end of the 14th or beginning of the 13th century BCE. Resuscitation of the site began immediately, with no gap in occupation. Shechem was now less densely populated and the quality of construction poorer. The excavators found considerable continuity between the Late Bronze and Iron I settlements, i.e., there was no destruction or no cultural revolution during the transition between those two periods (for the ceramic evidence, see Boraas 1986). They felt that this situation accorded very well with the absence of any tradition about a conquest of Shechem in the Bible and therefore concluded that the Israelite population had infiltrated the city in a peaceful manner. The Iron I settlement was destroyed in a massive conflagration that was attributed to Abimelech (Judges 9:45; on Iron I Shechem and the Abimelech narratives, see Na'aman 1986).

It is difficult, at present, to evaluate the contribution of the Shechem excavations to the study of the process of Israelite Settlement. For all practical purposes, the material thus far published is not conducive to learning about the material culture of the site in the Iron I period. It is, in fact, doubtful whether the results of the excavations have helped to clarify the history of Shechem during the period under discussion.

Mt. Ebal Site

Known in Arabic as el-Burnat (hat,in Arabic), the site covers 4 dunams on an extension of the northeast slope of Mt. Ebal. Zertal, who discovered it during a survey in 1980, has so far conducted five campaigns of excavations under the aegis of the Department of Archaeology of Haifa University (Zertal 1985c; 1986a; *Had. Arch.* 85, 1984:24–26 and especially 1986b:225–275).

Two phases, both belonging to Iron I, have been discerned. During the first, a temenos wall enclosed a large central courtyard, in the middle of which there was a round installation built of rubble, about 2 m in diameter. The later phase was the principal one (Fig. 24). Just inside the enclosure wall, a new and slighly narrower temenos wall was constructed. It had an entrance 8 m wide between two parallel walls. Three broad steps, paved with stone slabs, were built in the entryway.

In the center of the site, a full-fledged structure built of large field stones was erected over the earlier installation. This was a rectangular construction, with no entrance, measuring about 7 x 9 m; the walls, 1.5 m thick, were preserved to a height of about a meter. The corners of the structure were precisely oriented to the four points of the compass. The interior space of the structure, with two "piers," was filled with four layers of ashes, earth, and stones. There was no floor. Numerous animal bones were mixed in with the ashes. A kind of bench, 60 cm wide, was built around and against three sides of the structure; it was about a meter lower than the tops of the walls of the central structure.

Adjoining the building on the southwest side were two stone-paved courtyards in which various installations were built. These installations contained either ashes and animal bones or pieces of broken pottery. A wall about 7 m long and 1.2 m wide separated the two courtyards. Many installations were also found between the central complex and the temenos wall. The site was abandoned, with no destruction layer found. An Iron I settlement was recently discovered east of the "temenos," but has not yet been excavated.

Zertal concluded that this was a cultic site surrounded by a temenos wall. His main considerations were the plan of the site — an enclosure with an

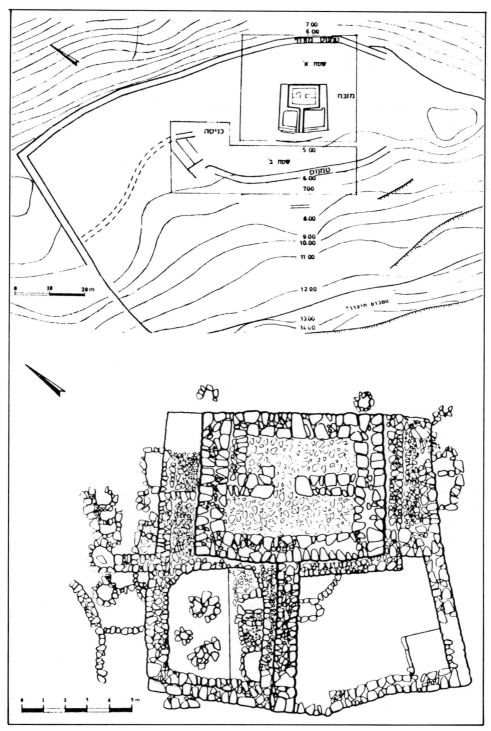

24. Mt. Ebal — general plan (above) and plan of the central structure (below) (*Had. Arch.* 85, 1984: 24–25).

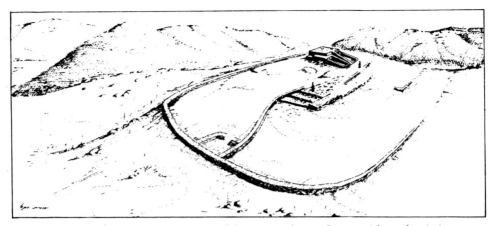

25. Mt. Ebal — Zertal's reconstruction of the site, a cultic enclosure with an altar in its center (Zertal 1985b).

isolated building in its center — and the finds — installations with ashes and large quantities of bones and pottery, which seemed to be the remains of sacrifices and offerings brought to the site. Zertal interpreted the central structure as a sacrificial altar (Fig. 25), some 3 m higher than its surroundings, filled with what he saw as the debris of the earlier cultic activity at the site. In his opinion, the wall separating the two courtyards served as a ramp leading up to the altar, and the bench around the central structure was a walkway for the priests.

Zertal found support for his hypothesis in ancient literary sources — the description of the altar in the book of Ezekiel and in the Mishnah *Middot* — and also in the faunal remains — all from unblemished, ritually prescribed animals, mostly young and male, which had been burnt in an open fire and cut near the joints, in compliance with the biblical injunctions governing sacrifices.

The excavator dated the early phase of the site to the second half of the 13th century BCE on the basis of two Egyptian scarabs found at the site, one of the 19th or early 20th Dynasty, the time of Ramesses II or Ramesses III, and the other from the time of Ramesses II. In his view, during the early phase this was a small cultic site belonging to a single family or perhaps to the inhabitants of the vicinity.

The main phase of the site, with the sacrificial altar, was dated by Zertal to the first half of the 12th century BCE. Zertal saw it as a central supratribal, perhaps even national, cultic site for the entire tribal confederacy and associated it with the biblical tradition of erecting an altar on Mt. Ebal (Joshua 8:30–31). In his opinion, it was the earliest, most complete Israelite cult site, the prototype of the sacred centers that were subsequently built. He connected the abandonment of the site with the establishment of the supratribal sacral center at Shiloh.

Indeed, some of Zertal's arguments would seem to indicate that there was an Iron I cultic site on Mt. Ebal (see Na'aman 1986, who identifies it with Migdal-Shechem and the house of El-berith in Judges 9). However, there are quite a number of problems in identifying the central structure as an altar (Kempinski 1986 even described it as a watchtower). Zertal raised some of these difficulties himself, especially the extent to which the structure is unlike other Israelite altars (1985c:39–40), but he suggested that these differences were related to the distinction between an isolated altar and an altar in association with a sanctuary.

There are additional problems in Zertal's reconstruction. Archaeologically, the thirty-four grinding stones that have been found at the site indicate that some kind of agricultural activity took place there (but this may be related to the nearby settlement). Chronologically, the ceramic assemblage must be understood to reflect material accumulated throughout the entire period of activity in each level. According to the matrial presented so far (Zertal 1986b Figs. 9–17), the end of Stratum II may be dated to the middle or even the second half of the 12th century (note the jar in Fig. 12:1 — its only parallels come from Qasile X(!) and Shiloh of the first half of the 11th century BCE), and Stratum I shortly after. From the biblical point of view, it is clear that the description of the altar on Mt. Ebal erected by Joshua actually reflects the reality of a much later period (Anbar 1985b). Historically, it is difficult to envision a supratribal Israelite cultic center as early as Zertal proposes, and none of the finds indicated that this site was a center for all of Israel. In any case, it is hard to take a stand concerning this important site before the completion of the excavations and the full publication of the findings.

Tirzah (Tell el-Far'a North)

One of the major sites in the hill country, Tell el-Far'a is strategically situated near an important crossroad and above the perennial water source at the head of the fertile Wadi Far'a. During the years 1946–1960, de Vaux directed nine seasons of excavations at the site on behalf of the École Biblique. The first final report, which deals with the Iron Age, was published recently (Chambon 1984). Several pillared houses were attributed to Stratum VIIa (in the new stratigraphic enumeration), which was dated to the 12th-11th centuries BCE. The published pottery plates show forms characteristic of the Iron I period, especially handles with holes and handles with incised decoration resembling a human face (Chambon 1984: Pl. 79:1–11; see Chapter 7). Amazingly enough, there are no drawings of collared-rim store jars, which were so widespread in the hill country at the time.

26. Figurine from the "Bull site" in Samaria (A. Mazar 1982b: 31).

The "Bull Site"

The site is located east of Qabaṭiya on a hill at the top of a ridge (map ref. 1807 2016). Following the chance find here of a bronze statuette of a bull, A. Mazar conducted brief excavations in 1978 and 1981 (A. Mazar 1982b). On the summit of the hill, which offers panoramic vistas, a single-period cultic site was uncovered. Little remained of the structure that once stood here, a wall composed of large stones enclosing an elliptical area (21 x 23 m) . In the eastern part, a large stone was installed upright and in front of it, there was a pavement on which, according to the excavator, offerings were laid. Mazar raised the possibility that a sacred tree had stood in the center of the enclosure.

The small amount of pottery recovered at the site was all of the Iron I period. On the basis of the cooking-pot rims, which resembled those of the Late Bronze tradition, Mazar dated the site to the first half of the 12th century BCE, although a few slightly later sherds were also found.

The most important find was, of course, the rare bronze statuette of a bull (Fig. 26) that inspired the excavation of the site. At 17.5 cm in length and a maximum height of 12.4 cm, the completely preserved statuette is the largest of its kind ever found in the Levant and is unique in its style of execution. It either was the object of a ritual or was brought to the site as an offering. Mazar postulated that the statuette came from one of the Canaanite centers that survived into the Iron I period. He saw the place as an open-air cultic site — of the kind mentioned in the Bible — erected by members of the tribe of Manasseh who settled in the area, but he judiciously refrained from suggesting which divinity was worshipped.

Dothan

The site was excavated between 1953–1960 under the direction of Free of Wheaton College, Illinois. From the preliminary reports that have been

27. Dothan — multihandled krater decorated with animal heads (Ussishkin 1975: 339).

published (summarized by Ussishkin 1975), it is difficult to reconstruct, with any accuracy, either the history of the site or the character of the settlement. In any case, the site was inhabited during the Middle Bronze, Late Bronze, Iron I and Iron II periods. The most important discovery, as yet unpublished, was a tomb that was used during the Late Bronze and Iron I periods. About 1,000 varied objects were discovered in it, most of them well-stratified ceramic vessels. A most unusual find from the tell was a krater with 14 handles, four of which terminated in stylized animal heads (Fig. 27).

Taanach

The mound of Taanach was first excavated in 1902–1904 by Sellin of the University of Vienna. In 1963, 1966, and 1968, P. Lapp directed three long seasons of excavations at the site on behalf of the American Schools of Oriental Research and Concordia Seminary of St. Louis.

The LB I settlement was destroyed by a fire that has been attributed to Thutmose III. While there was some activity at the site until the mid-14th century, there were no remains whatsoever from then until the end of the 13th century BCE. Taanach thus joined the list of cities mentioned in the conquest narrative in the Bible where no remains of a Canaanite city of the appropriate period have been found.

In the Iron I period, there were two principal phases of occupation; between them, according to the excavators, there was a gap. Each stage was further divided into two sub-phases (Rast 1978). Period IA was dated to the first half of the 12th century; its pottery still reflected Late Bronze traditions. This settlement was partly destroyed. During Period IB, dated 1150–1125 BCE, the extant buildings were reused and the settlement expanded. There is architectural continuity between these two phases. Following the destruction of Period IB, the excavators perceived a gap in occupation lasting most of the 11th century BCE.

Period IIA marked the renewal of activity at the site from 1020–960 BCE. There were only a few remains of this period, which preceded the overall revival of the site in Period IIB in the 10th century. The excavators believed that the inhabitants of both phases of Period I were Canaanites and that the destruction of Period IB was connected with the battle of Mt. Tabor described in Judges 4–5. In their opinion, Israelite Settlement began at Taanach only in Period IIA, during the time of David. Collared-rim store jars were no longer present in this phase, while hand-burnished red slip appeared on a limited number of vessels. The excavators rejected Albright's hypothesis (1971:117–118) that Taanach and Megiddo were alternately inhabited during Iron I and pointed, instead, to the similarity in the histories of the two sites during this period.

The precise dates assigned by the excavators were obviously based on their interpretation of the very vague biblical episode of the battle of Mt. Tabor. These dates cannot be accepted at face value. All that can be determined is that Period IA dated from the transition between the 13th and 12th centuries and that Period IB belonged more or less to the 12th century BCE. The absence of red-slipped pottery in Period IB and its presence in Period IIA may well indicate a gap in occupation at the end of the 12th century BCE or in the 11th. Since there was only a little red-slipped material in Period IIA, this level must be assigned to the middle or later 11th century, for at the end of that century, the amount of slipped and burnished pottery increased.

There does not seem to be sufficient data for determining unequivocally the ethnic identity of the inhabitants during the two main periods. On the one hand, there is the excavators' hypothesis — based, *inter alia*, on the mention of Taanach as one of the cities that the tribe of Manasseh did not inherit (Judges 1:27) — that Israelite Settlement at Taanach did not begin before the mid-11th century BCE. On the other hand, A. Mazar (1981b) raised the possibility that the inhabitants of Period I were already Israelites, both because the ceramic repertoire was relatively limited and meager compared to that of neighboring Megiddo and because pillared buildings were already present at Taanach at this time.

Before moving on to the surveys, it should be noted that Iron I remains have also been found in a limited excavation on the tell of Jenin (*Had. Arch.* 65–66, 1978:26).

Surveys

Zertal's survey of the hill country of Manasseh is one of the most important ever undertaken in the Land of Israel (Zertal 1986b). The results suggest that during Iron I, this region was more aggressively settled than any other part of the hill country.

About 1,000 km² have been thoroughly combed, which represents about two-thirds of the total area to be studied. Iron I pottery was picked up at 96 sites: 22 were tells and large ruins, 59 were medium-size ruins (5–15 dunams) described as villages; 13 sites were small "farms" (1–2 dunams), and two were defined as cultic sites. Most of the sites were located on the edges of the large valleys of the region; for example, 12 Iron I sites were found in the Dothan Valley alone (Zertal 1984:49). The arid desert areas on the east had few sites, except for the fertile and well-watered valleys of the Wadi Farᶜa and Wadi Maliḥ. In the desert fringe, however, the concentration of sites was quite large. The reason for the density of sites in the territory of Manasseh and their impressive size is no doubt rooted in the favorable geographical conditions prevailing in the region.

89

Zertal dated the beginning of the settlement process in Manasseh to the second half of the 13th century BCE. In his view, new groups penetrated at that time into the northern hill country from the east, via the valleys of the Wadi Far'a and Wadi Maliḥ. In the first stage, the newcomers settled in the eastern part of the Manassite territory, where pre-existing Canaanite settlement was sparse, and were occupied mainly with pastoralism. In a second stage of the process, in the 12th century, he believes that they moved into the inner valleys in the central part of the region. There they lived alongside the Canaanite population, and practiced herding together with cereal-crop agriculture in those parts of the fertile valleys that were not being used by the indigenous people. In Zertal's opinion, it was only in the third and later stage, when the settlement process intensified, that the new groups moved into the hilly areas of Manasseh also, mainly into the western part of the region, and shifted to a horticultural-based economy.

The general patterns of settlement revealed in the Manasseh survey are quite similar to the results of the Land of Ephraim project, especially in the slow movement of the population from east to west, which was accompanied by a change in their subsistence economy. However, we find it difficult to accept some crucial points of Zertal's interpretation: First, there is no clear-cut evidence in the survey of a 13th century date for the beginning of the settlement process in Manasseh. The fact that pottery in the tradition of the Late Bronze period was collected at a few sites is not conclusive proof, since these shapes appear also in the early phases of the 12th century BCE. (Hence, there is no reason to include the "Bull site" in the map of the Late Bronze period — Zertal 1986b: map 5). There is also no archaeological evidence whatsoever supporting his view that the new settlers penetrated the country from the outside steppe. The density of occupation in the well-watered eastern valleys does not indicate that they were the avenues through which the new groups moved into the hill country. As we shall demonstrate later, this pattern of settlement can be interpreted in a totally different way. Finally, Zertal does not deal with the complex demographic situation in Manasseh in the Iron I sufficiently, especially the role of the indigenous sedentary population who continue to inhabit the major Bronze Age tells.

Because the region is so fertile and suitable for habitation, it was also the most densely settled of the hilly zones already in the Late Bronze II period: some 22 sites are known in Manasseh, as opposed to only 5 in Ephraim and a smaller number in Judah. The Bible testifies to the strength of the Canaanite element in Manasseh in the early Israelite period, e.g., in the explanation of the relationship between Shechem and Manasseh and by including Shechem, Tirzah and Hepher, all large Canaanite cities, in the genealogical lists of Manasseh (Numbers 26:30–33; Joshua 17:2–3; see, e.g., Alt 1932:28–29; Noth 1958:145, 152–153; Y. Aharoni 1979b:246, 1982:64–65; Weippert

1971:20). There was, consequently, a certain continuity of occupation in the area from the Late Bronze period into the Iron Age.

The population during Iron I was composed of a sizeable sedentary element alongside which new groups settled in close proximity. Some of the Iron I sites in Manasseh, located on the major tells, were much larger than Israelite Settlement sites known from other parts of the country. Taking the above-mentioned factors into consideration, we arrive at the conclusion that these sites, or at least some of them (in which there was a continuity of occupation from the Late Bronze period), were inhabited by the sedentary Canaanite population, while close by, at small sites — and perhaps at large ones, too — other elements settled. In order to deal with this matter thoroughly, we obviously must await the forthcoming publication of Zertal's important work. It will undoubtedly shed new light on many of the topics crucial for the study of Israelite Settlement.

SHARON

Excavations

Tel Zeror

The site was excavated in four campaigns (1964–66, 1974) by an expedition of the Japanese Society for Near Eastern Research. The first three seasons were directed by Ohata, with Kochavi serving as field director; the fourth season was directed by Goto (Kochavi 1978:1224–1225).

The unwalled Late Bronze settlement was abandoned at the end of the period. The next phase was characterized by round pits, apparently silos, which were cut close together into the layers of the previous stratum. Although the pottery from these pits was relatively meager, Late Bronze ceramic traditions were perceptible. In the excavators' opinion, this 12th-century settlement consisted largely of huts and tents, and it was destroyed by fire. A citadel with a casemate wall was built at Tel Zeror in the 11th century. In the cemetery, stone-built cist tombs covered with stone slabs were disco-vered. Their rich finds included Philistine pottery. The excavators associated the scanty occupation level with the Israelite Settlement and Kochavi proposed connecting the citadel and cemetery with the Tjeker, a Sea People then centered at nearby Dor.

Tell Burgata

The site is located 5 km west of Tulkarm. In 1966, R. Gophna undertook a short salvage excavation here (Gophna and Kochavi 1966). The Late Bronze stratum was followed in the 12th century by pits, which were attributed to the Israelite settlers.

Surveys

During a brief preliminary survey conducted in the Sharon in 1966 by Gophna and Kochavi (1966), Iron I pottery was collected at seven sites (including Tel Zeror and Tell Burgata) to the west of the eastern alluvial plain (see also Porath, Dar and Applebaum 1985:55).

* * * * * * * * * *

The Sharon is one of those regions where the ethnic identification of the Iron I settlers is problematic. To the east, in the hills of Manasseh, there was intensive Israelite Settlement at the time, while historical sources indicate that on the coastal plain itself, one of the Sea Peoples (the Tjeker) settled. Kochavi and Gophna attributed the sites to the west of the eastern alluvial plain to Israelite Settlement. They blamed their brief duration on the appearance of the Sea Peoples in the area in the 12th century. The general picture, then, was of a brief attempt at settlement (or seasonal occupation?) in the eastern Sharon by Israelites, an attempt that was arrested with the establishment of the Sea Peoples in and around Dor. In this respect, the occupation pattern may have been similar to that which we observed in the eastern Shephelah.

JEZREEL VALLEY

Dozens of Iron I sites are known in the Jezreel and Beth-Shean Valleys, a considerable number of which have been surveyed and published (Zori 1962, 1977) and a few excavated. The latter include both small sites — Tel Qedesh, Afula, Tel Qiri, Tel Qishon and Tel Menorah (Stern and Beit-Arieh 1979; M. Dothan 1955; Ben-Tor 1979; Arnon and Amiran 1981:206–208; Gal 1979) — and the large centers of Megiddo, Beth-Shean and Taanach. Determining the date of the beginning of Israelite penetration into the valleys has important consequences for the study of the process of Israelite Settlement. Therefore, although in our opinion there was no Israelite Settlement in the Jezreel Valley before the beginning of the 10th century BCE, we nonetheless think it useful to briefly summarize the archaeological data from the region.

Megiddo is the key site for studying the history of the Jezreel Valley. The question that has perplexed scholars is, when did Megiddo become Israelite? The debate centers around the identity of the inhabitants of Stratum VI. After the destruction of the Canaanite city of Stratum VIIA, a relatively poor settlement, Stratum VIB, arose. This was replaced by the well- developed city of Stratum VIA, which was destroyed in a massive conflagration at the end of the 11th century BCE. The rich and varied ceramic assemblage included a limited number of both Philistine sherds and collared-rim store jars (see Chapter 7). Most scholars — e.g., Albright, Alt, B. Mazar, Yadin — emphasized the relatively high level of material culture of the inhabitants of Megiddo VIA and therefore classified it as a Cannanite-Philistine city, or even as the Philistine center in the Jezreel Valley (Engberg 1940; Albright 1940; Alt 1953; Yadin 1970:55; B. Mazar 1974:174; T. Dothan 1982:79–80). The destruction of this stratum was attributed to David's conquest.

Y. Aharoni reconstructed the history of Megiddo differently. In his opinion, there was a complete change in the plan of the city in Stratum VI, featuring the cessation of cultic activity in the eastern sector of the site (which had been a sacred area for almost two millennia). He attributed Stratum VI to Israelites and accordingly claimed that the entire center of the Jezreel Valley became Israelite before the end of the 12th century BCE. He explained the variety of the Stratum VI ceramic assemblage in terms of the proximity of the coast, rather than as a reflection of the ethnic identity of the inhabitants. On the other hand, his own views were based on the presence of collared-rim store jars, so typical of Israelite Settlement sites in the hill country (Y. Aharoni 1970:263–265), although the few vessels of this type could just as easily have reached the site through commerce.

A review of all the Iron I finds in the Jezreel Valley (Gal 1982a:80–83) indicates that at the beginning of the period, no major change in either the array of settlements or the material culture could be detected. On the contrary, there was a remarkable degree of cultural continuity until at least the mid-11th century BCE. As for Megiddo, the majority view that the site became an Israelite center only at the beginning of the 10th century best fits the evidence. Since there are no grounds for postulating Israelite Settlement in the Jezreel Valley before the 10th century, it follows that the local inhabitants continued to reside in this region in the 12th and 11th centuries BCE. On this matter, we agree with the comment of M. Dothan, who excavated Afula, that the area "seems to have been inhabited by an autochthonous 'Canaanite' population, and there is no reason to suppose that the Israelites occupied this area of the Jezreel Valley before the conquest of Megiddo and Bét Š'an" (1955:51). This view accords with the biblical evidence that the Israelite tribes were unable to take possession of the Canaanite cities of the Jezreel Valley (Judges 1:27; Joshua 17:11–12). Israelite occupation did not antedate the end of the 11th century and, in any case, mass settlement occurred only after the conquest of Megiddo VIA by David.

LOWER GALILEE

Data on the settlement pattern of Lower Galilee in Iron I come from the surveys recently undertaken by Gal (1980; 1982b). He divided the region into three geographical units of settlement (1982b:38–41):

1. Nazareth — Shefarᶜam - Netofa Unit, with the oak-covered chalk hills of Shefarᶜam and the fertile valleys of Beit Netofa and Turᶜān. The agriculture potential and available water sources made this area highly suitable for habitation.

2. Sakhnin - Beit ha-Kerem Unit, most of which is hilly, rocky and inhospitable.

3. Kokhav ha-Yarden — Ḥuquq Unit of eastern Lower Galilee, consisting primarily of basalt plateaus. These highlands were not easily habitable for the most part, so most of the activity in antiquity was concentrated along the wadis traversing the region.

Gal first worked in the plateau of Issachar, part of the third geographical unit. During the Late Bronze period, there were several sites here; Gal gave differing figures in his reports, apparently varying with the interpretations of the ceramic finds. In any case, this sub-unit was the most heavily populated area of Lower Galilee at that time. In Iron I, only isolated sites existed in the region. Not until late in the 11th century or early in the 10th did intensive settlement begin, with a total of 18 sites known (these were also originally dated to Iron I; Gal 1980:104). Gal linked the few Iron I sites with the Canaanite population that continued to exist in the valleys at the time and saw the wave of 10th-century occupation as the Settlement of the tribe of Issachar. In his opinion, the tribe of Issachar originated in northern Samaria, where it first settled together with the tribe of Manasseh. Only at the end of the 11th century, as Philistine strength in the valleys waned, did the tribe of Issachar begin to move onto the basalt plateaus of eastern Lower Galilee, which had previously been under the sway of the nearby Canaanite cities (Gal 1980:90–94; 1982a:82–83)

There were four Late Bronze sites in the Nazareth - Shefarᶜam - Netofa Unit (Gal mentioned only three, because he saw Rās ᶜAli as an Israelite Settlement site; see below). A major change in occupation came in Iron I, with 15 sites counted in the area (Fig. 28). In the Sakhnin - Beth ha-Kerem Unit, no Late Bronze sites were found, but five Israelite Settlements were discovered. In both Units 1 and 2, the sites were limited in area, generally with only a few houses each. Most of the sites in the Nazareth - Shefarᶜam - Netofa Unit were located near small springs.

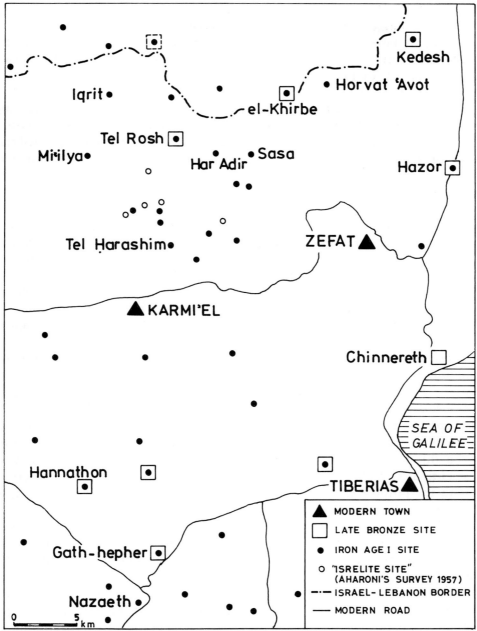

28. Late Bronze and Iron I sites in Galilee (except for Asher and Issachar).

As at the sites in the central hill country, the ceramic repertoire in the Nazareth — Shefar'am — Netofa area was scanty and comprised mainly pithoi and cooking pots. Interestingly enough, in this southern unit (#1), two types of pithoi — those with collared rims and the Galilean type (Chapter 7) — were found together, while in the northern unit (#2), only Galilean pithoi were found. Lower Galilee was thus both the northern limit of the distribution of collared-rim store jars and the southern limit of the distribution of Galilean pithoi (Gal 1982b:84).

Gal dated the beginning of Israelite Settlement to the second half of the 13th century BCE, based on the discovery of typical pottery of the Settlement sites together with Late Bronze pottery, including sherds of imported Cypriote vessels, at two of the sites surveyed (Gal 1982b:86). He attributed the sites of the Nazareth - Shefarᶜam - Netofa Unit to the tribe of Zebulun and connected those of the Sakhnin - Beit ha-Kerem Unit to the network of settlements discovered by Aharoni in Upper Galilee (see below).

The results of Gal's surveys shed light on the episode of Israelite Settlement in Lower Galilee and thereby fill a gap in our knowledge about the area between the central hill country and Upper Galilee. However, on the important issue of the date of the beginning of Israelite Settlement in the region, we find ourselves in disagreement with Gal.

His conclusions rest upon two arguments. First, in recent years, archaeological data from the central hill country were thought to indicate a date at the end of the 13th century for the beginning of Israelite Settlement. Second, at a few Settlement sites in Lower Galilee, characteristic Late Bronze pottery was picked up during the survey. For the first point, Gal relied heavily on the findings from ᶜIzbet Ṣarṭah and Shiloh, but understandably was not up-to-date on the work at these two sites (Chapter 9).

As for the second point, Gal has committed a methodological error in interpreting the survey results. If an assemblage of typical Iron I pottery will be discovered together with characteristic 13th-century pottery *in an excavation*, then this can be taken as evidence for an early date for the beginning of Israelite Settlement; so far, no such clear-cut coexistence has been observed (with the possible exception of Mt. Ebal and ᶜIzbet Ṣarṭah). But when Late Bronze and Iron I pottery are collected together *in a survey*, this simply means that the site was inhabited during both periods, especially since the two places Gal singled out were multi-period sites. The inescapable conclusion is that in Lower Galilee, as elsewhere, there is no indisputable evidence for dating the inception of Israelite Settlement to the 13th century BCE.

The sites Gal surveyed in central and western Lower Galilee should be assigned to the 12th century, and his meager ceramic material presents no obstacle to dating these sites even as late as the end of the 12th or beginning of the 11th century BCE. (At several sites, sherds of cooking pots belonging to the Late Bronze tradition were collected, but these vessels continued to appear in the 12th century and perhaps even down to the early 11th century BCE. Such a cooking pot was found, for example, in the destruction level of Shiloh, which can be dated on historical grounds to the mid-11th century BCE.)

As for the eastern sector of Lower Galilee, Gal's opinion that the influx of Israelites came only at the beginning of the 10th century seems valid, since it is based on the absence of collared-rim store jars at the sites in the area. This region was apparently populated some time before the destruction or abandonment of the Canaanite sites in the nearby Jezreel Valley, for otherwise it is difficult to imagine why the tribe of Issachar turned to the marginal zone of the basalt plateaus of eastern Lower Galilee instead of settling in the fertile valley.

WESTERN GALILEE

The coastal plain of western Galilee was, of course, beyond the limits of Israelite Settlement. This is clear both from the biblical testimony (Judges 1:31–32) and from the results of excavations (notably Tell Keisān). Information about the hilly part of western Galilee is drawn from the survey that Frankel has been conducting there for several years now. Frankel has generously shared the following data with us:

Over 200 km² have been thoroughly investigated (from longitude 174 westward), which comprises most of this topographical unit. Iron I pottery was gathered at 18 single-period sites and at 15 multi-period sites. About a quarter of the multi-period sites were located in the coastal plain, where the population could not have been Israelite. Of the one-period sites, seven are no more than stone heaps or isolated structures. The average size of the single-period sites was 4–5 dunams, with only two being larger. The sites were scattered in the heart of the hills of western Galilee, at a distance of several kilometers from the coastal plain, a situation significantly different from that of the western part of the central hill country, where Israelite Settlement sites were also found at the edges of the coastal plain.

The pottery collected from the sites in western Galilee appears to have been more or less contemporary with the material from Upper Galilee (see below), i.e, it dated not from the beginning of Iron I, but rather from the 11th century — or the end of the 12th century at the earliest. The incoming settlers here probably belonged to the tribe of Asher, as Frankel suggested (we will return to this point later).

UPPER GALILEE AND ḤULEH VALLEY

During the 1950s and 1960s, scholars dealing with the period of Israelite Settlement focused their attention on Galilee. Aharoni's survey in Upper Galilee and the excavations at Hazor yielded important finds that made it possible to present, for the first time, a comprehensive regional overview of the period.

However, opinions differ on the interpretation of the history of Israelite Settlement that came out of these projects, notably because the biblical information about the events that took place in this remote region in Iron I is extremely vague. It is difficult to use the episode of the battle against the kings of the north (Joshua 11) as a reliable historical document, and it is well known that the lists of cities and towns in the Book of Joshua reflect a later reality. As for the material culture, while the finds from Galilee perhaps resemble those of the central hill country in a general manner, they differ in many details. In this section, we will present the accumulated archaeological evidence and attempt to reassess it in the light of recent archaeological data, leaving aside those aspects of the biblical testimony that have hitherto hampered research.

Excavations

Hazor

Hazor, a key site for studying Israelite Settlement, is also one of the most imortant tells in the Land of Israel. Five campaigns of excavations at the site, from 1955–1958 and in 1968, were undertaken by the James de Rothschild Expedition, under the leadership of Y. Yadin, on behalf of the Hebrew University of Jerusalem.

The final Canaanite occupation, which extended over the large area of the Lower City as well, was destroyed by fire "during the thirteenth century BCE and not later than c. 1230..." (Yadin 1972:108; Stratum XIII in the Upper City and Stratum Ia in the Lower City). The lower date was derived from the chronology of Mycenaean IIIB pottery, which was found in this level. In an effort to be even more precise, Yadin proposed the second third of the 13th century as the time of the destruction of the last city, which was only slightly less developed than its immediate predecessor in the 14th century. Yadin attributed the devastation of the Canaanite city to Israelite tribes. Following the conflagration, the Lower City went out of use entirely, and subsequent occupation was confined to the Upper City.

Stratum XII, the first Iron Age level, represented the poorest occupation in the history of Hazor (Yadin 1972:129–130). There were no fortifications or public buildings — in fact, no real buildings were found at all, only the foundations of huts or tents, installations, and storage pits. The latter were the distinguishing feature of this stratum. In Area B alone, 22 of these pits were found; most appeared to be unlined, but the collapsed stones of their original linings were found within them. Many of these pits contained considerable quantities of pottery. "Galilean" pithoi dominated the ceramic assemblage from Stratum XII. Yadin saw the remains of Stratum XII as evidence of the

29. Hazor — bronze figurine of deity from Stratum XI (Yadin *et al.* 1961: Pl. CCCXLVI).

activities of a semi-nomadic population and dated this level to the 12th century BCE (see Geva 1984 for a proposed reconstruction of the socio-economic character of this stratum).

Stratum XI was exposed in Area B (Yadin 1972:132–134). Under the floor of a building that was cultic in character, a jar containing bronze votive objects had been buried; it may have been a foundation deposit. The contents included a figurine of a seated male deity wearing a helmet (Fig. 29) and a number of weapons. Bases of ritual stands were found in the vicinity of this building. Stratum XI was dated to the 11th century BCE, apparently to the second half.

The mounting number of comparable ceramic assemblages that have been excavated at various sites in the country now enable us to determine that there was a significant gap in occupation at Hazor between Strata XIII and XII. The absence of certain ceramic types — such as *cyma*-profiled bowls and hemispherical bowls — from Stratum XIII casts doubt on the occupation of the site in the second half of the 13th century BCE (Tufnell 1961:157; Kochavi 1985;

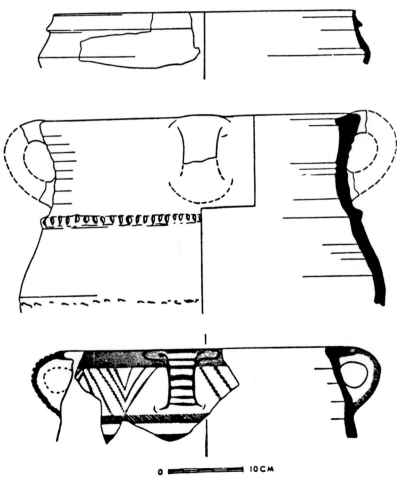

0 ▬▬▬▬▬ 10 CM

30a Hazor — pottery from Stratum XII.

Beck and Kochavi 1985:38; contra Fritz 1973, who attributed the destruction of Hazor to the Sea People). This cannot be explained away as a regional quirk' for these vessels were widespread throughout the country. Furthermore, the pottery of Stratum XII (Fig. 30) apparently did not belong to the earliest stage of Iron I (A. Mazar 1977:337, 1981a:35; Miller 1977:262). For example, cooking pots in the Late Bronze tradition, which were generally found at the earliest Iron I sites, are lacking. On the other hand, the Stratum XII cooking pots were of a later type, with a long, triangular rim (see below), and they were accompanied by slipped and burnished vessels and jars typical of a later stage of the period. Hazor Stratum XII should therefore be dated to about 1100 BCE or even into the 11th century. These data indicate that the gap in settlement at Hazor lasted for 150–200 years.

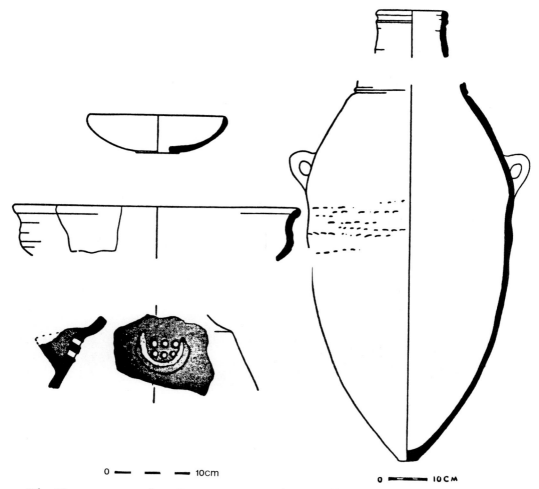

30b   Hazor — pottery from Stratum XII. On right, a "Galilean" pithos (Yadin *et al.* 1961: various plates).

Dan

Major excavations have been underway at Tel Dan since 1966, at first under the auspices of the Department of Antiquities and Museums and subsequently on behalf of Hebrew Union College; Biran has been the director throughout (for a summary, see Biran 1980). During MB II, Dan was an important fortified city. The sole find from the Late Bronze period was the "Mycenaean Tomb," so named by virtue of the many Mycenaean vessels found in it. The wealth of tomb offerings led the excavator to hypothesize that there was a large and prosperous settlement at Dan during this period, possibly located on the western part of the tell, an area that remains virtually untouched by excavation.

Stratum VI, the first Iron Age level, featured pits and silos, some of them lined with stones. In Area B (on the south) alone, some 25 of these storage pits were discovered. A particularly large and interesting one was exposed in Area Y (on the east); it contained 29 whole vessels, including "Tyrian" pithoi and kraters with many handles (Fig. 31). Biran thought the inhabitants must have lived in huts or tents, for almost no architectural remains have come to light. He viewed this stratum as the first settlement of the tribe of Dan on the mound and dated it to the 12th century BCE.

31. Dan — group of vessels from a Stratum VI silo. In background, "Tyrian" pithoi (Biran 1980: 176).

Stratum V resembled Stratum VI in character, but now the first buildings appeared. In addition, there was evidence of metallurgy. This level ended in a conflagration, which the excavator dated to the second half of the 11th century. Soon after, there was a renewal of activity (Stratum IV).

In shape, the pithoi of Strata VI and V resemble the collared-rim store jars of the central hill country.

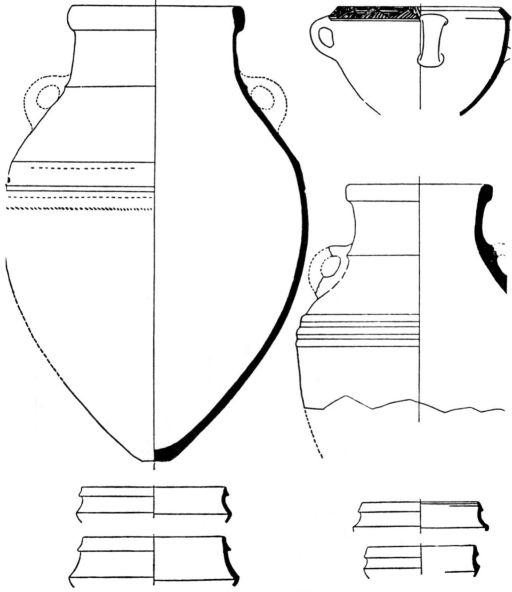

32.   Pottery from Tel Ḥarashim (Aharoni 1957: 22–23).

Tel Ḥarashim

Tel Ḥarashim (Khirbet et-Talil, map ref. 1814 2636) was examined in the framework of Aharoni's survey of Upper Galilee in the early 1950s. Aharoni then excavated it under the aegis of the Department of Antiquities and Museums (Aharoni 1957:18–24). The site covered 5–6 dunams on a hill south of Peqiʿin. In the Iron I level, one structure apparently served as a metallurgy workshop, for remains of a crucible and bronze slag were discovered in it. Among the few ceramic vessels found, the "Galilean" pithoi and a krater decorated with incisions around the rim (Fig. 32) are worth mentioning. Aharoni dated this stratum to the 13th-12th centuries BCE, as he dated comparable Galilean sites he surveyed. The parallel walls found in the Iron II level might have belonged to casemate fortifications.

Sasa

Iron I remains were found during the course of salvage excavations undertaken by Goz and Yogev in 1975 and 1980 on behalf of the Department of Antiquities and Museums (*Had. Arch.* 54–55, 1975:4–5; 76, 1981:9). A rock-hewn pit was full of pithoi of both northern types (see below); they were decorated with paint and reliefs. On the floor of a building of this period, a

33. The kernos from Sasa (courtesy of the Department of Antiquities).

beautiful kernos was found. This libation vessel consisted of a hollow ceramic ring, about 30 cm in diameter, on which six smaller vessels perched; two pomegranates, a bird and a cornet, all ornamented in black and red paint, are preserved (Fig. 33).

Har Adir

In 1975/76, Vitto and Davis conducted two salvage excavations on the summit of Mt. Adir (map ref. 185 270) under the aegis of the Department of Antiquities and Museums (*Had. Arch.* 59–60, 1976:9–10). Three strata were discerned. In the earliest one, a casemate fortification wall of a fortress, buttressed by a glacis, was discovered. The fill under the floor of one of the casemates yielded a rare and unique find: an intact bronze pick (Fig. 34) (Muhly 1982:45). Later, changes were made in the site, and the inner wall of the casemate fortification was dismantled. The site was dated to the span from the end of the 11th to the 9th centuries BCE.

34.   Iron axe from Har Adir (courtesy of the Department of Antiquities).

Ḥorvat ʿAvot

In 1980, Braun undertook a salvage excavation at the site (map ref. 1933 2763) on behalf of the Department of Antiquities and Museums (*Had. Arch.* 74–75, 1980:4; the following details were generously provided by the excavator, whom we thank). Two Iron I levels were exposed. At the outer edge of the site, there were several rectangular broad-rooms, measuring 3–4 x 7–10 m; they were not adjoining. From the sector excavated, one can project that the contour of the Iron I settlement was circular or elliptical with a diameter of about 75 m. The center of the site was not excavated, so whether it was an open courtyard or a built-up area remains unknown. Both types of northern pithoi were found.

Surveys

Aharoni's survey in Upper Galilee in the early 1950s was a landmark both in the development of survey methodology and in the study of Israelite Settlement. For the first time, an attempt was made to understand the history of occupation in a specific historical and geographical zone in the light of a modern archaeological survey. During that survey, 17 small sites (the largest was Tel Ḥarashim at 5–6 dunams) were dated to the 13th- 12th centuries BCE, and pottery of this period was also found at two tells in the area (Y. Aharoni 1957:8–34; our Fig. 28). These sites were located in the mountainous bloc of Upper Galilee, with 15 of them situated in the most rugged, isolated and difficult terrain of this region, i.e., south of Naḥal Keziv. To illustrate the extent of activity in this area in Iron I, Aharoni pointed out that during the Roman-Byzantine era, a time noted for its many rural settlements throughout the country, there were only 9 sites south of Naḥal Keziv.

As an adherent of Alt's "peaceful infiltration" theory, Aharoni claimed that during the Late Bronze period, occupation in Upper Galilee was concentrated in the flatter, lower and easier area north of Naḥal Keziv. When the members of the tribe of Naphtali — to whom Aharoni attributed the sites found during the survey — settled in the land they had inherited, they lacked sufficient strength to engage the Canaanite population in a direct confrontation over control of the region and were thus repulsed to the difficult area of southern Upper Galilee, where they devoted most of their efforts to overcoming natural obstacles. Only when they became powerful enough could the new settlers expand to the north. This, of course, brought them into inevitable conflict with the Canaanite cities. Ultimately, Naphtali prevailed, and an echo of these events is found in the description of the war of the kings of the north in Joshua 11. This conflict, in which Canaanite Hazor was destroyed, was initially dated by Aharoni (1957:118) to the end of the 12th century BCE.

The excavation of nearby Hazor began shortly after Upper Galilee was surveyed. A stormy debate raged between Yadin and Aharoni over the interpretation of the findings from the two projects. Yadin, a proponent of Albright's views on the Israelite conquest and Settlement, raised two main objections to Aharoni's theory. First, the ceramic evidence indicated that Canaanite Hazor had already been destroyed in the 13th century, much earlier than the date Aharoni advocated. Second, the pottery from the sites in Upper Galilee was identical to that of Hazor Stratum XII, which was the first Iron I settlement at the site and which, of course, followed the destruction of the Late Bronze city.

Yadin thus interpreted the settlement process in a manner diametrically opposed to Aharoni: The Israelites first destroyed Canaanite Hazor and only subsequently did they settle on its ruins and at the sites of Upper Galilee (Yadin 1972:131). As the argument continued, and in the light of the finds at

Hazor, Aharoni proposed elevating the date of the Upper Galilee settlements into the 13th century, i.e., before the destruction of Stratum XIII at Hazor (Aharoni 1982:178 and elsewhere; the debate is summarized by Yadin 1979:61–63).

Today, nearly 30 years later, new information can be adduced in order to clarify points pertinent to this ideological clash and, in fact, to take the sting out of it:

— As noted, there was apparently a significant gap in settlement at Hazor between the destruction of the Canaanite city of Stratum XIII and the meager occupation of Stratum XII.

— Yadin was correct in his observation that the pottery of Hazor XII was identical to that of the Upper Galilee sites. However, all these assemblages must apparently be dated to the 11th century. The characteristic vessels of the beginning of Iron I — especially cooking pots in the Late Bronze tradition — were lacking at Hazor and the Upper Galilee sites. On the other hand, the northern pithoi and cooking pots with elongated triangular rims seem to be closer in date to the 10th century than to the 13th century. At Tel Keisan (near Acco), these pithoi appeared in Strata 9a-b (1050 - 980 BCE), while the cooking pots turned up in Strata 11–8 (12th - 10th centuries BCE) (Briend and Humbert 1980: Pls. 55,57,63,77,81).

— A reexamination of the tells of Upper Galilee demonstrates that during the Late Bronze period, there were only a few centers in the region, Qedesh and Tel Rosh being the most important ones (contra Aharoni 1957:111, who claimed there were more). Nor, it seems, was southern Lebanon heavily populated during that period, for when the region was surveyed by Frankel and the author in 1981, indisputable Late Bronze sherds were found at only one site (el-Khirbeh east of Yarūn). On the other hand, during the same survey, Iron I sherds were collected at 11 sites. These data naturally change the picture of occupation in northern Galilee.

The issues of absolute chronology and the relationship between Hazor and the sites of Upper Galilee have thus been resolved to a considerable extent. At the same time, however, the matter of the ethnic identity of the founders of the Upper Galilee sites has become more problematic. Based on various elements of the material culture at these sites, Kochavi (1984:67–68) recently suggested connecting them to the southward expansion of the Phoenicians under the protection of fortresses such as the one found at Har Adir. Gal further raised the possibility that members of the tribe of Naphtali inhabited the sites of the Ḥuleh Valley, while the Upper Galilee sites were inhabited by Tyrian-Phoenician elements (1982b:90). We would like to expand upon this crucial question of ethnic identity according to some of the criteria we set for ourselves in Chapter 2:

1. *Historical data*. The only biblical source concerning Israelite activity in the region in Iron I is the description of the northward migration of the tribe of Dan (Judges 18). The list of settlements in the book of Joshua reflects, of course, a much later reality (for a summary of scholarly opinions, see Kallai 1967:2–13).

2. *Settlement pattern*. There is a great degree of similarity between the sites of Upper Galilee and the early Israelite Settlement sites in the central hill country in site size, in paucity of finds, and in the phenomenon of inhabiting areas with hilly and difficult terrain that had never before been so "densely" occupied.

3. *Finds*. Both the limited ceramic repertoire and the fact that the remains at Hazor XII and Dan VI were almost exclusively storage pits suggest that the people active in this region were in the early stages of the transition to complete sedentarization, and that they lived in isolated social and economic frameworks (Chapters 6–7).

Ceramically, there is no real difficulty in attributing these sites to Israelite groups. The sites were characterized by two types of pithoi: "Galilean" pithoi, which were decorated with horizontal ridges and incisions (Yadin *et al.* 1961:Pls. CLXVII-VIII) and which apparently developed from Late Bronze pithoi (e.g., *ibid.*, Pl. CCXCVIII); and "Tyrian" pithoi, which were ornamented with applied plastic "waves" and which probably originated outside the Land of Israel (see Bikai 1978:Pl. XL). These two types were not found together at every site. At Hazor and Tel Ḥarashim, for example, only the "Galilean" type appeared, perhaps due to chronological or geographical reasons. Neither type of pithos appeared south of the Jezreel Valley (*contra* Gal 1982b:58). Pithoi similar (but not identical) to collared-rim store jars — the typical vessels of the inhabitants of the central hill country during the 12th and 11th centuries BCE — have been unearthed in the north only at Dan.

There thus seems to have been a difference between the pottery of Galilee and that of the central hill country, but this distinction could be explained as regional rather than ethnic. More important are the similarities — the use of large pithoi in both regions and the limited repertoire of forms.

As for the architectural finds, the only unusual discovery to date is the fortress at Har Adir.[7] It is obviously difficult to associate a casemate fortress

---

7   Additional structures that have been regarded as Iron Age "fortresses" were found at Meiron (*Had. Arch.* 9, 1964:24), at Mitzpeh ha-Yamim (*Had. Arch.* 14, 1965:3), and at Mt. Kenaʿan (*Had. Arch.* 18–19, 1966:17). Kochavi (1984:67–68) attributed all of them to the influx of settlers into Upper Galilee during Iron I, but their dates have not been sufficiently well established.

with what we know about the typical patterns of Israelite Settlement. On the other hand, there is no compelling reason to connect the builders of this isolated structure with the inhabitants of the rest of the Iron I sites discovered in Upper Galilee (*inter alia*, the precise dates of the sites are not clear). In any case, the ceramic assemblage from Har Adir is relatively richer than that of any other site in the region.

In summary, then, it can be determined that some time after the destruction of Late Bronze Hazor, Upper Galilee (including its northern part) underwent a process of intensive settlement, in regions that had previously hardly been inhabited. The character of many of the new sites was consistent, in every respect, with what we know about Israelite Settlement sites, so there is no real problem in attributing them to the tribe of Naphtali. (On the other hand, a site like Har Adir may have belonged to a network ethnically related to the Phoenician coast.) This process of settlement took place in the 11th century, or no earlier than the end of the 12th century BCE. The pottery from the six excavations in the region suggests that the arrival of the settlers was not a single, one-time influx. The decisive vessels are apparently the pithoi, for the two types did not appear together at every site. Their distribution is summarized on the following table (based on oral communications from the excavators):

	Hazor	Dan	Adir	ᶜAvot	Harashim	Sasa
"Galilean" pithoi	X	X	–	X	X	X
"Tyrian" pithoi	–	Str. V only	X	X	–	X
collared-rim store jars	–	somewhat similar pithoi	–	–	–	–

This distribution raises the possibility that the "Galilean" pithoi made their appearance before the "Tyrian" pithoi, which is further strengthened by the resemblance between the "Galilean" pithoi and the Late Bronze store jars found at Hazor. This was followed by a period of overlap between the two types. Should this hypothesis be validated by future research (a statistical analysis of the appearance of these vessels at the various sites would be particularly important), it would follow that at Hazor XII, Dan VI and Tel

Ḥarashim, occupation ceased during an early stage of the process of settling Galilee; that Dan V, Ḥorvat ʿAvot and Sasa were settled during an intermediate stage; and that the site at Har Adir might have been the latest of this group. The significance of the appearance at Dan of pithoi resembling the collared-rim store jars of the central hill country is apparently historical rather than chronological (Chapter 10).

JORDAN VALLEY

The importance of the Jordan Valley for the study of the period of Israelite Settlement arises from its position as the bridge connecting the Transjordanian plateau with the central hill country. In those regions, hundreds of Iron I sites have been discovered, which make both of them the principal foci of the process of Israelite Settlement.

The archaeological data culled from two sides of the Jordan River are imbalanced. On the eastern side, there have been major excavations at two sites (Tell Deir ʿAllā and Tell es-Saʿidiyeh) as well as intensive surveys, while the western side has yet to be systematically investigated.

Excavations

Tell Deir ʿAllā

One of the most important sites in the Jordan Valley, Tell Deir ʿAllā is situated at the mouth of the Jabbok Valley (Wadi Zarqa) on the eastern side of the Jordan River. It is generally identified with biblical Succoth. Since 1960, eight campaigns of excavations have been conducted at the site, the first five directed by Franken under the aegis of the University of Leyden and the last three as a joint project of the University of Leyden and the Department of Antiquities of Jordan under the direction of Ibrahim, Franken and van der Kooij (for a summary of the results of the first campaigns, see Franken 1969:19–21).

During the Late Bronze period, a sanctuary was erected on an elevated artificial podium. Because no fortifications or ordinary buildings were found, Franken concluded that the site was an unwalled shrine that served the nomadic population of the vicinity. (On the sanctuary and the biblical tradition concerning the house that Jacob built at Succoth, Gen. 33:17, see B. Mazar 1984). The sanctuary was destroyed by an earthquake at the beginning of the 12th century BCE. Among the ruins was an Egyptian faience vessel bearing the cartouche of Queen Tewosret, the wife of Seti II (1193–1185 BCE, according to Wente and van Siclen 1977).

Soon afterward, new people came to the site. At this stage, during Iron I, there were still no houses but only open areas, pits and smelting furnaces. The excavator hypothesized that they reflected the winter activities of semi-nomads who engaged in metallurgy, agriculture and pastoralism, and who returned to the hills farther east for the summer months. These people lived in tents, for post holes are said to have been discerned at the site. Sherds identified as "Philistine" were found among the pottery of this occupation. A perusal of the published pottery indicates that no collared-rim store jars, so characteristic of Iron I sites in the hill country, were found at Deir ʿAllā (with the possible exception of one rim, Franken 1969: Pl. 50:100).

During the third phase, in Iron II, "new settlers" built a small walled city. The famous Aramaic inscription of Deir ʿAllā was found in the ruins of this settlement.

Tell es-Saʿidiyeh

The mound is located on the eastern side of the Jordan Valley, north of Naḥal Jabbok. Glueck's proposal to identify Tell es- Saʿidiyeh with the biblical city of Zarethan was accepted by Pritchard (on the problems of identification, see Oded 1971). Between 1964–1967, the University of Pennsylvania conducted four seasons of excavations under the directorship of Pritchard. On the western side of the tell, there was a cemetery dating from the end of the Late Bronze period and beginning of Iron I (Pritchard 1980). The Iron I burials were poorer in contents than the earlier interments. The excavators did not reach contemporary levels on the tell itself, and the history of the settlement during the period in question cannot be reconstructed on the basis of the evidence from the cemetery alone.

Surveys

As already noted, the eastern side of the Jordan Valley has been thoroughly surveyed, while our knowledge of the western side is no more than preliminary.

East of the Jordan. In the course of the survey conducted by Ibrahim, Sauer and Yassine in the northern part of the region, between Wadi Rajib and the Yarmuk River, 19 sites with "Iron I" occupation were investigated (including Tell es-Saʿidiyeh; only one of these sites was not known previously), as opposed to six sites with Late Bronze material and 17 with Iron II remains (Ibrahim, Sauer and Yassine 1976). Some of these sites, which were dated "Iron Ic", are from the 10th century BCE. The sites were scattered all across the area, from the foot of the hills right down to the Jordan River. In addition, about 20 other sites had been discovered by Glueck and attributed to this period (Glueck 1951:Chap. 5), but from the published pottery, it is hard to know just how many of them really gave evidence of activity during the period (*inter alia*, Glueck's "Iron I" included the 10th century BCE; *ibid.*: xix).

West of the Jordan. Glueck (1951) reported six Iron I sites north of Jericho. De Contenson (1964) added another site to the list. Six or seven more were found in surveys conducted in the wake of the Six Days' War (Porath 1968; Bar Adon 1972; Gophna and Porath 1972). Mittmann (1970) surveyed four sites of this period in the vicinity of Meḥollah, in the southern Beth-Shean Valley. Thus almost 20 sites have been located.[8] Only de Contenson published any pottery, so here, too, it is difficult to appreciate the extent of activity in Iron I.

* * * * * * * * * * *

To date, some 60 Iron I sites have been reported in the Jordan Valley, between the Dead Sea and the southern end of the Beth- Shean Valley.[9] Even if some of them would not meet modern criteria for inclusion in Iron I, there is still no doubt that this site density is impressive indeed. Since we lack sufficient information about the character of the sites, their distribution, size and precise dates, we cannot appreciate their significance in the network of Iron I settlements. Due to the climate and ecology of the region, however, it may well be that some of the sites were occupied seasonally, as Franken proposed for Deir ʿAllā. In other words, the inhabitants had not yet made the transition to permanent settlements, but spent winters in the Jordan Valley and summers in the hilly regions on either side of the valley.

TRANSJORDANIAN PLATEAU

The pioneer of modern research in Transjordan was Glueck, who investigated hundreds of sites in the course of his major survey during the years 1932–1947. The next important undertaking was the survey conducted by Mittmann in Gilead from 1963–1966. Although archaeological research in this region has intensified in recent years, these two projects — especially Mittmann's, which employed more modern methods — provide the basis of any

---

8   The situation at Jericho is unclear. H. and M. Weippert claimed that there was activity at the site in Iron I (1976:117, 144–145), but they published no clear-cut finds from this period. In any case, typical Iron I types are published in the final excavation report (Kenyon and Holland 1982: Figs. 215:1–2, 216:9, etc.).

9   Zori (1962) reported 44 Iron I sites in the Beth-Shean Valley. They should be considered together with the sites of the Jezreel Valley, and it is highly doubtful that they belonged to the framework of Israelite Settlement.

discussion of the settlement pattern of Transjordan. In any case, our knowledge of Transjordan is far less than that of Israel. We will attempt to summarize the archaeological data from relatively recent surveys and excavations and — despite the inherent difficulties — to evaluate their significance for the study of the period under discussion. It is only natural that we confine our remarks to the area between Naḥal Arnon (Wadi Mujaib) on the south and the Yarmuk River on the north — the arena of Israelite activity, according to the biblical source.

The main problem confronting all scholars who study the Iron I in the region is that at the same time, non-Israelite groups were also undergoing a process of consolidation in these areas of Transjordan, viz., Ammon and Moab. Because we are still virtually in the dark regarding differences in material culture among the various peoples who settled in Transjordan during the Iron I period, currently the only possibility of discerning the identities of the inhabitants of the sites excavated and surveyed is through historical and geographical considerations. Unfortunately, the historical data are not sufficiently clear, certainly not enough to permit unequivocal conclusions to be drawn.

Excavations

Heshbon

At Heshbon (modern Ḥisban, about 20 km southwest of Amman), five campaigns of excavations were undertaken between 1968–1976 under the aegis of Andrews University of Berrien Springs, Michigan, directed by Horn, Boraas and Geraty (Boraas and Geraty 1978:bibliography in n.3). The site was apparently first inhabited during Iron I, for pottery of this date was found in various places, and the excavators even attributed a fortification (?) wall found in one area to the period. Initially, the excavators hypothesized a gap in settlement spanning the 10th-7th centuries BCE, but they subsequently reported the finding of pottery of the 9th-8th centuries BCE. Absolutely no Late Bronze remains were found. Heshbon thus joins the list of sites that were mentioned in the biblical narrative of the conquest, but which lack any finds from that period.

Saḥab

Situated about 12 km southeast of Amman, Saḥab is the most important Iron I site thus far excavated on the Transjordanian plateau. Although this locale does not belong to the framework of Israelite Settlement, because finds from the site will be mentioned later on, we will here describe it briefly. Ibrahim directed three seasons of excavations at the site between 1972–1975 on behalf of the Jordanian Department of Antiquities.

The tell of Saḥab, which Ibrahim described as the largest pre-Roman site on the desert frontier of Transjordan, was already inhabited in the Middle and Late Bronze periods, but reached its floruit only in Iron I (Ibrahim 1972; 1974; 1975). Buildings of the Iron I period were uncovered at various places on the mound; in some of them, a few phases were discerned. Collared-rim store jars were found in these structures. A number of the rims bore rare and distinctive seal impressions (Fig. 94) of rosettes and animals (Ibrahim 1978; 1983). A similar stamped rim was recently found at Shiloh (Chapter 7). At Saḥab, collared-rim store jars were also used for burial. After the destruction of this settlement, activity at the site was limited; however, the Iron II settlement was better planned.

Iron I remains have also been excavated at *Aroer, Dibon* (a collared-rim store jar has been published), *Medeba, Khirbet el-Hajjar, Jerash, Irbid* and few other sites (Olavarri 1965:82–83; Tushingham 1972:Fig. 19; Harding 1953; Lenzen, Gordon and McQuitty 1985; Thompson 1972:62; see also Weippert 1979; Franken and Sauer 1971; Sauer 1982:81–82; 1986:10–12; Dornemann 1982:135).

Surveys

As noted, Glueck pioneered field research in Transjordan. In the southern part of this region, he reported more than 30 "Iron I-II" sites between Naḥal Arnon and Wadi Ḥisban (1934; 1939) and about 100 sites in the area between Wadi Ḥisban and the Jabbok River (Wadi Zarqa) (1939); in the northern sector, Glueck surveyed 65 sites of this period between the Jabbok and Yarmuk Rivers (1951) — altogether, some 200 sites.

However, there are serious problems confounding the use of the results of Glueck's surveys. First of all, Glueck did not exclude the 10th century in his definition of "Iron I" (1951:xix); nor did he separate Iron I from Iron II. Other difficulties involve his methodology. Because modern surveying was then in its infancy — and the purpose was to sketch the first picture of settlement in Transjordan — he made no attempt to sample the various areas in a balanced manner, did not always devote sufficient time to gathering sherds, and was sometimes even innaccurate in his ceramic identifications (for a critique of Glueck's survey, see Mittmann 1970:1–3). Moreover, he did not provide important basic data such as site size and relative proportions of pottery. As a result, it is hard to gain from Glueck's surveys a clear idea of the settlement pattern in Transjordan that would stand up to the criteria of modern research.

Two relatively recent surveys undertaken in the regions examined by Glueck have turned up dozens of Iron I sites. In the vicinity of Heshbon alone, Iron I pottery was reported at nearly 30 sites (Ibach 1976:122; 1978:206–209;

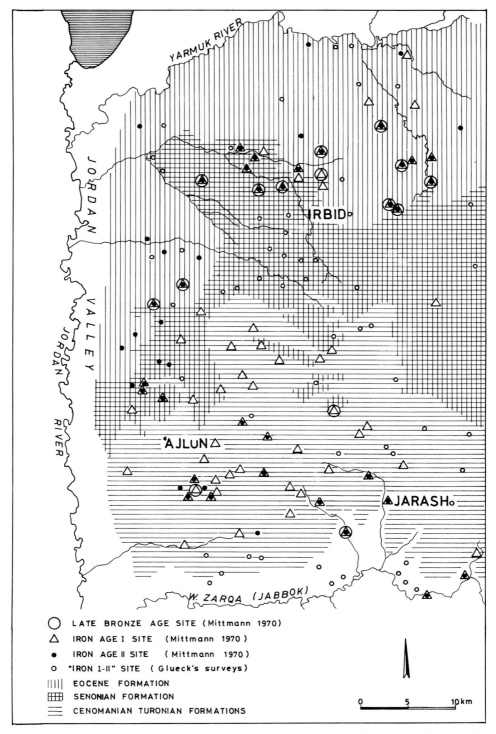

YARMUK RIVER

JORDAN VALLEY

JORDAN RIVER

IRBID

'AJLUN

JARASH

W. ZARQA (JABBOK)

○   LATE BRONZE AGE SITE (Mittmann 1970)

△   IRON AGE I SITE   (Mittmann 1970)

●   IRON AGE II SITE   (Mittmann 1970)

○   "IRON I-II" SITE (Glueck's surveys)

||||| EOCENE FORMATION

⊞ SENONIAN FORMATION

≡ CENOMANIAN TURONIAN FORMATIONS

0   5   10 km

35.   Late Bronze, Iron I and Iron II sites from Mittmann's Gilead survey, combined with Glueck's "Iron I–II" sites.

115

here too, the 10th century BCE may have been included in the "Iron I"). Mittmann systematically resurveyed the area between the Jabbok and Yarmuk Rivers (1970). He visited some 300 sites, only four of which had been investigated previously by Glueck. This sector thus became the best studied region of the Transjordanian plateau. Mittmann reported 73 Iron I sites (Fig. 35), as opposed to 15 Late Bronze sites and 49 of Iron II date.

From Mittmann's survey, which used a sufficiently large sample, several interesting trends emerge. While it would have been preferable to examine them in light of Glueck's findings as well, it is nonetheless worthwhile presenting the results on their own, bearing in mind that the picture is incomplete.

The area surveyed by Mittmann falls into two distinct geographical units: The *Plain of Irbid* in the north — except for the area of the deep wadis that descend to the Yarmuk and Jordan Rivers — is a topographically moderate plateau; composed of soft chalk, it was hospitable to settlement. The *'Ajlun bloc* in the south, is a higher and more rugged hilly region; consisting primarily of hard limestone, it was less amenable to settlement activities. The following table summarizes the data collected by Mittmann according to this bipartite geographical division:

		PLAIN OF IRBID	'AJLUN REGION
LATE BRONZE	# of sites	12	3
	%	80	20
IRON I	# of sites	31	42
	%	42	58
IRON II	# of sites	34	15
	%	69	31

These numerical data can be summarized as follows:

1. Most of the Late Bronze sites were concentrated on the Plain of Irbid in northern Transjordan, while only a few were found in the 'Ajlun region.

2. In Iron I, there was a strong wave of settlement throughout the area, but it was greatest in the 'Ajlun region.

3. During Iron II, the number of settlements remained stable in the Plain of Irbid, while declining sharply in the ʿAjlun region.

4. While settlement of the Plain of Irbid was relatively consistent through-out the time-span under review, the ʿAjlun region, which was less conducive to human activity, experienced rather extreme oscillations (Kochavi 1984:69–70).

The demographic implications of the results of Mittmann's survey are most interesting. During Iron I, there was an unprecedented revolution in the settlement of northern Transjordan, with a five-fold increase in the number of sites. More than half of the new sites were located in the difficult hilly region that had previously been practically uninhabited. This situation recalls the contemporary processes underway in certain regions west of the Jordan River, especially in Galilee. As the findings of Mittmann's survey are only partly published, we are unable to tackle the intriguing question of whether the process of settling Transjordan began while the Canaanite centers were still in existence or only after their destruction.

*   *   *   *   *   *   *   *   *   *   *

The results of surveys and excavations on the Transjordanian plateau indicate that during the Late Bronze period, the number of major urban centers was quite limited (see Sauer 1986:6, who mentions only five sites). During the Iron I period, this region experienced very intensive settlement, with dozens, or perhaps even hundreds, of sites founded. At present, the contribution of the findings from Transjordan is only partial, since the overall picture is currently quite foggy. However, we hope that further field work will add new dimensions to our knowledge of Israelite Settlement, especially concerning the question of the origin of the people who settled the Land of Israel at that time, the chronology of Settlement, and the sources of Israelite material culture. Furthermore, the pattern of settlement in Transjordan has direct bearing on the debate between the two schools of scholarship concerning the process of Israelite Settlement.

PART II:
THE REGIONAL STUDY OF THE TERRITORY OF EPHRAIM

The regional study of Ephraim, which began in autumn, 1980, comprises two archaeological projects: the excavation of Shiloh and the survey of the entire territory of Ephraim.[10] The results of these two projects, which are undertaken in the heartland of the central hill country, have major repercussions for the study of the period of Israelite Settlement.

Shiloh was the cultic center — apparently the first one — of the inhabitants of the central hill country at the time. The excavated material sheds light on a number of subjects concerning Israelite society in its early stage of organization, subjects that have long been central to the study of the history of the people of Israel and the roots of their material culture.

The intensive survey of Ephraim delineates the settlement pattern in the central hill country during Iron I. The concomittant environmental studies facilitate an understanding of the ecological and economic background to the process of Israelite Settlement.

10   The "Land of Ephraim Regional Project" is conducted by the Department of Land of Israel Studies at Bar-Ilan University. The four excavation campaigns at Shiloh took place during the summer months of 1981–1984. The project was under the direction of the author. The permanent excavation staff consisted of Sh. Bunimowitz and Z. Lederman (assistants to the director), P. Ben-Hanania, Sh. Yoseph, A. Demsky, M. Kislev, R. Kaufman, A. Cohen, A. Katznelson, B. Luttinger, A. Feldstein and M. Iron-Lubin. Participating in the survey were Sh. Bunimowitz (1981/1982–1984/1985), Z. Lederman (1981/1982, 1982/1983) and D. Eitam (1980/1981).

Many institutions and individuals facilitated the work of the Shiloh expedition: the National Council for Research and Development; the Israel Defense Forces; the Regional Council of Benjamin; the Cherna and Dr. Erving Moskovitz Chair for the Study of the Land of Israel (Bar-Ilan University); the Archaeological Staff Officer for Judea and Samaria; the Jewish National Fund; the Jewish Agency; the Dorot Foundation (USA); the modern settlement of Shiloh; L. Jesselson (USA); Dr. M. Strauss (Switzerland); and A. Ben-Ami. The survey was funded by the Israel Archaeological Survey, the Archaeological Staff Office of Judea and Samaria and Bar-Ilan University.

The two projects are integrated, and their results complement one another to produce a detailed comparative model — the only one of its kind — which helps clarify the problems surrounding the episode of Israelite Settlement throughout the entire country. Although our survey continues and further discoveries undoubtedly await us, the data currently available (after six years of field-work) enable us to present a reliable reconstruction of the pattern of settlement in the Iron I period. A preliminary report on the Shiloh excavations was recently published elsewhere (Finkelstein 1985); however, in order to give a full description of the Ephraimite regional project as a case study on the Israelite Settlement, we present it again here, with special emphasis on the Iron I period.

CHAPTER 4

THE SURVEY OF THE TERRITORY OF EPHRAIM

The survey covers an area of about 1,050 km². The limits approximated those of the territory of the tribe of Ephraim: the northern edge of the Beit Dajan Valley - Sahl Makhneh - Wadi Qana on the north; the Deir Dibwan - Ramallah - Beth Horon road on the south; the edge of the desert, just east of the last permament settlements on the east; and the 1967 border on the west. The additional area farther west, to the border of the foothills and the alluvial plain, was investigated by a survey unit from the Institute of Archaeology of Tel Aviv University, and this supplements our information down to the coastal plain.

The geographical unit defined above is located on the spine of the hill country, which explains its central importance in the history of the entire Land of Israel during the period of Israelite Settlement and the Judges. Its navel, so to speak, was at Shiloh, the most important religious, economic, and political center in the hill country during the Iron I period. Another focal site was located farther south, at Bethel.

The region is divided lengthwise by the major route linking Judah — and the important sites of Gibeah and Mizpah in Benjamin — with Shechem and the territory of Manasseh in the north. Important sites are scattered across the region, e.g., Kh. ʿUrmah — apparently biblical Arumah— southeast of Shechem; Tell Sheikh Abu Zarad — apparently biblical Tappuah — south of Shechem; Kh. Tibnah, which can be identified with biblical Timnath-heres, on the western slopes; and Upper and Lower Beth Horon in the southwest. Other central sites include the tells of Ṣarṭa, Ḥaris, and ʿAin Samiyeh (Kh. Marjama).

From an archaeological viewpoint, it suffices to note that of the nine principal sites of Israelite Settlement that have been excavated in the hill country, five are located in our region (Bethel, Ai, Kh. Raddana, Shiloh, and ʿIzbet Ṣarṭah), while two others are just to the south (Tell el-Fūl and Tell en-Naṣbeh). As we shall see, the archaeological surveys round out our knowledge and indicate that this was one of the most densely populated areas of Israelite Settlement. The archaeological picture is in agreement with the biblical evidence, which reflects the strength of the tribe of Ephraim before the United Monarchy (Noth 1958:59; de Vaux 1978:677; on the shift of the center of population density from Manasseh to Ephraim, see Kingsbury 1967).

Until 20 years ago, field work in the region consisted of scholars making excursions to investigate the central sites. Only in the late 1960s were the first modern surveys organized. The Shechem expedition investigated several sites at the northern end of our survey grid (Campbell 1968). Kallai, Gophna and Porath worked here in the framework of the 1968 Survey (Kallai 1972; Gophna and Porath 1972). Porath subsequently conducted another phase of this survey (Porath 1968). While these efforts marked an important breakthrough in research, they were insufficient as a basis for a full and comprehensive understanding of the history of the region for the following reasons:

— Only a few sites were actually investigated. If we take, for example, the sites marked on the maps, we find that of the 401 sites located on the survey grid, only 168 — 42% — were examined. The study of Arab villages, which are traditionally the locations of ancient sites, was even less rigorous. Of the 113 villages on our grid, only 34 — a mere 30% — were investigated. Nor were thorough surveys of representative areas undertaken.

— There was no planned geographical sampling of sites. As a result, coverage was relatively extensive in the northern part of the region, while the southwest was practically untouched. The data collected — however important in and of themselves — thus do not permit the creation of a comprehensive model of settlement.

— As for the survey methodology, it must be borne in mind that 20 years ago, important environmental factors were not taken into account; quantitative evaluations of the finds by periods were not attempted; and dating was sometimes based on body sherds and other non-indicative fragments. Periods of habitation should be determined solely on the basis of types that are unequivocal. A reexamination of the sherds collected in the territory of Ephraim during the 1968 Survey indicates that some 40% of the sites ascribed to Iron I had, in fact, yielded no clear evidence of this period. These sites will not be included in our discussion, unless the appropriate pottery was gathered when we revisited them. On the other hand, at a few sites that had not been dated to Iron I, we found pottery of the period. Some of the ceramic attributions of Campbell's survey in the Shechem area are inaccurate. For example, certain sites that were attributed to the Late Bronze period had actually produced no pottery earlier than the Roman period.

It is obvious, therefore, that a reliable picture of the history of settlement in Iron I cannot be drawn solely on the basis of the finds of these partial surveys (which does not, of course, detract from their importance).

The purpose of the survey of the territory of Ephraim is to achieve total coverage of the area delimited above. Figure 36 shows the areas where surveying has been completed (as of the summer of 1987), including the 1:20,000 Biddya map, which was surveyed before our arrival by D. Eitam (*Had. Arch.* 77, 1981:56; all the named sites of this map were revisited by our team). About three quarters of the area in the survey grid of Ephraim has been fully surveyed thus far. In the remaining area, we are now winding up the first phase, the surveying of all the sites marked on various maps. Combining all the

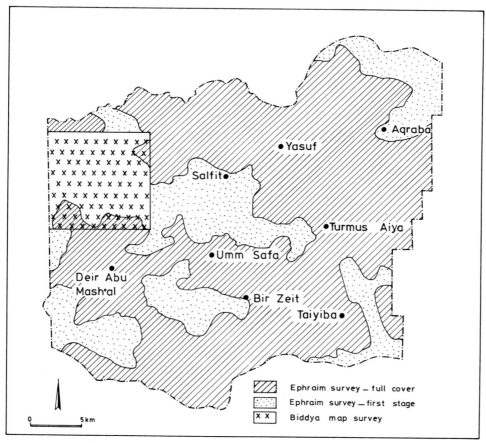

36. Territory of Ephraim — areas surveyed.

surveys, 552 sites have been investigated to date, including 385 (96%) of the 401 mapped sites and 104 (92%) of the 113 Arab villages. As indicated, we revisited many sites that had been surveyed previously. The following table breaks these figures down by topographical units, which will be described afterward.

TOPOGRA-PHICAL UNIT	Desert fringe	Northern central range	Southern central range	Northern slopes	Southern slopes	Foot-hills	TOTAL
Total # sites from all surveys	51	138	60	67	170	66	552
Sites surveyed for first time	34	87	42	30	123	35	351
Sites surveyed again	10	44	15	31	36	26	162
TOTAL SITES EXAMINED IN OUR SURVEY							513

Experience in the areas that were thoroughly surveyed taught us that the percentage of inhabited sites in our region that do not appear on any map is relatively small. In the vicinity of the northern intermontane valleys, for example, the percentage rises to about half, but drops to almost nothing in more difficult terrain such as the southern slopes (see below). In this respect, the territory of Ephraim is utterly unlike its northern neighbor, the territory of Manasseh, where the number of unmapped sites is much greater (*Had. Arch.* 77, 1981:53). The contrast between these two regions stems from differences in topography, rock formations and soil, i.e., the ecological settings are dissimilar. In summary, the data already at hand is sufficient, in our opinion, to produce a reliable model for the occupation of the territory of Ephraim during the various periods (Finkelstein, forthcoming d).

A few comments about our field methodology are in order:

— There were generally 5–7 surveyors, of whom 1–3 were archaeologists.

— The surveyors were systematically spread across the surface of the site, and sherds were collected from all terraces around the entire periphery, including the slopes.

— The ancient nucleus was identified in the Arab villages and every effort was made to survey its entire perimeter on the terraces immediately below the outermost houses.

— In general, all rim sherds were saved. A preliminary count of the indicative sherds was made at the site, the sherds were dated and the quantities were expressed in percentages by period. After this initial sorting, the sherds were taken away for further study. This method enabled us to check the appearance of popular types both quantitatively or geographically.

— The pottery was dated *solely* on the basis of unequivocal indicator sherds; body sherds, handles, bases and rim types that appeared during more than one period were usually not considered.

— The survey results are processed by computer. For this purpose, data sheets were prepared for use in the field, on which as much information as possible was filled in. These data included size of the site, elevation above sea level, landscape features, rock formation, geographical sub-unit, distance from nearest water source to site, road access, extent of building, quantities of pottery, etc. A separate sheet was used for recording the quantities of all types of pottery from each site. Those data that concern sites of the Iron I period will be examined in detail in this work.

As already noted, all the boxes of finds collected during both 1968 Surveys and listed as containing sherds of the Iron I period were opened and checked. Unequivocal indicator sherds of the period were found at only about 60% of these sites (at some 40% of the remainder, Iron I sherds were found when we revisited the sites themselves). We resurveyed all sites attributed by our predecessors to the Iron I period, even those where insufficiently clear evidence of the period had then been found. We also thoroughly reinvestigated all sites where they reported Iron II material.

It must be emphasized that since the amount of Iron I pottery is generally relatively small, it is possible that at certain sites, where Iron I activity was very limited, we may have failed to find the corresponding sherds. This cautionary note is particularly applicable for several Arab villages where evidence of the Iron Age was thickly covered by later periods.

Geographical Background

The territory of Ephraim is situated in the heart of the central hill country of the Land of Israel, in a region that is not very conducive to habitation. The landscape lacks the broad plateaus of Judah and Benjamin and the large valleys of Manasseh. Lithologically, the easily-worked chalk of the hill country of Manasseh is absent from Ephraim. The dissection of the area and the formations of hard limestone hinder both settlement and agriculture.

In terms of geography and human ecology, Ephraim is clearly divided into four distinct units. From east to west, these are the desert fringe, the central range, the western slopes and the foothills. The central range and the western slopes can each be further subdivided into north and south, so that we are ultimately dealing with a region comprising six topographical units. Each one has its own geographical, demographic and economic features, and these are of decisive importance for analyzing the settlement patterns of each period. We will briefly describe each of the six units.

Desert Fringe (DF)

In terms of area, this unit is the smallest: 103 km², or 10% of the survey grid. It is a long and narrow strip, whose eastern boundary is the outermost line of sites facing the desert and whose western limit is the simultaneous change in topography, climate, economy and demography occurring at the sharp escarpment (through part of which a north-south rift passes) that creates height differentials of 150–250 m. The amount of precipitation differs radically on either side of this escarpment and so, too, the subsistence base of the inhabitants. The top of the escarpment belongs, in all respects, to the central range, while its base is part of the desert fringe. In many places along the desert fringe, there are small valleys suitable for agriculture. The area has an elevation of 450–700 m above sea level and receives up to 400 mm of rainfall annually. The economy is based, as we shall see below, on cereal cultivation and pastoralism.

Central Range

This is the second largest topographical division in our region; its area is 329 km², which represents 31% of the survey grid. The eastern boundary is the abovementioned escarpment dividing it from the desert fringe. The western limits are not so easily defined, but must be placed at the beginning of the long and narrow ridges and the deep ravines of the Yarkon drainage system, which characterize the landscape of the western slopes. The entire region declines from south to north. The Jerusalem - Shechem road, which bisects its western side, was of critical importance in antiquity. As noted, the central range consists of two sub-divisions; the border between them is the escarpment north and east of the village Mazra°ah esh-Sharqiyyeh.

Northern Central Range (NCR)

This topographical unit, which is situated at 650–850 m above sea level, covers 222 km², about 21% of the survey grid. It is characterized by small intermontane valleys (Fig. 37), the most important ones being the valleys of Shiloh, Lubban esh- Sharqiyyeh, Qabalan, °Aqrabeh, Huwwara and Beit Dajan. Most

37. Typical landscape in the northern central range — the valley of Qabalan village.

of these valleys are relatively small — the Lubban esh-Sharqiyyeh and Qabalan valleys are each only about 2 km² in area — but they nonetheless were of primary importance for the development of settlement. In fact, each valley constitutes a distinct economic entity.

Southern Central Range (SCR)

In this unit, which covers 107 km², hospitable highlands continue the plateau of the hills of Benjamin. The area is higher than its northern neighbor, about 800–950 m above sea level. A formation of Amminadav limestone, exposed over a large area north of Deir Dibwan, creates stretches of rather harsh rocky terrain. In pre-Medieval periods, occupation here was virtually nonexistent. On the west, the slopes "penetrate" deeply into the central range.

Western Slopes

This is the largest topographical division: 473 km² or 45% of the total area. On the east, it borders the central range; on the west, it is separated from the

127

foothills by a moderate but very clear escarpment, which creates differentials in elevation of 100–150 m. The villages of Deir Qaddis and Deir Abu Mashʿal are situated at the top of the escarpment, while villages such as Zawiyyeh, Rafat and el-Lubban are located at its base. The most distinctive topographic feature of this region is the formation of ridges and wadis running east-west. Here, too, there are two sub-divisions, north and south, separated by the northern ravine of Naḥal Shiloh, which traverses the western slopes in the vicinity of Salfit. The difference between the sub-divisions consists largely in the degree of dissection in the area, which also affects the rock formations and the water sources.

Northern Slopes (NS)

This topographical unit comprises 150 km², about 14% of our region. The landscape here is relatively moderate. The ridges create flat areas and the wadis widen in some places to create narrow valleys. The topography in the northeastern part, in the vicinity of Jammaʿin, is especially moderate; this has resulted, *inter alia*, from the exposure of the soft rock formation. On the other hand, the slope down into Wadi Qanah in the north is wild and bare, both topographically and lithologically. The water sources in the northern slopes are very limited.

Southern Slopes (SS)

This is the largest topographical unit in the territory of Ephraim, covering 323 km², 31% of the total area. It is also the most rugged sector of the region. The landscape is characterized by long narrow ridges with rather flat tops, but very sharply sloping sides, which are separated by deep narrow wadis (Fig. 38). These ridges and wadis run east-west. Most of the settlements are situated on the ridges, with only a few found in the wadis. The main roads also traverse the ridges, so that travel along the east-west axis is relatively easy, while north-south movement is very difficult. The ridge is thus the characteristic economic entity of this part of Ephraim. The deep penetration of the wadis led to the exposure of aquiferous formations, so that the area is dotted with small springs.

Foothills (FH)

The eastern side of the foothills is demarcated by the escarpment described above; to the west, it reaches the coastal plain. Here we are concerned only with the eastern portion, for the demographic and economic features of the strip bordering on the coastal plain are completely different. The portion of

38. Typical landscape in the southern slopes, south of Salfit.

this topographical unit included in our survey (approximately up to the 150 longitudinal division) is 148 km², some 14% of Ephraim. The foothills differ from the hill country farther east topographically and, to a certain extent, lithologically. The landscape consists of low, generally moderate hills and continues the network of ridges and wadis of the area to the east. The area descends from east to west. Because there were no stable sources of water in the area, the inhabitants were entirely dependent on cisterns. Large sections of the terrain, particularly in the west, are rocky, which hampers agricultural exploitation.

DEMOGRAPHY AND SUBSISTENCE ECONOMY

In order to decipher a settlement pattern that arises from an archaeological survey, the geography of the area and its economic and agricultural potential must be examined. It is important to begin by building a settlement model for

129

which most of the necessary data exist; such a model, which should be as full and complete as possible, can then serve as the basis for comparisons with other periods.

The only reasonably complete model available is that of the Arab village at the beginning of the 20th century. Although on the threshold of a new era in the history of the Land of Israel, the distribution of villages, the number of their inhabitants, and their subsistence bases were then still determined almost exclusively by the natural conditions of the country. In other words, the considerations that dictated the choice of a particular locale and the diversification of the inhabitants into various branches of agriculture had not changed significantly since antiquity. We thus begin our discussion with a review of the economic potential of our region as reflected in the montane Arab villages.

Table 1 lists the number of villages and their populations according to the topographical divisions we established in the previous section. The data on the population of the villages are based on the census of 1931 (Mills 1933).

Table 2 is concerned with the economy of the villages. The data were taken from the *Village Statistics* (Government of Palestine, 1945). We collected the data for each and every village and rearranged them according to our own topographical divisions. For comparative purposes, we have presented the data for the large villages in the eastern central range and for the villages on the border between the foothills and the coastal plain (the line of Kafr Qasem, Majdal Yaba, Qula, etc.) in separate columns. For three of the areas, we also present calculations that ignore the urban population concentrations and the large villages.

Table 3 offers data on animal husbandry in the Arab villages of our region. The only information available that lists the number of animals by types for every village (i.e., the data we need for our discussion), comes from the early 1970s (Military Government of Judea and Samaria, 1974).[11] Of course, the number of animals has probably changed since the 1920s and 1930s, as have the methods of husbandry. But we assume that the relative proportions of the different kinds of animals within each topographical unit and between the units has not changed drastically. For this table, the population statistics were taken from the 1967 census (Israel Defense Forces Command, 1967) and were adjusted for the year during which the animals were counted according to the factor determined by Schmelz (1977) for the population increase in Judea and Samaria.

---

11   I thank M. Levy of the Civil Administration of Judea and Samaria for helping me acquire this material.

TABLE 1

(numbers in parentheses are percentages of the entire region)

TOPOGRA-PHICAL UNIT	Desert fringe	Northern central range	Southern central range	Total central range	Northern slopes	Southern slopes	Total slopes	Foot-hills	TOTAL
Area in km² **	103 (10)	222 (21)	107 (10)	329 (31)	150 (14)	323 (31)	473 (45)	148 (14)	1,053
Number of villages	4 (4)	24 (21)	12 (11)	36 (32)	13 (11)	43 (38)	56 (50)	17 (15)	113
Area per village in km² ***	25.75	9.25	8.9	9.1	11.5	7.5	8.4	8.7	9.3
Population	852 (1)	14,740 (22)	15,349 (23) 8,771*	30,089 (45) 23,511*	7,131 (11)	19,031 (29)	26,162 (40)	9,360 (14)	66,463
Average pop. per village	213	614	1,279 877*	836 691*	549	443	467	551	588
Average pop. per km²	8.2	66.4	143.4	91.5	47.5	58.9	55.3	63.2	63.1

* Without Ramallah and el-Bireh.

** For the purposes of this table, area was calculated according to the topographic units, rather than by adding up the extent of land of each village. The resultant distortion mainly affects the villages of the desert fringe and the eastern villages of the hill country (which own large fields to the east of the area of our survey) and also the villages of the foothills (some of which have property bordering on the coastal plain).

*** These figures are mathematical constructs, derived by dividing the area in km² by the number of villages per topographical unit. The actual area covered by each village will be provided in Table 2.

TABLE 2

(area measured in dunams; numbers in parentheses are percentages within topographical unit)

TOPOGRA-PHICAL UNIT	Desert fringe	Northern central range	Southern central range	Central range: 6 large villages in east *****	Northern slopes	Southern slopes	Foothills	Villages bordering foothills & coastal plain
Average pop. per village	270	860	1,557 1,069*	1,437	722	533	700	1,268
Avg. actual lands per village ******	23,929	16,252 9,586**	24,388 10,588***	58,582	12,889 11,116****	7,773	11,448	10,711
Avg. area hortic. (mainly olives) per village	701	2,236	4,088 3,780*	3,788	3,190	3,534	1,681	367
Avg. area cereals per village	5,487	4,949	6,285 5,786*	10,140	2,865	1,449	2,909	6,771
Average nonarable area per village	17,707	9,013 3,434**	14,459 3,493***	44,560	6,789 5,452****	2,752	6,827	2,891
Avg. land per person	88.6	18.9 12.1**	16 12.8****	40.8	17.9 16.3****	14.6	16.4	8.4

TABLE 2 (cont'd)

TOPOGRAPHICAL UNIT	Desert fringe	Northern central range	Southern central range	Central range: 6 large villages in east *****	Northern slopes	Southern slopes	Foothills	Villages bordering foothills & coastal plain
Avg. area hortic. (mainly olives)	2.6	2.6 2.7**	2.6 3.5* 4.5***	2.6	4.4	6.6	2.4	0.3
per person	(3.0)	(22.3)	(34.8)	(6.4)	(24.6)	(45.5)	(14.6)	
Avg. area cereals per person	20.3	5.8 5.0**	4.0 5.4* 4.0***	7.1	4.0	2.7	4.2	5.3
	(22.9)	(41.3)	(31.6)	(17.4)	(22.3)	(18.6)	(25.6)	
Average nonarable area per person	65.6	10.5 4.4**	9.3 4.2***	31.0	9.4 8.0****	5.2	9.7	2.3
	(74.0)	(36.4)	(33.0)	(76.0)	(52.5)	(35.4)	(59.1)	
Ratio of cereals to hortic. per village or person	89:11	69:31 65:35**	61:39 61:39*	73:27	48:52	29:71	64:36	95:5

* Without Ramallah and el-Bireh.
** Without ʿAqrabeh and Beit Furiq.
*** Without Ramallah, el-Bireh, and the 5 large eastern villages.

**** Without Deir Istiya.
***** Without ʿAqrabeh, Kafr Malik, Deir Jarir, Taiyibeh, Rammun and Deir Dibwan.
****** The areas of the villages sometimes extend beyond our topographical units.

TABLE 3
(SH/G = sheep + goats)

TOPOGRAPHICAL UNIT		Desert fringe	Northern central range	Southern central range	Central range: 7 large villages in east	Northern slopes	Southern slopes	Foot-hills
Average # per village	Cattle	66	79	21	88	57	15	83
	sheep	1,447	498*	686**	1,586	196	108	301
			297*	258**				
	Goats	802	369	496	921	422	171	440
			290*	299**		312***		
	Total SH/G	2,249	867	1,182	2,507	618	279	742
			587*	557**		517***		
	Draft animals	52	68	47	89	74	38	64
Per person factor (= avg. # animals per villager x 100)	Cattle	10	6	0.6	4	4	1.8	9
	sheep	293	36	19	72	15	13	32
			24*	19**				
	Goats	163	27	14	42	33	21	47
			24*	22**		25***		
	Total SH/G	456	63	33	114	48	34	79
			48*	41**		42***		
	Draft animals	11	4.9	1.3	1.4	5.8	4.6	6.8
Rel. % animal type per villager among topographical units	Cattle	32	19	2	3	13	6	28
	sheep	63	5*	4**		3	3	7
	goats	47	7*	6**	12	9	6	13
	Total SH/G	55	6*	5**	14	6	4	10
	draft animals	32	14	4		17	13	20
Rel. % animal type per villager within topographical unit	Cattle	2	12	3	3	9	5	10
	sheep	63	44*	45**	61	34	37	36
	goats	35	44*	52**	36	57	58	54

* Without ʿAqrabeh and Beit Furiq. ** Without Ramallah, el-Bireh, and the 5 large villages in the eastern central range. *** Without Deir Istiya.

We will now attempt to summarize the significance of the data presented in these tables for the appreciation of the economic and demographic potential of the topographic units in our region (see Figs. 39–40).

Desert Fringe

The few villages in this strip are relatively small in size. Their lands, however, are the most extensive, for the simple reason that they include the uncultivated pasture areas in the desert to the east. Cereals dominate the cultivated land. The area of field crops per person is greater than anywhere else in the territory of Ephraim, while the amount of land devoted to olives is relatively small.

Animal-raising here is the richest anywhere in our region. Sheep + goats are particularly noteworthy (55% of all the flocks in Ephraim), with sheep dominating (63% of all the domesticated animals in the desert fringe as well as 63% of all the sheep in Ephraim), despite the relative aridity. The absolute

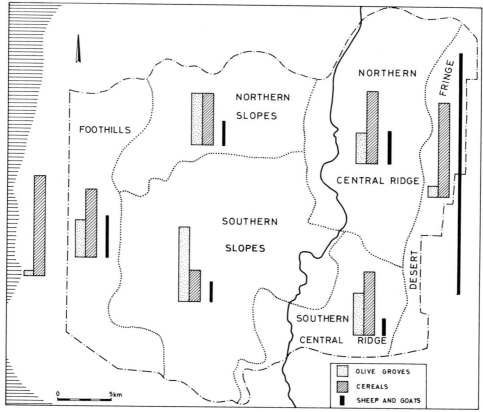

39. The proportion of cereal to olive growing areas and the relative number of sheep and goats in the various topographical units of the Territory of Ephraim.

135

number of cattle (32% of all cattle in Ephraim) and the number of draft animals are also relatively large, though in relation to other animals in the desert fringe, the proportion of cattle is relatively low.

This economic mosaic is influenced by a combination of climatological and topographical conditions: The climate is relatively arid; the many small plots are suitable for cereals but not for horticulture; and the desert edge offers broad pasturage.

Central Range

The phenomenon of large villages on the eastern side is noteworthy. These villages have two "faces," one directed toward the horticulture of the hills and the other toward the desert fringe to the east (on the village of Siʿir, which is similarly situated in the hills of Hebron, see Shmueli 1980:13–25). These are the largest villages and possess vast areas of land, a considerable proportion of which are located in the desert, cannot be cultivated, and serve as pasturage. (Yet the average amount of nonarable land per person is less than in the desert fringe.) Here, too, the areas of field crops per village and per person are very large — second in size after the villages of the desert fringe — and the areas devoted to horticulture are relatively small. In other words, here, as in the desert fringe, subsistence is based more on cereal-growing and pasturage.

Northern Central Range

The average number of inhabitants per village is very large, as is the population density per km^2. The main reason for this is, no doubt, the fertile interior valleys, which can support comparatively large villages. The proportion of land devoted to horticulture is relatively limited here and is the smallest of the four hill and slope topographical units. On the other hand, cereals are very prominent; the percentage of overall area per person planted with field crops is the largest in Ephraim. This, too, can be explained by the potential inherent in the interior valleys.

The number of animals is relatively small, especially if the two large villages in the east (ʿAqrabeh and Beit Furiq) are left out of consideration. Within this topographical unit, the proportion of sheep to goats is balanced (the steep sides of the valleys are difficult for sheep to maneuver), but when the two large villages are taken into account, the number of sheep is greater. Cattle constitute a relatively large portion of the animals here (12%).

Southern Central Range

In the unit proper (i.e., not including the desert pasturage belonging to the large eastern villages), the amount of land belonging to each village is

40. Territory of Ephraim — cereal versus olive-growing areas (1945).

relatively small, so that population density is comparatively high. The explanation for this is the concentration of the five large villages in the east and the presence of two cities, Ramallah and el-Bireh. Here, too, cereals are predominant, and the area devoted to horticulture is very restricted. Animal husbandry is on a smaller scale here than anywhere else in the territory of Ephraim. Within this unit, the proportion of cattle is miniscule. In the eastern villages, animals — mostly sheep + goats — are more numerous.

Northern Slopes

The few villages in this area are relatively small; consequently, population density is low. The average amount of land per person and the average amount of nonarable land per person are both large. This situation results from the fact

137

that the village of Deir Istiya owns broad areas in the rugged terrain near Wadi Qana most of which is exploited for pasturage rather than cultivated. The areas devoted to cereals and to horticulture are roughly equal. Animals are not numerous. There are fewer sheep than goats, apparently due to the difficult, rocky ground in the vicinity of Wadi Qana in the northern part of this topographical unit.

Southern Slopes

While the villages here are numerous, they are the smallest in the area of the survey grid, with the exception of those in the desert fringe. Population density per km² is sparse. This is olive country, and the area devoted to cereal growing per person is the smallest in Ephraim. The harsh topography has dictated the subsistence of the villages; it is easier to create terraces for vineyards on the slopes than to raise field crops. The village of Beit ʿUr el-Foqa offers a perfect example: Slopes and scarps constitute 92% (!) of the entire land of the village, and 73% of all the village lands are on declivities of greater than 36% (Dror 1979:20–21).
There are fewer sheep in this unit than anywhere else in Ephraim; nor are goats and cattle numerous. After the southern hill country, this area is the poorest in domesticated animals. Within the area itself, goats predominate even more than in the northern slopes, no doubt due to the difficult terrain.

Foothills

Although the villages are, on the average, relatively small, they are slightly larger than those of the slopes to their east. The area that is not suitable for cultivation is extensive, especially in the rocky region to the west of the villages (Finkelstein 1978). Horticulture plays only a small role in the economy, while field crops are the basis of subsistence. The topography is very moderate, and the relatively broad wadi beds are used for growing cereals. On the other hand, the rocky ridges are not suitable for orchards.

In the past, the rocky areas were exploited as pasturage, and even today, animal husbandry in the foothills is second only to the desert fringe (although if the villages of the eastern central range are considered as an independent bloc, they have relatively more animals than the foothills). Here, too, goats outnumber sheep, once again probably due to the rockiness of the terrain. In 1948, the villages of the foothills lost considerable pasturelands that were located between the border and the coastal plain. As a result, the total number of animals obviously declined, though the proportions within the flocks apparently did not change.

*   *   *   *   *   *   *

The principal branches of the economy can be summarized as follows:

Cereals — Field crops are predominant in the desert fringe, central range and foothills, but are very weak in the southern slopes.

Horticulture (today primarily olives, in the past, before the Moslem Occupation also grapevines) — These are very strong in the southern slopes, considerably widespread in the northern slopes, but of only minor importance in the desert fringe and in the villages of the eastern central range.

Animals — The pasture lands of the desert fringe and the villages of the eastern central range are very extensive; the pasturage available in the foothills and in the vicinity of Deir Istiya in the northern slopes is also considerable. Elsewhere in the central range and in the southern slopes, there is very little land for grazing. As for the composition of the herds, the number of cattle per person is greatest in the desert fringe (though cattle are only a tiny component of the animals within this unit). On the whole, from all aspects, cattle are quantitatively strongest in the foothills and weakest in the southern central range. The number of sheep in the desert fringe and in the villages of the eastern hill country is very large; they are also the dominant components of the herds in those areas. Sheep also predominate in the northern central range. On the slopes, their numbers are very small. The numbers of goats in the desert fringe and in the foothills are large, while these animals are scarce in the southern central range. Within the topographical units, goats are the dominant element in the herds of the slopes and the foothills. Flocks of sheep and goats, taken together, are of greatest importance in the desert fringe, in the foothills, and in the villages of the eastern central range.

SITES SURVEYED

On the following pages, we present a list of Iron I sites in the territory of Ephraim, including such well-known places as Shiloh, Bethel, Kh. Raddana and Ai. The sites are arranged by topographical unit (see Fig. 54) — since, as we saw, this division is of crucial importance for understanding the settlement pattern — and numbered within each unit. The following remarks concern the descriptions of the sites:

— Within each topographical unit, the sites are arranged according to the Survey of Israel, i.e., from northwest to southeast. The site numbers are also recorded according to the system of the Survey of Israel (Kochavi 1972a:13).

— An asterisk next to the site number indicates that the existence of Iron I occupation there is not absolutely certain (see also the table of finds).

— The Hebrew name follows the orthography of the 1:50,000 map, while the English name uses the transliteration of the Mandatorial 1:20,000 map. In a few cases, the names have been taken from the local villagers; these are presented in quotation marks.

— For large sites and Arab villages, the map reference is to a central point.

— By estimated area, we mean the total area of the site itself and not the estimated extent of the settlement in Iron I. For the Arab villages, no estimations are offered due to the difficulty in delimiting the ancient settlement accurately.

— The geological formations to which the sites belong have been taken from the works of Livnat (1971) and Dimant (1971), from the geological map of the Ramallah region (not yet published), from the geological map of the Jericho region (Begin 1974) and from additional unpublished field work.[12]

— For water supply, the distance (as the crow flies) to the nearest permanent source is given, but it must be borne in mind that there were cisterns at every site.

— Only the details important for our purposes are noted in the descriptions of the sites. Other information, notably concerning later installations and items, will be found in the full and final publication of the survey.

— With regard to the finds, the relative proportions among the different periods are reported only for the pottery that was collected during our survey. Disagreement between our findings and those published from earlier surveys means either that we have reexamined the finds and encountered no clear indicators for certain periods or that we revisited the site and collected sherds representing periods that had not been noted. The majority of the sherds listed as "UD" (undatable) belong to the Hellenistic, Roman, Byzantine or early Arab periods, within which certain types are difficult to distinguish. Arab pottery of recent generations is not noted.

— For the Iron I period, "large village" means 5–6 dunams or more, while "small village" means 3–4 dunams.

— For each site, the data are presented in the following abbreviated manner:

Left-hand column —
- topographical unit and cardinal number (DF = desert fringe; NCR = northern central range; SCR = southern central range; NS = northern slopes; SS = southern slopes; FH = foothills)
- site number
- Hebrew name
- English name

---

12   I thank the geologists Y. Rot, G. Shaliv, and N. Mittelfeld, who worked in the northern part of the territory of Ephraim, for all their assistance.

Central column —
- Israel grid reference
- UTM grid reference
- elevation in meters above sea level
- area in dunams

Right-hand column —
- topographical setting
- geological formation (when available)
- distance in meters from permanent water source
- character in Iron I

Then come three telegraphic paragraphs —
- description of the site
- finds, including the relative proportions (in %) of the periods represented, with a verbal summary of the quantity of sherds collected at the site on the right (Chalc = Chalcolithic; EB = Early Bronze; IB = Intermediate Bronze; MB = Middle Bronze II; LB = Late Bronze; Pers = Persian; Hell = Hellenistic; Rom = Roman; Byz = Byzantine; EA = Early Arab; Med = Medieval)
- reference(s) to previous modern surveys (even if their results differ, or Iron I sherds were not then found) or excavations; references to old field work that did not furnish accurate survey data are not given

No attempt is made here to identify sites mentioned in ancient sources.

DF 1	18475 17420	ridge
18–17 44/1	72320 56095	Ein Yorqeᶜam
	790	700
	1	isolated house / farmhouse

Heap of stones and courtyard area with cistern. Meager remains. Good view across desert fringe and Jordan Valley.

Iron I   medium

DF 2	18425 17385	slope
18–17 43/1	72270 56065	Soreq
חר׳ ינון	710	100
Kh. Yanun	4	small village

Terraced ruin on edge of small valley (Fig. 41). Building stones in terrace walls. No overview.

41. Kh. Yanun — the site (on the left) and the valley, looking east.

Iron I — 10; Iron II — 65; Hell — few; Rom — 20; Byz — few Porath 1968: 46–47		large

DF 3	18740 17325	hilltop
18–17 73/1	72585 56005	Amminadav; Moẓa on slope
חר׳ טנא א־תחתתא	309	550
Kh. Tana et-Tahta	8	few houses

Large ruin. Remains of later structures. No overview. EB — single sherd; MB(?) — single sherd; Iron I; Iron II; Hell-Rom — 85 Campbell 1968:31		large

DF 4	18435 17220	hilltop
18–17 42/1	72280 55900	Amminadav

| אינבי נון | 662 | 1,450 |
| En Nabi Nun | | summit site |

High peak with sheikh's tomb. Superb view across desert fringe and Jordan Valley. Sherds scattered over exposed bedrock. No architectural remains.

| Iron I; Iron II; Byz; Med | | small |
| Porath 1968:49 | | |

DF 5	18535 17105	slope of ridge
18–17 51/1	72390 55785	Amminadav; Moẓa on slope
חר׳ אל׳ג׳ריש	400	100
Kh. el Jarayish	7	few houses

Narrow ridge with steep slopes. Many building remains, some apparently fences or animal pens. Possible enclosure wall on western side. View of desert fringe and Gilead.

| EB — 40; Iron I — 10; Iron II — 50 | | medium |
| Porath 1968:52 | | |

DF 6	18695 16750	slope
18–16 67/3	72550 55430	
	325	2100
	1	few houses

Sherds scattered near a late animal pen. Heap of stones and remains of a single ancient wall. One wall of the pen is built of reused stones. No overview.

| MB; Iron I | | small |

DF 7	18595 16570	slope
18–16 55/1	72460 55245	
	420	1200
	3–5	few houses / seasonal site

Broad terraces doted with shreds, near a group of caves. In medieval times the caves were used by shepherds as seasonal campsite. View of Jordan Valley and Gilead.

| MB — 85–90 of ancient periods; Iron I; | | |
| Med | | medium |

| DF 8 | 18505 16485 | hilltop and slope |

18–16 54/1	72370 55165	Amminadav; Moẓa on slope
	610	1,000
	15	small village
	(area of sherd scatter)	

Site on top and eastern slope of hill. On summit, destroyed *weli* of esh-Sheikh Mazar. Terraced slope. Panoramic view encompasses desert fringe, Jordan Valley, and Moab. Iron I sherds on summit.

EB — 90+; Iron I — 5+; Iron II — few;	
Med — few	large
Porath 1968: 71	

DF 9	18400 16160	hilltop
18–16 41/1	72270 54840	Amminadav (above its soft element)
חר' אל מרג'ם	595	800
Kh. el Marajim	6	small village

Ruin partly converted into orchard. High fences with stones in secondary use. Collapse of two large square buildings in south. View through wadi opening to Jordan Valley.

| MB — single sherd; Iron I — 5; | |
| Iron II — 95 | large |

DF 10	18515 16150	slope
18–16 51/1	72385 54830	
חר' אדרחיא	545	400
Kh. er-Rahaya	3	few houses

Site on a steep slope. Heaps of fallen stones. Remains of walls. View of Jordan Valley and Transjordan plateau.

| EB — 22; MB — 16; Iron I — 10; Pers — 10; | |
| Hell — 42 | medium |

DF 11	18540 16060	slope
18–16 50/1	72420 54740	
	530	400
	2	few houses

A broad terrace on the upper slope of Wadi Fasayil. Heaps of stones apparently covering a building, retaining walls and a later building. View of Jordan Valley and Gilead.

EB; IB; Iron I; Byz   medium

DF 12	18460 15980	moderate hilltop
18–15 49/1	72335 54655	Vradim/Avnon interface
חר' ג'בעית	640	1,100
Kh. Jib'it	50	large village

Very large ruin with many later building remains. Cisterns, quarrying, and burial caves. View of Jordan Valley.

MB; Iron I; Iron II — large quantity;
Pers; Hell(?); Rom; Byz; Med — majority   large

DF 13	18160 15540	ridge in wadi
18–15 15/1	72040 54210	Amminadav
חר' מרג'מה	470	50
Kh. Marjama	30	large village

One of most important sites in Ephraim. On excavations, see A. Mazar 1982a; *Had. Arch.* 76, 1981: 19.

Kallai 1972:172

DF 14	18315 15100	edge of ridge
18–15 31/1	72200 53770	Shivta
חר' אנג'מה	610	3,650
Kh. en Najama	3–4	small village

Ruin at edge of rocky ridge east of fertile valley. Remains of walls of buildings and retaining walls. View of Jordan Valley.

Iron I — 80; Iron II — 20   medium

NCR 1	18100 17935	slope on valley edge
18–17 19/1	71935 56600	Amminadav/Moẓa interface
חר' א־שיח' נצראלה	500	900
Kh. Sh. Nasrallah	7	few houses

Ruin cleared of stones on slope. Terrace walls with stones in secondary use. Caves and quarrying. View across Beit Dajan Valley.

MB(?) — single sherd; Iron I — few;

42. Kh. Ibn Nasir — aerial view.

Iron II — 10; Pers — few;
Hell-Rom — 85; EA
Campbell 1968:26

large

NCR 2	18560 17860	ridge, valley edge
18–17 58/1	72400 56535	Giv'at Ye'arim
חר׳ שויחה	530	2,400
Kh. Shuweiḥa	6	large village

Ruin cleared of stones. Few walls poking up through ground. View across Beit Dajan Valley.

MB — 13; Iron I — 80;
Iron II — few; Rom — few
Campbell 1968:26

large

| NCR 3 | 17920 17835 | hilltop |
| 17–17 98/1 | 71755 56500 | Amminadav; possibly Kfar-Shaul on peak |

חר' אבן נצר (חר' דיב)	613	2,400
Kh. Ibn Nasir		
(Kh. Dhiyab)	3	small site

High peak with panoramic view of Shechem, Mt. Ebal, Mt. Gerizim, Sahl Mahneh, the Beit Dajan Valley, Kh. ʿUrmah, etc. Modern circular fence encloses summit. Ancient buildings perhaps spilled over somewhat onto the slope, but the ancient site was apparently also circular in plan. Architectural remains visible (Fig. 42).

Iron I — 90; Iron II — single sherd;	
Med — few	small
Campbell 1968:29; Kallai 1972:166	

NCR 4	17545 17600	slope of ridge
17–17 56/1	71385 56255	chalk (Menuḥa?)
חר' א׳נבי	620	350
Kh. en Nabi	12	large village

Sheikh's tomb and medieval village in center of large site.

EB — 8 (on summit); Iron I — 7;	
Iron II — 20; Pers; Hell;	
Rom — 45; Med — 20	large
Campbell 1968:32; Kallai 1972: 167	

NCR 5	18515 17590	valley edge
18–17 55/1	72360 56265	Beit Meir
חר' טנא אל־פוקא	530	2,100
Kh. Tana el-Fauqa	7	few houses

Sheikh's tomb next to medieval ruin. To south, 16 threshing floors (Fig. 43). View of Sarṭaba and Mt. Ebal.

Iron I — 7 (esp. in south);	
Iron II — 75; Hell — 18;	
Med (dominant but not	
included in % calculations)	large
Campbell 1968:31; Kallai 1972: 167	

NCR 6	17675 17405	hilltop
17–17 64/1	71520 56065	Beit Meir
תל אדרס	575	600
er-Ras	25	large village

Large tell with broad cultivated terraces on slopes. Building stones in second-

43. Kh. Tana el-Fauqa — the threshing floors.

ary use in terrace walls. Cisterns. Fortification line, constructed of large field
stones, visible on east. On west, complex of sheikh's tomb (Nebi ᶜUzeir).
Limited view of valley and its surroundings.
MB — 2; Iron I — 7; Iron II — 52;
Pers — 11; Hell(?); Rom — 27   large
Kallai 1972:167

NCR 7	18335 17385	flat-top ridge
18–17 33/1	72180 56055	Ein Yorkeᶜam
חר׳ ענם	810	700
Kh. Ghannam	7	few houses

Square fortress of Iron II, 85 m long on each side. Superb view of Shechem —
Jordan Valley road, desert fringe, and Jordan Valley south to Jericho.
Iron I — 5; Iron II — 95   medium
Porath 1968:46

| NCR 8 | 17335 17260 | slope |
| 17 — 17 32/1 | 71180 55910 | |

עינבוס   515   1000
cEinabus   large village

Arab village (on tell?). Most sherds collected on the southern slope. No overview.
MB — 12; Iron I — 32; Iron II — 8; Pers — 25;
Hell — 9; Rom — 8; med — 6   large
Porath 1968:48

NCR 9   18050 17265   ridge
18–17 02/1   71900 55940   Ein Yorkecam
חר' אל־ערמה   840   850
Kh. el cUrma   15   large village

High tell on ridge with steep slopes, linked by saddle to ridge to south (Fig. 44). Extensive view, especially toward north. Overlooks Shechem — Jordan Valley road. Few walls and piles of cleared stones. Ruins at head of eastern slope.
MB — 30; LB; Iron I — 5:
Iron II — 25; Hell;
Rom — 25; (UD — 10)   large
Campbell 1968:38–41; Kallai 1972:168

44. Kh. cUrma, looking northwest.

NCR 10	17290 17130	hilltop
17–17 21/1	71140 55780	Kfar Shaul
חר׳ עטרוד	690	1,700
Kh. ʿAtarud	12	relatively large village

Cultivated ruin. Panoramic view includes Sahl Maḥneh.

Iron I — 20; Iron II — 40;	
Hell — 10; Rom — 30	medium
Porath 1968: 50–51	

NCR 11	17415 17125	hilltop
17–17 41/2	71265 55780	Amminadav
חר׳ רסזיד	611	1,000
Kh. Ras Zeid	8	relatively large site

High site with panoramic view. Overlooks road along spine of hill country from Tappuah junction up to Shechem. On south, remains of buildings covered with heaps of cleared stones. Definite terrace wall bounds site on east.

Iron I — 85; Iron II — 15	small
Porath 1968:52	

NCR 12	17950 17190	hilltop
17–17 91/1	71795 55855	Amminadav
חר׳ רוג׳ן	710	600
Kh. Rujan	8	few houses

Ruin with well-preserved buildings. Walls with dressed stones. Most pottery from late periods. View of area of Mt. Ebal and Mt. Gerizim.

Iron I — few; Iron II; Rom;	
Byz; EA; Med	large

NCR 13	18265 17145	plateau
18–17 21/1	72120 55820	alluvium atop Moẓa
חר׳ אל־כרום	810	1,200
Kh. el-Kurum	3	small village

Site completely cleared of stones, with large stone heap in center. Panoramic view of Mt. Ebal, Mt. Gerizim, desert fringe, Jordan Valley, horn of Sarṭaba and Mt. Baal-hazor.

Iron I — 20; Iron II — 20;	
Pers — 25; Hell — 10; Rom — 25	medium
Porath 1968: 52	

NCR 14	17865 17000	hilltop
17–17 80/1	71725 55665	Amminadav
"דוארה"	713	1,300
"Dawara"	8	large village

Terraced site on high hill. Flat summit and broad terraces on slopes. Stones in secondary use in terrace walls. Heap of cleared stones on summit. Circular shape of site responsible for its name. View toward Mt. Ebal, Mt. Gerizim, Kh. ʿUrma, Aqrabeh, and Qabalan Valley.

| Iron I — 90; Iron II — 10 | | large |

NCR 15*	17660 16880	ridge
17–16 68/3	71530 55535	Amminadav
אל־חרבה	550	1,400
el-Khirbe	uncertain	few houses

Ruin on ridge descending toward Qabalan Valley. Two wells at top of site. Medieval buildings scattered along ridge.

Iron I — single sherd;

| Iron II; Hell-Rom; Med — 90 | | medium |

NCR 16	17990 16815	plateau
17–16 98/01	71850 55485	alluvium atop
		Amminadav; Moẓa
		on slope
מסלת א־שיח׳ חתם	810	1,000
Sheikh Hatim	10	small village

Flat area dotted with sherds. At southern end, remains of one or two buildings covered with tall heaps of cleared stones. Panoramic view to east and north.

Iron I — 10; Iron II — 70;

| Hell-Rom — 20 | | medium |

NCR 17*	18375 16805	slope
18–16 38/1	72235 55480	Amminadav (above its
		soft element)
	685	2,400
	10	few houses

Large ruin overlooking desert fringe. Many building remains buried beneath heaps of cleared stones. Buildings constructed of field stones. Cisterns. Good view eastward to desert fringe and Jordan Valley.

45. Tell Abu Zarad — the summit, looking north.

Iron I(?) — few;
Iron II — vast majority   medium

NCR 18	17195 16790	hilltop
17–16 17/1	71050 55440	Moẓa(?)
תל אבו זרד	680	250
Tell Abu ez Zarad	20	large village

High tell with distant panoramic vistas (Fig. 45). On summit, sheikh's tomb, grove, and enormous heap of cleared stones. Protruding terrace, with large stones visible at base, apparently hides fortification.
EB; MB — 15; LB; Iron I — 10;
Iron II — 45; Hell — 15; (UD — 10)   large
Kallai 1972:169

NCR 19	17520 16705	slope of ridge
17–16 57/2	71380 55360	Amminadav; Moẓa on slope
	570	550
	1	few houses

152

Sherd scatter on light-colored terraces in olive grove.
Iron I; Iron II — 95+;
Pers (?)   small

NCR 20	17740 16790	slope at valley edge
17–16 77/1	71595 55450	Amminadav
קבלן	600	600
Qabalan		large village, apparently

Arab village (Fig. 37). Ancient material collected on southwest slope of village nucleus.
Iron I — 33; Iron II — 66;
Med (dominant but not
included in % calculations)   small

NCR 21	18065 16765	moderate hilltop
18–16 07/1	71920 55430	Amminadav; Moẓa on slope
ג'וריש	813	200
Jurish		large village

Arab village. Ancient material collected on cultivated terraces on north and east sides. Good view toward Shechem and east to desert fringe.
EB(?); MB — 7; Iron I — 25;
Iron II — 30; Rom — 5; Med — 33   large

NCR 22	17605 16600	hilltop
17–16 66/1	71465 55260	Beit Meir adjacent to Moẓa
חר' א־שונה	725	750
Kh. esh Shuna		few houses

Ruin terraced and cleared of stones.
Iron I — single sherd;
Iron II — 95; few later body sherds   small

NCR 23	18025 16675	moderate hilltop
18–16 06/1	71885 55345	Amminadav; Moẓa on slope
חר' קרקפה	830	1,000
Kh. Qarqafa	3	small village

Ruin cleared of stones and cultivated. Good view to north and east.
Iron I — 35; Iron II — 65   small
Porath 1968:66

NCR 24	18115 16665	hilltop
18–16 16/1	72080 55340	Amminadav; Moẓa on slope
	790	1,600
	15	large village

Terraced hill with olive grove. Rock-hewn installations in north. Cisterns. Limited view of immediate surroundings.
Iron I; Iron II; Pers;
Hell(?); Rom; Byz;
EA (large amount)   large

NCR 25	17190 16560	ridge
17–16 15/3	71065 55205	Amminadav /Moẓa /Beit Meir interface
	520	600
	1.5	few houses

Hill with remains of terraces. About 10 cisterns on summit. Only scant architectural remains.
Iron I; Iron II;
Pers; Byz   small

NCR 26	17315 16530	plateau
17–16 35/1	71190 55180	Moẓa
	660	1,400
	4	few houses

Edge of plateau over Lubban esh-Sharqiyyeh Valley. Moderate terraces strewn with sherds. Panoramic view.
Iron I — few; Iron II — majority;
Pers   medium

| NCR 27 | 18015 16535 | ridge |
| 18–16 05/1 | 71875 55200 | Amminadav; Moẓa on slope |

חר' אל-קריק   882   650
Kh. el Qariq   8   few houses

Ruin cleared of stones.
Iron I; Iron II(?);
Pers (large amount); Hell   medium

NCR 28   18255 16565   hilltop
18 — 16 25/2   72020 55240
     762   2400
     5   small village

Hill with cultivation terraces and cistern. View of Jordan Valley and Transjordan plateau.
Iron I; Iron II sherds belong to a nearby
site.   medium

NCR 29   17375 16445   ridge at valley edge
17–16 34/2   71245 55090   Soreq
חר' צור   576   1,400
Kh. Sur   hard to estimate   village

Cultivated terraces and piles of cleared stones. Building remains not discerned.
MB — 30; Iron I — 50;
Iron II — 20   small
Porath 1968:71

NCR 30   17345 16250   saddle
17–16 32/1   71215 54915   Soreq/Kesalon
         interface
     675   1,200
     10   small village

Small tell at top of "Lebonah Ascent," overlooking the ascent and the valley
(Fig. 46). Entire site under cultivation. Large terraces, especially on north.
Active cistern in southeast.
Iron I — 10; Iron II — 85;
Pers(?) — single sherd;
Byz — few   medium
Porath 1968:72

NCR 31   17630 16200   slope

46. The tell at the top of the ascent of Lebonah, looking north-west.

17–16 62/01	71505 54865	Amminadav
	660	1,300
	12	few houses

Cultivated terraces on slope. Iron I material on top of site, where slope is relatively steep. Site may be connected with nearby Kh. er-Rafid (NCR 38).
EB — overwhelming majority;
MB; Iron I — few   large

NCR 32	17690 16280	slope
17–16 62/02	71565 54950	Amminadav
	650	400
	1.5	few houses

"Step" on slope at end of broadening of Wadi ᶜAli. Sherds strewn across area and in heaps of cleared stones.
MB; Iron I — 66; Rom   medium

NCR 33	17750 16260	hilltop

	71620 54910	Amminadav/Moẓa
חר' סילון (שילה)	714	interface
Kh. Seilun (Shiloh)	25	950

See Chapter 5

NCR 34	17980 16220	slope; valley edge
17–16 92/2	71850 54880	Amminadav
	730	1,300
	0.5	few houses

Small site on step of moderate slope on edge of Shiloh Valley. Buildings lean against fence. Monolithic pillars visible (see NCR 35).
Iron I — 15; Iron II — 50;
Roman — 35   small

NCR 35*	17950 16260	slope
17–16 92/3	71835 54920	Amminadav
	730	1,400
	1.5	few houses

Pottery strewn on terraces of slope, but no building remains. Site may be connected with NCR 34 (above).
Iron I — single sherd(?);
Iron II; Pers — 70; Hell; Byz   small

NCR 36	18035 16210	hilltop
18–16 02/1	71905 54880	
חר' נג'מת ח'ניפס	760	1100
Kh. Najmat Khuneifis	1.5	few houses

A large square heap of stones covers a rectangular building (ca. 15X20 m.) on top of the hill. Remains of other structures under heaps of stones. Late animal pens. View to south and west.
Iron I; Pers (?)   small

NCR 37	17290 16115	hilltop on ridge
17–16 21/1	71160 54770	Beit Meir
חר' ע'רבה	790	550
Kh. Ghuraba	10	few houses

Ruin largely cleared of stones. A few wall lines visible. Quarrying. View

northward to Mt. Gerizim, and Sheikh Abu-Zarad.
Iron I — few; Iron II;
Byz — majority   medium
Kallai 1972:169

NCR 38	17670 16180	ridge
17–16 61/1	71540 54845	Amminadav
חר' ארדפיד	700	1,700
Kh. er Rafid	3	few houses

Narrow, well-protected ridge. Remains of a large building at edge. Possible
building remains on broad terrace of lower level ending in scarp (see NCR 31).
EB — 75–80; IB (?); MB;
Iron I — 2 sherds;
Iron II — 5–10; Rom-Byz — few   medium
Kallai 1972:169

NCR 39	18120 16150	hilltop
18–16 11/1	71995 54825	
	775	1000
	3	small village

Moderate hill surrounded by cultivation plots. Oval peripheral wall, 1–2
courses high, not preserved all around the site. Building remains within the
site.
Iron I   medium

NCR 40	17270 15935	hilltop
17–15 28/1	71145 54580	Beit Meir
חר' עליתה	849	850
Kh. ʿAlyata	10	small village

Ruin on summit of gentle hilltop. Cultivated terraces and remains of walls.
Good view to north and west.
Iron I — 2; Iron II — 37; Hell — 6;
Rom — 20; Byz-EA — 10; Med — 3;
(UD — 22)   large
Kallai 1972:170

NCR 41	17980 15970	ridge
17–15 99/1	71850 54640	Kfar Shaul
	750	2,600
	1	single house

Remains of building covered by cleared stones, two wine presses and two cisterns on edge of small valley.
Iron I — single sherd; Iron II;
Rom; Byz   small

NCR 42	18215 15940	ridge
18–15 29/1	72095 54615	Vradim
חר׳ כולצון	795	3100
Kh. Kulesun	4	small village

Ruin on a ridge. Remains of structures. Cisterns. Good view: Judean desert, Transjordan plateau.
Iron I — 15; Rom — 45; EA — 35   large

NCR 43	17490 15870	hilltop
17–15 48/1	71370 54525	Beit Meir adjacent to Moẓa
חר׳ א־תל	840	600
Kh. et Tell	15	large village

Ruin on summit of isolated hilltop (Fig. 47). Buildings (mostly Medieval),

47.   Kh. et-Tell, looking north-east.

rock-hewn installations, other installations and pillars. View of Jerusalem Shechem road running through wadi below.
EB — few; Iron I — 9;
Iron II — 24; Hell(?);
Rom — 40; Byz — 10; Med — 10   medium
Kallai 1972:170

SCR 1	16825 15250	moderate hilltop
16–15 82/1	70715 53895	Soreq
חר׳ ביר זית	815	900
Kh. Bir Zeit	10	few houses

Site completely cleared of stones. Large medieval *khan* on summit. Ancient material found on western slope. Panoramic view.
Iron I — few; Iron II — 50;
Pers — few; Hell — few;
Rom — few; Byz; Med — 20   large
Kallai 1972:173–174

SCR 2	17845 15130	high hilltop
17–15 81/1	71735 53790	Menuḥa
א׳טיבה	863	1,200
Et Taiyiba		large village

Large Arab village on extensive site. Panoramic views of Judean Desert, Jordan Valley and across hill country.
Iron I — 20+ (mostly from western slope);
Iron II — 40–; Rom — 17;
Byz — 10; Med — 5; (UD — 8)   medium

SCR 3	17220 15075	slope
17–15 20/01	71115 53725	Beit Meir
חר׳ ע׳ריטיס	880	100
Kh. Ghureitis	2	few houses

Rom-Byz ruins cleared of stones. Remnants of buildings and burial caves. Nearby sheikh's tomb with adjacent threshing floors. The few earlier sherds found on southern edge of site.
MB — few; Iron I — few;
Rom — 30; Byz — 65   medium
Kallai 1972:176

SCR 4	17280 14815	moderate hilltop
	71175 53465	Amminadav, bordering
		on Moẓa
ביתין (בית־אל)	870	550
Beitin (Bethel)		large village
See Chapter 3		

SCR 5	17850 14840	hilltop
17–14 88/1	71745 53500	Menuḥa
רמון	750	1,700
Rammun		small village

Arab village. Panoramic views of Jerusalem, Judean Desert, Jordan Valley, Taiyiba, and Ai. Majority of ancient material collected on western slope.
Iron I — 25; Iron II(?);
Hell(?); Rom — 20; Byz — 5;
Med — 25; (UD — 20)   small

SCR 6	17485 14705	ridge
	71385 53365	Kfar Shaul/Amminadav
		interface
חר׳ א׳תל (העי)	850	500
Kh. et-Tell (Ai)	10–11	large village
	(Iron Age)	
See Chapter 3		

SCR 7	16930 14660	ridge
16–14 96/1	70835 53305	Soreq
חר׳ רדנה	871	250
Kh. Raddana	8–10	large village
See Chapter 3		

SCR 8	17020 14620	hilltop
17–14 06/1	70920 73260	Soreq
רס א׳טחונה	890	800
Ras et-Tahune	5	few houses

Ruin (not tell) within el-Bireh. Modern terraces. Panoramic view, south as far as Jerusalem area.
EB — single sherd; MB(?);
Iron I — few; Iron II — 75; Hell   small
Kallai 1972:178

SCR 9	17375 14690	moderate slope
17–14 36/2	71275 53345	Amminadav
	870	1,000
	1.5	few houses

Tops of walls protrude through three large heaps of cleared stones.

| MB — 36; Iron I — 57; Iron II — 7 | small |

NS 1	16005 17225	ridge
16–17 02/1	69855 55855	
עזבת אבו חליל"	365	400
"'Izbet Abu Ḥalil"	2	few houses/seasonal site

Seasonal site of shepherds from the village of Deir Istiya. A flat area sur-ruonded by stone fence; on its edge, a few animal pens. Cistern.

| Iron I | small |

NS 2	16795 17245	hilltop
16–17 72/1	70645 55885	Bina(?)
חר' אל־חוש	500	2,750
Kh. el Haush	12	large village

Retaining walls and piles of cleared stones on slopes of ruin. Later building on summit. Panoramic view, especially to west.

Iron I — 20; Iron II — 60;	
Rom — 20	small
Porath 1968:47–48	

NS 3	16005 17160	ridge
16–17 01/1	69860 55785	
	400	500
	1.5	few houses/seasonal site

Concentration of sherds on rocky hill.

| Iron I | medium |

NS 4	16760 17155	ridge
16–17 71/1	70615 55795	
זיתא	450	2300
Zeita		few houses

Arab village. Ancient pottery on north and south slopes.
Iron I — single sherd (+one sherd on the ridge west of the village — site 16 —
17 81/1); Iron II; EA;
Med   medium
Porath 1968:49

NS 5	16900 17080	hilltop
16–17 90/1	70750 55725	Menuḥa
ג׳מעין	540	4,100
Jammaᶜin		small village

Large Arab village. Most Iron Age material from west side. Panoramic view,
especially to west.
Iron I — few; Iron II — 20;
Rom — 10; Med — 70   medium
Porath 1968:53

NS 6	16415 17010	moderate hilltop
16–17 40/1	70265 55645	Bina(?)
	451	2,800
	10	scattered houses

Moderate hill. Stones from flat area of summit gathered into large heaps, some
of them long and straight, from which tops of walls protrude.
MB — 25; Iron I — 18;
Iron II — 35; Med — 12;
(UD-10)   small

NS 7	16385 16905	hilltop
16–16 39/1	70245 55540	Kfar Shaul(?)
חר׳ אתל	520	3,400
Kh. et Tell	30	large village

Large tell with panoramic view. Few walls visible on summit.
MB — 10; Iron I — 8; Iron II — 60;
Hell(?); Rom — 15; (UD — 7)   large
Gophna and Porath 1972:230

NS 8	17115 16910	slope
17–16 19/1	70970 55555	
	500	1,300
	8	few houses

Terraced slope with many sherds. Limited overview.
MB; Iron I — few; Pers — 95   medium

NS 9	15860 16810	elongated hilltop
15–16 88/2	69715 55430	Kfar Shaul(?)
אתל	386	3,900
et-Tell	20	large village

Terraced tell on hill, adjacent to village of Ṣarṭa. On one terrace, near flat area of summit, building remains (perhaps fortifications) protrude.
MB(?); Iron I; Iron II — 90;
Pers; Hell; Rom   large
Porath 1968:58

NS 10	16085 16080	slope
16–16 08/1	69945 55435	Bina(?)
חר׳ אל־ברק	450	2,900
Kh. el Burak		few houses

Byzantine ruin. Few earlier sherds on southwest side.
Iron I; Iron II;
Byz — 95+   medium
Porath 1968:58

NS 11	16890 16730	hilltop
16–16 87/1	70750 55375	
חר׳ רס׳קרה	660	1,600
Kh. Ras Qurra	5	small village

Ruin. Fences around perimeter create terraces for cultivation. Stone debris on upper slope. Panoramic view northward toward Mt. Gerizim, westward to Mediterranean, and southward to Farkha range.
Iron I — 8; Iron II — 50;
Pers — 42   medium
Porath 1968:61

NS 12	16755 16690	saddle
16–16 76/1	70620 55335	Amminadav
חר׳ א־שג׳דה	570	1,300
Kh. esh Shajara	10	small village

Well-preserved ruin entirely composed of tall heaps and massive walls of cleared stones (Fig. 48). Hard to discern original architecture. Another ruin,

48. Kh. esh Shajara — an aerial view, looking north-east.

smaller but of similar character, adjoins it on west; there, only Iron II is present.
Iron I — 10; Iron II — 90   medium

NS 13*	15965 16605	ridge
15–16 96/1	69820 55230	Bina (?)
חר׳ חמד	400	2,800
Kh. Hamad	6	few houses

Late ruin. Buildings, installations, and quarrying. A public building, apparently a church, on the south.
Iron I(?); Iron II; Pers;
Hell; Rom; Byz — majority   small
Porath 1968:64

NS 14	16335 16600	hilltop
16–16 36/1	70195 55230	Amminadav; Moẓa in wadi on south

ביר אֶתֶל	493	400
Bir et Tell	3	few houses

High hill with cliffs on south. Remains of massive walls and collapsed buildings. Defense wall visible along almost entire periphery. Iron Age olive presses cut into southern cliff face. Panoramic view.
Iron I — 8; Iron II — 77;
Pers — 9; Rom — 6   medium
Gophna and Porath 1972:230

NS 15	17060 16655	ridge
17–16 06/1	70920 55305	Moẓa
חר' ביר אל־חריב	640	1,250
Kh. Bir el Kharayib	approx. 5	small village

Terraced ruin planted with olive trees. Large active cistern on south.
Iron I; Iron II — majority   large

NS 16	16180 16510	ridge
16–16 15/1	70040 55140	Amminadav; adjoining Moẓa
חר' מטוי	455	700
Kh. Matwi	18	large village

Large ruin with many recent buildings. Panoramic view westward to coastal plain. Early material mostly from north side.

MB — 10; Iron I — 30;
Iron II — 40; Pers — 7;
Rom — 13; Med (dominant but not
included in % calculations)   large
Porath 1968:68

NS 17	16700 16530	ridge
16–16 75/1	70560 55170	Moẓa
סלפית	510	adjacent to springs
Salfit		large village

Arab town covering tell. On southern slope of ancient part, cultivated terraces with lots of pottery.
Iron I; Iron II — about 80%
of the ancient material;
Pers; Hell-Rom; Med   large

49. Kh. Banat Barr (on the top left, at the foot of the cliff).

NS 18	15535 16225	slope
15–16 52/1	69405 54840	border of Moẓa,
		Vradim and Bina
חר׳ בנת־בר	300	2,000
Kh. Banat Barr	approx. 5–6	few houses
	(main site)	

Ruins on the edge of a cliff above Naḥal Shiloh (Fig. 49).
For description of site, see Eitam 1980a:64–68.
MB — few; Iron I — little;
Iron II — majority; Pers;
Hell — little

large

SS 1	16410 16405	hilltop at end of ridge
16–16 44/1	70275 55040	Kfar Shaul
פרחה	600	800
Farkha		small village

Arab village impressively located at end of ridge with steep slopes. Many sherds in cultivated terraces. Ancient material found on northern slope. Panoramic view to west.
MB — single sherd; Iron I — few;
Iron II — 60–70% of pre-Med
material; Pers; Hell; Rom; Byz;
Med — majority   large

SS 2	15840 16240	ridge
15–16 82/1	69710 54865	Bina; Moẓa in wadi on north
"קלע"	433	450
"Klia"	6.5	few houses

On the site and its excavations, see Eitam 1980a:69–70; *Had. Arch.* 77, 1981:16–17.
Iron I — few; Iron II

SS 3	15935 16150	plateau
15–16 91/1	69805 54775	
דיר ע'סנה	470	1,000
Deir Ghassana		few houses

Arab village.
Iron I — few; Iron II;
Byz; Med
Gophna and Porath 1972:233

SS 4*	16625 16100	ridge
16–16 61/2	70500 54740	Givᶜat Yeᶜarim(?)
עְרורה	570	500
ᶜArura		few houses

Arab village. Ancient material collected from northwest slope.
Iron I(?) — few; Iron II — 50;
Rom — 50; Med — few   large

SS 5	16000 16000	ridge
16–16 00/1	69860 54625	Kfar Shaul
בית רימא	500	900
Beit Rima		small village

Arab village. Panoramic view to north.
Iron I — 7; Iron II — 23;

Pers — 2; Hell — 9; Rom(?);
Byz — 42; Med — 16   large
Gophna and Porath 1972:233

SS 6	15675 15990	ridge
15–15 69/1	69545 54605	Moẓa
	320	200
	5	seasonal site (?);
		few houses (?)

Small amount of sherds on ridge above springs in deep wadi adjacent to the village of ᶜAbud.
Chalc — 4; EB — 75;
Iron I — 4; Iron II — 7;
Rom — 10   small

SS 7	17365 15845	plateau
17–15 38/3	74240 54495	Moẓa, bordering on
		Amminadav
	900	700
	1	seasonal site (?);
		isolated house (?)

Sherds in field in large stone pile and in few fences of cleared stones. No architectural remains. Good view to north.
Iron I   small

SS 8	16035 15725	elongated hilltop
16–15 07/1	69915 54350	Kfar Shaul, bordering
		on Moẓa
חר׳ תבנה	540	adjacent spring
Kh. Tibna	35–40	large village

Large tell. Cultivated terraces with many sherds. Building stones in secondary use in terrace walls. Most of early material from northern slope; later material from summit of tell. Limited view.
Iron I — 6; Iron II — 50;
Pers — 2; Hell — 9; Rom — 8;
Byz — 8; EA + Med — 3;
(UD — 14)   large
Gophna and Porath 1972:234

| SS 9 | 16990 15680 | ridge |

16–15 96/1	70870 54325	Soreq
עטרה	820	100
ᶜAtara		large village (?)

Arab village at end of ridge. Panoramic view, northward as far as Mt. Gerizim.
Ancient material from east and west sides.
Iron I — 6; Iron II — 46;
Rom — 8; Byz — 36; Med — 4   medium
Kallai 1972:171

SS 10	16515 15555	hilltop
16–15 55/2	70400 54165	Kfira
כובר	650	300
Kaubar		small village (?)

Arab village. Limited view.
Iron I — single sherd;
Iron II — 48; Pers — 6;
Rom — 3; Byz — 30;
Med — 5; (UD — 7)   medium

SS 11	17015 15560	hilltop
17–15 05/1	70900 54205	Soreq
חר׳ טרפין	823	200
Kh. Tarafein	15–20	large village

Large ruin, mostly cleared of stones (Fig. 50). Fences and terrace walls.
Medieval village on southeast side. Architectural remnants on summit.
Ancient material on south. View across region.
Iron I — 30; Iron II — 60;
Pers — 10; Rom; Byz; Med
(proportions calculated only
for early periods, which together
constitute 30–40% of the material)   large
Kallai 1972:172

SS 12	16960 15405	ridge
16–15 94/01	70845 54055	Soreq
	760	300
	5.5	uncertain

Ridge with steep slopes. Wall that looks like long stone heap bounds the ridge

50. Kh. Tarafein, looking north-west. At the back — the village of ʿAtara.

on side of continuation of ridge and also continues along top of southern slope. In several places, width of 3.0–3.5 m was measurable. In center of site, heap of stones with architectural remains visible in it. Small quantity of sherds scattered over area, most body sherds.

Iron I   small

SS 13	15795 15350	hilltop
15–15 73/01	69680 53975	Kfar Shaul
	510	1,400
	2	few houses(?); seasonal site(?)

Sherds strewn across summit of hilltop.

Iron I   small

SS 14	15985 15270	hilltop
15–15 92/1	69870 53895	Kfar Shaul/Amminadav interface; Moẓa on slope
דיר עמר	530	300

171

51. The village of Deir 'Ammar.

Deir ᶜAmmar	4	small village or few houses

Small Arab village. Tall terraces and massive ancient walls (Fig. 51). Two Iron Age oil-pressing installations. Good view to distance.
MB — few; Iron I — few;
Iron II — 65; Pers;
Med — 35 large

SS 15	17160 15200	ridge
17–15 12/01	71055 53850	Beit Meir
אל מניטרה	740	800
el Mneitrah	3.5	small village

Hill planted with olive trees. Large heap of cleared stones at northern end. Most of pottery scattered in vicinity of stone heap, especially on terraces on north and northeast sides. Good view to north.
MB — 25; Iron I — 60;
later periods — few medium

SS 16	15890 15190	moderate hilltop
15–15 81/1	69775 53810	Kfar Shaul/Bina interface
חר' א־שונה	520	1,200
Kh. esh Shuna	35	small village or few houses

Large terraced ruin (Fig. 52). Remains of walls, pillars, tombs and other features. Thick cultivated steps with lots of pottery. Good views to Jerusalem hills and Ayyalon Valley. Iron I settlement may have been on eastern slope of adjacent hill (on the west), on summit of which there are pits cut into rock in manner of Gibeon "winery."
Iron I — few; Iron II — 30;
Hell — 15; Rom — 15; Byz — 20;
EA; (UD — 15)   large

SS 17	16030 15135	ridge and sddle
16–15 01/1	69920 53765	Beit Meir/Moẓa interface
חר' א־נבי עניר	440	250
Kh. en-Nabi ʿAnnir	30–35	small village

52. Kh. esh Shuna, looking east.

Large ruin. Sheikh's tomb and oak grove on saddle to north. Terrace walls with masonry stones in secondary use. Agricultural installations, pillar fragments, and tombs. Recent buildings on summit. Limited view.
Iron I — 5; Iron II — 10;
Pers — 5; Hell — 10; Rom — 10;
Byz — 45; (UD — 15)   large

SS 18	. 16335 14550	hilltop on ridge
16–14 35/1	70240 53180	Giv‘at Ye‘arim
חר' אל-חפי	670	400
Kh. el-Hafi	3	few houses

Terraced ruin. Building stones reused in terrace walls. Cisterns.
Iron I — 7; Iron II — 15; Pers — 30;
Hell — 48   large

SS 19*	16085 14360	hilltop
16–14 03/1	69995 52990	Kfar Shaul
בית עור אל-פוקא	590	500
Beit ‘Ur el-Fauqa	15	few houses

Small Arab village. Superb views, especially to west and south.
Iron I(?); Iron II — 60;
Pers — 5; Hell-Rom; Byz;
Med(?)   large

FH 1	15320 16665	moderate hilltop
15–16 36/1	69180 55275	Bina
חר' דיר קסיס	260	3,900
Kh. Deir Qassis	6	few houses

Later ruin crowned by buildings cleared of stones. Ancient material found on southwest side. View of coastal plain and foothills.
Iron I — single sherd;
Iron II — 44; Pers — 41;
Byz — 12; Med (dominant but not
included in % calculations)
Gophna and Porath 1972:230

FH 2	15240 16295	ridge
15–16 22/1	69105 54905	Vradim; Moẓa in wadi
		to south

| חר׳ צרצרה | 240 | 300 |
| Kh. Sarsara | 6 | large village |

Ruin. Collapse of buildings created heaps of rubble stones, especially on southern slope. Architectural remains also on summit. At northern end of flat area of summit, enclosure wall perhaps visible. Limited view.

MB(?); Iron I — 50;
Iron II — 13; Pers — 17;
(UD — 16)
Gophna and Porath 1972:231

medium or small

FH 3	15210 16215	ridge
15–16 22/2	69080 54830	
חר׳ דיר דקלה	271	600
Kh. Deir Daqla	8	small village

Terraced ruin. Stones in secondary use in terrace walls. On summit of hill, a large building into which ashlar stones are integrated. In north, a kind of crypt with loculi. Cisterns in west. Architectural elements. Site encompassed by massive terrace wall. View to part of coastal plain, a little to north, and to west.

Iron I — 6; Iron II — 57;
Byz — 37
Gophna and Porath 1972:231

medium

FH 4	15385 16290	hilltop and slope
15–16 32/1	69250 54905	Vradim
דיר אל־מיר	318	1,200
Deir el Mir	20	few houses

Well-preserved Iron II village. Houses buried under collapse. Installations on summit of hill. Panoramic view of foothills and coastal plain.

Iron I — few; Iron II — 85;
Pers — 15; Med — only on summit
Gophna and Porath 1972:232

medium

FH 5	15280 16160	ridge
15–16 21/1	69150 54770	Beit Nir; Moẓa on north
חר׳ ברעש	308	4,100
Kh. Burraʿish	8	small village

Ruin with medieval buildings on summit. Terrace walls on slopes. View to north and west.

Iron I — several; Iron II — 23;
Hell-Rom — 5; Byz — 17;
Med — 40; (UD — 10)   medium
Gophna and Porath 1972:233

FH 6	15325 16095	ridge and slope
15–16 30/1	69195 54715	Beit Nir
חר' עלי	300	3,800
Kh. ʿAli	10	few houses

Ruin with high terrace walls, built in part with stones in secondary use. Few
wall remains. Later agricultural installations. Extensive view to south.
Iron I — 1; Iron II — 16;
Pers — 1; Hell-Rom — 5; Byz — 55;
Med — 5; (UD — 17)   medium
Gophna and Porath 1972:233

FH 7	15275 16015	moderate slope
15–16 20/2	69150 54625	Bina
חר' אדור	269	4,200
Kh. ed-Duwwar	7	small village

Remains of Iron Age village. Structures collapsed. Panoramic view to south.
Iron I — 10; Iron II — 90   small
Gophna and Porath 1972:233

FH 8*	15380 16005	hilltop
15–16 30/2	69255 54620	Beit Nir
אלבן	300	2,800
el-Lubban		few houses

Arab village. Ancient material found on southeast side.
Iron I(?); Iron II — 50;
Pers-Hell; Rom; Byz — 25   medium

FH 9	15480 16090	slope of ridge
15–16 40/1	69350 54710	Bina; Moẓa in
		wadi on north
	310	800
	4	few houses

Remains of Iron Age settlement. See Eitam 1980a:68–69.
Iron I — few; Iron II;
Byz — few   small

FH 10*	15380 15475	top of ridge
15–15 34/1	69265 54085	Bina
שוקבה	300	2,000
Shuqba		few houses

Arab village. Ancient material found primarily on southeast side. Limited view.
Iron I(?); Iron II — 45;
Pers(?); Rom — 20;
Byz — 25; Med — 10   medium

FH 11	15075 14890	hilltop
15–14 08/1	68975 53495	
אדס	240	1,000
er Ras	hard to estimate	few houses

Cultivated tell. Panoramic view.
EB; Iron I; Iron II; Pers;
Hell(?); Rom; Byz; Med   medium
Gophna and Porath 1972:235

FH 12	15820 14465	flat ridge
15–14 84/1	69725 53085	Menuḥa
בית עור אל־תחתא	390	2,800
Beit ʿUr et-Tahta		small village or few houses

Arab village on tell. Most of pottery found on northern terraces. View to Beth Horon Ascent, Ayyalon Valley and western slopes of Judean Hills.
Iron I; Iron II — 28; Pers;
Hell(?); Rom; Byz — 7; Med   large
The Iron I sherds were found only in box in the Department of Antiquities. A. Mazar reports (oral communication) that he collected Late Bronze material at the site.

POTTERY

The ceramic material will be presented according to the types illustrated in Figure 53. Some of these types have variants that are not shown here. The two principal components of the ceramic assemblage are, of course, collared-rim store jars and cooking pots. At a limited number of sites, fragments of Iron I

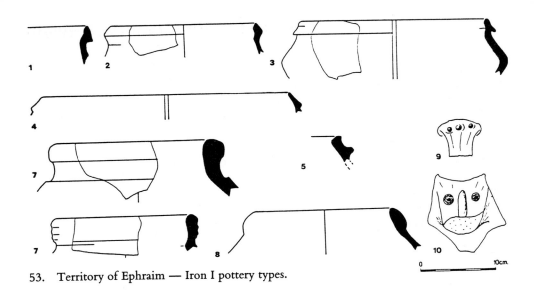

53. Territory of Ephraim — Iron I pottery types.

bowls and kraters were also found. It is our experience that the finding of even only a single Iron I sherd at a site is sufficient indication of some kind of activity during that period. In other words, unlike the situation during later periods (when the population in the region was very dense), isolated Iron I sherds should not be viewed as accidental finds or field sherds. The accompanying table itemizes the pottery found at each site according to the following type categories (the numbers refer to Fig. 53):

1. Cooking pot with everted rim.
2. Cooking pot with vertical rim. The form of the rim can be triangular, flattened or elongated. (Only one variant is shown on Fig. 53.)
3. Cooking pot with slanted rim, triangular in section.
4. Cooking pot with slanted rim, elongated and flattened.
5. This cooking pot appears only at those sites which also have Iron II pottery, but it apparently came into use during the 11th century BCE.
6. Other cooking pots.
7. Collared-rim store jars. To the best of our knowledge, it is very difficult to distinguish subtypes on the basis of sherds gathered in surveys. (The table also includes fragments with the ridge above the collar, even if the rim is lacking.)
8. Pithos with body widening below rim, i.e., neckless.
9. Punctured jar handles. Their attribution to this period was determined in the excavations at Mt. Ebal ʿIzbet Ṣarṭah and Shiloh, as well as at one-period sites from the survey (Chapter 7).
10. Jar handles with two holes flanking an incised vertical line creating what appears to be a schematic rendering of a face (see Chapter 7).
11. Miscellaneous sherds: bowls, kraters, jugs, and bases of jars (not shown on Fig. 53).

TABLE 4
DISTRIBUTION OF POTTERY TYPES PER SITE

SITE	S*	1	2	3	4	5	6	7	8	9	10	11 *****
DF	1	E			2			2	8***	3		1	1B+5
DF	2	SE		3		1	2		6	2	2	1	
DF	3	E					1		1(+1)	1			
DF	4	SE							1			1	
DF	5	SE		(1)			2(+1)	4	3(+1)		1		(1)K
DF	6	E		2		1							
DF	7	E							4–5				
DF	8	SE		6		4		2	15		2		
DF	9	E		3			1(+5)	1	5	1			
DF	10	E		2		1			2		1		
DF	11	E				1			2				
DF	12	E		(1)		2	2	2	6	1			
DF	13		E X C A V A T E D										
DF	14	E	1						1	1			1(+3)K
NCR	1	E					2		1				(1)K
NCR	2	E	1	5	1			5	36		2		2(+2)K 24B 12M Sh K 2U
NCR	3	E		2		1		1	3		8		1K
NCR	4	SE		3		2	5		6				
NCR	5	E		2		1			2(+1)		1		
NCR	6	E		1			2	1	3				1B 1K
NCR	7	E				1	5(+1)		6	1			
NCR	8	E		2					14–15		1		3B+2
NCR	9	SE	4	1					8	3			1S"Cj"
NCR	10	E		2	2	1	4–5		5(+1)	3	3		
NCR	11	SE		3	1	1			12		2	(1)	1Bc 1(+1)K
NCR	12	E							1(+1)				
NCR	13	E				1	1		7				
NCR	14	E		5			2		40***		2		4K
NCR	15	E								1			
NCR	16	E						3	5				
NCR	17	E					2			1			
NCR	18	SE		4	2	2	1(+1)		25	7	4	1	
NCR	19	E							1	1			
NCR	20	E					1		4				
NCR	21	E		1	1				15	3	1		
NCR	22	E							1				
NCR	23	SE		1	1		2(+1)		12	3(+1)	1		1K
NCR	24	E		1			2	2	6		1		
NCR	25	E							2				

(cont'd)

SITE		S*	1	2	3	4	5	6	7	8	9	10	11
NCR	26	E					1		1				
NCR	27	E		1		1			4				
NCR	28	E							15	1	1		
NCR	29	SE	1	17	1		1	1	17		1		(1)Bc (1)K
NCR	30	SE							12				
NCR	31	E		2									
NCR	32	E		1					4	1			
NCR	33			E	X	C	A	V	A	T	E	D	
NCR	34	E							5				
NCR	35	E							(1)				
NCR	36	E		2			1	2	4			1	1B 4
NCR	37	E							1(+1)				
NCR	38	E							2				
NCR	39	E							10		1–2		4U 2
NCR	40	SE		1				1	2	1			
NCR	41	E							1				
NCR	42	E					1	1	7				2
NCR	43	SE		1					3				(1)K
SCR	1	SE							3	1			
SCR	2	E	(1)	2					9	2			1K
SCR	3	E							1				
SCR	4			E	X	C	A	V	A	T	E	D	
SCR	5	E		1				1(+1)	2	2			
SCR	6			E	X	C	A	V	A	T	E	D	
SCR	7			E	X	C	A	V	A	T	E	D	
SCR	8	SE		2	1								(1)K
SCR	9	E		3					4–5				1K
NS	1	E				2		1				1	
NS	2	SE		1	2		1	1	6		1		
NS	3	E					2		4		1		IJ+1 IU
NS	4	S		1			1						
NS	5	S		(1)								1	
NS	6	E		(1)							1		(1)U 2Bs
NS	7	SE			2			2	3	(1)			
NS	8	E			1				(1)				
NS	9	SE			3				4				(1)K
NS	10	SE							3	1			
NS	11	E		1					3	1			
NS	12	E							14		1		

(cont'd)

SITE		S*	1	2	3	4	5	6	7	8	9	10	11
NS	13	E					1		(1)				
NS	14	SE					1	2	5	1			
NS	15	E		1		1			6	1(+1)			
NS	16	SE		4(+1)	2				14	(1)			
NS	17	E		1				1	5***				
NS	18	O						3(+2)	2				
SS	1	E							3				
SS	2	O								1			
SS	3	E							1				
SS	4	E							(2)				
SS	5	SE							4				
SS	6	EO				2			2***				
SS	7	E							11	1			
SS	8	SE		2	1		1	1	12				1S"Cj" 1K
SS	9	SE		1					3				
SS	10	E							2				
SS	11	SE					1		28	8(+1)			(1)K
SS	12	E							1				
SS	13	E							11				1U
SS	14	E		1					(1)	(2)			
SS	15	E		15					18				1U 2J
SS	16	E0		2				(1)	4(+1)				
SS	17	E		(1)				1	5				
SS	18	E		1				1	3	1			
SS	19	E							(1)				
FH	1	E							1				
FH	2	E0 **	1	9				3	30***	1	1	1	1S"Cj"
FH	3	E						1	3				
FH	4	E **							2		1		
FH	5	E							4(+1)				
FH	6	E							1				
FH	7	E0 **	1			1			3				
FH	8	E								(1)			
FH	9	O				1			(1)				
FH	10	E							(1)				
FH	11	E							1				
FH	12	S							1				

(cont'd)

Explanatory Notes

Sites are identified by the abbreviation for the topographical unit and number corresponding to the list of sites surveyed provided in the previous section.

Parentheses indicate uncertainty over attribution to the specific type or even to the period.

* Survey in which the Iron I sherds were collected. The following abbreviations are used in this column:
  S = 1968 Surveys of Samaria
  E = survey of Ephraim
  O = other surveys or study trips provided the information
** The boxes of sherds from the 1968 Survey could not be located.
*** Reed impressions on one of the rims (Column 7).
**** There was apparently activity at the site during the Late Bronze period.
***** The following abbreviations are used in Column 11:

B	= bowl	U	= jug
J	= jar	c	= *cyma*-profile
K	= krater	"Cj"	= "Canaanite jar"
M	= miscellaneous	h	= with holes
S	= base		

The following table summarizes the distribution of ceramic types in the territory of Ephraim by topographical units:

TABLE 5:
DISTRIBUTION OF POTTERY TYPES PER TOPOGRAPHICAL UNIT

TOP. UNIT		1	2	3	4	5	6	7	8	9	10	11	TOTAL
	A	1	19	2	10	14	12	57	8	6	3	10	142
DF	B	0.7	13.4	1.4	7	9.9		40.1	5.6	4.2	2.1		
								45.7		6.3			
	C		14.8			25		9.1	12.7	14.3			
	A	6	58	12	12	33	17	314	27	30	3	78	590
NCR	B	1	9.8	2	2	5.6		53.2	4.6	5.1	0.5		
								57.8		5.6			
	C		45.3			59		50.2	42.9	71.4			

(cont'd)

TOP. UNIT		1	2	3	4	5	6	7	8	9	10	11	TOTAL
SCR	A	1	8	1		1	2	20	5				
	B	2.4	19.5	2.4		2.4		48.8	12.2				
								61					
	C		6.3			1.8		3.2	7.9				
ALL CR	A	7	66	13	12	34	19	334	32	30	3	81	631
	B		10.5			5.4		52.9	5.1				
								58		5.2			
NS	A		11	11	3	6	12	71	7	4	2	7	134
	B		8.2	8.2	2.2	4.5		53	5.2	3	1.5		
								58.2		4.5			
	C		8.6			10.6		11.3	11.1	9.5			
SS	A		22	2	2	2	4	113	14			7	166
	B		13.3	1.3	1.3	1.3		68.1	8.4				
								76.5					
	C		17.2			3.6		18.1	22.2				
ALL S	A		33	13	5	8	16	184	21	4	2	14	300
	B		11			2.7		61.3	7				
								68.3		2			
FH	A	1	10	1	1		4	51	2	2	1	1	74
	B	1.3	13.5	1.3	1.3		5.4	68.9	2.7	2.7	1.3		
								71.6		4.0			
	C		7.8					8.1	3.2	4.8			
TOTALS		9	128	29	28	56	51	626	63	42	9	106	1147
%								54.6					

A = # of sherds
B = % of all sherds in topographical unit
C = % of all sherds of given type in all units

In the distribution of ceramic types in the territory of Ephraim by topographical units, certain differences are evident between north and south and between east and west. The most obvious one is the relative monotony of the repertoire of the south versus the relative variety of types in the north. This accords well with what we know from the excavations at Giloh and other sites in Judah and Benjamin, where the ceramic assemblage comprised a very limited number of types, as opposed to the greater diversity of types excavated, for example, at Shiloh. The explanation for this situation lies, apparently, in the geographical background: The southern sector of the hill country is much more isolated than the valley areas of the north. The proximity of Shechem and other centers in Manasseh also affected the relative variety of the northern assemblage.

As for the ceramic types themselves, although we are dealing with a sample that is not large, certain noteworthy trends seem to be evident:

— The paucity of Type 1 cooking pots found during the survey is surprising, especially in comparison to the large quantities excavated at Giloh, at other sites in Judah and Benjamin, and at ʿIzbet Ṣarṭah (Stratum III). At present, we are unable to explain this fact, which, if it is not simply a matter of chance, probably has chronological or regional implications.

— The cooking pot with vertical rim (Type 2) is generally the most widespread throughout the territory of Ephraim. According to the survey data, it was slightly more popular in the southern central range and in the desert fringe. (In the foothills this type was found at only two sites.) This may be of chronological significance, for this type of cooking pot was very common at the beginning of Iron I (A. Mazar 1981a:31), but subsequently declined in frequency (Finkelstein 1986:64–65).

— The other types of cooking pots are more prominent in the collections from the northern part of Ephraim, which is a logical consequence of our observation about the distribution of Type 1.

— The proportion of collared-rim store jars in the assemblage from the desert fringe is relatively small (40.1%); it increases in the units of the central range, foothills (where most of the material, however, is from a single site), and northern slopes; and it is greatest in the southern slopes (68.1%). As the table in the following page demonstrates, for each topographical unit, there is a high degree of correlation between the percentage of land devoted to horticulture (as opposed to cereals) and the percentage of collared-rim store jars in the ceramic assemblage (note the relative proportions among the topographical units).

Collared-rim store jars were thus more prominent in areas of horticulture and less frequent in areas where cereal cultivation was predominant. This correlation is of great importance in discussing the function of these vessels (Chapter 7).

— The profile of the rim of the collared-rim store jars has numerous variants.

	DF	NCR	SCR	NS	SS	FH
% land devoted to horticulture (vs. cereals) in each topo. unit	11	31	39	52	71	36
% collared-rim store jars in assemblage in each topo. unit	40.1	53.2	48.8	53.0	68.1	68.9

We have not yet perceived any chronological or geographical significance in these variations, but hope the matter will become clearer as we study the ceramic assemblage from the Shiloh excavations.

— The Type 8 pithos is most conspicuous in the southern central range and in the southern slopes. It is no accident, therefore, that the type was first noticed at Bethel (Kelso 1968:63).

— The phenomenon of handles ornamented with punctures and incisions is most evident in the desert fringe and in the northern central range. No such handles have been found in the southern part of Ephraim. This observation accords well with the information from neighboring areas: Only a few of these handles have been found in Judah and Benjamin, while they are very common in Manasseh and the Jezreel Valley (Zertal 1986b:289–291; Chapter 7).

The Settlement Pattern of the Iron I Period

The data on the following table indicate the comparative extent of settlement in each topographical unit of the territory of Ephraim during the Middle Bronze, Late Bronze, Iron I and Iron II periods (as of summer, 1987):

		DF	NCR	SCR	TOTAL CR	NS	SS	TOTAL S	FH	GRAND TOTAL
MB IIB-C	# of sites	10	18	9	27	12	10	22	1	60
	% all sites	17	30	15	45	20	17	37	1	100

(cont'd)

		DF	NCR	SCR	TOTAL CR	NS	SS	TOTAL S	FH	GRAND TOTAL
LB	# of sites	1	3	1	4	–	–	–	(1)	5–6
IRON I	# of sites	14	43	9	52	18	19	37	12	115
	% all sites	12	37	8	45	16	17	33	10	100
	% all sites surveyed in unit	27	31	15	26	27	11	16	18	–
	km² per site	7.4	5.2	11.9	6.3	8.3	17	12.8	12.3	avg. 9.2
IRON II	# of sites	19	64	10	74	35	37	72	25	190
	% all sites	10	34	5	39	18	20	38	13	100
	% all sites surveyed in unit	37	46	17	37	52	22	30	38	–

The data on this table limn the following picture:

— During the MB IIB-C periods, settlement activity was concentrated in the desert fringe, the northern central range — particularly around the intermontane valleys, the northern slopes and Bethel. In the southern slopes and the foothills, activity was limited. Some of the sites in the central range were relatively large, while the majority of the sites on the slopes were very small, testimony to the fact that these were the first attempts to inhabit this zone. It is possible that some of the small sites, especially those in the vicinity of Bethel, were occupied only seasonally. It is also possible that these sites did not all exist simultaneously (Chapter 11).

— There was a drastic drop in the number of sites during the Late Bronze period (Fig. 55). Activity was restricted to the central range. Every site on the western slopes was abandoned, and full-scale settlement did not resume there until Iron II. The Late Bronze sites in the central range — Bethel, Shiloh (which was not a genuine settlement; see Chapter 5), Sheikh Abu Zarad (Tappuah), Khirbet ʿUrma and Shechem on the border of our region — were located at roughly equal distances from one another in the Bethel plateau and in the vicinity of the fertile intermontane valleys. The settlements of Bethel

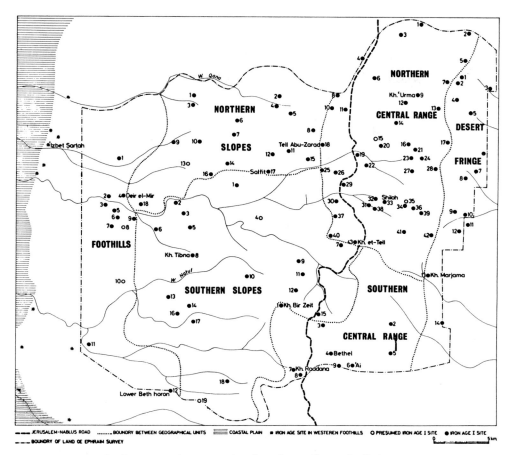

54. Territory of Ephraim — the Iron I sites (numbers refer to site list).

and Shechem were relatively large in size. For Khirbet ʿUrma and Sheikh Abu Zarad, the available information is insufficient to determine the size and nature of the Late Bronze settlements.

— During Iron I, an influx of settlers overran the region (Fig. 54). The desert fringe and the northern central range were densely crowded with sites, and sizeable concentrations existed in the northern slopes, the Bethel plateau and the vicinity of Rantis in the west. On the other hand, activity in the southern slopes and in most of the foothills area was very limited.

— During Iron II, settlement activity practically doubled. Only in the southern central range did the number of sites remain unchanged. Now there was a flurry of activity in the northern central range, the northern slopes and the northern part of the foothills. There was a certain decline in the relative proportion of the central range units in favor of the western slopes. Indeed, the

187

most important and significant change was the increase in sites in the western slopes (we will return to this later on).

The following table illustrates the development of settlement from Iron I to Iron II (see also the lists of sites earlier in this chapter):

	DF	NCR	SCR	TOTAL CH	NS	SS	TOTAL S	FH
# Iron I sites that expanded in Iron II	6	27	4	31	14	14	28	11
# Iron I sites that contracted in Iron II	2	8(+1)	2	11	1(?)	1(?)	2(?)	1
# Iron I sites abandoned	5	7	3	10	3	4	7	–
# of sites founded in Iron II	11	30	3	33	20	23	43	13
% of sites founded in Iron II	11	30	3	33	20	23	43	13

The table indicates that 76.5% of the Iron I sites continued to be occupied in Iron II, and that 66% of the Iron I sites increased in size in Iron II. The continuity between the two periods is thus undeniable.

Interestingly enough — and in complete contrast to the overall impresive increase in the number of sites in Iron II — there was a perceptible decline in settlement in the southern central range during the transition to the period of the United Monarchy. More than half of the Iron I sites in the Bethel plateau either shrank in size or were abandoned at that time (and only three new sites were founded there in Iron II). Two sites situated in the adjacent area of the western slopes (SS 11, SS 12) were also abandoned, and a neighboring site to the east (DF 14) contracted in size.

The excavators of Ai and Khirbet Raddana had dated the end of occupation at those sites to around 1050 BCE (Chapter 3), and it does seem that the area was adversely affected in the mid-11th century, perhaps in the wake of the Israelite defeat at Ebenezer. After the kingdom split, this was a sensitive border area between Israel and Judah. Occupation was concentrated in central sites such as Bethel, Beth Horon, Ophrah and Mizpah; unfortified villages or farms, like those founded in the neighboring areas to the north and south, did not exist here.

And further — 47% of the Iron I sites abandoned or diminished in size at the end of the period are located within the eastern strip of the area, i.e., the desert fringe and the eastern part of the central range units. This phenomenon is connected to the process characteristic of the Iron II period - the diminishing importance of the eastern periphery and, simultaneously, the increasing weight of the western units of the land of Ephraim.

In order to best understand the significance of the process of Settlement operating in the region during Iron I, I would make a bipolar chronological distinction between "early" and "late" in this period. Sites classified during an archaeological survey as "Iron I" could obviously date to the end of the 11th century or even to the beginning of the 10th century BCE, for the indicative pottery types continued to appear then. It is thus important to attempt to isolate those sites that were already inhabited at the beginning of the Iron I period (the 12th and early 11th centuries BCE) and to contrast their distribution with the late Iron I and Iron II settlement patterns (the latter reached its floruit in our region in the 8th century BCE).

We have separated out the sites belonging to the beginning of Iron I based

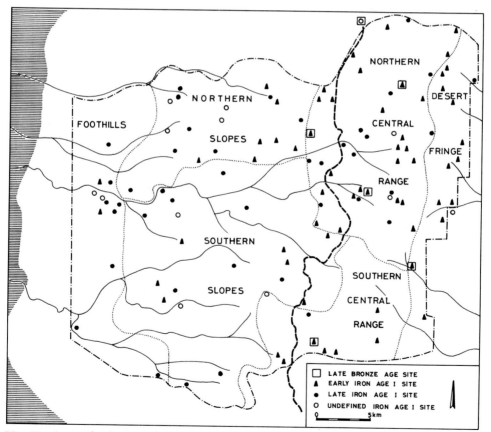

55. Territory of Ephraim — division into early and late Iron I sites.

either on the presence of Type 1 and 2 cooking pots, which characterized the early sites of Israelite Settlement in the hill country (e.g. A. Mazar 1981a:20–23), or, for sites where no cooking pot sherds were collected, based on the quantity of collared-rim store jars. We also took into consideration the appearance of early types, such as ornamented jar handles (Types 9 and 10), and late types, such as Type 5 cooking pots and Type 8 pithoi. The sites at which very few Iron I sherds were gathered were generally assigned to the later phase of the period.

Naturally, the situation is not clear-cut. Type 1 and 2 cooking pots were also found in later levels at ʿIzbet Ṣarṭah and in the destruction level of Shiloh. Moreover, at many sites, few Iron I cooking pots of any kind were found, so that the absence of Types 1 and 2 need not mean that a given site was unoccupied during the early phase of the period. Despite these reservations, plotting the distribution of sites belonging to the beginning of Iron I (Fig. 55) is worthwhile. The margin of error is unlikely to be very large, both because most cooking pots of the late 11th and early 10th centuries differed from their predecessors (Finkelstein 1986:64–71) and because the accumulated information from 115 sites is of undeniable weight.

The following table distinguishes between the earlier and later Iron I sites (see also Fig. 55). Most of the early Iron I sites were probably inhabited during the later phase of the period as well.

		DF	NCR	SCR	TOTAL CH	NS	SS	TOTAL S	FH	GRAND TOTAL
EARLY IRON I	# of sites	12	27	7	34	7	7	14	2	62
	% all sites	20	44	11	55	11	11	22	3	100
	% in unit	86	63	78	65	39	37	33	17	–
	km² / site	9	8	15	10	21	46	34	74	–
LATE IRON I	# of sites	1	14	1	15	8	10	18	8	42
	% all sites	2	33	2	35	19	24	43	19	100
	% in unit	7	33	11	29	44	53	49	67	–
IRON I UNATTRIBUTED		1	2	1	3	3	2	5	2	11

This chronological division clearly highlights the trends noted for all the sites of the period, both early and later. At the beginning of the process of Israelite Settlement in the territory of Ephraim, activity was especially strong in the desert fringe and in the central range, with 75% of all the sites then located in these sectors. The density factor in the desert fringe and central range was 9 km² per site, as opposed to 39 km² per site in the western slopes and the foothills.

It is also noteworthy that 10 of the 14 early sites in the western slopes bordered on the central range. If they are included, then 90% of the early sites were situated in the eastern part of the region. In the desert fringe and southern central range, virtually no new sites were founded later in the Iron I period (whereas 80% of the sites of the desert fringe and eastern central range were defined as "early Iron I"). In the western slopes and the foothills, at the beginning of Iron I, settlement was just starting; it increased considerably only later (62% of the sites founded in the later phase of Iron I were located in these sectors). These trends continued, as we have seen, during Iron II.

Another important factor in the deployment of settlements is the size of the sites. In most cases, the survey enabled us to appreciate the character of each site according to its size (if it was a one-period site) or according to its inclusive

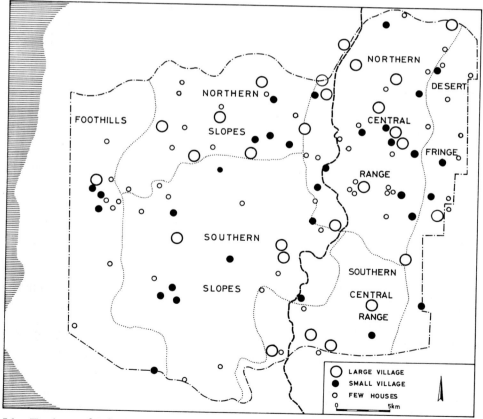

56. Territory of Ephraim — distribution of the Iron I sites according to their size.

area, location and the quantity of Iron I pottery collected (for multi-period sites). It was thus possible to attempt to determine whether the settlement of Iron I was a large central village, at least 5–6 dunams in area (e.g., Ai and Raddana), a small village covering some 3–4 dunams or a collection of a few houses (or tents?). This possibly reflects, to a certain extent, the social framework of the population according to the "folk model" of ancient Israel, i.e., the division into *bêt 'āb, mišpāḥot,* etc. (recently, Stager 1985b:17–23; Callaway 1985:43).

The following table indicates the size of sites within each topographical unit and the proportions within each unit and in relation to all units (see also Fig. 56):

		DF	NCR	SCR	TOTAL CR	NS	SS	TOTAL S	FH	GRAND TOTAL
LARGE VILLAGES	# of sites	2	11	4	15	5	3	8	1	26
	% all sites	8	42	15	57	19	12	31	4	100
	% in unit	14	26	44	29	28	16	21	9	
SMALL VILLAGES	# of sites	4	12	1	13	4	7	11	4	32
	% all sites	12	38	3	41	12	22	34	12	100
	% in unit	28	28	12	25	22	37	30	33	
FEW HOUSES	# of sites	7	20	4	24	9	9	18	7	56
	% all sites	13	36	7	43	16	16	32	13	100
	% in unit	50	46	44	46	50	47	49	58	
OTHERS		1	–	–	–	–	–	–	–	1

The majority of the large villages were concentrated in the central range and the northern slopes. The large villages of the central range were situated in the Bethel plateau, in the vicinity of the intermontane valleys and on the eastern side of these units, near the desert fringe — a location with obvious economic advantages. In the desert fringe, the southern slopes, and the foothills, most of the sites were small. The climate of the desert fringe and the limited areas suitable for cultivation were not conducive to the development of large settlements. The difficult terrain of the southern slopes dictated small settlements. The fact that in the western parts of Ephraim, the process of settlement began relatively late in the period also contributed to the small size of the sites.

Incidentally, this picture is remarkably similar to the situation obtaining in the region at the beginning of this century. Then, too, the largest villages were concentrated in the southern central range, while the sites decreased in size, respectively, in the northern central range, in the northern slopes and the foothills and, finally, in the southern slopes and desert fringe. The only major difference between Iron I and the recent past, in this respect, was in the size of the sites in the foothills.

The spatial relationship between the large and small sites is also of interest. In each topographical unit, the large sites were generally clearly spaced apart in a balanced manner (the reasons for the density in the vicinity of Bethel were apparently historical rather than economic or ecological). As a result, there was no more than one large site in each of the intermontane valleys of the northern central range. In many instances, one or two small villages and one or more sites with just a few houses were situated in geographical proximity to a large village. The pattern of settlement was thus one of prominent central sites with a peripheral populace connected to it, which means that by the end of the 11th century BCE, the patterns of rural life were already quite advanced.

However, the sites with a few houses each may reflect pastoralists, seasonal agriculture or very small permanent villages. A situation in which 49% of the sites fall into the category of "few houses" — which is the case in Ephraim in Iron I — seems to attest to the early stages of settlement of groups that did not have a background of urban or village life.

Another matter of significance is population size. This can be approximated by multiplying the estimated size of the Iron I sites by a density factor of 25 persons per dunam (Chapter 11). Site size is estimated by the scatter of the remains/pottery (in single period sites), or by a combination of the scatter of the remains with the ratio of Iron I pottery in the assemblage (in multi-period sites). Before proceeding to the data, four points must be noted:

1. The population of Iron I actually represents the situation at the height of the period, *ca.* 1050 BCE, before the destruction of Shiloh and the abandonment of Ai, Raddana, and other sites.
2. Understandably, pastoralists, who did not leave behind tangible remains, are not included in our calculations. During the Iron I period, this population was apparently still sizeable.
3. Our information about the Iron I sites is obviously still incomplete. For our purposes, the relationships among the topographical units, not just the absolute numbers, are important. (In any case, no drastic change in our conclusions is forseeable, since most of the large sites have already been surveyed.)
4. In order to calculate the population of the early Iron I sites, we have arbitrarily assumed that their surface area was then half of what it became by the end of the period.

	DF	NCR	SCR	TOTAL CR	NS	SS	TOTAL S	FH	GRAND TOTAL
population **TOTAL**	875	3,825	1,225	5,050	1,600	1,150	2,750	725	9,400
IRON I % all sites	9	41	13	54	17	12	29	8	100
population **EARLY**	450	1,825	625	2,450	350	450	800	125	3,825
IRON I % all sites	12	48	16	64	9	12	21	3	100

The table indicates that the estimated size of the population at the beginning of Iron I was only about 40% of its size at the end of the period. Early in Iron I, most of the inhabitants were concentrated in the central range (as in the Middle and Late Bronze periods), while the western slopes and the foothills were relatively sparsely populated. For the period as a whole, more than half of the people lived in the central range units. The most important development that took place during the course of the Iron I period was the population growth in the western slopes. If we compare our estimate with the known situation at the beginning of this century, we find that the relative contribution of the central range and western slopes to the total population is similar (but in recent times, population density was greater in the more southerly units).

The gradual expansion into the western parts of the Ephraim hill country, which was probably caused by population growth, had far-reaching implications for the social and political organization of the inhabitants. First, it was much easier to overcome the ecological difficulties of the slopes and the foothills in larger groups; secondly, as seen above, the western units of the region (and also other parts of the central hill country) are suitable mainly for horticulture, which probably forced the inhabitants to engage in barter with the neighbouring areas — oil and wine for grain and dairy products (Finkelstein, forthcoming c).

Another interesting and measurable parameter is the relationship between the Israelite Settlement sites and sources of water, a topic which in the past preoccupied scholars. It had long been known that early Israelite sites were not necessarily adjacent to permanent water sources; it was even hypothesized that the "invention" of plastered cisterns was responsible for the increasing number of settlements in the hill country (Albright 1971:113; Aharoni 1971b:58; Callaway 1984; 1985:40). However, as field work progressed, it became clear that already in the Bronze Age, sites had been established in locales with no immediately propinquous springs (Gophna and Porath 1971b:197).

We have now amassed considerable data on this subject. Figure 57 illustrates the distances between Israelite Settlement sites and reliable sources of water (the sites are not shown in the order of the list of sites surveyed). The same data are quantified on the following table (and compared to the situation during the Middle Bronze period:

		DISTANCE FROM PERMANENT WATER SOURCE (METERS)				
		0–500	501–1,000	1,001–3000	OVER 3,000	
MIDDLE BRONZE	# of sites	19	16	22	3	60
	% all sites	32	27	36	5	
		59		41		
TOTAL IRON I	# of sites	29	36	41	9	115
	% all sites	25	31	36	8	
		56		44		
EARLY IRON I	# of sites	15	22	21	4	62
	% all sites	24	36	34	6	
		60		40		
LATE IRON I	# of sites	12	12	15	3	42
	% all sites	29	29	36	7	
	%	58		42		

It is graphically apparent that the Iron I sites were not necessarily close to permanent water sources. This conclusion is equally valid for the beginning of Israelite Settlement. In the course of time from the Middle Bronze period to the end of Iron I, there was almost no change in the *average* distance between sites and water sources. This phenomenon was obviously connected first and foremost with the increase in activity in the northern slopes and the foothills. Zertal (1985a; 1986b:305–313) noted a similar trend in the settlement sites in the hill country of Manasseh. He associated the distancing of sites from

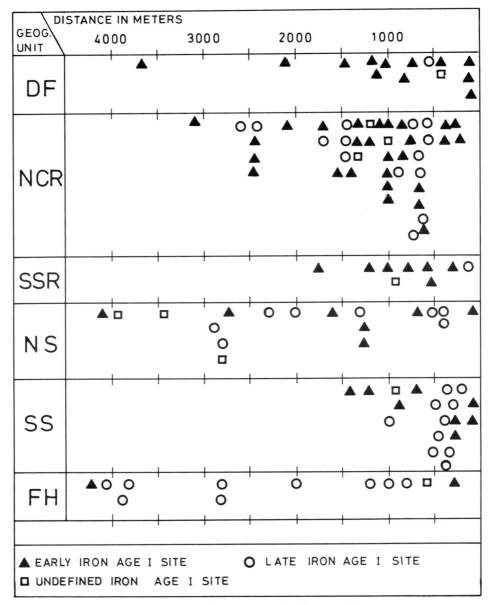

57. Relation between Iron I sites in the Territory of Ephraim and permanent water sources.

permanent water sources with the use of collared-rim store jars rather than with the digging of cisterns.

As settlement progressed westward in the direction of the slopes (especially the northern slopes) and foothills in the later stages of Iron I, the inhabitants had to deal with harder rock formations with more distant aquiferous layers.

The settlements themselves were generally founded on the more hospitable rock formations (Kfar Shaul, Moẓa, Beit Meir and Soreq) or on hard formations (e.g., Amminadav) in their immediate vicinity, for they created a relatively moderate landscape and provided reliable water sources or enabled cistern digging. (In this context, it is noteworthy that the sites of Taiyiba and Rammun were founded on the only two hills in the area that consist of Menuḥa chalk.) The creation of continuous agricultural areas was particularly difficult in the western topographical units.

We will now summarize the development of settlement in each of the six topographical units in our region:

Desert Fringe

Iron I settlement was relatively extensive, even at the beginning of the period. The majority of the sites were small and their population limited (which was also true at the beginning of the present century). They adjoined stable water sources. Settlement in Iron II was not as extensive as in Iron I.

Northern Central Range

While activity was relatively intensive during the Middle Bronze period, very few sites continued to exist in the Late Bronze period. This was the most densely settled unit during Iron I, with most of the sites founded at the beginning of the period. The number of sites increased by about 50% in Iron II; at that time, too, this unit was the most densely populated in Ephraim. Even in Iron I, there were already a number of large villages. The population — both at the beginning and at the end of the period —was the largest in the territory of Ephraim. The sites were close to water sources. Activity was focused in the vicinity of the small interior valleys: 8 sites around the valley of Shiloh, 1 in the small valley south of Shiloh, 5 around the Lubban esh-Sharqiyyeh — es-Sawiyyeh Valley (and a small valley to the south), 6–7 near the small valleys next to Quṣra and Jurish, 3 in the Qabalan Valley, 5–6 in Sahl Mahneh and 4 in the Beit Dajan Valley (totaling some 75% of all the sites in the unit).

Southern Central Range

During the Middle Bronze period, there was considerable settlement activity in the vicinity of Bethel; this important city also existed during the Late Bronze period. In Iron I, as well, most of the sites of this unit were concentrated in the area of Bethel. Almost every site was founded at the beginning of the period, and half of them rapidly became relatively large villages. Most of the sites were located near permanent water sources. Several of the settlements were abandoned at the end of Iron I, and in Iron II, there was no increase in the number of sites.

Northern Slopes

Of the western units of Ephraim, this is the most hospitable. The first attempts at settlement took place in during the Middle Bronze period, albeit at rather small sites. There were many settlements here in Iron I, and some of them (mainly on the east) were founded at the beginning of the period. The numbers of large villages, small villages and sites with a few houses were fairly well balanced. While the population at the beginning of Iron I was small, in the course of time it increased more here than in any other unit of Ephraim. The number of sites doubled in Iron II. In most of the unit, the inhabitants had to solve the problems of difficult rock formations and distance from stable water supplies.

Southern Slopes

Topographically, this is the most inhospitable unit in the entire region. As a result, activity in earlier periods was extremely minimal. In relation to its relatively large area, the number of Iron I settlements was low. Most were apparently founded at a late phase of the period. It was in Iron II that a major change took place here, with a twofold increase in the number of sites. Only later, however, did this unit really flourish. Most of the Iron I settlements were small, as was the population. While there were many sources of water in the unit, the difficult terrain was the decisive factor preventing greater development during the early periods.

Foothills

There are no permanent water sources, and the rock formations in most of the unit make settlement difficult. Activity prior to the Iron Age was thus extremely limited. Nor was the number of sites in Iron I large, and most were concentrated in a relatively small area (see below). The majority of the sites were founded toward the end of the period; most consisted of only a few houses each, with a concomittantly sparse population. The number of sites doubled in Iron II.

An examination of the archaeological data against the ecological and economic background of the region indicates that Israelite Settlement was initially concentrated in the units where subsistence was based on field crops and, in part, on animal husbandry. These were also the units most conducive to settlement in terms of topography: the desert fringe, the northern central range and the Bethel plateau. Throughout Iron I, from the beginning of the period, most sites were located in the vicinity of the small intermontane valleys, in the Bethel area and in the eastern part of the region.

Then, as today, the economy of the settlements in the desert fringe and in the eastern central range was based on a combination of pastoralism and cereal growing. These sites comprised 57% of the *early* Iron I sites in the desert fringe and the central range, and about 50% of all the Iron I sites in these units. The economy of the remaining sites in the central range — around the intermontane valleys and in the vicinity of Bethel — was apparently based on cereals. Interestingly enough, 2 of the 7 sites in the northern slopes, which were already inhabited early in Iron I, are located in the vicinity of two Arab villages (Zeita and Jamma'in) where field crops clearly dominate horticulture (in a 60:40 ratio) and where pasturage is available (near Wadi Qanah). The sites around 'Izbet Ṣarṭah are also situated in a region devoted to cereal-growing and pasturage (Rosen 1986).

Later in Iron I, settlement activity increased in the western slopes and spilled over into the foothills as well. In the northern slopes and in the foothills, cereal-growing was also considerable, and in the foothills, animal husbandry could be practiced. In the foothills, there was a concentration of sites in the area of Deir Balluṭ and Rantis (8 out of 12 sites, 67%). This, indeed, is cereal-growing country. At the beginning of this century, the ratio of field crops to horticulture in these two Arab villages was 86:14, as opposed to 59:41 for all the other villages of the foothills! The amount of nonarable land per person in these villages averaged 16.2 dunams in the 1930s, while the figure for all the other villages of the foothills dropped to 8.4 dunams per person. This land was primarily used for pasturage.

Settlement spread into the southern slopes — the classic region of horticulture — only later in Iron I and especially in Iron II. In the desert fringe and in the central range, the number of settlements grew by 41% in Iron II, while in the three western topographical units, there was a 100% increase.

These statistics hint at the socio-economic background of the people inhabiting the hill country during Iron I. The decision to settle in areas suitable for horticulture (during the pre-Islamic periods, there were undoubtedly vineyards as well) presupposes a sedentary populace that was prepared to wait many years before harvesting the fruit of its labors (e.g., Boardman 1977:189). On the other hand, a subsistence base of cereals and pastoralism did not require year-round occupation at permanent sites. The settlement pattern of Iron I, especially at the beginning of the period, thus suggests that the inhabitants came from a pastoral — rather than urban or village — background. This conclusion naturally has major repercussions for the debate over the origin of the Israelite population, and we will return to this matter in Chapters 8 and 11.

Admittedly, another explanation for this pattern of settlement is also possible. If the area was almost devoid of sites in the Late Bronze period, the settling groups would choose the eastern flanks of the region, the intermontane valleys and the Bethel plateau, simply because they are the most convenient areas for occupation. Most of these areas also enable their inhabitants to develop a well-balanced, self-sufficient economy. Their vegetation cover was not as dense as in the western units in the Iron I period.

However, the following data bring us to favor the first theory. 1. Since there is evidence for the activity of large groups of pastoralists in the hill-country in the Late Bronze period (Chapter 11), we may assume that the copice of the western units was not too dense; 2. early Iron I sites are found also in cereal-growing—pastoral units where there had been Late Bronze population (e.g. near Aphek at the west); 3. as shown above, even in the later stages of the process, when the better parts of the region were already densely occupied and new sites were established in the western units, areas with similar economic potential were preferred (e.g. in the vicinity of Rantis).

There is, of course, another aspect to Israelite Settlement in the hill country: confrontation with the natural forests. It is generally assumed that there was a total cover of vegetation in the the central range, the slopes and the foothills before the beginning of intensive settlement (Zohari 1959:338; Waisel et al. 1982:26; contra Callaway 1984). The results of the survey show that when the central range and the northern slopes were inhabited in the Middle Bronze period, these areas experienced extensive deforestation. During the following centuries of the Late Bronze period, arboreal vegetation partially renewed itself on the slopes, in areas not used intensively by pastoral groups. In any case, areas in the vicinity of the isolated settlements that continued to exist in the hill country — in the Bethel plateau and in the intermontane valleys of the northern central range — remained bare.

It follows that the earliest Israelite settlers — who inhabited the desert fringe, the eastern central range, the Bethel plateau and the intermontane valleys — were not faced with densely wooded areas; the remaining forests were located farther to the west, on the slopes and in the foothills. The final clearance of the western sector began at a later stage of the Iron I period and continued during Iron II. The survey results hint that the process of deforestation in the southern slopes lasted until the Roman period. (In any case, the large number of Arab villages in the area reflects the situation after the completion of this process.)

Against the background of these findings from the survey, we can now understand the complaints of the house of Joseph to Joshua about their narrow inheritance; in response, they were sent to clear the forest (Joshua 17:14–18). This episode reflects the situation not at the beginning of Israelite Settlement, as generally thought, but at a later phase, when the central range was thickly inhabited and the tribe of Ephraim began to penetrate into the partially forested areas of the western slopes, the second portion of its inheritance. The picture of settlement, albeit an incomplete one, arising from surveys in Manasseh, Benjamin, and Judah is one of a similar process (Chapter 3): Israelite Settlement began in the desert fringe and central range, and only later spread to the western slopes.

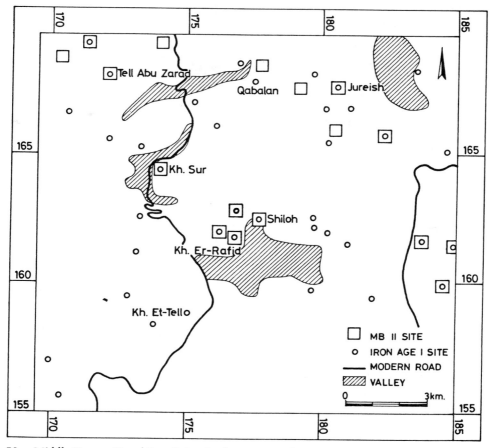

58. Middle Bronze II and Iron I sites in the vicinity of Shiloh.

The distribution map of Iron I sites highlights additional aspects that are important for appreciating the process of Israelite Settlement:

First, there is the matter of the relationship between the Iron I sites and the ancient routes in Ephraim. It can be assumed that the main roads then followed the same traditional courses that were used in the Roman period and that are still used today, for the topographical conditions that so obviously dictate the present thoroughfares have not changed. Less than half of the sites appear to have been adjacent to the main roads, while the others (e.g., in the southern slopes, around Salfit, and northeast and east of Shiloh) are quite far from these routes. In other words, in Iron I there was no particular tendency to locate sites along the principal arteries.

The map of Israelite Settlement sites indicates considerable site density in the vicinity of Shiloh (Fig. 58). In a radius of 5–6 km around Shiloh, 26 sites (over 20% of the sites surveyed) have been found. No other area of our survey

201

grid produced such a concentration. For example, within the same radius around Bethel (including the area in Benjamin to the south), only 12 Iron I sites are known. Since the site density emphasizes the demographic aspect of the centrality of Shiloh during the period, it comes as no surprise that excavations have recently shed light on Shiloh's economic importance in Iron I (see below). Interestingly enough, 40% of the sites around Shiloh seem to have been founded only at a later stage of the period. This accords well with the excavated finds, which indicate that Shiloh became an important center only in the latter half, or at the end, of the 12th century BCE.

The concentration of sites around Bethel also warrants our attention. This phenomenon may be explained by the ecological and economic advantages inherent in this area and also by the importance of Bethel itself, in whose vicinity daughter settlements developed. The centrality of Bethel during the Iron I period is hinted at in the Bible (Judges 20:18, 26; 1 Samuel 10:3), and Noth (1958:94–95) suggested that it was the next sacred center of the tribal amphictyony after Shechem. In any case, another possibility should be considered, even if it is difficult to demonstrate, namely, that for economic resons, settlement began in the periphery of Bethel while the Canaanite city was still extant (Chapter 11). The date assigned to the destruction of Canaanite Bethel, 1240–1235 BCE, was derived from irrelevant considerations (Chapter 9) and can easily be lowered. A similar and contemporary process of settlement may have been underway in the vicinity of Aphek (Finkelstein 1986:205–208); we will return to this matter later on.

In recent years, a new approach has developed, claiming that the spread of settlement in the hill country in Iron I was connected with the learned skill of terraces building (e.g., de Geus 1975; see also Gottwald 1979:658–659; Thompson 1979:66; Ahlström 1982; Stager 1982:116 n. 20; Callaway 1985:33. Stager 1985b:5–11 summarizes the importance of terraces and other technologies, e.g., cisterns and the use of iron tools, for overcoming the ecological obstacles of the hill country in Iron I. But see Hopkins 1985, who reduces the importance of the role these technologies played in the process of settlememt of the hill country in Iron I). The results of our survey, however, completely invalidate this view. In the western slopes, at least, settlement was obviously impossible without constructing terraces. So it follows that terraces must have been built already during the Middle Bronze period, if not earlier. Furthermore, Israelite Settlement initially took place in those sectors where cultivation was possible without building terraces, and at that time, there was, in fact, relatively little activity in the typical region of terraces.

The important points and significance of the survey can be briefly summarized by the following observations: Israelite Settlement in the territory of Ephraim took place in those regions most conducive to field crops and pasturage. This would suggest that most of the settlers came from a pastoral background. In the early phase of Iron I, the new settlements were concentrated mainly in the desert fringe, the Bethel plateau, the intermontane valleys of the northern central range and the western edge of the foothills (ʿIzbet Ṣarṭah and its surroundings, near Aphek). Because parts of the hill country were thickly forested, the new settlers went to the desert fringe or to those areas of the hill country that had already been cleared of trees by certain activities in the Late Bronze period.

It is difficult to determine whether Israelite Settlement began while the Canaanite cities of the region were still extant or whether it followed their destruction and abandonment. The fact that the earliest Iron I sites — even those close to the Canaanite cities — were not situated in their immediate vicinity, but rather at some distance, perhaps hints at the former possibility. In any case, if there was a period of coexistence (after settling down) with the Canaanite cities, it was short lived, since it left no clear imprint on the material culture of the Israelite Settlement sites. Furthermore, the Israelites established settlements at the former Canaanite sites from the beginning of Iron I.

During the second phase of Iron I, the most hospitable areas of Ephraim became relatively crowded, so settlements were established in areas that had previously been practically vacant — the western slopes and the eastern foothills. But even then, the focus of activity was in the central range, where most of the large sites were located; most of the contemporary sites in the western slopes and foothills were very small. Settlement in these western sectors intensified in Iron II, during the Monarchy, when olive oil production flourished in this region, which was ideal for horticulture (Eitam 1980a). In moving to the western slopes and foothills, the settlers had to overcome the obstacles of relatively dense forestation, distant permanent water supplies, and inhospitable and rocky terrain. Iron, which came into wider use during the course of the Iron I period (Waldbaum 1978:24–27; T. Dothan 1982:92), might have made these tasks easier (but see Stager 1985b:11 for a different explanation of how pyrotechnology helped bring about deforestation).

How better to close this chapter than with the words Albright wrote nearly 60 years ago, following an excursion through the western part of Ephraim. With his rare intuitive grasp of the character of the area, and without any basic field work, Albright pointed to a few of the dominant trends in the history of settlement in the region:

> One of the most important questions in Hebrew history is that of the occupation of Mount Ephraim by the Chosen People. This question cannot be separated from the parallel one: to what extent was Mount Ephraim occupied by a sedentary population in the Bronze Age?.... From the surface explorations it appears that there are very few Bronze Age mounds in Ephraim .... western Ephraim appears to be more destitute of

mounds than any other part of Palestine .... Owing to its exceedingly rugged character, and the abundance of rainfall on the western slope of the watershed ridge of Ephraim in normal years, it is quite certain that this region was heavily forested in antiquity. It was, therefore, down to the removal of the forests by the Israelites, not suited to become the abode of a sedentary population, but must have been occupied mainly by semi-nomadic shepherds.... (1929:3–4).

Albright's words have now been backed by archaeological investigations. Surveys and excavations at the central sites of the region have clarified the process of settlement in the territory of Ephraim — a region of critical importance in the heart of the Land of Israel — from the Middle Bronze through Iron II periods, and especially at the time of Israelite Settlement and the Judges.

CHAPTER 5

THE SHILOH EXCAVATIONS: PRELIMINARY REPORT

One of the most important sites in the central mountain ridge of the Land of Israel, Shiloh was the sacred religious center of the Israelite population in the central hill country during the first half of the 11th century BCE.

Neither the patriarchal narratives in the Bible (except for Jacob's blessing, Genesis 49:10) nor Egyptian literature of the New Kingdom include references to Shiloh. The site was mentioned many times, however, in the biblical accounts of the period of Israelite Settlement and the Judges (on the history of Shiloh during the biblical period, see Buhl and Holm-Nielsen 1969:58–60 and Ahituv 1976). It was at Shiloh that the tribal lands were apportioned (Joshua 18:10) and the Levitical cities appointed (Joshua 21:2). The people of Israel gathered here in times of trouble (Joshua 22:12). During annual religious festivities at the site, the young girls of Shiloh danced in the vineyards (Judges 21:19–21).

The importance of Shiloh both as a religious center and as the seat of leadership of the Israelite tribes reached its zenith during the first half of the 11th century BCE, at the end of the period of the Judges. Eli the priest and the prophet Samuel as a boy were active at this site, to which supplicants came bringing offerings (1 Samuel 1:3,24). Shiloh figured prominently in the dramatic events surrounding the battle of Ebenezer, an episode which culminated in the devastation of the site (1 Samuel 4). After defeating Israel in this campaign, which took place in the western approaches to the hill country, not far from the coastal plain, the Philistines apparently took advantage of their victory to press on up into the hill country and burn Shiloh to the ground. While the Bible does not explicitly describe the fiery end of Shiloh, the event was alluded to in a number of passages in the Books of Jeremiah (7:12,14; 26:6,9) and Psalms (78:60) and was also reflected in the excavations.

Once Shiloh was destroyed, the Israelite center moved south, first to the plateau of Benjamin and subsequently to Jerusalem (see Chapter 11). Shiloh itself remained deserted for a while, but by the reign of Jeroboam I, it was again inhabited (1 Kings 14:2,4). The site was still occupied at the time of the destruction of the First Temple (Jeremiah 41:5).

Shiloh was mentioned several times in rabbinic literature, in church texts, and in pilgrims' accounts of the Byzantine period (Thomsen 1907:105; Avi-Yonah 1976:96). Never again, however, did Shiloh attain the importance it enjoyed during the time of the Judges. The remains at the site indicate that it was occupied almost continuously until the later Middle Ages, and the location was still known in the 14th century CE, when the Jewish traveler, Eshtori ha-Parchi, found it in ruins (Luncz 1897:19 5–196). He and other Medieval visitors to the site would point out the tombs of Eli and his sons and a location known as the "dome of the *shkhina*."

LOCATION AND IDENTIFICATION

The identification of Khirbet Seilūn as ancient Shiloh was made without difficulty by Robinson in 1838 (Robinson 1891:84–89). As we noted, the site was still known during the Middle Ages. Moreover, historical sources indicated the location of Shiloh in relative detail.

An exceptionally detailed description was provided at the end of the Book of Judges: "...Shiloh, which is north of Bethel, on the east of the highway that goes up from Bethel to Shechem, and south of Lebonah" (Judges 21:19). Bethel was identified with the village of Beitin northwest of Ramallah; Lebonah was in the vicinity of the village of Lubban esh-Sharqiyyeh, just west-northwest of Shiloh; and the "highway," the ancient route, probably approximated the course of the modern Jerusalem-Nablus road (Fig. 59). Also helpful is the *Onomasticon* of Eusebius (4th century CE), which placed Shiloh "12 miles from Neapolis (= Shechem) at Acrabitene" (On. 156,28), i.e., in the district known by the town whose name is preserved in that of the Arab village of ᶜAqrabeh, northeast of Shiloh. As if all these literary references were not sufficient, the ancient name was preserved in the name of the village that stood here as recently as the 16th century CE (Hütteroth and Abdulfattah 1977:133) and of the adjacent spring — Seilūn. Finally, the excavated remains accord with the history of Shiloh as reflected in the written sources.

The mound of Shiloh is located in the heart of the territory of Ephraim, at the northern end of a fertile valley surrounded by hills, in the center of which stands the village of Turmus ᶜAiya (Figs. 58, 60). A large spring, 900 m northeast of the tell, supplemented the runoff rainwater collected in the cisterns within the settlement. The area of the tell (including its slopes) is about 30 dunams. The steep slopes surrounding the site on the north, east, and west made these sides easy to defend. Only on the south could the site be conveniently approached, and the main entrance was apparently located here in every period. Three factors were thus responsible for the choice of location: proximity to the fertile valley; availablilty of a dependable water supply; and defensiblity of the mound.

Remains of the Roman, Byzantine, and Medieval periods are prominent on the summit of the mound (714 m above sea level) and on the southern slope.

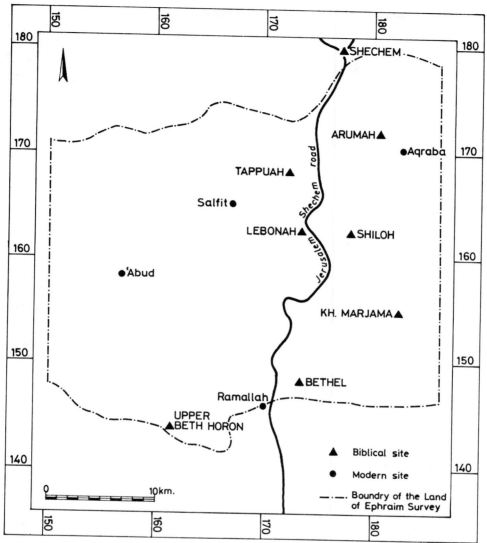

59. Location of Shiloh.

Other late buildings, including two Byzantine churches and two Moslem structures, were found in the area to the south of the tell.

THE DANISH EXCAVATIONS

Schmidt conducted the first archaeological soundings at Shiloh in 1922 (Albright 1923:10–11). This was followed by three seasons of excavations in

207

60. Tel Shiloh looking west: on the left — the mound; on the right — the natural terrace north of the mound.

1926–1932 by a Danish expedition under the direction of H. Kjaer, who published several preliminary reports on the results (1927; 1930; 1931). Due to his sudden death in 1932, the final publication was delayed by many years. In 1963, Holm-Nielsen undertook additional work at Shiloh and in 1969, together with Buhl, he published a final report on the pre-Hellenistic remains from all the excavation campaigns (Buhl and Holm-Nielsen 1969). This slim volume lacks many details, in part due to purely objective reasons. But there are also a number of basic errors, such as the dating of the collared-rim store jars from the site to Iron II (Shiloh 1971; 1973). In short, even after the appearance of the excavation report, little was known about the history of the site.

The Danish expedition worked in five sectors of the tell (Fig. 61). In 1926, rock-hewn caves and fragments of later buildings were exposed in the south. A trial trench on the summit in 1963 produced no earlier remains. In the northwestern sector, excavated in 1932, a fortification wall was uncovered and dated to the Middle Bronze period. Just inside this wall, there was a room containing a group of MB IIC storage jars. Unfortunately, these jars were lost when the excavation was hastily terminated following Kjaer's death; only a group photograph remained (Buhl and Holm-Nielsen 1969:40). In the northern sector, which was excavated in 1932 and again in 1963, another segment of the fortification wall was uncovered.

Only on the western side of the mound did the Danish expedition discover any remains of the Iron I period. This area was excavated in 1929, on the advice of Albright, who acted as archaeological advisor. His attention was drawn to this part of the tell by an impressive solid wall exposed on the surface; however, it turned out to be late in date, since Roman and Byzantine remains were found inside it. But when a trench was dug into a lower terrace outside this wall, two rooms were discovered (Buhl and Holm-Nielsen 1969:Pl. E). In the northern room, six of the seven famous collared-rim store jars from Shiloh

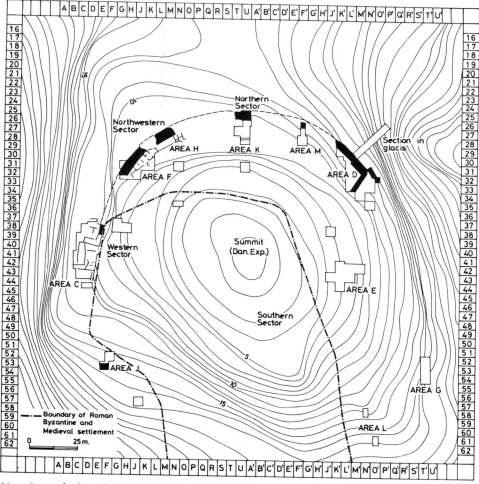

61. General Plan of Shiloh showing Danish and recent excavation areas.

62. Shiloh, the Danish expedition in the western sector 1929 — collared rim store jars in a destruction layer (Buhl and Holm Nielsen 1969: 33).

were found leaning against a wall, in the destruction layer (Fig. 62) that Albright and Kjaer attributed to the Philistines after their victory over Israel at Ebenezer (Albright 1929:4; Kjaer 1930:105). Only a limited area was exposed here. The excavations were not conducted in a systematic manner and penetrated down to the previous level. Nor was the architecture properly interpreted. The area was then abandoned, apparently because it defied the excavator's comprehension (Kjaer 1930:104).

The Danish excavations frankly added little to our knowledge of the site. The character of the Middle Bronze occupation was never sufficiently clarified, and the attribution of the fortification wall to this period was uncertain. The question of whether there was a genuine Late Bronze level at the site remained unresolved. With the exception of the discovery of the collared-rim store jars and the destruction level assigned to the mid-11th century BCE, virtually nothing was learned about Israelite Settlement at Shiloh in specific or in the hill country generally. Not even the slightest architectural hint of the Iron I center at Shiloh was found. Finally, the character of the renewed Iron II settlement remained unclear.

THE NEW EXCAVATIONS

During the years 1981–1984, an expedition sponsored by the Department of Land of Israel Studies at Bar-Ilan University fielded four seasons of excavations at Shiloh. The primary goal of this expedition was, naturally, to tackle the questions concerning Shiloh during the period of Israelite Settlement and the Judges: What was the character of the site in Iron I? What was Shiloh's role in the overall phenomenon of Israelite Settlement in the hill country? In the process, we hoped to investigate the entire history of the site, starting in the Middle Bronze period, in order to try to understand the circumstances that led to its transformation into an Israelite religious center.

Even before we began to excavate Shiloh, we were aware of two problems typical of hilltop sites. The summit had been badly eroded and bedrock was exposed in many places. Moreover, since the masons of every period attempted to lay the foundations of their buildings directly on bedrock, the activities of later periods — notably Roman, Byzantine, and Medieval — severely disturbed or even razed the earlier strata on the southern slope of the tell and on the summit. Of necessity, then, our efforts were concentrated on the edges of the tell and on the northern part, areas that had been spared the ravages of erosion and the damage of later construction.

63. Shiloh — an aerial view looking south; the letters mark excavation areas.

Altogether, we opened nine fields of excavation (Figs. 61, 63), the three principal ones being Area C on the western slope (where the Danish expedition had uncovered the famous collared-rim store jars in 1929), Area D on the northeastern side of the tell (where our goal was to expose more of the fortification wall and the accumulation along its inner face), and Areas F-H on the northwestern side of the tell (H was the continuation of the 1932 Danish sector). Six other areas were excavated in a relatively limited manner: Area E on the large terrace east of the summit; Areas G and L on the southeastern slope; Area J on the southwest slope; Area K at the northern end of the tell, adjacent to the Danish sector; and Area M, a short distance east of K. Because the areas we excavated were spread across the tell, we were able to obtain a reliable picture of its occupational history and of the layout of the various settlements that once existed there.

Before examining the Iron I finds, we will briefly describe the Middle and Late Bronze remains, which are of great importance for understanding the history of Shiloh (for full details, see Finkelstein 1985).

MIDDLE BRONZE PERIOD

Based on her impression of a few isolated sherds, Buhl fixed the beginning of occupation at Shiloh in the Early Bronze period (Buhl and Holm-Nielsen 1969:60). However, our excavations have not unearthed a single fragment of that era. It is even possible that Medieval sherds were mistakenly attributed to the Early Bronze period. The Early Bronze occupation of the fertile valley was at Khirbet er-Rafid, some 900 m southwest of the tell (Chapter 4, Site NCR 35).

The mound of Shiloh was first inhabited in the MB IIB period, and the settlement was apparently unwalled. The evidence for this period was strictly ceramic. MB IIB pottery was found in the large section cut in Area D within the glacis constructed in MB IIC and in earthen fills laid in MB IIC, including the make- up between the MB IIC floors and bedrock, inside the fortification wall at the northernwestern end of the tell. The builders of the MB IIC fortifications seem to have used the debris of the previous settlement for filling material.

In MB IIC, the site was bounded by massive defense works, which included a solid wall and a large earthen glacis. The Danish expedition had exposed two segments of the wall, in the northwest (= our Area H) and north (= our Area K). Our team excavated large sections of the fortifications in Areas D (30 m) and F (15 m). We also examined it in Areas C, J, and M and returned to Area H to check a few stratigraphic and architectural points. This field work, combined with an examination of aerial photographs, enabled us to reconstruct the course of this fortification wall around the entire perimeter of the site (Fig. 61), an area of about 17 dunams.

The fortification wall was founded directly on bedrock. It was constructed of large field stones, whose outer faces were occasionally slightly planed; the core was filled with stones of large and medium size. An enormous number of stones from this wall were utilized elsewhere on the site in all subsequent periods, making it a kind of "quarry" of stones for secondary use. Evidence of stone-robbing was found everywhere we dug. We also discovered that Rooms L and M, which the Danes had found in the fortification wall in Area H, had, in fact, been constructed later within such a robbers' trench.

The thickness of the Middle Bronze fortification wall varied from 3.0–5.5 m (Fig. 68). The upper part, which has not survived, was probably built of mudbricks. The preservation of parts of the fortification wall was most impressive: It was still standing about 8 m. high in the section cut against its outer face in Area D and 2.5 m high in Areas C and F.

The shape of the wall was no more uniform than its thickness. The Danes had uncovered a solid rectangular tower in the northern sector, which projected both inward and outward from the fortification wall. In Area D, the wall had been constructed in a "sawtooth" fashion, with a projection every few meters, a masonry technique that easily accommodated the topography of the mound. Elsewhere in Area D, we found a kind of large offset projecting outward toward the slope. The explanation for the variations in thickness and form must be sought in the various techniques employed in its construction and not in chronological phases during the time the wall was in use. Also in Area D, a massive wall, over 3 m thick, ran from the fortification wall toward the interior of the tell, in a southwesterly direction. It may be the remnant of an inner line of fortifications that demarcated the northern part of the tell.

We examined the glacis at a number of places around the periphery and learned that a variety of construction methods had been employed. In the large section cut down to bedrock (manually and mechanically) in Area D, on the eastern, steepest side of the tell, the glacis was especially impressive, both because of its strength and because of its colorful layers (Fig. 64). The base of the glacis extended about 25 m from the fortification wall to the edge of the slope. The height of the glacis next to the wall was 6.3 m and its angle of declination was 20–25°.

Buried within the glacis, at a distance of some 2 m from the fortification wall, there was a second wall, 90 cm thick and 3.2 m high. Two masses of large rough stones had been laid at the foundations of the outer edge of the glacis. These features served to stabilize the glacis and prevent it from sliding down the slope.

In Area D, the glacis consisted of four principal layers (from top down): hard reddish-brown earth; crumbly white material mixed with small stones (this layer was the main component of the glacis); brown, reddish, and light-

64. Shiloh — a section through the Middle Bronze IIC glacis in Area D.

colored earthen debris with tip-lines gently sloping *against* the direction of the slope; and yellowish-gray material found primarily next to the fortification wall and its nearby retaining wall. White "fingers" of the second layer, projected into the reddish-brown material above it. Before construction began, the bedrock was cleared of accumulated debris in order to strengthen the structure of the glacis. Hardly a sherd was present in the upper three layers of

65. Shiloh, Area F — the Middle Bronze IIC fortification wall (left) and the adjacent row of rooms.

the glacis, but in the bottom layer, a large amount of MB IIB pottery was found. In the white layer, we discovered a "Hyksos" scarab with a geometric design.

Elsewhere on the tell, the glacis was thinner and less complex. In Area C, for example, it consisted of a single, relatively skimpy white layer set directly onto bedrock.

A row of Middle Bronze rooms was constructed against the inside of the fortification wall in a belt about 115 m long, extending across the northern sector of the tell, from Area F on the west to Area M on the east. These rooms were first encountered by the Danish expedition in 1932 in their northwestern (= our Area H) and northern (= our Area K) areas (Buhl and Holm-Nielsen 1969:Pl. G). We continued to expose them on a large scale in Area F (Fig. 65) and in a limited sounding in Area M. The rooms were bounded on one side by the fortification wall and on the other by a wall that was visible only on the inside of the rooms, for on the other side of it, in the direction of the summit of the tell, a fill of dirt and stones had been dumped. In other words, these rooms were some kind of basement, a fact that explains their impressive preservation. In Area F, for example, where five rooms were uncovered, the walls (and fortification wall) stood at a height of 2.5 m above floor level. The floors themselves were composed of beaten earth; in a few places, traces of plaster were found. Between the floors and the bedrock there was a filling of light-colored earth, which was about a meter thick in Area F. Pottery of MB IIB, the period preceding the construction of the fortifications, was found in this fill.

These rooms apparently served as storerooms. While they contained a plethora of vessels suitable for storage, almost no daily domestic vessels, such as cooking pots, were present. In Area F, each room contained 12–13 pithoi as well as smaller jars and other vessels, completely filling the limited space of about 5–6 m² per room. The Danes had also uncovered one of these rooms full of pithoi (in our Area H), the vessels that vanished *en route* to Jerusalem when the excavation closed, leaving only their photographic image behind for posterity (Fig. 96).

In a corner of one room, we discovered a most interesting group of silver and bronze objects, some of which are the only examples of their kind ever found in Israel (Finkelstein and Brandl 1985). The bronzes included two large flat axes and a large shaft-hole axe of a type known principally in Anatolia and Northern Syria. The silver jewelry featured a large hammered pendant, 12 cm in diameter, displaying the "Cappadocian symbol" of a Hittite deity. The storerooms also yielded cultic stands, small votive bowls and a zoomorphic vessel in the form of a bull. All these finds suggest that the storerooms in Area F — and perhaps the entire row of rooms adjoining the fortification wall at the northern end of the site — were connected to a nearby sanctuary. Additional evidence for the existence of a sanctuary at Shiloh in the Middle Bronze period comes from the finds of the Late Bronze period, which will be described below.

Except for these rooms, no buildings of the Middle Bronze period were found at Shiloh. In Area D, a stone fill was laid in the space between the sloping bedrock and the inner face of the fortification wall. In the southern part of Area F, the space just inside the wall was filled with white earth. On the extramural side of the wall delimiting the inner side of the belt of rooms,

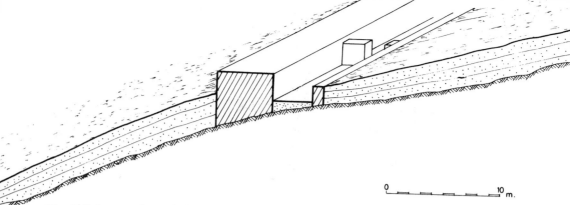

66. Shiloh — a schematic isometric section showing the various Middle Bronze elements on the northern edge of the site.

earthen fills were laid slanting upward in the direction of the summit. The following elements thus generally appeared in a section cut through the northern part of the tell (from outside to inside): an earthen glacis; a solid fortification wall composed of huge boulders; storerooms with floors laid on a fill of earth that descended to bedrock; the wall delimiting the inner side of these rooms; and earthen fills sloping up toward the summit of the mound (Fig. 66). Unfortunately, we cannot continue this description any farther inward, because intensive building activity on the upper part of the tell, from the Roman period on, resulted in the removal of all earlier remains down to bedrock.

Shiloh was destroyed at the end of the Middle Bronze period. Traces of burning were found in the row of rooms along the fortification wall, and mudbricks from the collapsing upper parts of the walls buried these chambers before the fleeing inhabitants could remove their contents. The date of the destruction was determined by the ceramic assemblage recovered from the storerooms in Areas F-H. Two sherds of "chocolate-on-white" ware found there were of particular importance, for this type did not antedate the 16th century BCE.

The Middle Bronze remains unearthed at Shiloh are of great interest for a number of reasons, a few of which we will mention briefly (for a full discussion, see Finkelstein 1985). First, there are signs that a shrine or sanctuary, perhaps situated on the summit of the tell, already existed here at this early date. If so, Shiloh would join the list of sacred Israelite sites where a cultic tradition had existed continuously ever since the Middle Bronze period.

The total lack of houses in the Middle Bronze period is certainly surprising. It is reasonable to suspect that the residential quarter was at the southern end of the site, an area that cannot be excavated because of the later remains covering it. It is also possible, though, that Middle Bronze Shiloh was, in fact, basically a cultic *temenos* rather than an ordinary settlement. In this connection, it is important to note that activity at the site during the following period (Late Bronze) was primarily cultic in character. As for the Iron I period, biblical and archaeological evidence are in agreement that Shiloh was essentially a sacred precinct.

The monumental construction projects undertaken at Middle Bronze Shiloh — including the massive stone fortification wall, the glacis, and the earth-and-stone fills inside the site — raise another question. Even if we assume that people lived at Shiloh as at an ordinary site, it is hard to imagine how such a small population managed to execute these impressive building operations. Calculating population density in the manner generally accepted today, no more than 400 people would have lived at a site of 17 dunams. Among these 400 people, there would have been fewer than 100 men. The inescapable conclusion is that people from all over the region must have participated in these labors.

LATE BRONZE PERIOD

Soon after the destruction of Middle Bronze Shiloh, there was renewed activity at the site. The Danish expedition had discovered a few objects dating to the Late Bronze period, but none were *in situ* (e.g., Buhl and Holm-Nielsen 1969:Pl. 6:64–65; few cooking pots on Pl. 7; scarab on Pl. XXIV). They assigned only one structure to the Late Bronze period — Wall A-A in their northwestern area, which they described as a fortification wall (*ibid.*:61). Our reinvestigation has demonstrated that it was a Byzantine terrace wall. Shortly after the publication of the Danish excavation report, Aharoni proposed that the few Late Bronze finds should be attributed to the level of very early Israelite occupation, which, in his opinion, existed at the site (Aharoni 1973:46; Aharoni, Fritz and Kempinski 1975:121).

During our excavations, it became clear that there was a genuine Late Bronze stratum at Shiloh, directly beneath the Iron I level. Apart from isolated sherds found in various places on the tell, remains of the Late Bronze period were encountered only in Area D. An accumulation of earth, ashes, light-colored material and stones, up to 1.5 m thick, extended over an area of about 200 m² inside and on top of the Middle Bronze fortification wall. This debris contained a very large quantity of broken pottery and animal bones, but could not be connected with any architectural remains. Much of the pottery dated from the Late Bronze I period. The ceramic assemblage was dominated by hundreds of shallow bowls broken into unusually large pieces (but sherds from a limited exposure generally cannot be rejoined into complete vessels). Also present were juglets, lamps, chalices, fragments of Cypriote vessels, local painted wares and a very few cooking pots. Several vessels were found intact, or nearly so, and filled with ash and bones (Fig. 67). Among the small finds were a female figurine, the impression of a cylinder seal on a jar handle and a piece of gold jewelry in the shape of a fly.

67. Shiloh, Area D — a Late Bronze jug with bones and ashes.

Data from all over the tell indicate that there was no real settlement at Shiloh during the Late Bronze period. Instead, there was apparently an isolated cultic place, perhaps on the summit of the tell, to which offerings were brought by people from various locales in the region. The vessels were deliberately broken after use. Together with the faunal remains (probably the bones of sacrificed animals), they were then collected — perhaps even buried — at a designated place on the summit. In Iron I, the accumulated debris was cleared off and dumped in a pit on the slope. The offerings may have been brought to the Middle Bronze sanctuary, which might have been renovated after its destruction. The steadily declining amount of pottery attests that activity at the site decreased, then ceased entirely, apparently before the end of the Late Bronze period.

The excavated evidence accords well with the picture emerging from our survey (Chapter 4): During the Late Bronze period, there was a drastic reduction in population all over the territory of Ephraim. The number of known sites dropped from 60 to 5, and even those surviving settlements were relatively smaller in size.

All these facts raise the possibility that the cultic site at Shiloh served a non-sedentary populace, i.e., groups of pastoralists active in the vicinity. Support for this hypothesis may be garnered from the animal bones found at Shiloh. Faunal analysis indicates that the proportion of sheep/goat to cattle in both the Middle Bronze and Iron I periods were basically the same — 79.2:17.4 (percentages) in the Middle Bronze IIB, 85.7:12.8 in the Middle Bronze IIC and 76.5:23.4 in the Iron I — while in the Late Bronze period, the ratio of sheep/goat to cattle was a skewed 92.3:6.6 (Hellwing 1985). The abundance of sheep/goat and the small amount of cattle are indicative of flocks belonging to people leading a pastoral existence (Chapter 11).

IRON I PERIOD

Israelite Settlement at Shiloh began during the course of the 12th century BCE, after the site had been abandoned for some time. Iron I remains were found virtually everywhere we dug. Structures in Areas C and E and stone-lined silos and other remains elsewhere. However, since the various excavation fields were not stratigraphically linked, we cannot presently determine whether all the remains were contemporary or whether they represent more than one phase within the Iron I period.

In Area D, adjacent to the inner face of the uppermost course of the Middle Bronze fortification wall, we exposed a rough pebble floor (Fig. 68). The top of the stone portion of the fortification wall was so well preserved here that it was leveled off with small stones and converted into the continuation of the pebble floor. Collared-rim store jars lay crushed on the floor. Since no evidence of permanent structures associated with this floor was discovered, it might have served as a base for huts or tents or as a work surface. A large seal (4 cm in diameter) was found on the floor. Made of black stone, it displayed two chiastic arrangements of galloping horned animals. A similar but smaller seal stone was found in the Iron Age level at Tell el-Farᶜa near Shechem (de Vaux 1955:581).

The most impressive structures of the Iron I period were unearthed in Area C, at the western end of the mound. They indicate that knowledge of construction techniques was well developed at a relatively early stage of Israelite Settlement. In a small exposure in this area in 1929, the Danish expedition had uncovered "Houses" A and B, one of which contained the famous collared-rim store jars. Digging proceeded no further because, by the excavators' own admission, they failed to understand the character of the area.

Our team opened a field immediately to the north of the Danish excavations; we subsequently expanded to join the two areas. The Iron I buildings

68. Shiloh, Area D — Iron I floor (right) adjacent to the Middle Bronze IIc fortification wall (left).

uncovered here had been erected outside the perimeter of the well-preserved Middle Bronze fortification wall, which served as their rear wall. During construction, a portion of the Middle Bronze glacis was removed, and the side walls of the later buildings leaned against the continuation of the glacis. As a result, the Iron I buildings were actually "sunken" into the Middle Bronze glacis. (The Middle Bronze pottery picked up by the Danish expedition in "Houses" A and B must have originated in the remnants of the glacis beneath

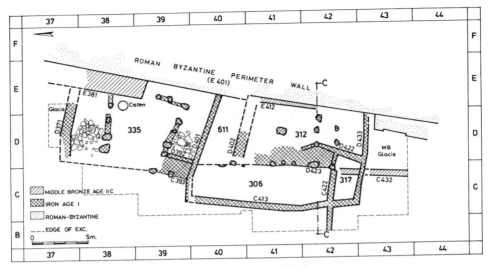

69. Shiloh, Area C — schematic plan of the Iron I buildings.

the floors.) The Middle Bronze fortification wall evidently also served as a retaining wall for additional Iron Age structures higher up on the slope.

The steep slope outside the Middle Bronze fortification wall necessitated the creation of two building levels with a terrace wall between them (Figs. 69–71). The terrace wall consisted of multilithic pillars — built of rough stone drums — alternating with a filling of small and medium field stones. The filling continued behind the terrace wall to make up a solid area with a flat surface on which stood the upper-level Iron Age structures: two pillared buildings (312 and 335) separated by a corridor. The entrance to this building complex must have been on the eastern (summit) side, with access gained by means of steps or a breach in the Middle Bronze fortification wall. Unfortunately, a massive later wall covering part of the eastern side of this complex prevented us from clarifying this problem.

In Building 335, the northernmost one on the upper level, there was a courtyard with a beaten earth floor flanked by two rooms carefully paved with stone slabs. The courtyard was separated from the side rooms by two rows of multilithic stone pillars, preserved to a height of a meter or more; a low partition wall connected the pillars within each row. Two additional pillars stood in the eastern part of the courtyard, between the above-mentioned rows of pillars. A rock-hewn plastered cistern and two installations were discovered in the courtyard. The northern wall of the building was still standing at a height of 2 m. On its western side, this building ended in a massive terrace wall, into which multilithic pillars were integrated.

Building 312 to the south had four parallel aisles separated by three rows of

70. Shiloh, Area C — isometric reconstruction of the Iron I buildings.

multilithic stone pillars. The flooring consisted of bedrock, stone slabs, and crushed white material from the Middle Bronze glacis.

A large hall (306) apparently functioned as the basement of Building 312. It had a floor of beaten earth over pebbles; in the center of the room, there was an ash pit. This basement was entered by means of a ladder or steps from the corridor or from Building 312. However, any evidence of steps was destroyed by a Byzantine kiln, which damaged the terrace wall at this point. The western wall of this hall was also the outer wall of the site on the side of the slope.

The ceramic assemblage from the Area C complex is the richest ever discovered at any early Israelite site. We have unearthed about 40 vessels that were either whole or represented by large pieces; 10 others had been recovered by the Danish expedition. Dominating the collection are collared-rim store jars, the storage pithoi that characterized Iron I sites in the hill country (see Chapter 7). The Danes found six of these store jars in 1929 in "House" A

71. Shiloh, Area C — aerial view, looking east.

72. Shiloh, Area C — collared rim jars in the southern side unit of Building 335.

(Fig. 62), i.e., in the southern part of Hall 306, and extracted another from the southeastern corner of Building 312 (Buhl and Holm-Nielsen 1969:Pls. 15,16,XXII,XXIII). We uncovered a row of seven collared-rim store jars in the southern side unit of Building 335 (Figs. 72–73); others were found in Hall 306. Altogether, more than 20 collared-rim pithoi have been found in Area C, every one of them leaning against walls and many with their bases inserted into the floor.

73. Shiloh, Area C — assemblage of vessels from the southern side unit of Building 335, after restoration.

The pottery from Area C also included smaller jars. The handles of one of them had been stamped with a scaraboid bearing a geometric design. There were also jugs and kraters, one of which had many handles. Cooking pots were discovered in the ash pit in Hall 306. Several grinding stones were found in these buildings as well. A pile of carbonized raisins was revealed on the floor of the northern side unit of Building 335 (Fig. 74).

The building complex was destroyed in a fierce conflagration. Burnt floors were found throughout. Collapsed burnt bricks accumulated on these floors to a height of over a meter. Some of the bricks had been baked by the blaze that

74. Shiloh, Area C — carbonized raisins from the northern side unit
     of Building 335.

raged here. Roof collapse was discernible in many places. Taking into
consideration the chronological evidence and the geo-political situation in the
central part of the country in the 11th century, it seems that one must follow
Albright and associate all this dramatic evidence of combustion with the
destruction of Shiloh by the Philistines in the mid-11th century BCE.

The accumulated debris on top of the brick collapse in the northern part of
Building 335 contained a large quantity of animal bones and Iron I pottery.
Two sherds bore animal figures in relief: the head of a lioness on a cooking pot
rim, and a ram's head at the base of a krater handle (Fig. 101). There were also
fragments of a cultic stand with applied images of a horse, a lioness, and a scene
of a leopard attacking a deer (Fig. 75; see also Chapter 7).

In Area E, where only a relatively limited area was excavated, we discovered
the remains of an Iron I structure and a rock-hewn installation with several
collared-rim store jars inside. Fourteen stone-lined silos of this period, averaging 1.5 m in diameter, were found in Area D. They had been dug into the Late
Bronze debris. Two of them contained a large amount of carbonized wheat. A
similar silo was encountered in the southern section in Area H; it had been cut

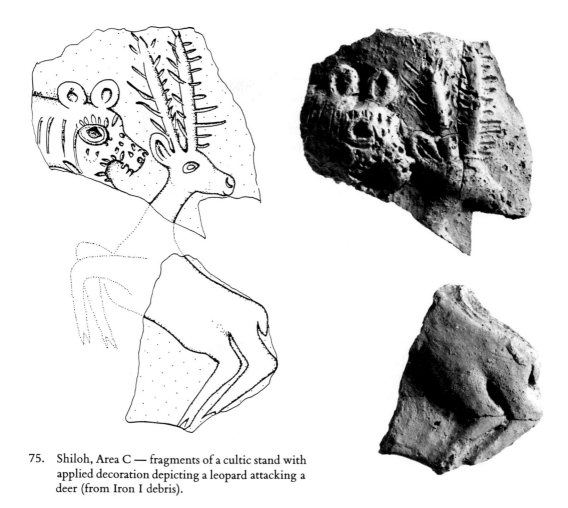

75. Shiloh, Area C — fragments of a cultic stand with
     applied decoration depicting a leopard attacking a
     deer (from Iron I debris).

into the Middle Brnze brick collapse. In Area K, we cleared three more silos
that had been dug into Middle Bronze fills.

At the southern end of the tell, in a section in the lower part of Area J, we
found thick debris with a great quantity of Iron I pottery. This accumulation,
which was about 2 m thick and slanted in the direction of the slope, seems to
be the refuse of buildings at the edge of the site that had been dumped down
the slope. As such, it described the southern limit of the Iron I settlement.
Among the finds from this debris was a practically complete rim of a collared-
rim store jar with three rosettes stamped on it (Fig. 95). Comparable impressions were found at Sahab in Transjordan (Fig. 94; Chapter 7). To the best of
our knowledge, this is the first time such stampings have been found west of
the Jordan River.

Iron II Period

After the destruction of Shiloh in the middle of the 11th century BCE, the center of Israelite population moved southward, to the hill country of Benjamin. Shiloh lost its claim to prominence, and, indeed, no important town ever arose here again. Following a period of abandonment, the site was reinhabited in Iron II. Remains of this village were encountered at various places on the mound: a few walls in Area E; a building severely damaged by erosion and later construction in Area G; isolated remains in Areas C and D; and a few structures from the end of the Iron Age on the flat area immediately to the north of the tell (excavated by Yeivin: *Had. Arch.* 77, 1981:19–20).

Shiloh During the Period of Israelite Settlement and the Judges: Preliminary Conclusions

The excavations at Shiloh, the survey of the surrounding area, and the regional projects in different parts of the hill country have all shed light on a number of crucial topics concerning the general social, political and economic role of Shiloh in the period of Settlement and the Judges as well as the specific nature of the site as an Israelite sacred center.

The first problem concerns the history of Shiloh before Israelite Settlement. The Bible makes no mention of any pre-Israelite cult at Shiloh (nor did the Danish excavations add anything in this respect). The absence of earlier sacral associations perplexed a number of scholars (e.g., Noth 1958:95), while others saw the transformation of a previously inconsequential site into an early Israelite cult center as the very reason for its subsequent importance (e.g., Bright 1981:169).

However, there are now increasing indications of cultic continuity at Shiloh from the Middle Bronze II period onward, i.e., there were pre-Israelite sacred traditions at the site. The evidence we adduced earlier in this chapter leads us to conclude that a shrine or sanctuary already stood at Shiloh in the Middle Bronze period. Moreover, this cult center may well have been the principal reason for the development of the site. Even after the destruction of the fortified Middle Bronze occupation, cultic activity continued in the Late Bronze period, despite the apparent absence of any real settlement. We have already hypothesized that during the Late Bronze period (especially LB I), Shiloh may have become a central cultic site serving pastoralists of the surrounding area, people whose way of life has not yet become sufficiently well known through either excavation or survey (Finkelstein 1985:166–167). Naturally, the more that is understood about the history of Shiloh during the Bronze Age, the better our ability to appreciate why it was chosen as an Israelite sacred center.

Na'aman (1985), on the other hand, does not see any continuity in the sacred tradition from the Bronze Age into the Iron Age. In his opinion, the cult places of the Settlement period were deliberately established outside the ancient urban centes, evidence of the revolutionary nature of the Israelite religion in the period of the Judges and the beginning of the Monarchy. This theory encounters two difficulties: (1) it is not clear why and through what progress the outdoor cult centres were eventually transferred into the cities of the Monarchial period; (2) the central hill country has by now been almost completety explored by archaeological surveys, which have revealed hundreds of Settlement sites, but not a single cultic installation has been found in the vicinity of the ancient Middle and Late Bronze centres such as Bethel and Hebron.

Whether the sanctuary at Shiloh was strictly local in purview or whether it served as a central shrine of a much broader populace is the basic and crucial question about the site. Noth, the chief proponent of the maximalist approach, saw Shiloh as one of the central sanctuaries — the latest chronologically — of the amphictyonic league of the tribes of Israel. The existence of such sanctuaries was, according to Noth, a *sine qua non* for the creation of an amphictyony (Noth 1958:93ff; in support of the opinion that central shrines existed in the early Israelite period, see, *inter alii*, Albright 1942:102, 1966a:54–55; Kraus 1966:126–127; Alt 1966:58,193; supporters of Noth's chronological scheme — Shechem, Bethel, Gilgal and finally Shiloh — included Kraus 1966:127 and Kingsbury 1967:134–136). Others opposed this view, and even doubted that there was any central Israelite sanctuary at the time (Basters 1965; Irwin 1965; Orlinsky 1962:375ff; de Geus 1976:195–199; Mayes 1974:34–35; de Vaux 1978:704–709; Lemche 1985:303. See recently Miller and Hayes 1986:133, who claim that Shiloh "was one of the numerous local shrines that dotted the palestinian hill country during the early tribal period"). Some scholars arranged the main cult sites of the period of Israelite Settlement and the Judges in a different chronological order. Lemaire, for example, saw Shiloh as the earliest — rather than latest — center (1973:242–243).

We take an intermediary position. Archaeological data from all over the Land of Israel indicate that during the first half of the 11th century BCE, when Shiloh reached its zenith, Israelite Settlement was just beginning in many areas (e.g., Upper Galilee, the Beersheba Valley, and, to a certain extent, the Judean Hills), while other regions (e.g., the plateau of Issachar) were still completely uninhabited. In other words, when Shiloh was at the peak of its prosperity, some groups were still in the process of settling down or moving from the central hill country to more distant areas (Chapter 10). It is therefore hard to imagine that at this early stage of Israelite socio-political organization, Shiloh would have acted as a center for distant groups occupying isolated areas such as Upper Galilee or the Beersheba Valley. On the other hand, the well-developed architecture and the hints of very advanced planning revealed by the excavations at Shiloh would suggest a sphere of influence greater than the narrow limits of the territory of Ephraim. The presently available information thus suggests that the sanctuary at Shiloh served the Israelite population in the central hill country and its vicinity, with most of the people involved dwelling in the territories of Benjamin, Ephraim and Manasseh. This is not to say that Shiloh was the *only* cult place in the hill country at the time, but it was probably the most important one.

The distribution of Israelite sites is the decisive factor for determining the chronological order of the major Israelite cult centers as well. We have seen (Chapter 3) that most of the Israelite population was concentrated in the central hill country between Jerusalem and the Jezreel Valley, in the Jordan Valley and on the northern Transjordanian plateau. Over 300 Iron I sites have been recognized in these areas alone, representing about 75% of all the known Settlement sites in the entire Land of Israel. These statistics, of course, reflect the situation at the end of the 11th century, on the eve of the Monarchy. To the extent to which we can make distinctions among the Iron I ceramic types, it appears that during the early stages of the period, the picture was even more extreme: We estimate that upwards of 90% of the 12th century sites were located in the above-mentioned principal areas of occupation.

If we confine ourselves to the central hill country, we find that 85–90% of the Iron I sites were situated in Ephraim and Manasseh. Only later in the period, at the end of the 11th century BCE, did the process of settlement gain momentum in the southern half of the hill country — in Benjamin, Judah and even the Beersheba Valley. So *a priori* we would expect that an important cult center serving the montane population would be located in the heart of the most densely settled region, i.e., in Ephraim or Manasseh. The logical consequence of this is that the center at Shiloh antedated places like Bethel and Gilgal (i.e., Gilgal during the days of Samuel and Saul), which rose to prominence only during a later phase of Iron I, following the destruction of Shiloh, when the main arena of Israelite settlement and religious activity shifted to the south. Regarding the chronological order of the most important shrines, we therefore opt for Lemaire's approach over Noth's, a conclusion which has significance for understanding the process of Israelite supratribal organization.

The place of Shechem in early Israelite traditions is a Pandora's box we shall refrain from opening here. Suffice it to note that the biblical account and archaeological evidence agree that a strong Canaanite population continued to be present in the city of Shechem and its surroundings in the Iron I period (from the standpoint of biblical history, see Bright 1981:170, who felt that Shechem's non-Israelite background rendered it unsuitable as a central shrine; see also Wright 1965:123–141; Nielsen 1955; on the archaeological evidence from Shechem, see Toombs 1979; Ross 1963; on Shechem in Israelite traditions, see B. Mazar 1974:144–151).

In summary, we believe that Shiloh was the first inter-regional cult center in Israel. De Vaux (1961:304; 1978:707) also saw Shiloh as the first shrine of the God of Israel, but he was of the opinion that there were additional contemporary shrines. Other scholars viewed Shiloh as the sole — or principal — religious center during the period of the Judges (Albright 1942:103–105; Bright 1981:169–170; Nielsen 1955:36; Liver 1971:196; Cross 1947:56; Woudstra 1965:127,133).

Another issue involves the date at which Shiloh became an important religious and economic center. Whether there were one or two occupation phases in Iron I, we are obviously concerned with the stage during which the impressive buildings on the western side of the site were erected, for these structures may have been part of a complex of annexes to the sanctuary (see below). The pottery found in the buildings was obviously that in use at the time of the destruction, so we must resort to architectural considerations in attempting to date the erection of the complex.

Based on the results of excavations at Iron I sites throughout the central hill country and its surroundings, it appears unlikely that advanced pillared buildings, such as those uncovered in Area C, could have been constructed before the mid- 12th century BCE (Chapter 7). At early Israelite Settlement sites, e.g., ʿIzbet Ṣarṭah Stratum III and Giloh, no developed pillared buildings were found. These structures, which were gradually becoming regularized at the time, achieved a more developed and uniform appearance in the hill country, e.g., at Khirbet Raddana, Ai and Shiloh, at a somewhat later stage of Israelite Settlement; a date at the end of the 12th century or beginning of the 11th seems to fit all the evidence.

Our estimated date for the foundation of the cultic center at Shiloh — not before the second half of the 12th century BCE — is the earliest one that can presently be deduced for the formation of an inter-regional Israelite framework on the basis of the material culture. (This timetable does accord with the fact that we presently have very little real archaeological evidence for Israelite Settlement before the 12th century; see Chapter 9.) The importance of this phase for the crystallization of hill country society from isolated groups of settlers into an organized kingdom is obvious.

Why, among all the sites in Ephraim and Manasseh, was Shiloh chosen as the first cult center? The early sacral traditions associated with the site and the absence of a flourishing Late Bronze Canaanite city here on the eve of Israelite settlement must have been contributing factors. In addition, as a result of differences in geographical setting and historical background between Manasseh and Ephraim, the Israelites in Manasseh had to settle alongside an indigenous sedentary population, which was still sizable in Iron I, while Ephraim was practically uninhabited by sedentary groups just prior to the extensive Israelite Settlement. At the beginning of the period, Shiloh was thus an outstanding candidate among the sites in the hilly regions because it was an ancient cult site that now stood deserted in an area of dense Israelite Settlement but very sparse autochthonous sedentary population.

The floruit of Shiloh was not long in duration — no more than a century and probably even less, spanning the second half of the 12th century and first half of the 11th. There is no reason to dispute the view of Kjaer and Albright that Shiloh was destroyed by the Philistines in the wake of their victory over Israel at Ebenezer. Buhl's erroneous dating of the buildings on the western slope to Iron II (Buhl and Holm-Nielsen 1969:3 3–34,60–62) was one of the reasons why Pearce (1973) hypothesized that the agents of the destruction of Shiloh alluded to by Jeremiah (7:11,14; 26:6,9) were the Assyrians in the 8th century BCE. This theory has no archaeological foundation whatsoever (nor any biblical basis; see Day 1979). Shiloh in Iron II was a small and insignificant village, in which no evidence of a destruction has ever been discovered. Consequently, there is also no ground for the assumption that Shiloh "emerged as a sanctuary of national importance" only in the days of Saul (Miller and Hayes 1986:133).

Information accumulated from different parts of the mound enables us to clarify various points connected with the nature of the site in Iron I and its layout. In the Iron I period, Shiloh did not exceed 12 dunams in area, which was the size of contemporary large villages in the hill country, such as Ai. While Iron I pottery was found all over the mound, we can delimit the extent of the built-up area more precisely. Area C was at the western boundary of the site. The eastern end could not have been much farther east than Area E, since no architectural remains of the period were found in Area D and no Iron I finds of any kind were unearthed in Area G. Only silos represented Iron I at the northern end of the tell, so the built-up area must have commenced south of Area K. It would have ended just north of Area J, where the garbage dump was discovered. In any case, a large portion of the surface area was probably occupied by the cultic complex and its auxiliary buildings.

Was Shiloh also an ordinary settlement, or was it strictly a sacred *temenos* with annexes? Assuming that most of the sacred complex stood on the summit (see below), the answer to this question should be found on the southern slope of the tell. Unfortunately, it is precisely this area that was so damaged by later construction as to render the chances of uncovering any early architecture there exceedingly slim. So, while the question of the nature of the occupation at Shiloh must remain open for the time being, there are hints that in Iron I, as in the Bronze Age, the principal activity at the site was connected with the cult center located there.

Although we lack sufficient data to reconstruct the site- plan with certainty, we can sketch in a few features. A tremendous amount of effort was expended in erecting the buildings of Area C. A segment of the Middle Bronze glacis was removed, and the steep slope had to be counteracted — all the more astonishing given that large flat surfaces convenient for construction were available on the northern side of the mound. This strongly suggests that these were no ordinary houses. The pottery discovered in these buildings lends further support to this view, for the overwhelming majority of the vessels were designed for storage. In an area of 250 m², 20 pithoi were found, as well as a great many kraters and jars. Therefore at least parts of the buildings must have been designated for storage: Hall 306 and the southern room of Building 335 were almost filled with pithoi. Furthermore, the buildings were very precisely oriented along the north-south and east-west axes. All of this evidence bolsters the probability that the pillared buildings of Area C were connected to a larger complex of buildings that continued to their east, in the direction of the summit. The Middle Bronze fortification wall, which became the eastern wall of the Area C buildings, also served as a terrace wall for an upper level of construction.

This brings us to the question of the location of the Shiloh sanctuary. Over a century ago, Captain Charles Wilson, the British explorer, proposed that the Tabernacle stood on the natural rock terrace just north of the tell, where he observed many indications of hewing (Wilson 1873:38; see also Kaufman 1981). The excavations of Z. Yeivin in this area have refuted this hypothesis, for he found no remains whatsoever of the Iron I period (*Had. Arch.* 77, 1982:19–20).

Nor have our excavations on the mound itself provided an unequivocal answer to the question of the location of the sanctuary. Our best clues consist of negative evidence from the northern part of the tell and from the eastern and western slopes. Assuming that the sanctuary was situated on the tell itself — and this would be hard to dispute — the only possible locations remaining for it are the summit and the southern slope.

Circumstantial evidence would seem to favor the summit. It is hard to understand why so much effort was invested in the constructions on the western slope unless they were planned as part of a larger complex of buildings. Moreover, just as the cult site of Shiloh in the Middle and Late Bronze periods apparently stood on the summit of the mound, so it is probable that the Israelite sanctuary was erected on or close to the same place.

Some support for this line of reasoning may be garnered from the debris found overlying the collapsed bricks of Building 335 in Area C. As noted, the ceramic material included fragments of a cultic stand and two vessels orna-mented with animal heads in applied relief. This pottery and the many animal bones may have been the remains of offerings. All this refuse must have been dumped down the slope at a later period, when the adjacent area on the east (in the direction of the summit) was cleared in preparation for new construction. In summary, in all probability the sanctuary was erected more or less on the summit of the mound, and the pillared buildings of Area C might have been related to it.

If we are correct in our belief that the constructions in Area C were no ordinary houses, then they represent the only public buildings ever discovered at Israelite Settlement sites. The quality of their construction and the sophisticated manner in which they solved the problem of the steep slope represent Iron I Israelite architecture at its finest, and may even hint at the physical character of the sanctuary itself. In the past, scholarly opinion has been divided over whether the first few chapters of 1 Samuel indicated that the sanctuary at Shiloh consisted of a genuine architectural construction (e.g., Kraus 1966:176; Eissfeldt 1957:146, 1975:564–565) or not (Woudstra 1965:135–139; Noth 1958:95; Haran 1962:22–24; Cross 1981:173–174). The results of the excavations would seem to lend credence to the former interpretation.

The renewed excavations have therefore helped unravel various knotty problems concerning Shiloh and its history during the period of Israelite Settlement. It has become increasingly clear that Shiloh had a tradition of cultic activity dating back to the Middle Bronze period. We have been able to shed new light on the special position of Shiloh as the first religious center of Israelite population in the hill country. Finally, the rich ceramic finds and well-developed architecture uncovered in the western part of the tell have contributed greatly to our knowledge of the material culture of the inhabitants of the central hill country during the Iron I period.

PART III:
MATERIAL CULTURE

CHAPTER 6

EARLY ISRAELITE ARCHITECTURE

In recent years, our knowledge about architecture at the beginning of the Iron Age has increased considerably. New information from sites in the Beersheba Valley and Negev Highlands has been supplemented by a wealth of new and important data from the central hill country, thanks to excavations at Ai, Khirbet Raddana, ʿIzbet Ṣarṭah, Khirbet ed-Dawara, and Shiloh. A fresh look at the results of earlier excavations at Ai and Tell en-Naṣbeh has also proved instructive.

The time has come, therefore, to attempt a summary of the development of architecture during the period of Israelite Settlement. Needless to say, this summary is preliminary, for although we are presently able to discern many features of Iron I construction, quite a few aspects remain vague, and satisfactory solutions to certain problems have yet to be found. First, a number of methodological points must be clarified:

— Most previous discussions about early architecture in the Land of Israel have employed the traditional approach: observing typological development (in dated constructions). Without denigrating the importance of either typology or chronology — they are, after all, the cornerstones of all research of this type — we wish to bring to the fore important aspects that have hitherto been neglected. These concern environmental factors and the human and social elements; the people who lived in and used the structures. We will thus place special emphasis both on geographical parameters in the regions of Israelite Settlement and on the socio-economic background of their inhabitants.

— A principal feature of Israelite Settlement was the transition from a pastoral to a sedentary way of life (Chapter 11). We will therefore adduce modern examples of analogous processes and explore their architectural expression.

— Because of the similarity in site-plans — and, as far as we know, in the processes of sedentarization as well — between the central hill country and the Negev Highlands in the Iron Age, we will occasionally make reference to southern sites, even though they were not part of the phenomenon of Israelite Settlement and were somewhat later in date than most of the sites under discussion.

— In describing the development of early Israelite architecture, we speak of several "phases." By this we mean a given architectural situation reflecting both the socio-economic background of the inhabitants and environmental data. These "phases" need not always have chronological implications, and their development was not necessarily linear. In other words, groups with similar social conditions — even if differing in geography and date — were likely to have arrived at similar architectural solutions, while groups in dissimilar social situations — even if adjacent and contemporary — were likely to have developed dissimilar building styles.

Various types of settlements would thus have coexisted. A good example of this is the great disparity in construction and site-plan between Giloh, on the one hand, and Khirbet Raddana and Ai, on the other, despite the geographical and chronological proximity of all three sites. The divergences reflect the differing socio-economic frameworks of the inhabitants. It follows, then, that we cannot speak of a single model for the process of sedentarization; nor can we expect every Iron I site in the hill country and in the south to fit into the classification scheme we shall outline below.

— Especially since we are dealing with groups undergoing a change in lifestyle, the individual house should not be divorced from its setting. In our considered opinion, the individual house and the overall site-plan developed together in an organic and complementary manner.

Elliptical Sites: The Transition to Sedentarization

One of the earliest Israelite sites — if not the earliest presently known — was ʿIzbet Ṣarṭah Stratum III (Chapter 3), whose founding we date to the end of the 13th or beginning of the 12th century BCE. Its early date and special layout, make it a key site for studying the development of Israelite architecture. Thus we begin our discussion by describing the site once again and citing parallels to its plan.

Stratum III consisted of an elliptical band of rooms surrounding a broad central courtyard, in which a number of stone-lined silos (but nothing else) were discerned (Fig. 76). The basic architectural element was the peripheral wall enclosing the courtyard. On the outer side, the parallel wall was neither uniform nor even; rather, it was created by linking the outer walls of the rooms, which varied in width.

Portions of eight rooms were uncovered, as well as the entryway into the site. The rooms, which were generally of the broadroom type, resembled casemates; they opened onto the courtyard. There was no direct access from one room to another. Along the inner wall, the rooms averaged 6 m in length. Since the projected circumference of the peripheral wall was 135–140 m, 22–

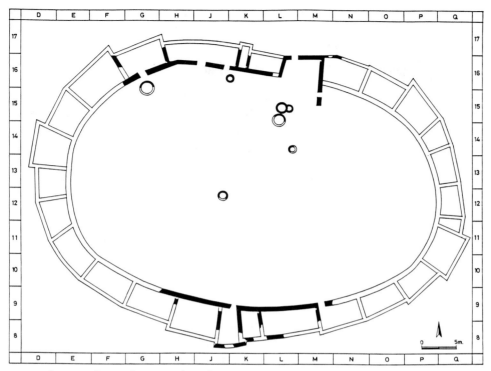

76.   ʿIzbet Ṣarṭah — schematic plan of Stratum III.

24 rooms — in addition to the entryway — could be reconstructed. The depth of the rooms is difficult to determine with certainty, but from the stumps of outer walls found on the south and northeast, we estimate 5–6 m.

The total size of the site in Stratum III was thus about 47 x 60 m, encompassing an area of some 2,200 m² (2.2 dunams). Of this, the courtyard comprised about 1,450 m² and the built-up area covered 750 m², a ratio of 65:35. This figure is very significant for determining the socio-economic character of the settlement, since it indicates that the focus of activity was the large open-air courtyard in the center. The situation changed in Stratum II, which was founded at the end of the 11th century BCE.

There are a number of parallels to the architecture of ʿIzbet Ṣarṭah Stratum III:

Ḥorvat ʿAvot

Located in Upper Galilee (map ref. 1933 2763), the site has been partly excavated (Chapter 3). At the outer edge of the Iron I settlement, a number of rectangular broad-rooms, measuring 3–4 x 7–10 m, were uncovered; they were not contiguous. From the sector excavated, it appears that the contour of

239

the site in Iron I was circular or elliptical, about 75 m. in diameter. The center of the site was not excavated, so whether it was an open-air courtyard or a built-up area remains unknown.

Khirbet et-Tina

This Iron I site (map ref. 1654 2666) was surveyed by the Western Galilee Survey Unit under the direction of R. Frankel (who kindly provided the following information). The site was located at an elevation of 150 m above sea level, about 1.5 km east of the boundary between the hills of Western Galilee and the coastal plain. Elliptical in outline, it covered an area of about 1,250 m². Here, too, there seems to have been a central courtyard encircled by rooms, and the principal circumvallation was apparently the inner wall (i.e., the one between the rooms and the courtyard); there may have been structures in the courtyard as well. Since the area of the courtyard was about 900 m², the estimated ratio of open-air courtyard, if there were no structures in it, to built-up space is about 70:30.

Enclosures in the Judean Desert

During the 1968 Survey, enclosures of different periods were discovered in the Judean Desert. At least two of them, whose plans have been published, resemble our early Iron I sites in layout (Bar-Adon 1972:106,118). The most interesting one is #19–13 23/3 D (Fig. 77), dated to "the Israelite period"

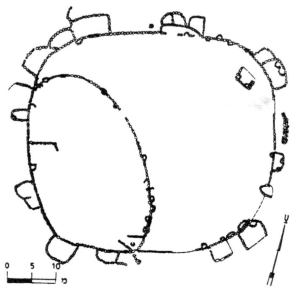

77.   An Iron Age courtyard site in the Judean Desert (Bar-Adon 1972: 118).

(i.e., the Iron Age). Measuring about 54 x 57 m, the site-plan was rounded in form and covered an area of about 2,400 m². The dimensions of the courtyard were 45 x 50 m, a surface area of 1,750 m². The basic architectural element was the inner wall, to which the rectangular rooms were joined. Some of the rooms had rounded corners. According to the published plan, these rooms did not form a continuous band, but without excavation, it is difficult to be certain

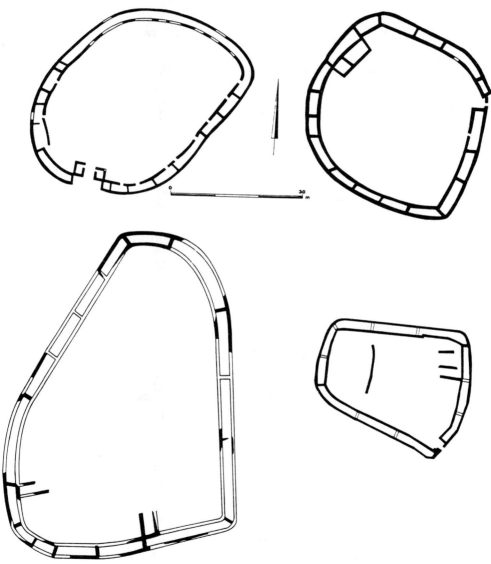

78. Iron Age Courtyard sites in the Negev Highlands: top left — Ein Qadeis; right — Atar Haroʿa; bottom left — Raḥba; right — Ketef Shivṭa (Cohen 1979: 64).

of this. If we mentally fill in the spaces along the perimeter with rooms, then the ratio of courtyard to built-up area was roughly 75:25.

Sites in the Negev Highlands

Among the Iron Age sites of the Negev Highlands, which date from the end of the 11th or the beginning of the 10th century BCE, a number are almost identical in plan to Stratum III at ʿIzbet Ṣarṭah, viz. Atar Haroʿa, ʿEin Qadeis, Raḥba, and Ketef Shivṭa (Fig. 78). They are similar in overall plan, in size, in the shape of of the casemate-like rooms and in ratio of courtyard to built-up area (65:35 - 75:25).[13]

Because the Negev Highlands sites are very important both in helping us to understand the character of Stratum III at ʿIzbet Ṣarṭah and its parallels and in deducing the socio-economic background of the inhabitants, we will return to them later. At this juncture, we wish to note only that in contrast to the popular notion that these Negev sites were Israelite "fortresses" (Cohen 1979), we follow Rothenberg and Eitam in seeing them as settlements of desert nomads (Finkelstein 1984).

In addition, we wish to mention two other southern sites already discussed in Chapter 3: Beersheba Stratum VII and Tel Esdar Stratum III. For despite significant differences in the character of their built-up areas, their overall plans do bear a certain similarity to ʿIzbet Ṣarṭah Stratum III and its parallels: Both sites featured a large open courtyard surrounded by a belt of constructions opening onto it.

Beersheba Stratum VII

When a 70–meter long segment of the southern end of the site was excavated, it became apparent that a chain of casemate-like broad-rooms ringed the perimeter of the site (Herzog 1984:78–82). At least some of them seem to have been the rear rooms of three and four-room houses constructed around the periphery. While the broad-rooms did form a belt around the settlement, their outer walls did not create a smooth and uniform line. Rather, the houses were separate but contiguous. Each "casemate" was 1.25–1.75 m in width and 9–12 m in length, with an outer wall 1 m thick. Since parts of 5 such "casemates" were uncovered, it was estimated that there would have been 18 units surrounding the courtyard. Access to the site was through a real gate structure, consisting of two chambers flanking a passage 1.5 m wide. Stratum VII belonged to the end of the 11th century BCE.

13   Another site resembling the elliptical sites of the Negev Highlands has been found in southern Transjordan, in the area of Wadi el-Ḥasa (MacDonald 1980:171,Pl. CIII). Most of the pottery collected at the site was Iron I in date.

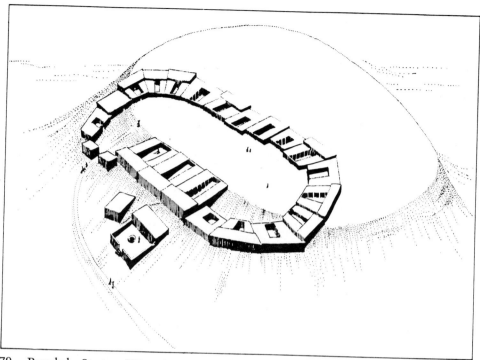

79.   Beersheba Stratum VII — isometric reconstruction (Herzog 1984: 80).

Herzog reconstructed an elliptical site composed of four-room houses whose rear rooms created the peripheral belt of casemates (Figs. 4, 79). This would leave only about 900 m² in the center for the courtyard — if the band of houses continued around the perimeter. The size of the site was estimated at 50 x 80 m, an area of a little more than 3 dunams. Additional buildings were found outside this complex, next to the well. The excavator remarked upon the resemblance between this settlement and the sites in the Negev Highlands, even though at none of the latter did a belt of multichambered houses adjoin the peripheral casemates.

Tel Esdar Stratum III

The resemblance between this site and ʿIzbet Ṣarṭah is restricted to the general plan: structures surrounding a central courtyard. However, at Tel Esdar these were real buildings, not simply casemates (Kochavi 1969a:23–26; our Fig. 3). It is not known whether these buildings created a smooth line or whether there were spaces between them. Eight of them were excavated and two others were discerned on the surface of the mound.

Aharoni (1976a:69) reconstructed a total of about 20 rectangular houses encircling the summit of the hill; their long walls paralleled the perimeter. The houses opened onto the courtyard, which was devoid of construction. With dimensions of about 55 x 85 m, the site covered an area of 3,750 m², of which 2,800 m² was the courtyard. The proportion of courtyard to built-up area was thus about 75:25. Stratum III at Tel Esdar was inhabited during the 11th century BCE.

The site of Giloh is also worth mentioning in this connection; while its plan is unrelated, the division of the surface area between buildings and courtyards is reminiscent (Fig. 8). The excavator viewed the site as a "fortified herdsmen's village" with a number of families or small clans dividing up the area in such a way that each had houses bordering on a large courtyard in which the flocks were kept (A. Mazar 1981a:12,32; 1980a:36–38).

Elliptical "courtyard sites" have thus been found in diverse regions of the country, from Western Galilee and the foothills of Ephraim through the Judean Desert (and perhaps Transjordan as well) and into the Negev Highlands. While the majority date from Iron I or early in Iron II, it would not be surprising if similar sites from other periods should turn up in the future.[14] Apart from the general resemblance of their overall plans, the outstanding feature common to all these sites was the dominant position of the courtyard: The estimated ratios of courtyard space to built-up area range from 65:35 to 80:20. The large courtyard obviously played a central role — figuratively as well as literally — in the daily life of the inhabitants, undoubtedly as a shelter for their flocks.

In summary, then, the occupants of "courtyard sites" were people whose primary economic activity was herding. All of these sites were located in classic grazing areas — the Negev Highlands, Beersheba Valley, Judean Desert, foothills of the Yarkon basin, and Western Galilee (Zeligman et al. 1959:51). The reasons for building them in this specific layout were strictly socio-economic; neither ethnic nor chronological explanations need be sought. The special architectural form reflected the subsistence base of the inhabitants and their social organization.

Dealing with the elliptical sites of the Negev Highlands, we have attempted to show that they represented an early stage in the sedentarization of desert nomads, with both the outline of the individual tent and the layout of the group encampment translated into stone construction. At that time, their economy was still based on pasturage (Finkelstein 1984). The same seems to

---

14   In fact, there is a distinct resemblance between these settlements and EB II and Intermediate Bronze sites in the Negev and Sinai, whose plans were also based on a central
courtyard surrounded by residential units. The resemblance stems from similar social and
economic functions; we shall return to this matter.

have held true for similar sites in the Judean Desert and in other regions of the Land of Israel.[15]

It is widly excepted that nomads in the process of sedentarization retained traditions from their pastoral existence, at least initially. An obvious example is the transference of their tradition of dwelling in portable tents made of perishable materials to their permanent architecture. The same line of reasoning has been applied to the translation of the residential tent form into stone buildings that did not serve as habitations. In a well-known example, the typical *yurt* (tent) of the nomadic Central Asian tribes is thought to be the origin of the Seljuk *turbeh* (mausoleum) (Talbot Rice 1961:141–142). All the more so is this approach valid when dealing with the transition from residential tent to residential architecture.

Fortunately, comparable processes can still be witnessed in the region today. Shmueli made the following observations on the sedentarization of the Beduin on the fringe of the Judean Desert:

> The transition from tent to house meant a revolution in the life of the people who ceased being nomadic and built houses for themselves, but the influence of the tent on the life of the Beduin in the process of sedentarization has not ceased. The entrance of the house in Beduin settlements generally faces east, which was the customary direction for the opening of the tent. A considerable proportion of the buildings in a Beduin settlement, especially the first ones erected, were actually no more than stone walls replacing the flies of the portable tent. The functions of the various rooms of the houses are identical to the functions of the spaces into which the tents had been partitioned. The lifestyle in these houses is influenced by the way of life in tents, even decades after the transition to permanent dwellings (1980:154– 155; see also Katakura 1977:73; Kay 1978:143).

On the tent-camp, Shmueli commented:

> ....Beduin villages differ from other permanent settlements in their physical structure, in their location and in the plan of the individual house. In this respect, the settlement is a copy of a Beduin encampment executed in building materials (1980:83).

The literature dealing with the lifestyle of nomads in our region in the 19th and 20th centuries indicates that in cases of enclosed encampments, the tents were arrayed linearly, in the form of a crescent, or were pitched in a circular or

---

15 In various discussions connected with the excavations at Tel Masos, Kempinski (1978:36; Kempinski *et. al.* 1981:176) and Fritz (1977a:44,n.48; 1977b:64; 1981:65) drew attention to the influence of the traditions of the tent and tent-camp on construction at a stage following sedentarization (see below). However, we fail to detect evidence of a nomadic past in the well-developed material culture of Tel Masōs.

80. Tent encampment in Transjordan, after a picture published by Musil (1908: 131).

81. Tent encampment in the Judean Desert (Dalman 1939: Pl. 12).

elliptical arrangement. In some regions, the latter were even called *duwwar*, "circle" in Arabic.

Two photographs of *duwwar* encampments taken at the beginning of this century enable us to study their structure and size. The first (Fig. 80), elliptical in outline, was located in Transjordan (Musil 1908:131), and the second (Fig.

81), rectangular or trapezoidal in form, was found in the Judean Desert (Dalman 1939:Ph. 12). The surface area of the encampment and the number of tents are similar in both cases. The tents opened onto the large central courtyard. There were one or two entrances into the encampment. (Such a tent-camp was described by Conder 1878:275; see also Cunnison 1970:321–323, Nijst et al. 1973:23–30).

As for the factors dictating the outline of the encampments, Musil (1908:130) noted that when conditions were secure or when the encampments were large, the arrangement was linear, while in hostile locales, the tent-camp was laid out in the form of an ellipse in order to protect the flocks in the center. Raswan (1934:153) offered a different interpretation: The tents of camel-raisers were arrayed in long parallel lines, while the encampments of shepherds were arranged in crescents or circles. Both explanations are reasonable, but neither seems to be complete, since the layout of the tent-camps was probably also influenced by other factors, such as climatic conditions and geographical setting. (On the various forms of Beduin encampments, see Burkhardt 1831:33; Musil 1928:73; Dalman 1939:27; Montagne 1947:56,64; Dickson 1949:83; Ashkenazi 1957:146; Marx 1974:148; Ben-David 1978:52; Bar-Zvi 1979:623; Amiran et al. 1979:658).

The similarities in detail between the elliptical "courtyard sites" and the enclosed Beduin encampments are illustrated by the following table; we have also included data from Tell Esdar Stratum III and Beersheba Stratum VII, despite the differences between these two sites and the others (see below).

	ʿIz. Ṣarṭah III	Haroʿa	Ein Qadeis	Raḥba	Tel Esdar III	Beer-sheba VII	tent camp Musil (Fig. 80)	tent camp Dalman (Fig. 81)	tent camp Conder
Size (m)*	47x60	42x50	37.5x50	60x75	55x85	50x80	c.40x70	c.50x70	22x63
# of tents, casemates, or bldgs	22–24	17	20	c. 20 est.	c. 20 est.	18	19–22	20–23	20–30
width (m) of tents or casemates	6 avg.	5.5–10	5.5–10	5–10		9–12	6–12	6–12	6–12

* The "casemates" at the built sites adjoin one another, while at tent sites, there are spaces between the tents. The sizes of the encampments in Figs. 80 and 81 have been estimated by multiplying the estimated size of an individual tent.

Another important feature of the elliptical sites requires an explanation: At the sites in the Negev Highlands, both the inner and outer perimeter walls formed straight and smooth lines, while farther north, at ʿIzbet Ṣarṭah and, apparently, et-Tina, only the inner wall (which delimits the courtyard) created such a line. This inner wall was the basic structural element of the settlement; rooms of variable depth were adjoined to it, giving the site an outer line of alternating projections and recesses. The explanation for this difference may lie in the difficulties inherent in the hilly terrain of the northern sites, where support on the slopes was required. This phenomenon seems to have continued in the constructions of the central hill country even later in the Iron I period (see below).

From our hypothesis that the elliptical site originated in the nomadic encampment, it follows that the individual unit of construction — a broad-room or "casemate" — reflected the individual desert tent. In this connection, it should be stressed that the tradition of the tent shape was apparently even stronger than stone construction, for it was deeply rooted in centuries of an unchanging lifestyle and consistent geographical setting (Faegre 1979:3). It is therefore unlikely that the shape of the desert tent in our region was altered over the course of time. It remained a broad "structure" that generally opened to the east, because the wind blows from the west. The dimensions, especially the length, varied according to the size and means of the family: 2.5–4.5 x 6–12 m. The main supporting poles were set in a row through the long axis of the tent.

The interior of the tent was usually divided by curtains into two unequal spaces. The smaller one was for men and guests and the larger one was for women, household tasks, and family living quarters. Sometimes the division was tripartite, with the third area serving as a sheepfold or pen. The curtains

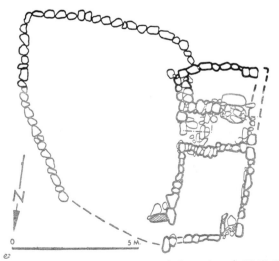

82. Ramat Matred — Structure A (Aharoni *et al.* 1960: 34).

83.   Tent and pen in Samaria.

were hung along the short axis of the tent on one or more rows of wooden poles, depending on the size of the tent. (On the tent form, see Musil 1928:72; Dalman 1939:1–58; Epstein 1933:12–13; Feilberg 1944:65–72; Weir 1976:1–7; Kay 1978:12–14; Faegre 1979:19–22.)

Another model for the transition from tent to fixed architecture — the individual house deriving directly from the individual tent — seems to be exemplified at Ramat Maṭred in the Negev (Fig. 82; cf. Fig. 83). There, Aharoni and his colleagues first discovered in survey, then excavated, a broad-room (A) measuring 2.9 x 7 m. In the long wall facing east, there was an opening onto a courtyard enclosed by a stone wall (Aharoni et al. 1960:34,Fig.8). That this building was closer to a pastoral stage of existence than the others at the site is demonstrated by the ratio of courtyard to dwelling space: 63:37 versus 52:48 for Building C, for example (Fig. 87)[16]. Additional individual units of this type have now been surveyed in the Negev Highlands, but they have yet to be published (Had. Arch. 80–81, 1982:62).

In conclusion, there do appear to be rather striking similarities between the individual tent and the isolated broad-room and between the *duwwar* tent-

16   On different, but contemporary stages in the transition from tent to permanent house in modern-day Beduin settlements in the Negev, see Amiran and Ben-Arieh 1963:173.

camp and the elliptical "courtyard sites." The resemblances are evident in general layout, details of plan, function of units, and dimensions. The inhabitants of the "courtyard sites" must have become sedentary only recently, and their residential customs, as well as their subsistence base, were still connected to their former pastoral mode of living. The rounded or elliptical layout had clear advantages for such groups of people: relative security and a convenient area for sheltering their flocks.[17]

SITES WITH A PERIPHERAL BELT OF PILLARED BUILDINGS

The next major step in the development of the Iron I site layout is reflected in settlements characterized by a belt of houses, most of them of the three or four room type, built around the outer edge of the site. Because the rear room of each house was a broadroom, a row of such rooms created a kind of casemate effect. The interior space of the house generally included free-standing pillars. Ai and Beersheba Stratum VII are good examples of such sites. This type of site-plan apparently originated in the elliptical settlements discussed in the previous section. Now, however, several points of difference can be discerned between the central hill country and the Negev Highlands.

In the Negev Highlands (and central hill country as well, apparently), monolithic pillars first appeared during this phase of architectural development. They were integrated into the inner walls of the casemates (Fig. 84). Perhaps initially, as at Refed (Meshel and Cohen 1980:72), there was no further construction toward the open courtyard in the center of the site. Eventually, however, the casemate-with-monoliths became a longitudinal (!) unit in a building that developed on the courtyard side, as at Ḥatira, near Refed (Meshel and Cohen 1980:77). A similar phenomenon was observed in Units 80, 81, 86, and 90 at Tel Esdar (Kochavi 1969a:23–26), but there the pillars were more freestanding, the houses were independent units rather than

17 In the peripherally-protected tent camps of nomads, Kempinski saw the archetype of Stratum II at Tel Masos, for, in his opinion, the inhabitants used just such a camp during the semi-nomadic phase preceding their sedentarization (Kempinski et al. 1981:176; Kempinski 1978:35). This analogy is invalid for the following reasons: 1. In the circular encampment of nomads, the entrances always face inward, while at Tel Masōs, the majority of the openings were directed outward (which, incidentally, attests to the relative security and lack of any need to organize in a defensive formation). 2. At Tel Masōs, the center of the site was built up, while nomadic tent camps are characterized by the large open courtyard in the middle. 3. The material culture of the inhabitants of Stratum II at Tel Masōs had already advanced far beyond the nomadic stage assumed for their forebears. On the other hand, the houses at Masōs were constructed in a layout of enclosed groups, separated from each other by open spaces. This may reflect the nomadic background of at least some of the inhabitants.

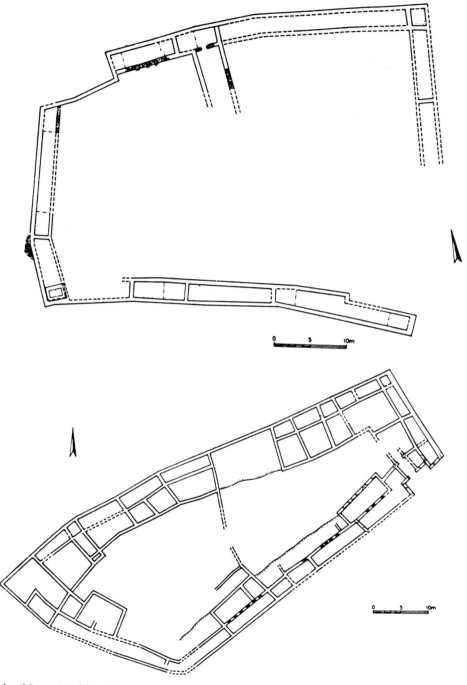

84. Negev Highland sites — Refed (top) and Ḥatira (bottom) (Meshel and Cohen 1980: 72, 77).

251

casemates-like rooms, and these units may have been propinquous rather than contiguous.

The main point is that in the Negev Highlands, the houses ringing the courtyard were parallel to the peripheral line of defense, with the casemates serving as longrooms. At first glance, the appearance of monolithic pillars in the casemate walls would seem to hark back to nomadic housing traditions, when a row of wooden poles supported each tent. But the real reason was probably the obvious architectural one — simply reinforcing the wall (see below).

In the central hill country, a very similar development took place. Here, however, the houses, which were definitely attached to one another, were arranged perpendicular to the peripheral line of defense. The "casemates" thus served as the broadrooms of these houses. The reason for this basic difference between the sites of the hill country and those of the Negev appears to have been topographical. The main obstacles to construction in hilly areas has always been the steep rocky slopes. The problem was solved by building terraces, with the result that some of the houses stood on two levels. In these circumstances, it was undoubtedly preferable to erect buildings perpendicular to the slope, with their entrances on the upper (summit) side,[18] as every typical montane Arab village demonstrates.

A good example of this construction method in Iron I was encountered on the steep western slope of Shiloh (Figs. 69, 70; see Chapter 5), where the buildings were erected on two levels separated by a solid terrace wall. The fact that these structures were not ordinary private houses makes no difference. There was a large broad hall on the lower level, and two pillared buildings on the upper level; pillars were embedded in the western terrace wall of the latter, facing the slope. Integrating monolithes into terrace walls (a method still in use today in the hill country for agricultural terraces), helped withstand the pressures that built up atop and behind these walls.

The aggregate outer walls of houses constructed on the sloping ground of the hill country did not form a smooth line, but rather protruded and receded in accordance with the topography or with the need for buttressing. This too, is evident in contemporary montane Arab villages. A good Iron I example is Ai (Marquet-Krause 1949:Pl. XCVII; Shiloh 1978:45). On the outer edge of the village, a group of contiguous two-to-four room houses was unearthed. Their broad-rooms (which were occasionally double) formed a peripheral belt of casemates (Fig. 85). Seen from the outside, the wall would have appeared to have had offsets and insets. At Tell en-Nasbeh, too, portions of offsets from the

---

18   It follows that since the entrances to the constructions on the outer edge of Tel Masos faced outward, the building layout there could not have originated in the hill country. Instead, there are various hints that the building methods were influenced by the southern coast (Kempinski 1978:36).

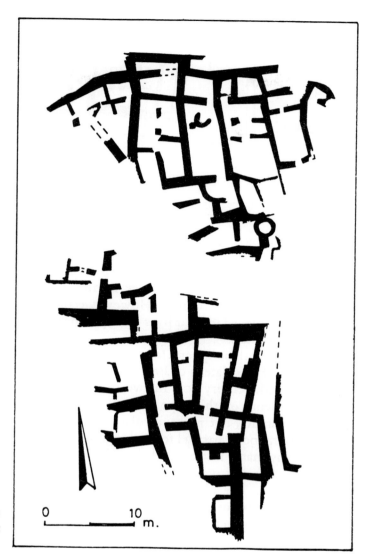

85. Ai — the Iron I village, Marquet-Krause excavations (*idem.* 1949: Pl. XCVII).

0   10 m.

line of the two-to-four room houses of the early settlement could be discerned (Fig. 12). At all three sites, the center of the settlement was built-up, but such an arrangement of the outer line of the settlement was also known at courtyard sites, e.g., ʿIzbet Ṣarṭah Stratum III.

The plan of Stratum VII at Beersheba seems to be intermediate between the plans of central hill-country sites and those of sites in the Negev Highlands. Although not many walls of Stratum VII were exposed, it is clear that the longrooms of the houses were perpendicular to the "casemates" (which protruded and receded), as at sites in the central hill country. The courtyard,

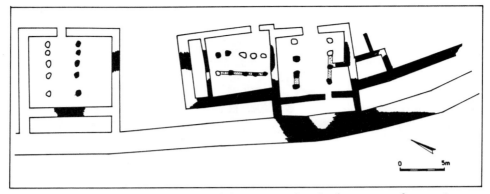

86.   Kh. ed Dawara — schematic plan of the remains after the first season of excavations.

however, was empty, as at sites in the Negev Highlands. The explanation for this is very simple. Because the inhabitants of Beersheba VII were Israelites who apparently came from farther north, they were influenced by the architecture of the hill country. However, economic reality — the primary role that flocks played in their lives — required that a large and open courtyard be left in the center.

Another site with peripheral four-room houses is Khirbet ed- Dawara on the desert fringe of the plateau of Benjamin, which was established at the second half of the 11th century BCE. In two respects, however, it differed from the other settlements of this type (Fig. 86). First, some of the houses were apparently parallel, not perpendicular, to the outer line of the site. In such instances extra room, parallel to the longitudinal units of the building, created a kind of "casemate" instead of the rear broadroom. Second, the outer wall of the row of casemates was surprisingly thick, creating a real fortification wall around the site. The plan of Khirbet ed-Dawara illustrates, therefore, that historical factors or local ecological conditions could cause deviations from the normative development of settlement types in Iron I.

In summary, the development of early Israelite architecture was influenced by two overriding factors: the pastoral background of most of this society prior to sedentarization, and the special topographical conditions prevailing in the central hill country, which was the principal locus of Israelite Settlement.

ON THE ORIGIN OF PILLARED FOUR-ROOM HOUSES

The typical four-room house with pillars, the principal architectural entity in the Iron Age, was already widespread early in the period — at Tel Masos, Ai, Khirbet Raddana, Tell en-Nasbeh, ʿIzbet Ṣarṭah and Giloh (on the different elements of the house and their social function see Stager 1985b:11–23).

Scholars have wrestled with the problem of the origin of these buildings (summarized by Shiloh 1970), but with inconclusive results. Determining that this house type was indeed Israelite (Shiloh 1970) still did not explain how the idea developed.

Concerning the origin of the four-room house, two main theories have arisen. According to the first — whose principal proponents are Kempinski, Fritz and Herzog — the type developed at the beginning of the Iron Age. All of them agree, in one way or another, that this house originated in the pre-sedentary nomad's tent (but see reservations expressed by Stager 1985b:17). The second theory posits that the phenomenon already began in the Late Bronze period.

Kempinski (1978:36) hypothesized that the four-room house developed from two- and three-room houses, which in turn originated in the plans of tents in use prior to sedentarization. In other words, the tent plus courtyard became the broad-room plus courtyard (which was later divided into few spaces). The most concrete example of the transition from tent (which generally lacked a defined courtyard[19]) to stone house with courtyard is, as we have already seen, Building A at Ramat Maṭred (Fig. 82).

However, the other structures at the site, which illustrate the development of more complex buildings, contradict to some extent, Kempinski's theory: Building B had two rooms separated by a row of pillars, while Building C was a genuine three-room house, with two longrooms flanking a row of pillars perpendicular to a broadroom (Fig. 87). In both cases, the buildings were entered from a courtyard enclosed by a stone fence (Aharoni *et al.* 1960:34–36). In other words, the building type did not develop at the expense of the courtyard, but rather, the courtyard varied in size relative to the house, while its form and location remained unchanged.

Fritz (1977a:43–44; 1977b:60–64; 1980:125; 1981:65) considered two possibilities for the origin of the four-room house. Either (like Kempinski's theory) it developed from a broad-room plus frontal courtyard , or else it grew out of broad pillared buildings, such as Building 167 at Tel Masos and Building 90 at Tel Esdar, which in turn originated in nomads' tents with parallel rows of wooden poles. Fritz favored the second possibility: In his view, the entrance to the building was transferred to its narrow side, and two rooms - a longitudinal unit and a broad-room - were added. One of the long units became a courtyard.

There are several objections to this idea. Fritz' theory was based solely on two buildings bearing only a partial resemblance to one another, both from sites in the south, which is not where this type of building developed. Nor did he explain the strange process he described: adding a longroom, moving the

---

19   On the enclosing of courtyards with fences by Beduin in the process of sedentarization, see Baily 1969(?):151.

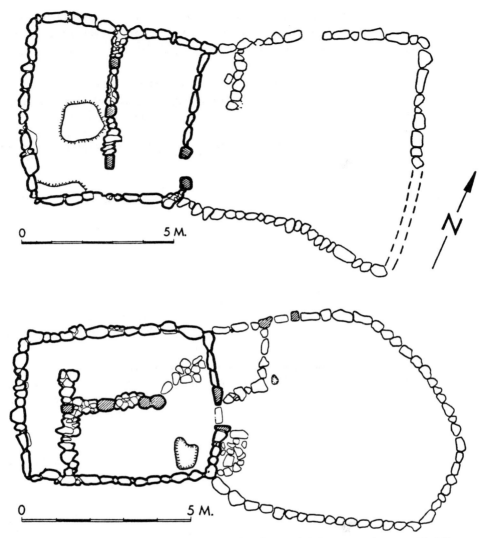

87.   Ramat Matred — Buildings B (top) and C (bottom) (Aharoni *et al.* 1960: 35, 36).

entrance, and adding a broadroom. In fact, Fritz has really advocated the *de novo* creation of a house type rather than its development from an existing form.

In Herzog's opinion (1984:76–77), the four-room house developed from the broadroom, which was the principal and constant feature of this house type. During Iron I, the broadroom may have been influenced by the tent form, and its facade may have initially been only a row of pillars instead of a real wall (like Building 81 at Tel Esdar). Later, a courtyard was added to the broad-room. The courtyard was enlarged as the process of sedentarization took root, and it was eventually divided into three parts. However, as we have seen, the need for a large courtyard lessened as sedentarization became more firmly established, and as the base of subsistence underwent a transition from herding to farming.

At Tel Baṭash in the Shephelah, a pillared building dating from the Late Bronze period was unearthed (Kelm and Mazar 1982:9–12), once again raising the possibility that the pillared buildings of the Iron Age had antecedents in the preceding period (Ahlström 1984a:42–48; A. Mazar 1985a:67–68; see also Wright 1985:295–296, who argues that elements of the concept can be traced already to the Middle Bronze period). We find this view hard to accept at present. Except for the discovery at Tel Baṭash, no similar building has ever been excavated at any of the main Late Bronze sites. It is especially significant that no such building has turned up in any of the hilly areas, where most of the pillared buildings of the Iron Age have been found.

The following points should, in our opinion, be emphasized in the search for the origin and development of the pillared buildings, most of which have four rooms:

— As Kempinski and Herzog have shown, the core of the four-room building was its broadroom, and this element probably originated in the nomad's tent. However, the four-room house did not grow directly from the tent. There was, instead, an intermediate stage in which broadrooms were constructed along the periphery of the site, an arrangement that echoed the nomadic tent camp.

— The building did not develop in isolation, but as an integral part of the entire Iron I site layout.

— The building developed by the addition of longrooms to the broadroom. Sometimes the longitudinal units were created by means of two rows of pillars, which may have continued the pillars embedded into the wall of the broad-room.

— The use of pillars was prominent in hilly terrain because they facilitated construction on terraced slopes.

— At first glance, it would seem logical that the massive use of pillars (usually monoliths) in the central hill country and Negev Highlands, just when the people of these regions were in transition from nomadism or semi-nomadism to sedentarization, arose from their portable "building" traditions, i.e., from wooden tent poles. However, it is precisely at the elliptical sites in both the Negev and the central hill country — which we believe to be typologically closest to the pre-settlement stage — that no freestanding pillars have been found.[20]

— The widespread use of pillars in Iron I can be explained first and foremost by the influx of settlers into the hilly regions of the Land of Israel at that time. It follows that during earlier periods, this construction technique was not frequently employed for the simple reason that these areas were relatively sparsely inhabited.

— The distribution of the four-room house is inextricably linked to the question of its origin. The most important considerations are quantitative (and not simply whether or not this type occurs at a given site) and chronological (see below). Since Ahlström (1984a:42–43) and Braemer (1982:105) did not take these issues into account, the views they advocated are difficult to accept.

To go further than the points noted above would, at present, be to enter into the realm of far-fetched speculation.

The dating of the pillared buildings also warrants clarification. In the central hill country, houses of this type were already constructed in the 12th century BCE. A. Mazar dated the building at Giloh to the beginning of the 12th century (1981a:11), and the pillared buildings of Shiloh were erected toward the end of the 12th century (Chapter 5).

The houses at Ai and Khirbet Raddana probably belonged to the second half of the 12th century as well. Had we accepted the excavators' 13th century dates for the foundation of these settlements (Callaway 1976:19; Cooley 1975:7), we would be forced to seek the source of this building type in the Late Bronze period, for the pillared houses at Ai and Khirbet Raddana were already well-developed in form. On the other hand, the pottery from these two sites ruled out any date much later than the second half of the 12th century.

Turning to the southern part of the country and the coastal plain, the dates assigned by Fritz (1980:121) to Stratum II at Tel Masos are preferable to the earlier dates advocated by Kempinski (Kempinski *et. al.* 1981:177); in short, the well-developed pillared houses were erected in the course of the 11th century BCE. At Beersheba and the Negev Highlands and at Tell Shariᶜa (Oren 1978:1064) and Tell Qasile (A. Mazar 1977:Plan 19) in Philistia, pillared buildings were first constructed only in the 11th century, and generally toward its close. Because the pillared four-room house is too specific a type to have

---

20 On the other hand, there were periods during which nomadic desert societies in the process of sedentarization employed freestanding monolithic pillars in their constructions. Specifically, we are referring to the EB II period in southern Sinai (Beit-Arieh 1977:87–88; 1981) and the Intermediate Bronze period in the Negev (Kochavi 1967:34–35). In both cases, the site-plans largely comprised rooms surrounding a central courtyard, with the rows of monoliths (where there is more than one pillar) almost invariably ranged down the longitudinal axis of the building (like the main poles of nomads' tents).

undergone parallel and independent development in several regions, we must conclude that the building made its massive debut in the hill country, and then, still in Iron I, spread from there to the Beersheba Valley, Negev Highlands, Philistia, northern coast (Tell Abu Huwam IV; Hamilton 1935:Pl. IV), and Transjordan (Sauer 1986:10). The inhabitants of Tel Masos thus borrowed this architectural type from the hill country to their north, just as they learned Egypto-Canaanite building styles from the coastal plain to their west.

The Influence of Iron I Hill Country Architecture on Construction During the Monarchy

The architecture of Iron I in the hill country exercised a decisive influence on Israelite architecture in Iron II. Some of the elements known from Beersheba Stratum II (Fig. 88) and other sites, which had hitherto been regarded as evidence of advanced urban planning during the Monarchy period (Aharoni 1978:190–192; Herzog 1978), had, in fact, already appeared centuries earlier in rural settlements in the hill country; there they underwent a slow develop-

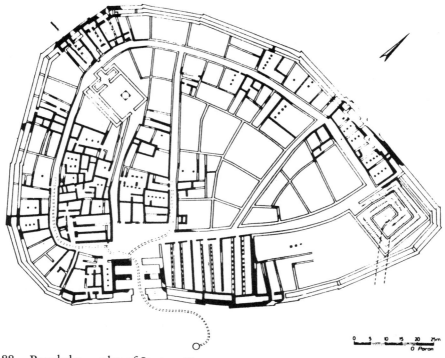

88. Beersheba — plan of Stratum II.

ment that was clearly influenced both by the socio- economic situation of the populace and by environmental conditions.

The prototype of the peripheral belt of two-to-four room houses, with their broadrooms serving as casemates, is evident at sites such as Ai (Shiloh 1978:45–46) and Tell en-Naṣbeh (and also Beersheba Stratum VII). The effect of shallow insets and offsets incorporated into the casemate wall was already created at these sites and elsewhere by contiguous houses that alternately protruded outward and receded inward. The peripheral street, which gave access to the houses adjoining the wall, probably originated in the path following a contour line around a hilltop village.

The prototype of storehouses with rows of pillars (especially storehouses adjoining casemates at the edge of a settlement) might be sought in the pillared buildings we excavated at Shiloh, at least parts of which were used for storage. On this point, too, we find Fritz' explanation untenable. He felt that the storehouse also developed from the broadroom house with pillars, such as Building 167 at Tel Masos, as follows: the entrance was moved to a short side and a parallel longroom was added (Fritz 1977a:44).

So by the middle of the 11th century BCE at the latest, hill-country sites already featured many of the characteristics of "royal" construction known from the important Iron II centers. This realization is hardly surprising. For although settlements such as Shiloh and Ai were destroyed or abandoned before the 10th century, at most sites occupation continued throughout the entire Iron Age; some 80% of the Iron I sites in Ephraim, it should be recalled, still existed in Iron II. During the course of these centuries, there were no architectural upheavals. The well- developed settlement at Tell en-Naṣbeh provides an excellent example of this continuity: The village was first established in the Iron I period, and the only subsequent additions in Iron II were, the big fortification wall and a few large buildings erected at important places within the circumvallation (Chapter 3). At Beersheba, too, we can follow certain ideas of town planning from Stratum VII through Stratum V and down to Stratum II. The same holds true for Tell Beit Mirsim B and A.

In many respects, then, we can trace the development of Israelite architecture from the beginning of the period of Settlement in the hill country down to the end of the Iron Age.

THE QUESTION OF FORTIFICATIONS

It was long assumed that Israelite Settlement sites were either completely unfortified or at most surrounded by a simple boundary wall (e.g., Callaway 1975:49; Kochavi 1982:5). A. Mazar, however, recently expressed a different opinion (1981a:16–17) in light of both his own work at Giloh and his reevaluation of the results of excavations at Gibeon, Shiloh, Bethel, Beth-zur and ʿIzbet Ṣarṭah. He concluded that there were fortified settlements in the central hill country in the 12th and 11th centuries BCE, and that the skills of constructing defenseworks developed in Israelite culture from the outset. The need for fortifications arose, in his opinion, from the complicated ethno-political situation in the Jerusalem region at the time — when different groups of Israelites settled alongside Jebusites and Hivites — and also from the external threat posed by the growing power of the Philistines.

Before taking a stand on this important issue, we will review the evidence from the above-mentioned sites:

The most interesting site in this context is *Giloh* (Mazar 1981a:12–16, Fig. 2). A double defense wall was uncovered in the northern part of the site (Fig. 8). The outer wall was 1.9 m in width. Parallel to it at a distance of 2.5 m ran the inner wall, which was 1.85 m wide. Both walls were solidly built. The void between them was filled with earth and small stones on top of a beaten earth floor. No partition walls were found linking the two parallel walls. Additional segments of the peripheral wall were discovered on the eastern and southern sides of the settlement during a surface survey of the site. Excavations in Area F revealed that the wall there was 1.5 m, but no sign of a parallel wall was found. There were, however, remains of a building erected 1.8 m inside and parallel to the defense wall. Mazar interpreted the differences in the construction of the fortification wall as evidence that it was built in segments, perhaps by the various families living there. He estimated the total area of the settlement within the "fortifications" to have been about 6 dunams. In the double wall of Giloh, he saw the origin of the 10th-century casemate walls.

To recapitulate our discussion of *Gibeon* in Chapter 3, Pritchard assigned the "early wall," which was 1.6–1.8 m wide, to Iron I (1964:34–39). Elsewhere, however, he attributed the more massive "late wall" to this period without mentioning the second defense wall (1962:101–104). On the basis of form alone, the "late wall" would belong to the Middle Bronze Age, or perhaps Iron II (on the latter possibility, see Albright 1966b:33). Iron I remains have been found Inside the "early wall," toward the interior of the site. But because the area excavated was too small to permit any unequivocal conclusions, it is uncertain whether or not Gibeon was, in fact, fortified during the Iron I period.

Our renewed excavations at *Shiloh* have proven, beyond a shadow of doubt, that the site was not fortified during Iron I. The buildings on the western slope were erected outside the well-preserved Middle Bronze fortification wall (Figs. 69–70); their western wall, which was the outer wall of the site, consisted of a single row of field stones only 60–75 cm thick (Chapter 5). In Area D, Iron I pavements ran over the Middle Bronze defenses (Fig. 68).

The excavators of *Bethel* dated to Iron I repairs that were made in the Middle Bronze fortification wall. Their reasons included the finding of a few silos leaning against it (Kelso 1968:16–17). Obviously, no new defenseworks were constructed in the Iron I period, and from the use made of the old MB II wall while cutting silos, it does not necessarily follow that it functioned as a fortification wall.

On the basis of two loci in which Iron I material was found, the excavators of *Beth-zur* claimed that the Iron I inhabitants had reused the Middle Bronze fortification wall. They further noted that no remains of Iron I were found outside the line of fortifications (Sellers *et al.* 1968:7). However, the two loci were not ceramically clean (*ibid.* :20,25), and the area excavated was too small to be definitive.

'Izbet Sartah was not fortified. All that can be said about Stratum III is that its perimeter was outlined by a wall consisting of a single row of stones, a mere 50–60 cm thick (Finkelstein 1986:7–12). Stratum II (Fig. 21) lacked even a boundary wall (see Chapter 3).

A most interesting late Iron I site, where a genuine fortification wall has recently been discovered, is *Khirbet ed-Dawara* (Fig. 86). A solid defense wall, 2–3 m wide, constructed of large field stones was unearthed. Walls of the adjoining four-room houses were bonded into it. This single-phase settlement was established in the 11th century, apparently in the second half, which determines the date of the fortification wall as well.

At all the other sites excavated in the regions of Israelite Settlement, no fortifications have been discovered. Beersheba Stratum VII, Ai, and Tell en-Nasbeh were delimited by the combined outer walls of the contiguous houses at the edge of the site. Not even such a line marked the boundary of other settlements, e.g., Arad, Tell Beit Mirsim, Khirbet Raddana, Tell el-Fūl, Hazor, Dan, Tell Harashim, Sasa and Horvat 'Avot.

Giloh, then, is presently the only early Iron I Israelite Settlement site which may have been surrounded by some sort of defence wall. At some sites, the old Middle Bronze fortification wall was reused, but not necessarily for the purpose of defense, while at other sites a rather thin wall simply delimited the boundary of the settlement. For many sites, the perimeter was not demarcated in any way.

We are under the general impression that there was no systematic attempt at fortification during early Iron I. It is possible that the security situation in most of the areas of Israelite Settlement did not require fortifications. But the case of 11th century 'Izbet Sartah Stratum II — which was unfortified despite its location opposite Philistine Aphek — perhaps suggests that the inhabitants of some small villages assumed themselves so powerless in the face of an enemy that they simply erected their outer buildings next to one another in order to create a kind of boundary wall. However, in a few places, such as Giloh, local conditions may have necessitated the construction of a defence wall; but this seems to be the exception that proves the rule.

The first real massive fortification wall of Iron Age date in the hill country found so far — at Khirbet ed-Dawara — was not built until the second half of the 11th century. The bulwarking of this small site with a solid wall up to 3 m thick was probably connected to the mobilization of the Israelites for the impending struggle against the Philistines over control of the hill country in general and the plateau of Benjamin in specific (see 1 Samuel 13). The fortifications of Khirbet ed-Dawara were actually the composite of a solid wall with casemate-like rooms built against it. At this early stage, it seems that no clear distinction was drawn between these two methods of fortification.

This leads to the issue of the origin of the casemate fortification wall. It had been widely accepted that this type of circumvallation first appeared in Anatolia in the 15th century BCE; from there, the concept was presumably brought to Syria by Hittites and then eventually reached our region in the 11th or 10th century BCE (e.g., Albright 1971:121). A few scholars subsequently observed that casemate-like fortifications appeared in the Land of Israel as early as the end of the Middle Bronze period (summarized by N. Lapp 1978:47).

The proponents of an Anatolian origin have failed to explain the lengthy time lag between its inception there and its appearance in Israel. On the other hand, it is also difficult to see the two segments of "casemates" adjacent to the Middle Bronze gates at Hazor and Shechem (at a time when this technique was not used in city walls proper) as the prototype of the casemate fortification walls surrounding Iron Age cities and towns (which would require an even longer time lag).

Other scholars have sought the origin of the casemate wall locally. Shiloh (1978:44–46) and Kempinski (1978:35–36) claimed that this type of fortification evolved from the broadrooms of four-room houses, which joined together to create a line of defense at the edge of sites such as Ai. A. Mazar (1981a:17) raised the possibility that casemate fortifications developed from peripheral boundary walls similar to those he unearthed at Giloh.

Our review of the evidence suggests a somewhat different line of development. The broadrooms of sites whose plan consisted of broadrooms around a central courtyard, e.g., ʿIzbet Ṣarṭah Stratum III and elliptical sites in the Negev Highlands — a plan which in turn was an outgrowth of the tent camps preceding sedentarization — was the source of the casemate concept. Four-room houses also developed from these peripheral casemate-like broadrooms — and not *vice versa*. The architectural progression, therefore, would have been from courtyard sites encompassed by a row of broadrooms, to sites with a peripheral belt of adjoining two-to-four room houses, and finally to the well-developed casemate fortification walls of the 10th century BCE. The fortification of Khirbet ed-Dawara might be an intermediate stage between villages like Ai and Beersheba Stratum VII and sites surraunded by genuin casemate walls.

Silos

One of the most outstanding characteristics of Israelite Settlement sites is the proliferation of pits for storing grain (on Iron Age silos in general see Currid 1986). They have been found at virtually every site excavated, from Beersheba in the south to Dan in the north. Generally, they were dug into the ground and lined with stones, but rock-cut silos have also been reported. So while the typical silo was stone-lined, in places where the bedrock was soft and the earthen accumulation insufficient, the alternative was to hew silos into the living rock. At many sites, the number of stone-lined silos was particularly striking.

At *Tell en-Naṣbeh*, more than 50 silos were encountered, the majority of them in the space between the "early wall" and the Iron II fortification wall. A fine exemplar was found in the courtyard of Building 2, a four-room house. The density of silos was quite remarkable in places: In squares AG 26 and AG 27 (Fig. 12), for example, in an area of 60 m^2 there were five complete silos and portions of three others (McCown 1947a:62,210,218–219).

Dozens of silos were excavated at *Tell Beit Mirsim*. Most of them belonged to Stratum B, which spanned Iron I and the 10th century BCE (Albright 1932:53,60–61; 1943:Plan of Stratum B). A quarter of these silos were associated with Stratum B1, which was believed to represent an occupation by Israelites before the Philistines took over that region (Chapter 3). In the southeastern sector, measuring about 2 dunams, 20 silos of Stratum B were found. At Tell Beit Mirsim, as at ʿIzbet Ṣarṭah, we are confronted with the phenomenon of silos cutting other silos. This indicates that the network of silos at a given site was subject to change. Actually, since our plans illustrate the aggregate of silos throughout the life of a stratum, it is probable that they were not all in use simultaneously.

At *Shiloh*, silos were uncovered in the northeastern and northern parts of the mound (Chapter 5). In a space of about 150 m^2 in Area D alone, we discovered 14 stone-lined silos, two of them filled with carbonized wheat.

Stratum 8 of Area X at *Aphek*, dated to the 10th century BCE, was the first Israelite level at the site. While the concentration of silos in it was less dense than at other sites, the silos themselves were larger (see below). A group of complete jars was discovered in one of them (Kochavi 1981:84).

At *Tel Zeror* (Stratum 8, Area C), many grain pits had been dug into the Late Bronze stratum (Ohata 1966:24).

Numerous pits were found in Stratum XII at *Hazor*. The field stones found inside them probably represent the original silo linings, which had collapsed over the course of time. In Area B alone, 22 of these pits were found in an area of only 575 m^2 (Yadin 1972:129–130).

At *Dan*, 25 silos of Stratum VI were encountered in Area B, some stone lined (Biran 1980:173).

89. ʿIzbet Ṣarṭah — Stratum II silos.

Large rock-cut pits that may have been used as silos were found at *Beersheba* in Stratum IX, the first occupation level at the site (Herzog 1984:10–11,70–71), and also at *Tell el-Fūl* (N. Lapp 1978:56–62), where they cannot be dated precisely (nor is it certain that all of them were used to store grain).

The site with the most impressive examples of Iron I silos is undoubtedly *ʿIzbet Ṣarṭah* (Finkelstein 1986:18–20, 124–128). A few silos had been dug in the central courtyard as early as Stratum III (12th century), while in Stratum II (late 11th century), 43 (!) silos were discovered. The latter were crowded together closely (sometimes even touching one another) in the space between the four-room house in the center of the site and the houses on the periphery of the settlement (Figs. 21, 89). These silos were lined with small and medium-size stones. They were paved with small pebbles, or else, the flat bedrock surface served as floor. Their diameters varied between 1 and 2 m, and their circumferences were round or elliptical in shape. Some of the silos leaned against the walls of buildings, which broke their curvilinear outlines. In a few places between the silos, remnants of the courtyard floor were encountered; it consisted of hard, thick, compacted plaster of a light color.

What is the meaning of this veritable explosion of silos in the period of Israelite Settlement? In the preceding Late Bronze period, only isolated silos were found at a limited number of sites, especially in the Shephelah (e.g., Tell Beit Mirsim, Albright 1932:51,61; Tel Ḥalif, Seger 1983:6; Beth-Shemesh, Grant and Wright 1939:55). The phenomenon was similarly scarce during the succeeding Iron II period.

The explanation is quite simple. A proliferation of silos generally characterizes groups in the process of sedentarization or societies organized in local rural frameworks. This phenomenon can be observed today in the settlements of newly-sedentarized Beduin at the edge of the Judean Desert and in the Negev, where the first structures erected were for the storage of grain and straw (Shimeoni 1947:133; Amiran and Ben-Arieh 1963:168: Shmueli 1973:33). Silage is the first problem for which such societies must find a permanent architectural solution.

On the other hand, in urban societies or under governmental organization, small silos are not encountered because better storage solutions have been found. In the royal centers of the Monarchy period, for example, large central storehouses or silos were established. Suffice it to note that the volume of the huge stone-lined silo (1414) at Megiddo was about 450 m^3 (Lamon and Shipton 1939:66), which meant it could hold three times more grain than all the silos of ʿIzbet Ṣarṭah combined. In other words, the proliferation of silos is, to a great degree, yet another clue to the socio-economic background of the inhabitants of these sites.

In our present state of knowledge, it is difficult to generalize either about the relationship between silos and buildings at Israelite Settlement sites or about the placement of silos in the overall site-plan. At many sites, the silos were discovered in architecturally-poor strata, leading their excavators to conclude that the inhabitants dwelled in huts or tents (e.g., Ohata 1966:30; Yadin 1972:129; Biran 1980:173). Yet these silos have also been found at well-developed villages such as Tell en-Naṣbeh and ʿIzbet Ṣarṭah Stratum II. It is possible that at some sites only the sectors devoted to storage have been excavated, and this would be the explanation for the seeming lack of houses.

The location of the silos within the settlement may have varied according to local conditions. In Stratum II at ʿIzbet Ṣarṭah, for example, the reason why the silos were dug in the area between the central building and the peripheral houses could have been the insecurity felt in a settlement situated near the Philistine coastal plain. Alternatively, the accumulation of earth toward the summit of the hill may have simply made it easier to dig silos there than in the bare rock just outside the houses.

Most of the silos found at Tell en-Naṣbeh were beyond the limits of the early village (i.e., before the big fortification wall was constructed), apparently because the houses had been built so close together. Similarly at Shiloh, the silos seem to have been dug outside the main building complex. At Shiloh, the silos were concentrated on the eastern side of the site, while at Tell en-Naṣbeh, they were found on the eastern and southern sides. The Iron I inhabitants may have prefered to locate their silos on these sides because they were warmer and less moist and hence more favorable for storing grain.

At other sites too, the silos may have been concentrated in one area, as suggested above for Hazor and Dan; at Tell Beit Mirsim, silos were found between the houses. There is no reason to suspect that the presence of these subterranean granaries would have interfered with the functioning of the open spaces between buildings (e.g., Tell Beit Mirsim and ʿIzbet Ṣarṭah), for the tops of the silos had been sealed and plastered over. Even if the ceilings of the silos were slightly domed, this would not have hindered human or even animal traffic in the area (Hyde *et. al.* 1973:18).

Only at Dan and Aphek were groups of ceramic vessels discovered inside the storage pits. The large number of vessels, some of them pithoi, found in the large grain pit in Area Y at Dan (Fig. 31) suggests that this pottery had, for whatever reason, been thrown in when the pit was no longer in use. The absence of ceramic vessels from the storage pits at other sites indicates that grain was typically stored either loose or in sacks to take full advantage of the silo's capacity. Provided that the granary was tightly sealed, carbon dioxide (CO_2) would have formed and repelled noxious pests.[21]

The size of the silos also varied according to local conditions. A comparison between ʿIzbet Ṣarṭah and Aphek illustrates this point. At ʿIzbet Ṣarṭah, where the earthen accumulation was not great, many shallow pits were cut, while at nearby Aphek, with its thick accumulation, the silos were larger, deeper, and spaced farther apart. But the overall storage capacity per dunam was similar at both sites:

	Avg. volume per silo	# silos per dunam	Avg. volume per dunam
ʿIzbet Ṣarṭah	1.28 m³	28	36 m³
Aphek (Area X, Str. 8)	3.40 m³	10	34 m³

The average silo capacity in Stratum B at Tell Beit Mirsim was 5.1 m³. Since there were about 10 silos per dunam, the average volume per dunam was 51 m³, which is approximately 45% greater than the two sites in the Yarkon region.

---

21 Despite these precautions, pests destroyed up to 20–25% of the grain stored in Arab villages at the beginning of the present century (Ilan 1974:26).

At a site like ʿIzbet Ṣarṭah, where a large part of the settlement was excavated and the plan is clear, silos may enable us to reconstruct various aspects of the local and regional agrarian economy. The surface area of the band of silos between the central building and the peripheral houses in Stratum II covered roughly 1,100 m². We excavated about 425 m² — 38% — of this area and found 43 silos. By extrapolating these results, we arrive at an estimate of 110 silos at the site. Where the courtyard floor was preserved, the average volume of the silos was 1.4 m³; multiplied by 110 silos, the total storage capacity would have been about 150 m³.

Rosen (1986) used this figure to estimate the amount of grain stored at the site, the acreage under cultivation, and the size of the population. Taking data about crop yields per dunam in the Land of Israel at the beginning of the present century and assuming that the relative ratio of wheat to barley — 2/3 to 1/3 — would not have been very different in antiquity, Rosen concluded that in an average year, 54 tons of wheat and 21 tons of barley, the harvest of 1,100 sown dunams, would have been stored away. If cereals were grown on a given plot only every other year, then the village would have had 2,200 dunams of land available for field crops. Subtracting the amounts of grain destroyed by pests and reserved for seed (some 30% of the yield) and taking into account the commonly accepted consumption factor of 200 kg per person per year, Rosen concluded that there had been about 190 inhabitants at ʿIzbet Ṣarṭah Stratum II.

By employing three other methods for calculating population size, lower estimates are obtained:

1. The size of the site in Stratum II was about 4 dunams. Using the widely accepted density factor of 25 persons per dunam (Broshi and Gophna 1984:148; Brawer 1984:8–15), the population would have been about 100 villagers. (A density of 25 persons per dunam may even be a bit high for open agrarian settlements such as ʿIzbet Ṣarṭah.)

2. According to Naroll (1962), each person requires about 10 m² of built and roofed living space. In Stratum II at ʿIzbet Ṣarṭah, an area of 1,550 m² was built up, and of this, some 1,150 m² were covered. Dividing by his constant, the village would have had about 115 inhabitants.

3. In Stratum II, according to our estimates, there were about 20 ordinary houses around the perimeter of the village and one large house in the center. If an average of 4.2 people lived in each house,[22] the population of the settlement would have numbered 90–95 residents.

---

22 In the 1920s, each household in the Arab villages in the hill country had an average of 4.4 members (calculated according to data from Mills 1933). In 1871, the average was even

These three methods of calculation lead us to the conclusion that the inhabitants of ʿIzbet Ṣarṭah Stratum II — about 100 people, not 190 — enjoyed a large surplus of grain. This accords well with the agrarian character and geography of the region. Data from the period of the Mandate show that Arab villages in the vicinity, similarly situated on the border between the foothills and the coastal plain, were primarily involved in raising field crops, devoting 95% of their cultivated lands to cereals (see Table in Chapter 4). Calculating the volume of grain produced in the five villages closest to ʿIzbet Ṣarṭah (according to *Village Statistics*, 1945), we find that on the average, they had twice as much grain per person as they could consume — similar to the nearby ancient site. The inhabitants of ʿIzbet Ṣarṭah would have traded their surplus grain, probably to the small villages established by then on the slopes of the hills, where the topography was not conducive to growing field crops (Chapter 4), receiving olive oil and wine in exchange.

The data from ʿIzbet Ṣarṭah may be compared to those from another site that was almost entirely exposed: Tell en-Naṣbeh (McCown 1947a:Plan). While we cannot determine when in the course of the Iron Age the silos there were cut, even if we assume, for the sake of argument, that they were all in use in Iron I, the results are instructive.

Just over 50 stone-lined silos were discovered at Tell en- Naṣbeh. If we assume (based on the published plan) that there had originally been 70–75 silos, each with an average volume of 1.9 m³, then the total storage capacity was similar to that of ʿIzbet Ṣarṭah Stratum II. The area of the early village at Tell en-Nasbeh (inside the "early wall") was roughly 22 dunams; at about 25 persons per dunam, there would have been approximately 500 inhabitants. Even if we have underestimated the storage capacity, the amount of grain per person at the site was still considerably less than at ʿIzbet Ṣarṭah. It is therefore doubtful whether the wheat produced in the vicinity of the site met the needs of its inhabitants. So the people of Mizpah must have been seriously engaged in horticulture. They would have supplemented their insufficient yields of wheat by trading olive oil and perhaps wine for cereals with the villages of the desert fringe, for example (for the socio-political implication of such exchange see Finkelstein, forthcoming c).

lower — 3.6 persons per family (calculated according to data from Sochin 1879). It follows that the figure used by Shiloh (1980:277) — 8 persons per household — is far too high.

CHAPTER 7

IRON I POTTERY IN THE CENTRAL HILL COUNTRY

OVERVIEW

During the Iron I period, there were striking differences between the ceramic assemblages of the coastal plain, the Shephelah, and the northern valleys on the one hand, and the hilly interior regions on the other (A. Mazar 1977:345). The lowlands can be divided into two "ceramic units": the southern coastal plain and the Shephelah, where the Philistines and their distinctive pottery were strong; and those areas where a significant Canaanite presence meant the continuation of Late Bronze ceramic traditions. The pottery of the hill country, where the Israelites settled, had been somewhat distinctive already during earlier periods; now, however, it differed sharply from the pottery of the low-lying regions. The causes of these regional ceramic differences were environmental, social, economic and cultural.

While excavating at Tell el-Fūl in the 1920s, Albright identified, for the first time, the ceramic features of the new material culture that appeared in the central hill country of the Land of Israel in Iron I. Chief among these was the collared-rim store jar, which many came to regard as the prime criterion of an Israelite Settlement site. Six decades later, many aspects of Israelite Settlement pottery in general and the collared-rim store jars in specific, still need clarification.

The manner in which the results of the older excavations at Beth-zur, Bethel, Tell el-Fūl, Shiloh and Ai were published precludes any quantitative examination of the advent of pottery types — and without such analyses, our understanding cannot be advanced. Other excavations either remain unpublished (e.g., Khirbet Raddana and the new work at Ai) or else the finds were very meager (e.g., the "Bull Site" in Samaria). At present, the only sites offering a full ceramic perspective are Giloh, Kh. ed-Dawara, Mt. Ebal and ʿIzbet Ṣarṭah (A. Mazar 1981a:18–31; Zertal 1986b:251–265; Finkelstein 1986:38–93). While their finds elucidate a few aspects of early Israelite pottery, before a synthetic work can be undertaken we must await the systematic publication both of excavations at other sites in the central hill country and Galilee and of the intensive surveys currently underway all over the country.

Since we thus cannot discuss the pottery of Israelite Settlement comprehensively, we will confine ourselves to exploring several aspects that have been illuminated by recent excavations. In evaluating the pottery of Iron I in the hill country — or of any other period and place, for that matter — five variables must be considered: the prevailing environmental conditions, the socio-economic status of the populace, relations with neighboring regions, the influence of the preceding period, and the previous socio-economic and environmental background of the groups under discussion.

It has long been apparent that the repertoire of vessels at Israelite Settlement sites in the hilly regions was extremely limited (see the recent discussion by Kempinski 1985). In both Upper Galilee and the central hill country, the overwhelming majority of the vessels in Iron I ceramic assemblages were pithoi and cooking pots (e.g., A. Mazar 1981a:31; Sinclair 1960:Pls. 20–21).

Regionalism was a prominent feature of Iron I ceramics. Assemblages from Israelite Settlement sites in different sectors of the country betray their local character, which is perceptible in the shapes of vessels and sometimes in the variety of the repertoire. For example, the pithoi of Upper Galilee were different in form from those of the central hill country, and these differences arose from the influence of local ceramic traditions in each region. The pithoi in Upper Galilee were of two subtypes (Chapter 3): the "Galilean," which recalled the Late Bronze pithoi of Hazor (Fig. 30); and the "Tyrian," which was apparently influenced by the Phoenician coast (Fig. 31). In the central hill country, on the other hand, the pithoi — none other than the famous collared-rim store jars — recalled the ones in use there during the Middle Bronze period (see below).

The differences between cooking pots are primarily evident in their rims. In the Beersheba Valley, for example, a cooking pot with a simple rim, barely convex on the outside and slightly concave on the inside (Fig. 7:5), was popular toward the end of the 11th century BCE, while in Upper Galilee, the contemporary cooking pot rim was slanting, elongated, and sometimes slightly concave on the outside; it terminated in a long tongue (Figs. 30, 32). Both of these types were virtually unknown in Ephraim, where the typical cooking pot rim was vertical and varied in profile (Chapter 4). Although most widespread in the 12th century, it was still found in considerable quantities in the mid-11th century, e.g., at Shiloh on the eve of destruction. As we noted in our discussion of the pottery from sites in Ephraim (Chapter 4), minor local variations in the shapes of vessels could be detected even within a relatively limited geographical area.

Another striking feature of the pottery from Israelite Settlement sites, especially in the central hill country, is the tremendous variety of rim profiles within each type. Two identical pithos rims or two identical cooking pot rims are virtually never encountered, even in a rich assemblage such as that unearthed during the recent excavations at Shiloh.

There were pronounced differences in the degree of variety within a ceramic repertoire from one region to another. This observation may have chronological implications. In any case, it sheds light on the connections between the inhabitants of the various geographical regions and their surroundings. Fewer types were present in the assemblages from the interior hilly areas of the country than at sites in the vicinity of the coastal plain and the valleys; within each region, however, the repertoire at earlier sites was more limited than that at later sites. The following table, which demonstrates these factors (data reflect percentages of entire assemblage), will also be quoted in later discussions.

Site	Giloh	ʿIzbet Ṣarṭah**			Mt. Ebal***		Kh. ed-Dawara**
Stratum		III	II	I	II	I	
Date	early 12th cent.	12th cent.	late 11th cent.	early 10th cent.	late 13th–early 12th cent.	late 12th cent.(?)	late 11th–10th cent.
Source	Mazar 1981a	Finkelstein 1986			Zertal 1986b		unpub-lished
Cooking pot with everted rim	14.8	1.9	0.7	0.5	1.8	1.2	0.6
Cooking pot with vertical rim	11.8	3.1	4.4	3.1	2.6	5.0	4.0
Other cooking pots	–	8.2	10.2	17.3	–	–	18.7
Bowls and kraters	9.4	27.9	15.7	18.6	20.0	25.3	9.9
Jugs	11.8*	8.0	19.0	14.6	19.3	17.3	17.0
Collared-rim store jars	33.7	4.8	2.6	2.3	28.5	30.0	6.8
Other store jars	16.6	13.0	11.1	11.6	11.6	6.0	5.7
Other vessels	–	33.1	36.3	32.0	16.2	15.2	37.3
Slipped/burnished material	–	2.9	9.1	16.6	–	–	1.7
Handles with incisions and holes	one pub-lished	–	two handles	–	3.2	7.3	–

* With juglets.
** Bases were also included in the calculation.
*** The fact that Mt. Ebal was a cultic site also influenced the nature of the assemblage.

Giloh — a remote and isolated early 12th-century settlement on rocky terrain — clearly illustrates this point. Cooking pots and collared-rim store jars

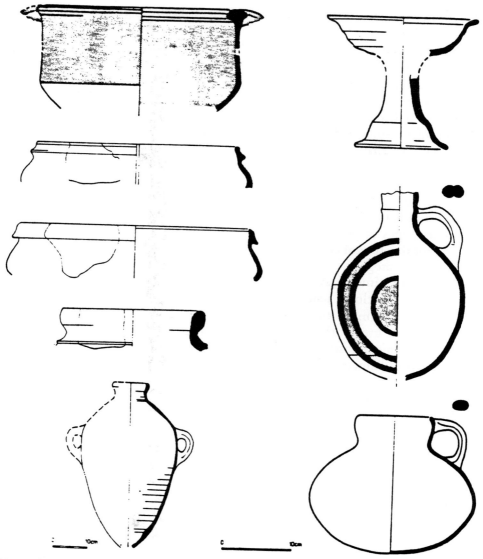

90. ʿIzbet Ṣarṭah — pottery of Stratum II.

comprised 60% of the ceramic assemblage. There was more variety in the mid-11th century at Shiloh — and perhaps at Bethel and Tell en- Naṣbeh as well. In stark contrast to Giloh, the repertoire at ʿIzbet Ṣarṭah, near the coastal plain, was much more diverse. In Stratum III, cooking pots and pithoi comprised only 19% of the assemblage. At this site, too, the assemblage became richer in time (Fig. 90). Kh. ed-Dawara represents a pottery assemblage from the heart of the hill country from a somewhat later Iron Age date. Of special interest is

273

the limited number of slipped/burnished sherds in this region even in the 10th century BCE.

The reasons underlying the special character of the Settlements sites pottery must be sought in the social background of the Israelite settlers. At the beginning of the sedentarization process, they comprised small and isolated groups, who settled down in relatively inhospitable regions that were difficult to traverse and were engaged in an ongoing struggle against natural elements. The meager resources of these groups, their lack of social organization beyond the clan level, the absence of a well-established ceramic tradition, their isolation from the prosperous regions of the country, the presence of pockets of Canaanites among the blocs of Israelite settlers, and the relative isolation from other sites even within regions of Israelite Settlement — all these factors led to a situation whereby the inhabitants used only the most basic and necessary types of pottery: pithoi and cooking pots; on the other hand, the strictly local nature of ceramic manufacture led to the great variety of subtypes within each category.

The more time passed and the phenomenon of settlement became entrenched, the closer a site was to the coastal plain or northern valleys, the better the economic situation, and the broader the social frameworks that evolved — the greater the variety of forms in the ceramic repertoire. It follows that the ceramic industry of the Iron II period in the hill country was, in many respects, the diametric opposite of its Iron I predecessor. The number of different types was greater, but within each type, the vessels were remarkably uniform, with few subtypes and variants. Organization into a state spelled the end of regional isolation. Trade and other connections between the various regions increased, and centralized workshops apparently supplied at least a portion of the vessels in use.

In recent years, several scholars have described the pottery of the Israelite Settlement period as the direct descendants of Late Bronze ceramics (Miller 1977a:255,262; Franken 1975a:337; Kempinski 1985:403). Proponents of the "sociological school" of thought have siezed upon such pronouncements to support their view that the Iron I Israelites originated directly from the Canaanite centers of the preceding period (e.g., de Geus 1976:167; Ahlström 1984a:49). While this is no doubt a reasonable description of the ceramic situation in the regions where occupation was continuous from one period to the next — as in the northern valleys and parts of the coastal plain — it is not as applicable to the pottery of the hill country.

Although it is possible to point to a certain degree of continuity in a few types, the ceramic assemblage of the Israelite Settlement sites, taken as a whole, stands in sharp contrast to the repertoire of the Canaanite centers: a few coarse vessel types with numerous variants *versus* a plethora of well-formed shapes, each of which was quite uniform throughout most of the country. Nor is it surprising to find points of similarity to Canaanite pottery, for groups lacking an established ceramic culture would, when undergoing the process of sedentarization, be likely to absorb traditions from the well-developed cultures in their vicinity, especially if they had contacts with the settled people before their sedentarization. In any case, differences in pottery should not be explained away as simply ethnic in nature, but must instead be seen in the broader socio-economic and cultural setting (more on this in Chapter 11).

COLLARED-RIM STORE JARS

By "collared-rim store jar," we refer strictly to the type found in the central hill country (Fig. 91), not to the jars from Upper Galilee, although many have

91. Collared rim jars at Shiloh (Area C).

erroneously discussed both types in the same breath (Sinclair 1960:18; Rast 1978:9; Ibrahim 1978:122; Callaway 1969a:9; Gal 1982b:58). The term "collared-rim store jar" was coined by Albright in the 1920s, when he excavated at Tell el-Fūl, and it was he who realized that it was characteristic of the material culture of the central hill country in Iron I (Albright 1937:25; 1940a:548; 1971:118). In recent years, the collared-rim store jar has returned to the limelight, with discussions focusing on its origin, the date of its debut, its division into subtypes, and, especially, the ethnic identity of its makers. Given the amount of new evidence that has been unearthed, a fresh summary of the subject is now in order, even though unequivocal answers to these questions are not yet within our grasp.

Division into subtypes

This was a major preoccupation of scholars in the past. In light of the *Tell el-Fūl* excavations, Sinclair claimed that a type transitional between the collared-rim store jar and the later Iron Age jars was abundant in fortresses I and II. In his opinion, this transitional type overlapped briefly with the collared-rim store jars in the middle of the 11th century BCE (Sinclair 1960:16–18). But an examination of the published plates to which he made reference shows that all of these vessels are simply classical collared-rim store jars with slight variations in rim form.

The excavators of *Bethel* discerned two types of Iron I jars, one with a folded rim and high collar, and a later one with a heavy folded rim incurving at its lower end. In their opinion, the former was used in the first three building phases of Iron I, while the latter appeared at that time, but continued into Iron II (Kelso 1968:63).

At *Ai*, Callaway (1969a:8–9) distinguished two phases of Iron I (Chapter 3), each with its own subtype of collared-rim store jar (Fig. 92). The first jar had a short neck, relatively narrow rim and long collar reaching down to the shoulder. While this type continued to be present in the second phase, the typical store jar now had a folded rim, which was previously unknown.

Rast (1978:9) described two similar subtypes at *Taanach*, but his chronological order was the inverse of Callaway's: the earlier type (which he thought to be still influenced by Late Bronze jars) had a thick rim and long neck with a ridge at its lower end, while the later type had a short neck, thinner rim, and ridge closer to the lip. He dated the former to the 12th century, while the latter continued, in his opinion, to the end of Iron I.

The excavations at Giloh, ʿIzbet Ṣarṭah, Mt. Ebal and Shiloh have shown that there are no grounds for a clear-cut chronological ordering of the appearance of subtypes of collared-rim store jars (A. Mazar 1981a:28–29; Finkelstein 1986:77–84; Zertal 1986b:254). At *Shiloh*, for example, in the destruction layer of the mid-11th century, jars with narrow and thick rims, tall

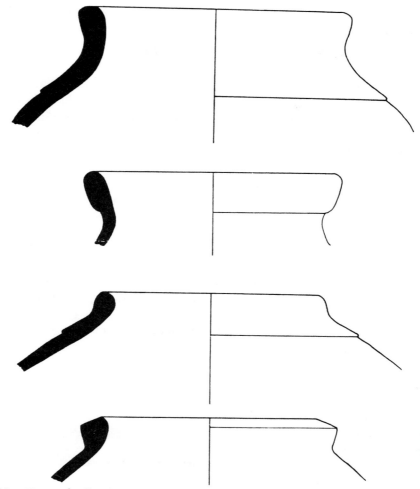

92. Types of collared rim jars at Ai according to Callaway (1969a: 8. Scale 1:3).

and short necks, etc., were all found together (Fig. 73). While a statistical analysis may some day indicate quantitative variability of the subtypes over the course of Iron I, the 'longevity' of these huge pithoi may impede any such analysis.

In any case, at 'Izbet Ṣarṭah we attempted to analyse quantitatively the different rim forms in the three strata. Since the rim generally survived with the ridge broken off, unless the entire profile could be restored, the relative placement of the ridge could not be determined (this also holds true for the Callaway's second subtype at Ai). We therefore chose rim thickness as the variable to test. The number of samples was not large, so it is possible that the results are random, though I feel they are significant. In Stratum III, the thick folded rim dominated the thinner, less profiled lip: 62.5% *versus* 37.5%, while in Stratum I, the thinner rim was most common: 80%.

Decoration

To date, ornamentation has been found on only the handles and rims of collared-rim store jars.[23] Decoration on the handles consisted of holes (Fig. 53:9), varying in number and arrangement; perhaps these variations had some kind of administrative significance. Two types of decoration have been found on the rims:

1. Reed impressions — These usually appeared in an evenly-spaced row, although the size of the reed marks and the distance between them varied from jar to jar. Since a complete rim of this type has not yet been discovered, we do not know whether the decoration continued around the entire circumference. Rim sherds with one, two, or three impressions have been found in the Manasseh survey, at Mt. Ebal (Zertal 1986b Figs. 14:7, 26:7), Shiloh (Fig. 93) and at five sites surveyed in the territory of Ephraim (Chapter 4, Table 4, Column 7 with ***). Another was found at Tell el-Fūl (Sinclair 1960:Pl.20:2), where a collared-rim displaying a row of punctures was also unearthed (Albright 1924:Pl.28:24; see Zertal 1986b Figs. 21:24, 22:11 for similar rims).

93.   Shiloh — rims of collared rim jars decorated with reed impressions.

---

23   Except for a jar from Taanach (Rast 1978:Fig.35:1), whose body bears incisions like those on northern pithoi (e.g., Yadin *et al.* 1961:Pls.CLXVII-CLXVIII).

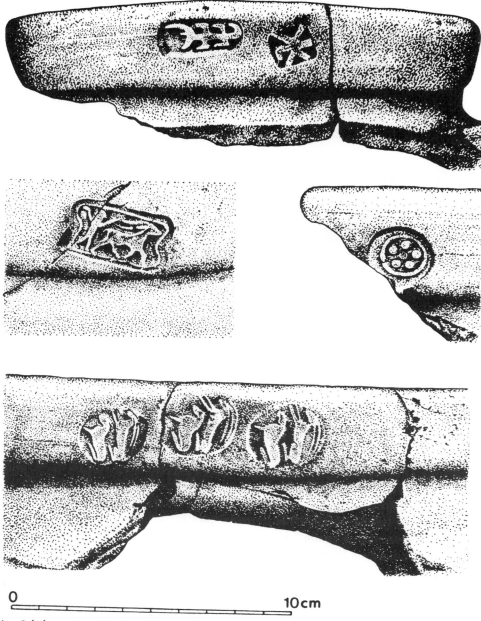

94. Saḥab — rims of collared rim jars decorated with seal impressions (Ibrahim 1978: 120).

Interestingly enough, these reed impressions have also been found on the rims of pithoi from Galilee. A rim with three marks arranged in a triangle was

95. Shiloh — rim of collared rim jar decorated with impressions.

found at Khirbet Shufnîn in Upper Galilee (Aharoni 1957:Pl.V:3), and a sherd with a single reed impression was found at Ḥorvat ᶜAvot.[24]

2. Seal impressions — This type of rim decoration has so far been found at only two sites. At Saḥab in Transjordan (Fig. 94), Ibrahim found collared-rim store jars whose rims had been stamped with seals bearing images of animals (and a human figure). One rim displayed three identical rosette impressions, while another bore a single rosette (Ibrahim 1978:117,120–121; 1983:48–50). At Shiloh, we recently found an almost complete rim with three impressions of rosettes or stars (Fig. 95).

Chronology

Albright thought that collared-rim store jars were in use between 1175 BCE and 1050–1020 BCE (1940a:548; 1971:118; see also Sinclair 1960:26). Today, however, it is clear that this span must be extended in both directions. The earliest example presently known was found in the destruction level of the Egypto-Canaanite governor's residency of Aphek (Beck and Kochavi 1985:34, 40), a building that was destroyed in the second half or at the end of the 13th century BCE (*ibid*; Kochavi 1981:78–79; on the chronological implications of this find, see Chapter 9). Sherds from collared-rim store jars have been unearthed in transitional LB-Iron I levels at Megiddo VIIB (Loud 1948:Pls.64:8,83:4; see Yadin 1979:64) and Tell Keisan, where it appeared

---

24 I thank E. Braun, the excavator of the site, for permitting me to mention this find.

together with Mycenaean IIIC1a pottery (Balenci 1981:399).[25] However, both strata should apparently be dated to the early 12th-century.[26]

Collared-rim store jars clearly reached their zenith in the 12th and 11th centuries BCE, but they were still recovered from strata of the first half of the 10th century: Taanach IIB, Megiddo VB, Tell Qasile X-IX, and ʿIzbet Ṣarṭah I (Rast 1978:Pl.35:1; A. Mazar 1977:297 (Qasile), 298 (Megiddo); Finkelstein 1986:76–77). Because these huge jars were placed upright and left stationary, they were likely to remain in use for a long time. They would thus be found in 10th-century levels even if their manufacture had ceased by the end of the 11th century. The quantitative evidence from ʿIzbet Ṣarṭah is instructive here as well. The proportion of jars with collared-rims among all types of jars decreased from 27% in Stratum III to 17% in Stratum I. As a percentage of the total ceramic assemblage, collared-rim store jars decreased from 4.8% to 2.3% during this span (Finkelstein 1986:76).

Distribution

This important issue has repercussions for the questions of source, use, and ethnic affiliation. To date, only the geographical distribution of collared-rim store jars has been examined (Ibrahim 1978:121–122; A. Mazar 1981a:23–29), but the quantitative aspect is no less significant.

Geographical distribution — Collared-rim store jars have been found from the desert fringe of Transjordan west to the Mediterranean, south to the Hebron Hills and northward into Lower Galilee.

In Transjordan they are presently known from Khirbet Abu- Banna in the south (Weippert 1982:Fig.8:9) to the Yarmuk River in the north. As for Israel, not even one collared-rim store jar has been published from any of the four Iron I sites in the Beersheba Valley, so the southernmost site where such rims have been found is Khirbet Rabud near Dhahariyeh (Kochavi 1974:Fig.5:12).

They were used as far north as the Jezreel Valley — at Megiddo, Tel Qiri, Afula, Beth Shean — and near Acco at Tel Keisan (Loud 1948:Pl.83:4; Ben-Tor 1979:109; M. Dothan 1955:Fig.11:25; Fitzgerald 1930:Pl.XLIV:18; Briend and Humbert 1980:Pl.68:1), as well as at sites in southern Lower Galilee (Gal 1982b:58,84). But they were unknown either in the northern part of Lower Galilee or in Upper Galilee — except at Tel Dan, where a type close to the collared-rim store jar of the central hill country was found (Biran 1980:174; 1985:187,Pl.24:c).

25 In order to date the infant burials in collared-rim store jars at Tel Zeror (Beck and Kochavi 1985:34; Kochavi 1978:1224), we must await the publication of the finds discovered in them.

26 It should be recalled that a fragment of a statue of Ramesses VI was discovered under a wall of Stratum VIIb (Loud 1948:135,n.1).

Collared-rim store jars reached the coast in the vicinity of the Yarkon River and to its north (A. Mazar 1977:297; Stern 1978:68,Fig.19:4). In the Shephelah, however, they did not traverse an imaginary line running from Beth-Shemesh to Tell Beit Mirsim; none have been found at Gezer or Tel Baṭash (A. Mazar 1981a:28).

Quantitative distribution — At early Iron I sites in the central hill country, collared-rim store jars comprise up to a third of the ceramic assemblage (A. Mazar 1981a:31; Zertal 1986b:254), but as one approaches the edges of the hills and the neighboring regions, their number decreases. Thus this type made up only 2.3–4.8% of the assemblage at ʿIzbet Ṣarṭah, depending on the stratum, or 3.2% of all the pottery excavated at the site (Finkelstein 1986:76). Only a few of these jars were found at Tell Beit Mirsim and Beth Shemesh in the Shephelah (Albright 1971:18; Grant and Wright 1939:129). During all the years of excavation at Tell Qasile, a grand total of five sherds and one complete jar of this type were unearthed, leading the excavator to the justifiable conclusion that they were foreign to the site (A. Mazar 1977:296–297). The relative amounts of collared-rim store jars in and around the Jezreel Valley are not yet certain, but the quantities do not seem large. Their numbers within a given assemblage also decrease at late Iron I hill country sites, e.g. Kh.ed-Dawara (see table).

In summary, only in northern Transjordan and in the central hill country of the Land of Israel were collared-rim store jars widely used. The geographical distribution must therefore be connected either to the function of these jars or to the identity of the people who manufactured them and used them extensively.

Function

As we observed in summarizing the distribution of the various types of vessels collected during the survey of Ephraim (Chapter 4), collared-rim store jars comprised a relatively small proportion of the pottery in the desert fringe (40%), while on the southern slopes, these jars were very frequent (68%). In other words, they were more popular in areas where horticulture was extensive than in areas devoted to field crops.

This generalization is valid for other areas of Israelite Settlement as well. At ʿIzbet Ṣarṭah, located in a strictly grain-growing region (Chapter 4, Table 2, right-hand column), collared-rim store jars were few in number, while they were completely lacking in the Beersheba Valley. Their geographical distribution thus indicates that collared-rim store jars were primarily associated with hilly regions, and within them, with those areas where horticulture predominated, as the following observations further indicate:

In Areas C and E at Shiloh, a large number of complete collared-rim store jars were unearthed *in situ* in the debris of the fierce conflagration; none of them contained any carbonized grain. There is definite evidence at Shiloh that cereals were stored in silos. On the other hand, in Area C, near the collared-rim store jars, a pile of carbonized raisins was discovered (Fig. 74), and in Area E these jars were found in a rock-hewn industrial installation.

Based on the settlement pattern arising from the survey in the hill country of Manasseh, Zertal has recently (1985a; 1986b:305–313) raised the possibility that the collared-rim store jars were used primarily for storing water. In his opinion, it was these jars, not rock-hewn cisterns, which enabled the Israelites to settle in places distant from permanent water sources. One flaw in this theory is the fact that in Ephraim, these jars were common at sites in areas with abundant and stable supplies of water nearby.

All of these observations combine to indicate that collared-rim store jars were used for storing various types of liquids: olive oil, wine and water. (On their use for burials at Saḥab and Tel Zeror see Ibrahim 1978:122–123; Beck and Kochavi 1985:34).

Origin

The question of origin is one of the knottier problems concerning collared-rim store jars. To the best of our knowledge, they did not appear in strata of the Late Bronze period, with the single exception of the jar from Aphek. It may be, however, that even before that site was destroyed in the second half of the 13th century BCE, new elements had already begun to settle on the hills to the east of the city, and these groups could have been the source of the jar found at Aphek (Chapter 9). In any case, none of these jars has ever been found at Bethel, Dothan, Tell Farᶜa or Shechem (Toombs 1979:70), the principal Late Bronze sites in the hill country that have been excavated. Accordingly, there is no validity to Kempinski's theory (1985:401) that pithoi were manufactured in Canaanite centers for Israelite villages.

On the other hand, we cannot ignore the resemblance between collared-rim store jars and MB IIB-C pithoi from sites in the hill country. (Many scholars have seen parallels in Late Bronze store jars from Hazor, but such comparisons are valid only for the Galilean pithoi.) Collared-rim store jars are similar in size to Middle Bronze pithoi, which were common in the central hill country. Some Middle Bronze jars also had thickened rims and occasionally even a ridge on the shoulder (Fig. 96), although it was less pronounced than the ridge on Iron I collared-rim store jars. In this context, it should be recalled that many of the Israelite Settlement sites in the central hill country had previously been occupied during the Middle Bronze period. This was true, for example, of all 12 Iron I sites in the Dothan Valley (Zertal 1984:153,155) and of about a quarter of the Israelite Settlement sites in the territory of Ephraim. We therefore cannot preclude the possibility that the new settlers copied older

96. Shiloh — a group of Middle Bronze IIC jars (Buhl and Holm Nielsen 1969: 40).

pithoi, whose sherds were scattered all over these sites, and even reused jars found still intact.[27]

Ethnic affiliation

This, of course, has become the Big Question. Albright was the first to recognize that collared-rim store jars were characteristic of Iron I sites in the central hill country, but nowhere did he claim that they were exclusive to the Israelite population. Aharoni had no such qualms; for him, the discovery of collared-rim store jars in Stratum VI at Megiddo was proof that Israelites already inhabited the site (1970:264–265). In light of his excavations at Saḥab in Transjordan, Ibrahim rejected the notion that collared-rim store jars represented a single ethnic group, preferring to connect their use with certain socio-economic traditions (1978:124; see also Weippert 1971:134–135).

27 In Building 335 of Area C at Shiloh, seven collared-rim store jars were found standing in a row, together with one additional smaller jar (Fig. 73, lower left), which had rope decoration around its neck and, on both of its handles, impressions of a geometric Egyptian seal of a type known elsewhere in the hill country during the Middle Bronze period. In this case, at least, the people of Shiloh apparently reused a jar that was centuries old!

Summary

The data we have presented demonstrates that the distribution of collared-rim store jars was densest in the regions of Israelite Settlement, and at these sites, this type generally dominated the ceramic assemblage. Collared-rim store jars were unknown in these regions prior to the commencement of Israelite Settlement. On the other hand, collared-rim store jars have been found — albeit in small quantities — at sites in the coastal plain, the northern valleys and Transjordan (e.g., Tell Qasile, Megiddo and Saḥab), locales where, as far as we know, Israelites did not settle at the time. Therefore, the discovery of collared-rim store jars at a given site cannot be used to indicate the ethnic identity of its inhabitants. The jars were manufactured primarily in the regions of Israelite Settlement, but also traveled to neighboring districts — Ammon, Philistia and the Canaanite enclaves.

Collared-rim store jars made their debut at the end of the 13th century BCE. In certain respects, they resemble the large storage vessels in use during the Middle Bronze period. How extensively the collared-rim store jars were used also depended on the nature of the regional economy, for this vessel was generally typical of areas of the hill country that were engaged in horticulture.

Collared-rim store jars vanished in the 10th century BCE, at the beginning of the Monarchy period. At first glance, this would seem to be surprising, for it was precisely during that era that the olive oil and wine industries flourished in the hill country. However, large pithoi, which were too awkward to transport, were more suitable for use in a relatively self-sufficient society, that did not conduct trade on a very large scale. But during the period of the Monarchy, when trade and commerce between the various regions of the country was lively and entire families and settlements became specialized (Eitam 1979), the jars of choice were smaller and more convenient for marketing.

Further advances in knowledge about the pottery of Israelite Settlement sites in general, and collared-rim store jars in specific, must await the systematic publication — including quantitative data — of additional excavations in various regions of the country, especially at sites where stratigraphic distinctions within the Iron I period can be drawn. In this respect, we are especially anxious to broaden our knowledge of Transjordanian pottery. Great importance should be attached to the results of petrographic studies which, we hope, will enable us to grapple with the questions of the origin of these vessels, the methods of their manufacture, and the commercial habits of the people who made them.

HANDLES WITH INCISIONS AND HOLES

Handles of pithoi, jars, and jugs, marked with incisions or holes before firing (Fig. 97), were very common at Israelite Settlement sites in the hill country.

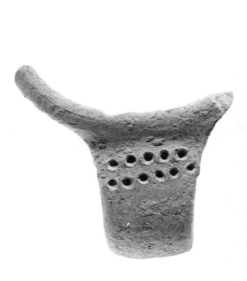 

97. Punctured handles from Shiloh.

The punctured handles featured either a single punch, two or three holes arranged in a vertical or horizontal line, or an array of many perforations. At Shiloh, we found handles with as many as 7–11 holes arranged in rows.

Punctured handles are known from Giloh, Tell el-Fūl, Tell en-Naṣbeh, Bethel, ʿIzbet Ṣarṭa , Mt. Ebal, Tell el-Farʿa, Taanach, Afula and Megiddo (A. Mazar 1981a: Fig. 9:7; N. Lapp 1978: Pl. 50:33–35; McCown 1947a: 252; Kelso 1968: Pls. 40,72:468; Finkelstein 1986: 15:28; Zertal 1986b. Figs 13,16; Chambon 1984: Pl. 79; Rast 1978: Figs. 6:1,26:2,31:6,32:2; M. Dothan 1955: Fig. 11:32,16:27; Lamon and Shipton 1939: Pl. 42). Many were excavated at Shiloh and picked up during surveys in Ephraim and Manasseh. In Ephraim (Chapter 4 Table of pottery types), most of these handles were found in the northern part of the region, which accords well with their frequency in the neighboring territory of Manasseh, where the decorated handles are popular mainly in the eastern part of the region. In Ephraim they were found at 26% of the sites, while in Manasseh they are more common — 44% of the sites surveyed (Zertal 1986b:289–294).

As for chronology, punctured handles made their debut at the beginning of the 12th century (Giloh, Mt. Ebal, Taanach IA) and continued to appear into the 10th century (Taanach IIB, Megiddo V) and perhaps even later (Yadin *et al.* 1958: Pl. LXXXIV:8–10). In any case, in Ephraim, they were never found at single-period Iron II sites. Zertal has suggested that they originated in eastern Manasseh and later dispersed to neighbouring regions (1986b:293).

Whether the holes had some kind of administrative significance or whether they were purely decorative is impossible to determine until more examples of complete vessels with these handles come to light. To date, the collection of whole vessels consists of a complete jug from Taanach IIB with three punctures on its handle (Rast 1978:Fig.16:2) and two collared-rim store jars from Shiloh, one with 7 holes perforating a handle and the other with 11 bores on one of its handles. Since a jug handle bearing 11 perforations was also found at Shiloh, the number of holes apparently had nothing to do with the capacity of the vessel.

Another handle, found only on pithoi and jars, was marked with a pair of holes flanking a vertical incision, giving the appearance of a schematic human face (Fig. 98). Zertal (1985:42) was the first to discern this type, which we subsequently found to be typical of Iron I during our survey. They have been found at Tell en-Naṣbeh (McCown 1947a:252:37), at Shiloh, in the northern reaches of Ephraim (Chapter 4, Table 4), and in the hill country of Manasseh. These markings seem to be strictly ornamental; insufficient evidence currently prevents greater certainty.

98.   Shiloh — handle with an incised schematic face.

Vessels Decorated with Figures in Relief

The phenomenon of relief images ornamenting ordinary vessels (as opposed to zoomorphic vessels) was known all across the country in Iron I. We shall first describe the finds from Israelite Settlement sites in the hill country:

99. Tell en-Naṣbeh — a sherd with applied relief of an animal (courtesy of the Department of Antiquities).

A small sherd bearing the relief of a horned animal (Fig. 99) was discovered at *Tell en-Naṣbeh* (Wampler 1947:186,Pl.79:1834; on sherd 1836 there also appears to be relief decoration; see also *ibid*: 186). The same site yielded the handle of a large vessel with an animal head at its lower end (McCown 1947a:Pl.89:23). Neither piece could be dated accurately.

On a multihandled krater[28] from *Khirbet Raddana* (Fig. 15), a kind of tube

28 The multihandled krater was widespread throughout the country during Iron I, especially in the hill country. The krater from Dothan (see below) had 16 handles. On half of a krater from Raddana there were 8 handles. At Shiloh, we found a krater with 7 handles on one half (Fig. 73). A fragment with 8 handles was published from Tell en-Naṣbeh (Wampler 1947:Pl.65:1480).

Outside the hill country, multihandled kraters have been found at Jenin (Zori 1977:Fig.17), Megiddo VIA (Loud 1948:Pl.79:2), Tel Qiri (Ben-Tor 1979:44), Kfar Yehoshua (Druks 1966:215), Tell Jemmeh (Petrie 1928:Pl.LI:289) and Tel Masos (Fritz and Kempinski 1983 Pl. 150:7). A different type of multihandeled kraters was encountered at Beth Shean (Fitzgerald 1930 Pl. XLVI:13,14), Dan (Biran 1980:176), Taanach IIB (Rast 1978: Fig. 41) and elsewhere (on this subject, see Kempinski 1985:402).

100.   Bethel — handle decorated with a human face in relief (Kelso 1968: Pl. 44).

encircles the entire vessel just below the rim and opens to the inside via two bovine (?) heads (Callaway and Cooley 1971:15–19).

A human face was modeled at the base of a jar handle from *Bethel* (Fig. 100). The handle has been dated to about 1100 BCE (Kelso 1968:65,Pl.44:b).

Two fragments were found at *Shiloh* (Fig. 101): a cooking pot rim with a lioness(?) in relief and a krater handle with a ram's head at its base (for the findspots, see Chapter 5).

Stratum III at *'Izbet Ṣarṭah* produced a krater sherd on which the head of a horned animal was applied in relief (Fig. 102). Facing it is the edge of another relief. This might be a unique example of the "palm and ibex" motif in relief!

A sherd with the head of a bull(?) in relief was found on *Mt. Ebal* (Zertal 1985b:32).

A multihandled krater was found at *Dothan* (Fig. 27). The upper end of four

289

101. Shiloh — rim of a cooking pot with a head of a lioness(?) (left) and a handle with a ram's head (right).

102. ʿIzbet Ṣarṭah Stratum III — fragment of a krater decorated with applied relief depicting a head of a horned animal.

of the 16 handles terminated in stylized animal figures, apparently lions (Free 1954:17–18).

Outside the hill country, the figure of a lioness appeared on a sherd from the rim of a bowl at Deir ʿAlla (Franken 1961b:Pl.12). Various vessels with images in relief came from Megiddo VIIA-VA (Loud 1948:Pl.70:10, 90:10,249). At Tel Qishyon, a bowl sherd was found bearing two bulls' heads; one head projected inward near the bottom of the vessel, while the other faced outward from the rim (Zori 1977:Fig.46a). Others have turned up at Tel Qedesh in Upper Galilee (Aharoni 1957:Pl.VI:24) and at Tell Qasile (A. Mazar 1980b:79,81).

Ornamentation with figures in relief was also common on cultic stands of Iron I and the 10th century. In the hill country fragments of a stand with images of a horse, a lioness and a scene of a leopard attacking a deer (Fig. 75) were found at Shiloh; a cultic stand decorated with paws was unearthed at Ai (Marquet-Krause 1949:Pl.LXIV; our Fig.17); and two others were discovered at Taanach (Sellin 1904:XII; P. Lapp 1969:42–44).

As we have seen, vessels decorated with relief figures were not exclusive to the areas of Israelite Settlement, although they were widespread and relatively numerous in the hill country. This is particularly impressive in contrast to the paucity of forms in the ceramic repertoire of these same regions. Without delving into the question of the origin, relief decorations seem to be the only surviving artistic expression of the Israelites in the Iron I period.

The fact that these reliefs were prevalent on ritual stands suggests that the other vessels they graced were also involved in cultic practices, perhaps as offerings. In this connection, it is noteworthy that the majority of sites in the hill country where these vessels or sherds were found — Shiloh, Bethel, Mizpah and Mt. Ebal — were well-known cult sites and perhaps even pilgrimage centers.

PART IV:

THE PROCESS OF ISRAELITE SETTLEMENT

CHAPTER 8

ARCHAEOLOGICAL EVIDENCE AND
THE SCHOOLS OF SCHOLARSHIP

Reconstructing the character of Israelite Settlement has naturally preoccupied scholars of the period more than any other topic, for it is the very heart of the problem. But after decades of research, no agreement has been reached. Quite the contrary, differences of opinion have become even sharper, and the "traditional" archaeological evidence has only engendered further confusion.

As noted in the introduction (Chapter 1), three ways of understanding the process of Israelite Settlement have crystallized over the years. Two of them — the "unified military conquest" and the "peaceful infiltration" hypotheses — were formulated already in the 1920s and 1930s, while the "sociological" school originated in the early 1960s. In time, as the body of research grew, these theories took on various nuances — but their basic outlines have remain unchanged. In this chapter, we will briefly describe each of the three approaches and evaluate them in light of the latest archaeological evidence. (For surveys of the the various schools, see Weippert 1971:5–62; Miller 1977a:268–279; Gottwald 1979:192–219; Soggin 1975:1–30; Lemaire 1982; Chaney 1983:41–61.) Our own view will be set forth in full in Chapter 11.

THE UNIFIED MILITARY CONQUEST THEORY

The archaeological aspect of this line of inquiry was first formulated by Albright and his students starting in the 1930s (Albright 1935; 1937; 1939; 1950:24–34; Wright 1940; 1962:69–84; P. Lapp 1967; Kaufmann 1953; Malamat 1976b and, slightly more flexibly, 1983; Yadin 1979; 1982). This approach adhered closely to the description of the conquest of Canaan in the first chapters of the Book of Joshua, whereby Canaanite city-states throughout the country were subjugated in a series of battles and many of them were destroyed by fire. In the wake of their victories, the Israelites, who had come up from the desert, settled down in these areas. Three kinds of evidence were adduced in support of the unified conquest theory:
— the literal description in the Bible;
— the destruction levels at the close of the Late Bronze period encountered at sites such as Lachish, Tell Beit Mirsim, Bethel and Hazor, which were

attributed to the invading Israelites (e.g. Albright 1939:20–23; P. Lapp 1967; Kelso 1968:32,47–48);

— historical parallels to nomadic tribes with low levels of material culture which, nonetheless, caused the collapse of strong and highly developed urban societies (e.g., Isserlin 1983).

G.E. Wright, one of the most prominent and orthodox advocates of the unified military conquest theory, described the events in these words:

> There was an Israelite campaign of great violence and success during the 13th century. Its purpose was to destroy the existing Canaanite city state system, weakening local power to such an extent that new settlement, especially in the hill country, might be possible (1962:70).
>
> The manifold evidence for the terrific destruction suffered by the cities of Bethel, Lachish, Eglon, Debir (Kiriath sepher), and Hazor during the 13th century certainly suggests that a planned campaign such as that depicted in Josh. 10–11 was carried out....We may safely conclude that during the 13th century a portion at least of the later nation of Israel gained entrance to Palestine by a carefully planned invasion... (1962:84).

Traditionally, proponents of the unified military conquest theory claimed it was the best explanation for the archaeological evidence, while their opponents, primarily Alt's students, rejected the notion that excavating the large Canaanite tells could contribute to the reconstruction of the process of Israelite Settlement (Noth 1938; 1960). This objection is as valid today as it was given the evidence available in the 1930s and 1940s, for the scholars of the Albright school were preoccupied with the devastation of the Late Bronze cities rather than with the Settlement of the Israelite tribes.

However, not only does archaeological evidence contribute decisively to our understanding of the period, but the data unearthed actually contradict the theory of a unified military conquest. In reviewing the evidence, we will emphasize the distinction between sites in the hill country and those in the lowlands. This distinction was critical during the period under discussion, although it has not been accorded due recognition.

Absence of LB remains

No evidence of the Late Bronze period was ever unearthed at a number of sites central to the biblical account of the conquest of Canaan. For certain sites, this embarrassing state of affairs has been known for decades — and with the expansion of archaeological investigation, the phenomenon has turned out to be even more widespread than anyone imagined. This subject has been discussed by others (e.g., Miller 1977b), so we will treat it only briefly.

Although the nature of *Jericho* in LB II has been discussed over and over, no unequivocal conclusions about the size of the settlement or the date of its destruction have been reached; the character of this important site remains shrouded in fog (Kenyon 1957:256–263, summary by Avigad 1965:851–855).

There was a gap in occupation at _Ai_ between the Early Bronze and Iron I periods (Callaway 1975:49), and no Late Bronze site has been discovered in the surrounding area (problem summarized by Yeivin 1971c:180–181).

Late Bronze material was found in the cemetery at _Gibeon_ (Pritchard 1963:72). But because no remains of the period have been found on the tell itself (Pritchard 1962:157–158), it is hard to envision an important city there at the time.

To date, only the lower city of the Early Bronze period has been excavated at _Tel Yarmuth_. However, the site has been surveyed and no sherds of the Late Bronze period were picked up (Richardson 1968:12). Two hard-to-date sherds collected during Ben-Tor's excavations were hesitantly attributed to the Late Bronze period (Ben-Tor 1975:73). In short, there appears to be no evidence of Late Bronze occupation at the site.

Arad experienced a gap in occupation from the end of the EB II period until the 11th century BCE (Aharoni 1975:82:88). The absence of LB II remains from any of the intensively excavated tells of the Beersheba Valley (Aharoni 1976a:59) has effectively quashed the contention that Late Bronze Arad must be sought elsewhere in the vicinity (Aharoni and Amiran 1964:14 4–147; B. Mazar 1964: 2–3).

The earliest remains excavated during all the campaigns at _Heshbon_ in Transjordan date from the Iron I period (Geraty 1976:42). The proposal to identify Canaanite Heshbon with Tell Jalūl, some 10 km from Ḥisban (in Miller 1983:123–124), is unacceptable from the standpoint of historical geography (Miller 1983:124–125; for various attempts to solve the "problem" of Heshbon, see Geraty 1983).

To the best of our knowledge, _Taanach_ was also uninhabited during the Late Bronze II period (Rast 1978:3; P. Lapp 1969:5).

Proponents of the unified military conquest theory initially attempted to minimize the gravity of the problem. Kelso, for example, wrote

> The Jericho and Ai narratives present knotty problems to the students of Joshua's military campaign, but the over-all conquest itself is now one of the most striking findings in all Palestinian archaeology (1968:47).

Some of the attempts to explain or excuse the absence of Late Bronze levels at these sites were utterly ridiculous:

> The walls were apparently of mud bricks, and in both cases they have disappeared through wind and rain erosion.... Jericho is in a strong wind zone where the air currents of cold Mt. Hermon, 9000 feet above sea level, are sucked down to the hot dead sea, 1300 feet below sea level (Kelso 1968:48).

Obviously we are not dealing with an isolated absence of LB II remains, which could be explained away somehow, whether by recourse to the powerful erosive forces of rain washing away the Late Bronze level at Jericho; by attributing the conquest of Ai to the destruction of nearby Bethel (Albright 1939:16); by identifying the Canaanite king of Arad as a chief of nomadic tribes (Glueck 1959:114); or by searching elsewhere for the cities mentioned (see above; also Callaway and Nicol 1966). This phenomenon must be discussed on a broad and comprehensive a level, rather than in the conventional site-by-site manner.

For example, at three of the sites mentioned in the biblical account — Arad, Yarmuth and Ai — great cities lay deserted from the time of their destruction in the Early Bronze period until small villages were founded on them in the early stages of the Iron Age. This has led various scholars, many of them associated with the German school of biblical research, to seek an etiological solution to the problem (e.g., Noth 1935; 1953:23ff.; Dussaud 1935; Zevit 1983:32). In this view, the tales of the conquest of these cities appearing in the Book of Joshua had been created over the years in order to explain the awesome ruins encountered by the first Iron Age settlers. Yadin, the most outspoken contemporary advocate of the Albright school, tried to harmonize the negative archaeological evidence with the biblical conquest narratives:

> Wherever we find agreement between the biblical narrative and the archaeological evidence, there is no reason to doubt the historicity of that particular biblical source. On the other hand, wherever the archaeological evidence bluntly contradicts the biblical narrative — as in the case of Ai — we should examine the possibility that that particular chapter in the bible is either etiological, a later interpolation or an editor's misunderstanding... (1979:66–67).

But if so, the archaeological data listed above leave the episode of Israelite Settlement almost bereft of "historical" evidence!

Geographical distribution

The deployment of the principal Canaanite cities and of the Israelite Settlement sites is highly significant. Many of the cities mentioned in the biblical account of the conquest were located in the coastal plain, the Shephelah, and the northern valleys — precisely those areas which have yielded virtually no evidence of Israelite Settlement in the Iron I period (Chapter 3). On the other hand, the central hill country, the heartland of Israelite Settlement, is hardly represented at all in the tradition of the unified campaign of conquest. Archaeological and historical evidence clearly indicate that the spread of the Israelites into the lowlands began only toward the end of the 11th century, and this expansion was largely a phenomenon of the 10th century, during the

United Monarchy (Tell Beit Mirsim B3, Beth Shemesh IIa, Gezer VIII, Aphek X-8, Megiddo VB).

At the end of Late Bronze period and during Iron I, the coastal plain, the Shephelah and the northern valleys were the scene of great disturbances. Many cities suffered damage, and a new ethnic entity, the Philistines, appeared on the scene. However, in these areas there were no drastic changes in either the density or the extent of occupation. The revolutionary demographic upheavals of that era took place in the central hill country, which experienced an unprecedented flood of settlers. Suffice it to recall that in the entire territory of Ephraim, there were only five Late Bronze settlements, while for the Iron I period, 115 sites are known thus far. The situation in other hilly regions was similar.

Succession of occupation

Had there been a unified conquest of all or most of Canaan, we would expect to find Israelite Settlement to be most intense in the fertile and hospitable regions of the country, atop the ruins of the devastated Canaanite cities. And so the situation appeared to the advocates of the military conquest theory (Yadin 1979:5 8–59). But definite evidence of sparse Israelite Settlement on the remains of a freshly-destroyed Canaanite city has been found almost exclusively in the hill country (at Bethel), though possibly also at Tel Zeror in the Sharon, and Tell Beit Mirsim and Beth Shemesh in the Shephelah (at these sites, either the ethnic affiliation of the new settlers or the archaeological evidence is insufficiently clear).

At *Hazor,* which was previously regarded as a classic paradigm of this reconstruction, a considerable gap in occupation separated the destruction of Stratum XIII from the beginning of Stratum XII (Chapter 3). The situation at nearby *Dan* is uncertain: The Late Bronze occupation there has yet to be located, and Stratum VI, with its plethora of stone-lined silos, which was dated by the excavator to the beginning of the 12th century (Biran 1980:173–174), can just as easily be later in date, based on the examination of a group of vessels found in one of the silos (although this furnishes only a *terminus ante quem*). So it is possible that at Dan, too, the sparse occupation of Iron I followed the destruction of Canaanite Laish only after a period of abandonment.

Tell Beit Mirsim, Beth Shemesh and *Tel Zeror* are the only sites in the lowlands where there may have been a brief Israelite occupation immediately after the destruction of the Late Bronze city. However, it is noteworthy that the first two sites were located right on the border between the hill country and the Shephelah, and the Israelites (if they had settled there) were soon expelled from all three sites by the Sea Peoples. The situation at other sites in the coastal plain, the Shephelah, and the northern valleys that were mentioned in the conquest narratives and which have been satisfactorily excavated, can be summarized briefly:

Opinions are divided concerning the history of *Megiddo* during this period, especially over the question of when the site became Israelite. In any case, what is certain is that the pattern of succession differed both from that of Hazor and from that of Tell Beit Mirsim. The last Canaanite city, Stratum VIIA, was still viable during the second half of the 12th century BCE, and it is doubtful that its unfortified successor, Stratum VI, was Israelite (Chapter 3).

A new element with a highly developed material culture settled at *Aphek* following the destruction of the Egypto-Canaanite governor's residency in the second half of the 13th century BCE. Soon afterward, the site fell into the hands of the Philistines. There is no evidence of Israelite occupation before the beginning of the 10th century BCE (Kochavi 1981:82).

At *Gezer*, there was apparently a "partial hiatus in occupation" at the end of the 13th and beginning of the 12th centuries BCE, in the wake of the destruction of the Canaanite city; next came the Philistine phases (so summarized by Dever 1976:439; with reference to Stratum XIV, dated to the 13–12th centuries BCE, the picture is unclear: Dever *et al.* 1970:22–24; 1974:50–52; Kempinski 1976:213).

A long gap in occupation succeeded the destruction of the last Canaanite city, Stratum VI, at *Lachish* in the first half of the 12th century BCE (Ussishkin 1983:168–170).

Tell Halif (we accept its identification with Hormah: Naaman 1980:136–143) was continuously inhabited during the transition from the end of the Bronze Age into Iron I (Borowski 1982:59).

To summarize the archaeological evidence presented thus far, out of over 10 cities in the coastal plain, the Shephelah and the northern valleys mentioned in the conquest narrative (which were all identified with relative certainty and excavated in an orderly manner), only two, Hazor and Dan, offer any indication that a new entity, poor in material culture, settled above the ruins of the Late Bronze city. Even at these sites, the newcomers probably arrived only after some time had elapsed. Elsewhere, there was a lack of either Late Bronze occupation, Iron I remains, or evidence of new settlers — or else the picture was too hazy and indecipherable.

Chronological evidence

In recent years, important chronological data has accumulated from sites in many parts of the country. This new evidence exercises a decisive influence on the historical reconstruction of the events occurring in the region at the end of the 13th and beginning of the 12th centuries BCE. It is becoming increasingly clear that the main Canaanite centers were not wiped out in a single campaign, but rather that they succumbed gradually over the course of at least a century (Ussishkin 1985; Kempinski 1985:404, table of estimated dates). Noth, it will be recalled, had already hypothesized such a scenario nearly 50 years ago (1938:20).

The devastation of *Hazor* apparently took place no later than in the middle of the 13th century, for characteristic pottery of the end of the 13th century was lacking in Stratum XIII (Chapter 3). According to a tablet from Ugarit found in the destruction level of the Egyptian-Canaanite governor's residency, *Aphek* was destroyed in the second half of the 13th century (Chapter 9).

On the other hand, a metal object bearing the cartouche of Ramesses III, which was found in the area of the city gate of Lachish, testifies that Stratum VI there was destroyed no earlier than that Pharaoh's reign, i.e., around the middle of the 12th century BCE (Ussishkin 1983:168–170; 1985), several decades *after* Israel was mentioned in the Merneptah stele. Such a late date was already adumbrated during the excavations at Lachish in the 1930s (e.g., Tufnell 1958:36–37), but it was then rejected by scholars who were wedded to the preconceived notion that all of the Canaanite cities had been destroyed simultaneously at the end of the 13th century (e.g., Albright 1939:20–21).

Megiddo Stratum VIIA was devastated even later, apparently in the second half of the 12th century BCE, according to the statue base of Ramesses VI discovered beneath a wall of Stratum VIIB (!) (Loud 1948:135 n.1).[29]

For other cities destroyed at the end of the Late Bronze period, the chronological evidence is not clear enough to decide whether, for example, Tell Beit Mirsim C was savaged at the end of the 13th century or, as at nearby Lachish, only in the first half of the 12th century.

Archaeological evidence for dating the establishment of the Israelite Settlement sites in the hill country to the second half of the 13th century is hardly abundant (Chapter 9). However, the Mt. Ebal site, ʿIzbet Ṣarṭah Stratum III and probably Giloh and other sites as well were already in existence prior to the destruction of Lachish, an important Canaanite city around which an unambiguous tradition of conquest had arisen. It is also not unreasonable to hypothesize that the Israelite Settlement sites in the vicinity of Aphek were founded even before the Egypto- Canaanite city was destroyed (Finkelstein 1986:206–208).

Other historical events

The reflexive attribution of all or most of the destruction levels *ca.* 1200 BCE in the Canaanite cities of the Land of Israel to a campaign of conquest by the Israelite tribes has caused a blind eye to been turned toward other historical possibilities: Egyptian military campaigns, such as the one led by Merneptah; local conflicts between rival Canaanite city-states; and the Philistine inflitration of the southern coast and the Shephelah during the first half of the 12th century BCE (already Noth 1938:19–20, see also Fritz 1973; Schoors 1985).

---

29   It was hard to separate the walls of Stratum VIIA from those of Stratum VIIB in Area CC, but even if the statue base was found under a Stratum VIIA wall, it is still a decisive piece of chronological evidence.

Naturally, these events occurred primarily in the coastal plain, the Shephelah, and the northern valleys, where many of the cities mentioned in the conquest narratives were also concentrated.

To remain faithful to the archaeological evidence, while at the same time adhering steadfastly to the theory of a unified military conquest, requires the following reconstruction of events: The Israelite tribes gained dominion over most of Canaan by means of a military campaign, during the course of which the major Canaanite cities were destroyed. Special efforts were expended in vanquishing the Shephelah, the Judean Hills, and certain areas of the coastal plain and the northern valleys. At the end of this military campaign, the victors failed to exploit the opportunity to settle in these fertile areas, at least some of which were almost vacant. Instead, they preferred the topographically difficult hill country, with its rocky terrain and thick forests. Obviously it is hard to swallow such a reconstruction, although more than one scholar has been imprisoned by it.

Nature of the relations between settled groups and nomads

Needless to say, this is probably the most convincing argument against a united military conquest. Our present knowledge of the society of the ancient Near East, especially of the relations between sedentary people and pastoral nomads, does not permit the romantic reconstruction of hoards of desert nomads invading the settled lands and devastating their inhabitants (see below and Chapter 11). Therefore, even if there were archaeological evidence for the contemporaneous destruction of many Canaanite cities at the end of the 13th century BCE, the identification of the agressors would have to be sought elsewhere than among obscure desert tribes.

THE PEACEFUL INFILTRATION THEORY

The results of recent excavations and, even more so, the data from comprehensive surveys throughout the central hill country accord well with many of the tenets of the peaceful infiltration school of thought. The most notable exception is the issue of the origin of the new settlers. On this score and in various details, this reconstruction of the process of settlement needs to be "brought into line" with the accumulating socio-historical and archaeological evidence.

The originator of the peaceful infiltration theory was Alt (1925), who examined the episode of Israelite Settlement against the political, territorial, and demographic situation in the Land of Israel during the Late Bronze period, as reflected in the Bible and in New Kingdom Egyptian sources. He described Israelite Settlement as the peaceful infiltration of pastoral groups into the sparsely populated regions of Canaan, part of a routine pattern of transhumance between the desert fringe and the central hill country (Alt 1939; see also Meek 1936 and, more recently, Klengel 1972:181–182).

Alt was thus the first scholar to recognize the value of geography, ecology and sociology as tools for studying Israelite Settlement, and in this respect, adumbrated contemporary scholarship. Both Alt and Noth, his student and successor, regarded the hill country of the Land of Israel as the place to search for solutions to the problems of the period.

Noth was the principal critic of the unified military campaign theory. He understood the snare in which that approach had become trapped: Biblical scholarship was bound up in the interpretation of the archaeological finds by the archaeologists themselves, who, in turn, relied on the biblical source! He viewed as "naive" the way in which archaeological evidence was used in the 1930s to verify the "conquest of Palestine". Instead, he felt that the situation at each site and in every region must be judged on its own merits, and thereby became the first to advocate a regional approach to the study of the period.

Noth's understanding of the biblical account was based on the distinction between the condensed description of the conquest in the first half of the Book of Joshua, which he regarded as a late composition, and the other, sometimes contradictory traditions scattered through Joshua 15 and Judges 1, which he tried to evaluate in light of archaeological evidence. Noth, then, regarded the episode of Israelite Settlement as an intricate, complicated, multifaceted process that continued for a long time (1938; 1957; 1960).

A turning point for the peaceful infiltration theory occurred in the 1950s, when Aharoni, who pioneered field work on Israelite Settlement, produced archaeological data that gave a fresh impetus to this approach. In recent years, Weippert has represented the German school and investigated the potential contribution of archaeology to the study of Israelite Settlement (1971; 1976; and, for a slightly different tack, 1979; see also Herrmann 1985, for the opinion of another of Alt's students).

As noted, Alt's views were firmly anchored in a thoroughgoing knowledge of both the physical and human landscape of the country, which enabled him to appreciate the ecological setting and social frameworks involved in the process of Israelite Settlement, even if he did not employ the terminology in use today.

For Alt, the process was a slow one. It began in the annual pastoralist routine of wintering in the desert fringe of Transjordan and summering in the central hill country, during the course of which links were forged with the sedentary population. The penetration of the sown areas was, according to Alt, generally peaceful and did not interfere with the lives of the existing residents, since the new settlers came to those areas of the hill country where Canaanite occupation was sparse. The search for pasturage repeated itself year after year, until the herders began to transfer the focus of their activities to the settled areas, at the same time creating a network of agreements with the inhabitants. The newcomers gradually switched over to agriculture, although at first, while this activity was confined to the small areas available in the hills, they did not forego shepherding. As they began to clear the forests the new settlers became more firmly established in the hill country, and the economic importance of flocks waned.

Rowton (1965; 1967a; 1967b; 1973a; 1973b; 1974; 1976) has dealt extensively with pastoralism in the ancient Near East, expanding on the topics that Alt only touched upon. He placed particular emphasis on the importance of the forested areas of the hill country. According to him, the best grazing lands in our region were not in the desert fringe, but in the hilly enclaves of the settled sectors of the region. In these hilly areas, the combination of trees, bushes and pasturage served as a drawing card for both infiltrating nomads and uprooted elements from the nearby urban system. The pastoralists active in these areas maintained a symbiotic relationship with the permanent inhabitants of the proximal regions. The rugged zones of the hill country were difficult to control, which facilitated the process of infiltrating them. But once the tribes gained control of large plots of land, they affected both commerce and agriculture adversely and led to the contraction of the cities. As the city-states became weaker, nomads spread out farther, larger groups shifted to this form of nomadism ("enclosed nomadism," in Rowton's terminology), and penetration into the settled areas became more aggressive.

In Alt's view, the factual basis of the biblical description of the conquest was the second and later stage of the process, the period of territorial expansion that followed the phase during which the new settlers dwelled alongside the Canaanite population. When the biblical descriptions were redacted during the Monarchy, memories of the wars of expansion were still fresh. And since most of the territory was acquired in those campaigns, they were associated with the initial stage of Israelite Settlement. Thus, according to Alt, the story of Israelite Settlement was dramatized during the period of the Monarchy.

Weippert proposed (1979:32–34) that Alt's pastoral groups should be identified with the Shosu, nomadic groups living in the frontier regions, who are mentioned in Egyptian sources from c. 1500 to 1050 BCE. In his opinion, population growth within these groups undermined their nomadic subsistence economy and drove them to sedentarization.

Criticism of the peaceful infiltration theory came mainly from the advocates of the sociological school. Mendenhall, Gottwald and others pointed out the basic deficiency of Alt's theory — the inability to trace the origins of the pastoral groups in the steppe, outside the country (see below).

Admittedly, Alt's *weltanschauung* must be reconciled with this last issue; to the best of our knowledge, Israelite Settlement was not connected with the infiltration of any major new elements from the east. Rather, it represented a long process of sedentarization undergone by groups of pastoralists who, during the Late Bronze period, had lived in various marginal zones within the Land of Israel, including the central hill country. This description, of course, requires certain changes in some details of Alt's reconstruction of Israelite Settlement, as we shall see in Chapter 11.

Aharoni was the first to try to examine Alt's views in the light of new and varied archaeological data. Based on his work in Galilee and in the Beersheba Valley, he offered a model of slow and peaceful Israelite Settlement in the remote, marginal, and inhospitable regions that were devoid, or nearly devoid, of Canaanite inhabitants; the settlers had initially to struggle against harsh environmental conditions, but not against an indigenous population (e.g., 1957:115–119; 1982:153–180; also Aharoni, Fritz and Kempinski 1975:121; B. Mazar 1981; Kempinski 1981; 1985).

This matter, too, must be "updated" to some extent, for it now appears that compared to the central hill country, Israelite Settlement in the regions investigated by Aharoni took place relatively late and was more limited in extent. Moreover, while Israelite Settlement did indeed commence in regions with a sparse — but nonetheless extant — Canaanite population, within them, the comparatively hospitable areas were preferred, even though these were naturally close to the Canaanite centers. The penetration into remote, virtually uninhabited, and inhospitable regions occurred only in the second phase of the process (Chapter 10).

Zertal seems to be the prominant archaeologist supporting the peaceful infiltration theory today (1986b). Based on the results of his Manasseh survey, he believes that the groups which settled in northern Samaria in Iron I came from the steppe. He thinks that they entered the region along the fertile valleys of Farʿa and Maliḥ and settled in the eastern part of the Manassite hill country. He interprets the finds at Mt. Ebal as evidence for the supra-tribal organization of these groups already in a very early stage of their sedentary activity. However, the results of the Manasseh survey are quite similar to the patterns uncovered in the survey of the land of Ephraim, and can be interpreted in a completely different way (Chapter 11)

Of late, Fritz has attempted to consolidate an independent approach to tracing the course of Israelite Settlement, based largely on the results of the excavations at Tel Masos (1980; 1981; 1982; Fritz and Kempinski 1983:231–233).

According to him, none of the current models fit the new data. Instead, the first Israelites were semi-nomads who entered the Land of Israel in the 15th and 14th centuries BCE; who spent the 13th century in a symbiotic relationship with the urban Canaanites, in whose territories they were already living; and who then settled down in the 12th century.

Fritz attributed the connections between the material culture of the inhabitants of Tel Masos — who were Israelites, in the eyes of Fritz and Kempinski — and that of the Canaanites to the phase preceding sedentarization, when these people lived in groups adjacent to the Canaanite centers. Fritz, in fact, took elements from the sociological school and grafted them on to Alt's model; in other words, he concurred that the process was basically peaceful.

The refutation of Tel Masos' status as an Israelite Settlement site (Chapter 3) leaves Fritz's theory out on a limb, since it was based entirely on the highly developed material culture of that site. Nonetheless, certain elements of his reconstruction are close to our own, as we shall see. In any case, the main deficiency in his approach is that he sought the origins of the new settlers in the desert, which, as we have already explained, is no longer plausible.

THE SOCIOLOGICAL SCHOOL

G. Mendenhall's groundbreaking article in the *Biblical Archaeologist* in 1962 laid the foundations for the sociological approach (1962; also 1973; 1976). This school of interpretation was developed through the work of Gottwald in the 1970s (esp. 1979:191–233; also 1974; 1975; 1978a; see also, with slight differences: Dus 1975; de Geus 1976; Ahlström 1982; 1986; Halligan 1983; Chaney 1983; Lemche 1985). In this view, Israelite Settlement did not occur in the wake of a campaign of military conquest of Canaan; nor could it be characterized as the peaceful infiltration of pastoralists into sparsely populated regions of the country. For Mendenhall and Gottwald,[30] the oppressed and exploited groups at the bottom of the social strata of the royal Canaanite city-states rebelled against the ruling class — and therein lay the origins of Israel. Persecution by the upper classes caused the lowest social stratum to drop out of urban society by deserting the large cities of the coastal plain and the valleys in favor of the hill country, where these newcomers organized themselves in new frameworks. A slightly different version of this school of thought sought the origin of the Israelites in the pre-existing rural communities of the hill country, rather than among those of the plains (de Geus 1976:172–173; Halpern 1983:239).[31]

Mendenhall and Gottwald particularly stressed two points which, in their opinion, precluded a reconstruction of the Settlement process according to either Albright's or Alt's model: First, the basic social conflict in the Land of Israel was not between the Desert and the Sown or the Shepherd and the Farmer, but between the Village and the City (Mendenhall 1962:70; Gottwald 1979:461). Second, the nature of nomadic pastoralism in our region has been

---

30 The views of Mendenhall and Gottwald are lumped together here, despite the sharp attack on Gottwald issued recently by Mendenhall (1983).

31 In his review of Gottwald's book, Lenski (1980) proposed a somewhat different sociological model for the process by which Israel came into being, viz., a revolt by peasants and marginal elements of the population, but Gottwald (1983) rejected this hypothesis.

misunderstood: At that time, this mode of existence was of secondary importance, a kind of offshoot of village life, and not the lifestyle of a population originating in the desert (esp. Gottwald 1979:436–442,448–451).

The sociological school may be briefly summarized as an approach based on a new evaluation of the relations among pastoral, rural, and urban societies, and this, in turn, was largely based on information from the archives at Mari, in North Syria, dating from the early 2nd millennium BCE (Luke 1965; for an up-to-date review of the literature concerning the implications of the Mari documents on the research of the Settlement process, see Anbar 1985a:11–29).

The fresh insights presented by Mendenhall and Gottwald necessitate a reexamination of the entire issue of Israelite Settlement. Two of their points should be accepted:

— Before the domestication of the camel, there was not any significant populace living deep in the deserts of the Near East. Therefore, the origins of the Settlers should not be sought in those areas. (The dating of the domestication of the camel is still a controversial issue. For an earlier dating see Ripinski 1985 and for a late 2nd millenium dating see Albright 1971:20 6–207; Zeuner 1963:364–365; Zarins 1978. For a summary of the problem see Luke 1965:42–43; Bulliet 1975:ch. 2. It seems that the available evidence does not support the earlier date, especially not for the use of the camel as a subsistence animal in the "deep" desert).

— As a corollary of the above, shepherds/nomads and sedentary elements must have lived in proximity and engaged in reciprocal economic and social relations. In the past, as today, coexistence, rather than ongoing confrontation, characterized the relationship between the two groups. As we shall see, this has crucial implications for reconstructing the process of Israelite Settlement.

In other respects, however, it is hard to accept the views of Mendenhall, Gottwald and their followers. In particular, their claim that the people who settled in the hill country in Iron I came *directly* out of the social framework of the sedentary Canaanites in the lowlying regions must be rejected (Chapter 11).

The discussions by the adherents of the sociological school are noticeably deficient in two respects: The environmental aspect is treated only theoretically, and the archaeological contribution — both material culture and settlement patterns — is virtually ignored. (Further criticism is expressed by Hauser 1978 from the biblical standpoint and by Thompson 1978 and Lemche 1985 from the sociological angle; see also Herion 1986:14, who warns that modern, social science assumptions, can sometimes play a decisive role in shaping reconstructions of the past). Moreover, their acquaintance with the natural setting of the Land of Israel is strictly superficial and limited. By this we refer to the physical geography of the region and its influence on the inhabitants; the economic potential of the various zones; and the traditional lifestyle still followed today by some elements of the population, which can help us understand social phenomena of the past. This is especially true of the hill country and the desert fringe, which are obviously critically important.

Mendenhall completely disregarded the archaeological evidence, while Gottwald made use of only the hackneyed evidence from the large Canaanite tells, without bothering to acquaint himself either with the results of excavations at the Israelite Settlement sites themselves or with the information coming from the comprehensive surveys undertaken all over the country. By failing to reconstruct the material culture and settlement pattern of the Late Bronze and Iron I periods, advocates of the sociological school foreclosed important avenues of inquiry into the question of Israelite Settlement.

Human ecology and environment

The model of Israelite Settlement constructed by Mendenhall and Gottwald is utterly divorced from the socio-ecological reality of its environment. Mendenhall's article could just as easily concern some other geographical — and perhaps even historical — setting, while Gottwald's work never comes "down to earth," as it were, and the few examples he adduced are essentially irrelevant to our region.

These flaws are especially evident in their critique of Alt's school. While Alt's approach, as his writings attest, was grounded in a thoroughgoing knowledge of the physical and human background of the central hill country, the arena of the principal events connected with Israelite Settlement, his critics related only to purely theoretical aspects and thus ended up cavilling over terminological nuances of minor importance.

The degree to which the proponents of the sociological school are removed from the scene of the events they purport to explain is particularly conspicuous with regard to the desert areas and the hilly regions of the country, which are of critical importance for the Settlement episode. They never bothered to consider whether the sedentarization of Beduin or the relations between the Beduin and nearby permanent settlements could help illuminate similar processes in antiquity (although extensive literature on both aspects had been in existence for decades).

Their contention that the desert regions bordering the country could not support a population of any significant size (e.g., Gottwald 1979:443) — their main reason for rejecting other possible origins of the Settlers — is refuted by the fact that in the 1920s and 1930s, 200,000–250,000 Beduin lived in these very regions (data from Shalem 1968:1–17; Muhsam 1966; Shmueli 1980:73), and their subsistence was based on flocks, not camels. Gottwald's claim (1979:444) that in our region only the Syrian desert was suitable for nomadic pastoralism is purely arbitrary; the Negev Highlands and certain areas of Transjordan and Sinai offer no less favorable ecological conditions (Marx 1974; Perevolotsky 1979).

The argument that regions where the annual precipitation is below 100 mm cannot support flocks is not accurate either. The quality of available grazing land is determined not only by the amount of rainfall, but also by both elevation and underlying rock formations, which affect the catchment of the runoff water and its accessibility. Thus, for example, excellent pasturage is found high up in the Sinai, although the annual precipitation there is relatively negligible.

In summary, Gottwald's fundamental error is that he took a body of data from North Syria at the beginning of the second millennium and applied it, without the slightest reservation or hesitation, to the Land of Israel at the end of the second millennium — heedless to the totally different geographical and historical settings involved (Lemche 1985:162 and see Anbar 1985a:188, who claims that Mari offers an analogy only to theories of peaceful infiltration by outsiders).

Gottwald's aquaintance with the heartland of Israelite Settlement is also insufficient. His assertion (1979:447,658–659) that springs and irrigation agriculture were important for settlement in the central hill country is astonishing, since the practice of irrigation agriculture was, in fact, utterly negligible in the region, and even today has been attempted in only a few villages.

No less bizarre is the theory — which has made a big splash among proponents of the sociological approach — that the knowledge of how to build terraces was the most important factor in the spread of settlement in the hill country in the Iron I period (Gottwald 1979:658–659; de Geus 1975; Thompson 1979; Stager 1982). Ahlström (1982) went even further and contended that the newcomers to the central hill country in Iron I brought this knowledge with them; he thus concluded that the settlers came from an agricultural — rather than semi-nomadic — background.

Intensive archaeological surveys completely contradict this notion. In the first place, the earliest Israelite Settlements turned out to be located in the very areas where terraces were less essential, while the classic terraced regions were practically devoid of Settlement sites. Second, terraces were obviously in use long before Iron I, at least since the beginning of relatively dence occupation in the hill country in MB II, especially on the western slopes; the need to build terraces was simply a function of topography and population growth (Chapter 4).

Surprisingly, those studies professing to examine the process of Israelite Settlement from a *sociological* perspective utterly fail to pursue the far-reaching implications of contemporary habitation in the hill country — the traditional Arab village, its setting, and its economy — for research into the processes of settlement in antiquity.

Settlement patterns

Gottwald anticipated the future direction of research — regional studies in the hill country — when he wrote:

> The aim is to survey and/or sound all the sites in a given region so that they may be viewed contexually or ecologically. The results of such systematic area studies in depth should be of immense value for historical reconstruction... (1979:202).

> ...However, Israel emerged into the light of history from the countryside not the city.... It is precisely this germinative early Israelite rural hearland that archaeology has neglected. Happily there is at last some movement toward bringing the full powers of archaeology to bear an reconstructing the socio — economic organization of rural Israel (1978b:6).

Indeed, recent years have witnessed comprehensive field studies in many areas of the Land of Israel, including the central hill country. The distribution of Iron I sites in the territory of Ephraim, one of the two main regions of Israelite Settlement in the hill country, demonstrates that at the beginning of the period, there was a marked preference for the desert fringe, the interior valleys of the northern hills, and the Bethel plateau. Some 70% of all early Iron I sites were found in these regions (Chapter 4), where subsistence was primarily based on field crops and also, in many areas, on flocks. A similar picture arose from the 1968 preliminary survey in the territory of Benjamin, where almost all Israelite Settlement sites were located on the edge of the desert, and from Zertal's survey in Manasseh, where most of the early Iron I sites were locaed in the eastern part of the central range (Chapter 3). Conversely, the horticultural areas of the hill country were only relatively sparsely inhabited at that time. The settlement choices made by the Israelites were therefore at odds with the theories of the sociological school. The economic background of the newcomers was closer to that of pastoralists in the desert fringe than to sedentary dwellers in the plains and valleys.

Had the new settlers in the hill country been fugitives from the Canaanite polity, they would have been more likely to seek refuge in the rugged, relatively inaccessible regions of the western slopes — which were also devoid of Canaanite settlements. Our survey, however, paints a very different picture. Israelite Settlement sites were concentrated in the comparatively hospitable areas of the hill country, close to the few Late Bronze Canaanite cities in the region: Shechem, Bethel, Tappuah, etc. (on the similar situation in Lower Galilee, see Gal 1982:88–89). In Manasseh, too, the new settlements were established close to the main Canaanite cities. The explanation for this distribution seems to lie in the desire of the new settlers to exploit the already deforested areas in the vicinity of the Canaanite cities, where it was possible to begin agricultural activities without first having to overcome environmental obstacles. (The question of whether Israelite Settlement developed in these areas before or after the destruction of the Canaanite cities remains unresolved.)

As for other matters raised by the sociological school, there is no archaeological basis for the supposition of a conflict between Village and City in the Land of Israel during the Late Bronze period. The rather sparse population of the country was concentrated primarily in the major cities and, to a lesser extent, in their immediate periphery. Small, unfortified, outlying settlements were virtually nonexistent (see Gonen 1984; Naaman 1982; Lemche 1985:421). If this phenomenon of the "country side" (to use Gottwald's term) existed at the time, it has not been detected in archaeological surveys, not even in the lowlands (with the possible exception of the southern coastal plain, e.g. Oren and Morrison 1986:74–75). Needless to say, the evidence from recent surveys, showing that the hill country was almost devoid of Late Bronze permanent settlements, rules out any theory that the Iron I settlers originated from pre-existing rural groups in that area (i.e. de Geus 1976: 172–173; Halpern 1983:239).

The most densely settled regions during the Late Bronze period were the southern coast and the Shephelah. In contrast to other areas of the country, almost no demographical crisis was felt in these regions in the Late Bronze period. One would expect that people fleeing them would settle in the hilly bloc of Judah to the east, for this region was elevated, isolated and uninhabited; indeed, in other periods, it functioned as a consolidated and isolated unit of habitation. The catch is that archaeological evidence indicates otherwise. There were, in fact, very few Settlement sites in the Judean Hills — only about 10 have been found (Chapter 3), as opposed to 115 in Ephraim and 95 in Manasseh (though ecological factors probably affected this too). Based on the number of sites in the various regions of the country and their dates, we conclude that the region densest in Israelite Settlement sites was the central hill country, between Jerusalem and the Jezreel Valley. From this nucleus, the Israelites spread south into Judah and north into Galilee during the second stage of the Settlement process (Chapter 10).

Field work undertaken in the border area between the hill country and the coastal plain also has a contribution to make. In the foothills opposite Canaanite (and later Philistine) Aphek, a group of seven Israelite Settlement sites was surveyed, and one of them, ʿIzbet Ṣarṭah, was excavated extensively (Chapter 3). For the purpose of this discussion, it is immaterial whether these sites were established before or after the destruction of Canaanite Aphek in the second half of the 13th century BCE, because in either case it is obvious that if their inhabitants were uprooted from the Canaanite polity, they would have sought refuge in the hill country, and not on the periphery of the Canaanite settlements that continued to exist in the plain.

311

Material culture

The theory that the inhabitants of the central hill country in Iron I were fugitives from the oppressed lower rungs of Canaanite society requires a demonstration of continuity of Canaanite material culture at Israelite Settlement sites (e.g. Ahlström 1986:26–36,57). Advocates of the sociological school apparently found succor in statements such as:

> Nevertheless, with one outstanding exception Philistine pottery, the techniques and styles of Iron I suggest more of a cultural continuum from LB than a cultural break (Miller 1977a:255).

It is clear, however, that once again such determinations were made almost exclusively on the basis of excavations at the large tells in the Jezreel Valley and the coastal plain. Since there was no Israelite occupation in these regions during the early phases of the Iron Age, such statements are devoid of significance regarding the process of Israelite Settlement.

Callaway (1976), Cooley (1975) and Ahlström (1984a; 1984b, 1986:26–36, 57) were the first who discussed the finds from the hill country and the Beersheba valley, in an attempt to support the sociological approach.

Callaway (1985) interpreted the finds from his Ai and Khirbet Raddana excavations as evidence that the inhabitants of the hill country in the Iron I period came from rustic, rather than nomadic background. In his opinion, at the end of the Late Bronze period villagers from the lowlands (the coastal plain and Shephelah) were forced to emigrate eastwards, to the sparsely populated hill country. This movement, he claimed, was the result of demographic pressure, possibly following the arrival of the Sea Peoples.

Callaway accepted Alt's reconstruction of the Settlement process as basically correct, but he had reservations concerning the sociological approach (1985:33). However, his own reconstruction has absolutely no bearing on Alt's theory of a slow infiltration of groups of pastoralists into the hill country in a process of seasonal grazing. To the contrary, Callaway sounds the sociological approach nearly to the letter and the same arguments expressed against it below hold true for him as well (see also chapters 6 and 7). In any case, the archaelogical evidence he presents to consolidate his views can not be used to support either theory, since it may be interpereted as evidence for trade with the neighboring areas, rather than as proof of the ethnicity or origins of the inhabitants.

The transition from Late Bronze to Iron I in the hill country was, in fact, characterized by an unmistakeable change in material culture — in both pottery and architecture — as well as by a wholly new pattern of settlement. Archaeological data debunk all claims of a *direct* connection between the Late Bronze centers of the lowlying regions and the Iron I sites in the hill country.

Two prominent and typical features of Iron I architecture in the hill country were pillared buildings, mostly of the four- room house type, and a special site plan in which the peripheral houses formed a defensive belt around the settlement (e.g., Ai, Tell en-Naṣbeh). This site layout has no antecedents whatsoever at any of the Late Bronze sites excavated throughout the country, and pillared buildings were practically unknown there as well. The reasons are simple: Israelite architecture was rooted in the pastoral mode of existence preceding sedentarization, and it developed by adapting to the environmental conditions of the hill country. It is particularly significant that the influences of both the tent and the encampment are perceptible in the plans of several early Israelite sites.

At most Israelite Settlement sites, a third feature, the presence of dozens of stone-lined silos, was also frequently encountered. A proliferation of silos is also typical of a society in the early stages of organization.

Another architectural issue which Mendenhall's and Gottwald's approach ignores is the problem of defense. Had the founders of the hill country sites come from the Canaanite polity, with its firmly established traditions of construction, we would expect them to build fortification walls around their settlements. Yet there is almost no evidence of genuine fortifications from early Iron I sites in the hill country. At most, the outer buildings of some of the sites were contiguous (details in Chapter 6).

Some aspects of the pottery of Israelite Settlement sites do suggest a certain relationship to Late Bronze ceramic traditions, but here we must emphasize two important factors that scholars have all too often neglected: regionalism, i.e., the local traits evident in pottery, and the quantitative distribution of the various types.

A resemblance to the pottery of the Late Bronze period is understandably most recognizable at sites near the coastal plain and the northern valleys, e.g., ʿIzbet Ṣarṭah adjacent to Aphek. On the other hand, the pottery of Israelite Settlement sites in the hill country is completely different from that of the Canaanite centers. Whereas the repertoire of Late Bronze types was rich and varied, the number of types found at Israelite Settlement sites in the hill country was comparatively small. But while Late Bronze pottery was uniform in appearance throughout the country, Israelite Settlement pottery was characterized by locally divergent subtypes.

These differences undoubtedly reflect the contrasting socio-economic situations of these two groups: an urban society bound together by commerce versus a dispersed and isolated tribal society. They also show that the links between the two cultures were not very strong. Even types which were thought to have developed from the preceding period, such as the cooking pot, manifested distinctly new traits. (In any case, some connection to the preceding culture, even in a newly established society, should be expected). Nor should we forget that the collared-rim store jar, which is the most characteristic type at Israelite Settlement sites in the hill country — comprising 35% of

313

the assemblage in some places — made its debut at this time (Chapter 7).

The inescapable conclusion is that the subject of Israelite Settlement, which involves the reconstruction of complex historical and demographic processes, cannot be discussed without a direct knowledge of at least one of the regions involved and without keeping abreast of the latest developments in archaeological field work. Recent studies on settlement patterns in different parts of the country in the Late Bronze and Iron I periods, as well as the accumulating data about the material culture of Israelite Settlement sites in the hill country, make it impossible to accept a theory claiming that the people responsible for Iron I settlement in the hill country came *directly* from the sedentary Canaanite society of the lowlying regions. Finally, another crucial point that is usually forgotten in the heat of the debate is the simple fact that no process of the type hypothesized by Mendenhall and Gottwald can be traced in any ancient Near Eastern source. To sum up, some of the points discussed above are stronger than others, but the general picture that emerges is what is of primary importance. Other points raised by the sociological school are valid, however, and we shall return to them later.[32]

32 After this manuscript was ready for publication, Lemche's important book on *Early Israel* appeared (1985). Although large parts of his work are devoted to sharp criticism of Gottwald's *Tribes of Yahweh* (e.g. *ibid*: 407–410), Lemche basically agrees with almost all the views of the sociological school. He too seeks the origins of Israel in the socio-political situation in the Late Bronze period. From the 14th century BCE the hilly regions of the country were inhabited, in his opinion, by para-social elements who originated in the city-states of the lowlands. Since these groups were not sedentary, they are archaeologically invisible. Technological innovations in the beginning of the Iron Age made their sedentarization in the hill country possible (*ibid*: 416–432). The strongest and most impressive part of Lemche's research is the socio-anthropological data which has been incorporated into the book. On the other hand, the treatment of the archaeological material is artificial and insufficient.

#### CHAPTER 9

CHRONOLOGICAL PROBLEMS OF ISRAELITE SETTLEMENT

Due to their isolation, Israelite Settlement sites, especially the earliest ones, almost never yield objects of chronological significance. The meager ceramic repertoire and the absence of clear historical *points de répère* make it difficult to get a handle on the chronology of the period. This is especially true for determining the date of the beginning of the process of Israelite Settlement and for discerning phases within Iron I. Our ability to assign relative dates to the sites of this era is thus very limited.

ARCHAEOLOGICAL EVIDENCE FOR DATING THE BEGINNING OF THE PROCESS

Disputes over the date of the beginning of Israelite Settlement have always been central to research into this period (see, most recently, Kempinski *et al.* 1981:121; Yadin 1979:63–65). Two positions, related to the historical outlook of their advocates, have consolidated over the years.

Proponents of the Albright school of a unified military conquest placed the destruction of the Canaanite cities in the 1230s BCE (Albright 1933:78–79; 1937:24; Kelso 1968:32; Yadin 1972:108) and the founding of the first Israelite Settlement sites shortly afterward, in the 1220s BCE (Kelso 1968:xiv; Callaway 1976:19; Cooley 1975:7). For them, two factors were decisive: The finding of imported Mycenaean IIIB pottery together with very late local Late Bronze wares in the debris of the last Canaanite levels required a date as late as possible in the 13th century for these destructions. On the other hand, the mention of Israel as a group of people in the Merneptah stele, which had been dated to about 1220 BCE, was taken to mean that Israelite Settlement had begun by this date. (On the Merneptah stele, the possible identification of "Israel" in the reliefs of Merneptah, and the currently accepted date of 1207 BCE for this campaign, see Stager 1985a; for a different interpretation of the name "Israel" on the stele see Ahlström and Edelman 1985).

In the 1970s, Aharoni, who followed the Alt school in advocating a slow and peaceful infiltration by new elements into the hilly sparsely inhabited areas while the Canaanite cities still flourished, claimed that there was archaeological evidence to date the beginning of Israelite Settlement in the 13th century, if not before.

One way or another, however, chronological positions were based largely on indirect historical and archaeological considerations (see Aharoni 1982:171–174), some of which themselves lacked clear and independent dates. It follows that the dates of the destruction of the Canaanite cities and of the founding of the Settlement sites rest on shaky grounds. The problem is all the more serious because certain ceramic assemblages, which were dated on the basis of inconclusive historical data, became, in turn, the grounds for dating strata at other sites. In short, to a great extent, the issue of chronology can be compared to a dog chasing its tail.

But once we break free from the restraints of the various historical interpretations, we are left with no means for assigning precise dates to Israelite Settlement sites. We cannot, in fact, determine whether Bethel was destroyed in 1250 BCE or, say, 1175 BCE. A good illustration of the problem concerns the dating of the destruction of Stratum VI at Lachish. It was long accepted that this occurred in the second half of the 13th century — until it recently became clear that Stratum VI still existed during the reign of Ramesses III, in the first half of the 12th century (Ussishkin 1983:168–170).

Moreover, even at sites that have yielded objects of chronological significance, there still remains considerable room for maneuvering. For example, the Ugaritic tablet found recently in the destruction layer of the "governor's residency" at Aphek (Owen 1981) has been dated to *ca.* 1230 BCE on the basis of the personal names recorded in the text (Singer 1983). But this still provides only a terminus post quem for the destruction of Aphek; it does not tell us whether the devastation took place in 1230 BCE or, say, 1200 BCE.

In like manner, even if we adhere closely to the views of the unified military conquest school, we cannot determine whether the village at Ai was established in 1210 or 1125 BCE. A somewhat more precise date might be possible if certain aspects of the material culture of the settlement were taken into account; however, most of the evidence remains unpublished.

Aharoni's survey of Galilee in the 1950s intensified the debate over the chronology of Israelite Settlement. Based on both Alt's peaceful infiltration theory and the settlement pattern in Upper Galilee, Aharoni hypothesized that the Galilean sites were founded before the destruction of Canaanite Hazor. When it was realized that Hazor was devastated already in the second third of the 13th century BCE (Yadin 1972:129–131), Aharoni proposed raising the dates of the Galilean sites to the earlier 13th or even the 14th century BCE (1957:115–119; 1982:177–178; 1971b:114–120). Since then, scholars have been preoccupied with the question of whether there exists archaeological evidence (other than settlement patterns) for dating the Israelite Settlement sites of Galilee or the central hill country before the 12th century BCE. This question naturally has important repercussions for reconstructing the course of

Israelite Settlement and for investigating the origins of the material culture of the period.

Lo and behold, ever since the 1950s, but especially in the 1970s, direct archaeological evidence for raising the date of the beginning of the occupation of the central hill country and the Beersheba Valley has purportedly come to light at the Israelite Settlement sites themselves. Aharoni even found support for his 14th-13th century dating in the results of excavations conducted years before (1973:41–46; 1979a:211–212; 1982:150,153,171–174; Aharoni, Fritz, and Kempinski 1975:118, 121; see also Fritz 1980:134; Kempinski *et. al.* 1981:175; Kempinski and Fritz 1977:146; Kempinski 1985). But most of this evidence was subsequently overturned. So we are essentially right back where we started, for the Israelite Settlement sites themselves still provide almost no direct chronological data about their foundation.

The following points have recently been regarded as important archaeological evidence for raising the date of Israelite Settlement:

Settlement pattern of the Galilean sites

The deployment of settlements — which was the foundation of all arguments in favor of raising the dates of Israelite Settlement sites — lost its value once it became clear both that the last Canaanite city at Hazor, Stratum XIII, no longer existed by the second half of the 13th century BCE and that the sites of Upper Galilee and Stratum XII at Hazor (the first Israelite occupation) should be dated to the end of the 12th century or perhaps even the 11th (Chapter 3).

Raddana inscription

Three letters in proto-Canaanite script were incised on the handle of a jar from Khirbet Raddana (Fig. 103). Aharoni (1971a) dated it — supposedly on paleographic grounds — to the 14th century BCE and then used it to determine the commencement of activity at the site. Cross and Freedman (1971) dated it, on the basis of paleography, to about 1200 BCE, and later Cross (1979:97 n.2) specified the end of the 13th century. What some of the dates proposed for the Khirbet Raddana graffito have in common is that they are permeated with historical considerations. In other words, the date assigned to the jar handle depended on a given scholar's views about the chronology of Israelite Settlement; accordingly the Raddana inscription cannot then be used as independent evidence for dating the beginning of Israelite Settlement!

Tel Masos scarab

A scarab found in Stratum III at Tel Masos (Fig. 104) was dated by Giveon (1974) to the time of Seti II. This reading, combined with the pottery from the stratum, was the basis for dating the foundation of the site to the end of the

103. The Kh. Raddana inscription
(Cross and Freedman 1971: 19).

104. The Tel Masōs scarab
(Giveon 1974: Pl. 5).

318

13th century BCE (e.g. Kempinski *et al* 1981:176, but see Fritz and Kempinski 1983:229–230 for a more cautious dating). Brandl (1982), however, has argued that the scarab dated from the reign of Ramesses X, and the ceramic assemblage could just as easily belong to the early 12th century. But even if Giveon's earlier attribution is accepted, we are no further enlightened concerning the chronology of Israelite Settlement because Tel Masōs was hardly a typical Israelite Settlement site (Chapter 3).

Ceramic evidence from Shiloh, Tell en-Naṣbeh and Tell el-Fūl

Since the Danish expedition found no evidence of a Late Bronze city at Shiloh, Aharoni (e.g., 1973:46) proposed that the small amount of Late Bronze pottery at the site should be associated with an early phase of Israelite occupation in the 14th century BCE. Our renewed excavations have indicated, however, that there was activity at Shiloh in the Late Bronze period; that this activity was part of the Canaanite cultural sphere; that the site was abandoned at the end of the late Bronze period; and that there is no evidence from the assemblages of the subsequent occupation that Israelites were present at Shiloh before the beginning of the 12th century BCE (Chapter 5).

Aharoni also singled out several vessels and sherds from Tell en-Naṣbeh and Tell el-Fūl as evidence that Israelite Settlement at these sites already began in the Late Bronze period (1982:174; also Aharoni, Fritz, and Kempinski 1975:121), but all of these vessels were either cooking pots with everted rims or *cyma*-profiled bowls, types which also appeared in the 12th century BCE.[33]

Mycenaean sherd from ʿIzbet Sartah

Supreme importance was initially attached to this small fragment (Fig. 105) with regard to the chronological quandry of the beginning of Israelite

105.   ʿIzbet Ṣarṭah Stratum III — the Mycenaean sherd.

33   In one place in the excavation report (McCown 1947a:180), Wampler noted that Cypriote sherds were found at Tell en-Naṣbeh. It is impossible to know what he meant by this; at any rate, nothing Cypriote appears among the published pottery.

Settlement, for it was thought to furnish the first unequivocal ceramic evidence that an early Israelite site had existed in the 13th century BCE (Kochavi and Finkelstein 1978:268). However, this evidence, too, must apparently be dismissed, for V. Hankey has examined the sherd and classified it as a fragment of a Late Mycenaean IIIB vessel in the "Simple Style," the latest exemplars of which date from the 12th century BCE (Hankey, 1986).

Other clues

The finds discussed above did not help resolve the chronological debate[34]. This leaves us with only three archaeological hints — two from the vicinity of Aphek and ʿIzbet Ṣarṭah — that Israelite Settlement began already in the 13th century BCE.

Among the pottery of ʿIzbet Ṣarṭah Stratum III were local vessels manufactured in the Late Bronze tradition (Finkelstein 1986: Figs. 8–13). But these vessels can just as easily be dated to the beginning of the 12th century as to the end of the 13th. Either way, this would appear to be the earliest clean assemblage thus far unearthed at an Israelite Settlement site.

When this assemblage is combined with a piece of evidence from nearby Aphek, the earlier date appears preferable. The vessel in question is a whole collared-rim store jar, which was found in the destruction level of the Egyptian governor's residency (Beck and Kochavi 1985:34,40), along with the cuneiform tablet from Ugarit (Owen 1981) that provided a *terminus post quem* of around 1230 BCE for the destruction of the palace (Singer 1983). The ceramic assemblage from Aphek cannot date the destruction of the Canaanite city any more closely than the late 13th century.

Collared-rim store jars were totally and utterly lacking at contemporary sites in the hill country, the region where the greatest quantities of these jars turned up not long afterward. This makes it very difficult to associate the earliest use of the type with a Canaanite population at the end of the 13th century BCE. The most logical way to explain the collared-rim store jar from Aphek is to assume that during the last third of the 13th century, collared-rim store jars

---

34 A few other sites have been mentioned lately in connection with the date of Israelite Settlement. For Kempinski's proposal to relate Tel Ṣippor in the Shephelah to the Israelite Settlement movement of the 13th century and the reasons why it must be rejected, see Chapter 3. The evidence from Lower Galilee adduced by Gal in order to raise the dates of Israelite Settlement was also commented on in Chapter 3.

Recent reports from Tel Dan speak of finding Late Bronze pottery, including Cypriote import and a Mycenaean fragment, together with such "Israelite I" pottery as pieces of pithoi with collared rims (*Ḥad. Arch.* 72, 1979:12; 85, 1984:4; for a different wording of this announcement, see Biran 1985:187). Before evaluating the significance of these finds for the chronology of the Israelite Settlement period, we must await their full publication and their stratigraphic assignment.

were already in use by the groups which settled in the foothills to the east of Aphek. For this reason, a late 13th century date for the founding of Stratum III at ʿIzbet Ṣarṭah seems preferable.

The third clue comes from the Mt. Ebal site, where two Egyptian scarabs were recently discovered, one from the time of Ramesses II or III (Zertal 1985c:42) and the other from the reign of Ramesses II (Zertal 1986a:52–53). Unless later parallels to these scarabs will be found, they constitute the single, direct, definite piece of archaeological evidence for the existence of an Israelite Settlement site as early as the late 13th century BCE. (The theoretical possibility that these scarabs were hierlooms brought to the site later is exceedingly remote). The pottery of Stratum II at Mt. Ebal may also be dated to the beginning of the 12th century BCE.

Feeble though these clues appear to be, they do offer circumstantial evidence for the existence of a new sedentary population in the hill country and its fringes by the end of the 13th century BCE.

The data for assigning the beginning of Israelite Settlement to the 13th century are therefore few and inconclusive. To the best of our knowledge and understanding of the character of Israelite Settlement, the process began at a time when the Canaanite cities still existed in the lowlands — and apparently in the hill country as well (Chapter 11) — regardless of whether this occurred in the mid 13th century, late 13th century or even the early 12th century BCE.

In any case, the fact that the material evidence pointing to the coexistence of permanent Settlement sites and Canaanite centers is far from abundant, indicates that the beginning of the Settlement process cannot be pushed back to the 14th or even the first half of the 13th century BCE. Had there been such a long period of overlap between the two cultures, it would have found clearer expression in the finds from both the Canaanite cities (such as the Aphek pithos) and the sites in the hill country. (Although it is possible that two contemporary and neighboring groups could have different material cultures due to their different socio-economic frameworks).

We look forward to new chronological evidence on this matter as Israelite Settlement sites are investigated further. It is important to note that thus far, only genuine settlements have been excavated, although the groups who occupied these sites had been active in those regions in a pre-sedentary phase of pastoral existence. This phase has yet to be detected archaeologically, but should, nonetheless, be taken into account in any chronological discussion. We are of the opinion that the intensive surveys underway in the regions of Israelite Settlement will ultimately show us the way to identify such sites in the field.

Relative Chronology of Israelite Settlement Sites

The virtual absence of historical anchors during a period spanning two centuries or so, from the beginning of the Settlement process to the inauguration of the Monarchy, makes it extremely difficult to determine both absolute and relative dates for Israelite Settlement sites. Nonetheless, there are a few bits of evidence, some still rather shaky, which are likely to be of assistance.

The only historical event that apparently expressed itself archaeologically was the defeat of Israel at Ebenezer in the mid-11th century BCE. Kjaer and Albright were correct in attributing the destruction level at Shiloh to the Philistines following their victory in this battle (Chapter 5). Other sites in the hill country were probably also destroyed or abandoned at this time, as suggested by the ceramic assemblages from Ai and Khirbet Raddana and by the results of our survey in southern Ephraim (Chapter 4).

The other chronological evidence comes from the material remains of the Settlement sites themselves. With respect to the pottery, the closeness of a few assemblages to Late Bronze ceramic traditions is very important. The resemblance is particularly striking in Stratum III at ʿIzbet Ṣarṭah, where the proximity to the coastal plain explains the richness of the assemblage. But it is also perceptible at Giloh, Mt. Ebal and other sites in the hill country. However, vessels recalling ceramic types of the 13th century — cooking pots with everted rims and jars similar to "Canaanite jars" — were found in the destruction level at Shiloh, i.e., as late as the mid-11th century BCE. It follows that the quantitative dimension of the appearance of various types at Israelite Settlement sites is also significant.

The presence or absence of characteristic pottery types of the second half of the 11th century BCE must also be considered. By this we mean red-slipped and burnished pottery and decorated Philistine material. Here, too, we must add a cautionary note to the effect that burnishing was relatively common in the vicinity of the coastal plain and the valleys (on the appearance of burnishing, see A. Mazar 1985b:45, 83–84), but became increasingly rare as one ascended into the hills. Similarly, Philistine pottery was less frequent in the heart of the hill country than at sites bordering on the coastal plain. Nonetheless, the presence or absence of these features is still meaningful: slipped and burnished pottery was found neither at Giloh, and Mt. Ebal nor in the large assemblage from Shiloh and apparently not at Ai and Khirbet Raddana either.

Philistine sherds have been published from only three sites in the hill country: Tell en-Naṣbeh, Bethel and Beth-zur (T. Dothan 1982:44,48,54). On the other hand, the assemblage recovered from the destruction layer at Shiloh — the richest collection ever unearthed at an Israelite Settlement site — included only one possibly Philistine sherd. None were encountered at Ai and Khirbet Raddana (based on the preliminary reports). It appears that

Philistine pottery reached the heart of the hill country only in the second half of the 11th century BCE, with the expansion of Philistine political power into the region following their victory at Ebenezer and the establishment of footholds in the Hills of Benjamin. Another logical consequence is that sites where no Philistine pottery was discovered, despite extensive excavation, must have been destroyed or abandoned no later than the mid-11th century BCE.

Further progress in discerning chronological nuances in the pottery of Israelite Settlement sites must await a statistical analysis of the ceramic assemblages, especially those from sites where clear architectural phases within the Iron I period can be distinguished.

The conclusions about relative chronology that can be drawn from the architectural evidence at the Israelite Settlement sites have already been presented (Chapter 6). Suffice it here to recall that a courtyard site such as ʿIzbet Ṣarṭah Stratum III probably represents the stage when the inhabitants were still close to their pre-sedentery pastoralist way of life, although this observation does not necessarily have any direct chronological significance. On the other hand, it is doubtful whether sites with developed pillared buildings could have belonged to a very early stage of Iron I.

In summary, the ceramic and architectural evidence both lead to the conclusion that the earliest Israelite Settlement sites (archaeologically speaking) known thus far are Mt. Ebal, Giloh and the beginning of Stratum III at ʿIzbet Ṣarṭah (see also A. Mazar 1981a:33; Kempinski 1981:64). Other sites founded early in the course of Settlement in the central hill country include Beth-zur, Tell el-Fūl, Tell en-Naṣbeh and Bethel. At all these sites, the influence of ceramic traditions of the preceding period is apparent in such features as cooking pot rims and jar bases. The developed architecture of the villages at Ai and Khirbet Raddana prevents the attribution of their main phases to a very early stage of the period; we would thus assign them to no earlier than the end of the 12th century BCE. Shiloh, and probably Ai and Khirbet Raddana as well, were destroyed or abandoned in the middle of the 11th century BCE, while activity at other sites, such as Tell en-Naṣbeh, Bethel and Beth-zur, continued into the second half of the 11th century, even if these sites had also suffered damage ca. 1050 BCE.

CHAPTER 10

THE MAGNITUDE OF ISRAELITE SETTLEMENT

The archaeological data presented in Chapters 4–5 make it possible for us to examine two issues of crucial importance that have hitherto received only passing mention due to the lack of a sufficient factual basis for discussion. Specifically, we are referring to a quantitative chronological survey of the spread of groups of settlers through the country and an estimation of the size of the Israelite population during the Iron I period. Both of these matters bear directly on virtually every aspect of the study of Israelite Settlement; in fact, unless they are taken into account, no progress can be made in reconstructing the historical processes that took place in the country during the Iron I period. This is especially true when considering the nature of Israelite Settlement and the origins of the settlers.

THE EXPANSION OF THE ISRAELITE POPULATION IN CANAAN

Previous attempts to deal with this complex issue on the basis of abstruse and disputed sources were doomed to total failure (e.g., Yeivin 1971a). Instead, our discussion will be grounded in field-work data: the number of sites found in archaeological surveys and their dating according to evidence from excavations and surveys. In the future, it will be possible to return to the literary sources and to reassess them on the basis of these data.

In general, the principal region of Israelite Settlement was the northern part of the central hill country, between Jerusalem and the Jezreel Valley — especially in Ephraim and Manasseh. Almost 70% of all the known Israelite Settlement sites west of the Jordan River were surveyed in these two tribal territories; they also represent 90% of all the sites known in the entire central hill country, from the Beersheba basin to the Jezreel Valley. This was, in many respects, mirrored by the Iron I site density in the eastern Jordan Valley and in the Transjordanian plateau, where, as we have seen, the majority of the Iron I sites were concentrated in Gilead, which paralleled the Ephraim-Manasseh bloc on the other side of the Jordan.

At the beginning of the Iron I period, most of the Israelites resided along the spine of the central hill country and its eastern flank (Fig. 106). The western slopes of the hill country, the Beersheba Valley, Upper Galilee and the eastern

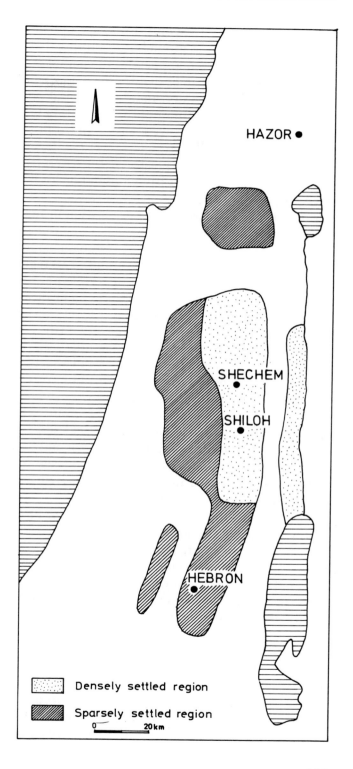

106. Map of the Israelite
Settlement — early stages.

Lower Galilee were settled only during later phases of the period (Fig. 107). It follows that there are no grounds for claiming that the "House of Joseph" was not settled until the second phase of the period (e.g., Alt 1939:47–49).

Israelite Settlement can be divided into three schematic historical stages: the beginning, the 11th century, and the territorial expansion at the beginning of the Monarchy. Initially, most of the population was concentrated in Ephraim and Manasseh. A few sites were also founded in Benjamin, Judah, the upper Shephelah (?), the Sharon (?) and Lower Galilee. Between Jerusalem and the Jezreel Valley, activity was greatest in the desert fringe, the highland plateaus, and the intermotane valleys from Shiloh northward. The western slopes were barely inhabited at all.

Most striking is the paucity of occupation in Judah. This is no archaeological accident, but has been substantiated by considerable research. For example, comparing the number of sites in Judah to an equivalent area in Ephraim, we find ten times as many sites in Ephraim! The regions adjacent to the Judean Hills reinforce this picture: The upper Shephelah experienced few, if any, attempts at settlement; no Israelite Settlement sites are known in the southern Hebron Hills (*contra* Kempinski *et al.* 1981:175); and in the Beersheba Valley, Israelite Settlement did not begin until the 11th century BCE — and even then, only on a limited scale. Had the Judean hills been thickly settled already in the 12th century, or even in the 11th, we would have expected to find evidence of a steady flow of people farther south, into areas that were then practically uninhabited by "non-Israelite" elements.

The plateau of the Judean Hills was seemingly conducive to settlement. In the first place, there was a broad marginal area to the south and east, with extensive areas available for growing cereals and for pasturage, similar to those regions of Ephraim that were favored at the beginning of Israelite Settlement. Second, there were hardly any Canaanites living in this part of the country; Debir was the only center south of Jerusalem in the Late Bronze period.

The explanation for the scarcity of occupation in Judah during the entire Bronze Age as well as during Iron I must be geographical and ecological: The proportion of rocky terrain to areas suitable for agriculture was relatively high, and the ground was covered with dense coppice. Analogies to modern times cannot be drawn for this region, since the present situation reflects millennia of intensive cultivation dating back to the Iron II period, when the area was heavily inhabited for the first time.

The small population in Judah of the Iron I period either arrived in a thin trickle from the principal areas of Israelite Settlement to the north, or included sedenterizing pastoral groups who had already been active in the region. Both processes swelled toward the end of Iron I and at the beginning of the Monarchy. Judah's transformation into a beehive of activity thus occurred relatively late, starting only during the United Monarchy. The demographic picture painted by archaeology has its counterpart in the biblical accounts, which indicate clearly that during the 11th century, activity in the hill country was pretty much restricted to Ephraim and Benjamin, where all the major centers were located — Shiloh, Gilgal, Bethel, Mizpah, Ramah, and Gibeah. On the other hand, very little information is offered about Judah before the time of Saul and David. (The emphasis on the importance of Ephraim and Benjamin in the Bible is also due to the personalities of Samuel and Saul, who are the focus of 1 Samuel.)

The penetration into Judah from the north is perhaps hinted at in the story of Judah and Simeon setting out from Manasseh to invade the Judean Hills (Judges 1:4–9; see de Vaux 1978:541–542). A clearer reflection is the appearance of the form "Ephrati(m)" [מ] אפרתי in connection with Bethlehem and Kiriath-yearim, which indicates that Ephraimite clans settled in northern Judah (Na'aman 1984; on the biblical evidence for the consolidation of Judah, see, e.g., Cohen 1965:94–98).

That leaves the problem of the biblical tradition of the penetration into Judah from the south (Aharoni 1979:220; Herrmann 1975:91; Miller 1977a:284; de Vaux 1978:539,541–542,674). The surprising dearth of sites in the Beersheba Valley and in the southern Hebron Hills seems to preclude any large-scale influx of elements from that direction. If there were connections with southern groups (Na'aman 1984:325–327), their archaeological expression was negligible.

Another indication of the spread of settlement into Judah involves the sacred centers of the Israelites. Archaeological and biblical evidence combined suggest a process by which these centers gradually moved southward, simultaneous with the expansion of occupation in that direction. Our excavations have validated the theory that Shiloh was the earliest center of the hill country groups (disregarding the hazy tradition concerning Shechem). After the destruction of the site in the mid-11th century BCE, Gilgal, where Samuel and Saul were active, came to the fore, with other important towns in the mountain ridge of Benjamin. At the end of the 11th century, the Ark of the Covenant was lodged in Kiriath-yearim (1 Samuel 7:2). Only at the beginning of the 10th century BCE, as settlement in Judah burgeoned, did the southern centers rise in importance: Hebron and David's selection of Jerusalem as his capital.

With the increasing concentration of population along the spine of the central hill country, the process of Settlement became firmly rooted and needed room for expansion. Meanwhile, due to the pressure of the Philistines and other elements farther north, those groups which may have settled in the upper Shephelah and eastern Sharon retreated eastward. The Israelite population was now caught on the horns of a dilemma. On the one hand, the best areas in the central hill country — along the intermontane valleys of Ephraim and Manasseh — were already relatively densely settled. On the other hand, the inhabitants of the hill country had not yet amassed sufficient strength to take control over the coastal plain, the Shephelah, or the northern valleys.

As a result, in addition to the intensification of settlement in various areas of the northern central hills, in Judah, and in Lower Galilee, there now began a movement into uninhabited marginal zones. The remote and harsh western slopes had previously been avoided, due to the difficult geographical conditions: a rugged landscape; distance from permanent water sources in some cases; formidable rock formations; and relatively thick forests (Chapter 4). Now, however, settlers overcame the natural obstacles of these marginal regions. A few sites were established in the Beersheba Valley, and Israelite Settlement got underway in Western Galilee, as well as in the hilly, dissected, forested heart of Upper Galilee.

The expansion into these frontier regions had far-reaching implications for the socio-political system of the hill country groups. The struggle with ecological obstacles, the beginning of horticulture cultivation that speeded agricultural specialization, and the territorial confrontation with neighbouring entities to the west and south necessitates better administration and military organization, and brought about the emergence of the monarchy (Finkelstein forthcoming c).

The archaeological data thus indicate that the main force of Settlement was felt in the areas of the "House of Joseph," and that this was the core from which many groups fanned out into other regions. However, there obviously were groups that settled down directly in these peripheral zones, without passing an interim period in the central hill country. The Bible also hints of the outward spread of population from the northern central hill country (as noted as early as Luther 1901; Meyer 1906:506).

In addition to the expansion into Judah, the following sould be noted. There is evidence that the tribe of Issachar (which, as Gal has shown, settled in the basaltic highlands of eastern Lower Galilee only in the 10th century) originated in northern Samaria (Gal 1982a). A strong tradition emphasizes the roots Asher had in the southwestern hills of Ephraim (e.g., Malamat 1976a:64; de Vaux 1978:665).[35] The northward migration of the tribe of Dan via the hill country of Ephraim has apparently received some archaeological support (Chapter 3).

The last stage in the expansion and organization of the Israelite entity began at the end of the 11th century and peaked in the early 10th century, when the last Canaanite enclaves in the Jezreel Valley were subdued and when the Philistines were repulsed from certain areas of the Shephelah and the southern

---

35 However, the archaeological evidence also permits another interpretation. Only few Israelite Settlement sites have been found in the region mentioned in the genealogical list of Asher in the southwestern part of the territory of Ephraim (I Chron 7:30–31). It may be that the biblical source reflects northward expansion in Iron II or else, movement from the north into the central hill country during that period.

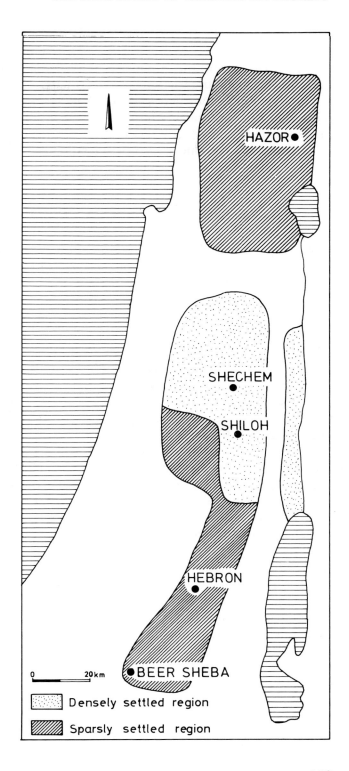

107. Map of the Israelite Settlement — end of 11th century BCE.

HAZOR

SHECHEM

SHILOH

HEBRON

BEER SHEBA

0   20km

Densely settled region

Sparsly settled region

coast. Israelite groups were then able to penetrate into these previously closed regions.

Territorial expansion, which had already begun in the 11th century, obviously created more friction between the Israelites and the relatively strong groups living in the northern valleys, the coastal plain and the Shephelah. The skirmishes that unavoidably broke out were among the factors leading up to the watershed event of the political history of the country: unification of most of the Land of Israel under a single government.

THE SIZE OF THE ISRAELITE POPULATION IN IRON I

Estimating the size of the Israelite population in Iron I is of critical importance in discussing the characteristics of the historical and demographic processes underway in the Land of Israel at the time, and it also occupies a focal position in the debates among the three schools of interpretation of Israelite Settlement.

Advocates of the sociological school made no bones about the centrality of this issue:

> The major question, upon which all else depends, is what were the sources of that population of the Twelve Tribes that Albright years ago estimated as approximately a quarter million, only a generation or two after the time of Moses (Mendenhall 1976:155).

In other words, the large number of Israelite Settlers involved precluded, in their opinion, any origin in the desert fringes bordering the country.

In the past, scholars had to make do with biblical census data and other indirect historical sources, most or all of which required considerable explication before they could be used and were therefore liable to lead to extremely contradictory results. Even if they never admitted it outright, most scholars operated under the *a priori* assumption that a large mass of people entered the Land of Israel one way or another at the time.

Albright's opinion was naturally given great weight. He estimated that the number of inhabitants in the Land of Israel at the beginning of the period of the Monarchy, i.e. at the *end* of the Settlement process, was about 750,000 (1925:20–25). Elsewhere, Albright hypothesized that during the United Monarchy, the population doubled from 400,000 to 800,000 souls (1950:56, 60 n. 75). He reckoned the Israelite population "a generation or two after the time of Moses" at about 250,000 (in McCown 1947b:435). In Baron's view (1971:869), the number of inhabitants in the country in the year 1000 BCE stood at some 1,800,000. Based on population figures during the Roman-Byzantine period, Avi-Yonah claimed that it was "possible to estimate the number of inhabitants during the time of the Israelite Monarchy at one and a third million, and at no less than a million at the time of the conquest" (1972:146).[36]

More recently, considerable information has accumulated from comprehensive field studies all over the country, providing the means to make a more realistic estimate of the population in the Land of Israel in antiquity, one based on solid archaeological data rather than on vague literary sources or intuitive, sometimes emotional, perceptions. The numbers previously bandied about for earlier periods have turned out to be way too high (Broshi and Gophna 1984; 1986; Shiloh 1980). We must, therefore, reexamine the population estimates for the Iron I period as well, based on the data presented in Chapters 3–4.

These data, even when incomplete, accurately reflect the pattern of Israelite Settlement west of the Jordan River. Regions such as western Galilee and eastern Lower Galilee have been thoroughly surveyed; for other areas, such as the Beersheba Valley, Ephraim, Manasseh, and Upper Galilee, the data are very satisfactory. Although the Judean Shephelah, the Judean Hills, central Lower Galilee, the Jordan Valley and Benjamin have been less rigorously explored, drastic changes in our appreciation of these areas are highly unlikely.

Several aspects of our method for calculating population size need to be clarified:

— Methods for estimating the population of a single site according to water or grain consumption (Rosenan 1978; Currid 1986:221–228; Rosen 1986:171–174), or by measuring the roofed built-up area (Naroll 1962), are not applicable for estimating population of large territories. The only appropriate system for this task is one that calculates the total inhabited area of all the sites of a certain period and multiplies by a density factor.

— We have sufficient information to provide us with a very clear notion of the physical size of one-period Israelite Settlement sites. For multi-period sites, it is obviously much harder to deduce the surface area during the Iron I period, but we can make educated guesses using both data from the one-period sites and the relative proportions of Iron I pottery among the sherds picked up in surveys at these sites. From our work in the territory of Ephraim, we reached the conclusion that the size of a given site in Iron I was no more than half the size it attained in Iron II (which was often the predominant period in the hill country sites), and it was usually considerably less.

— We have used a density factor of 25 persons per dunam. This figure has been found to be realistic; the higher multipliers previously used produced inflated results (summarized in Broshi and Gophna 1984:148; 1986:74). Even the figure of 25 persons per dunam may be a little too high, especially at sites

---

36 But in reference to the number who took part in the Exodus from Egypt, there were also minimalists, who spoke in terms of only a few thousand (Petrie 1906:208–221; Lucas 1944:166).

representing a society in the process of sedentarization, where architecture was relatively sparse (e.g., Giloh, where the open areas were extensive).[37]
— A numerical summary of the Iron I sites actually reflects the situation around the year 1000 BCE, for the ceramic types that characterized the period continued to appear until the end of the 11th or beginning of the 10th century BCE.
— Only permanent sites have been included in our calculations, for obvious reasons. However, at least by the end of the 11th century BCE, on the eve of the inauguration of the Monarchy, the role of various nomadic elements of the population should not be exaggerated. At the end of the Ottoman period, for example, when the number of Beduin was relatively large, they still did not constitute more than 15% of the entire population (Shmueli 1980:73).

The following table summarizes the information from the various regions of Israelite Settlement:

REGION	DATA[a] P	E	IRON I STAGE[b] E	L	# KNOWN SITES	EST. POP.	CORR. FACTOR[c]
Beersheba Valley	X			X	2–3	150–200	2
Judean Hills	X	X		X	10 (?)	1,250	2
Judean Shephelah[d]	X		X		2(?)	500	3
Judean Desert	X		unknown		few (?)	100	3
Benjamin	X		X	X	12	2,200	1.5
Ephraim		X	X	X	122[e]	9,650	1.25
Manassehe[f]		X	X	X	±74/96(?)	16,500/ 29,000	1.25
Sharon[d]	X		X		± 10	1,250	2

37 According to the 1945 *Village Statistics*, the population density in montane Arab villages was less than 20 persons per dunam (see also Brawer 1984).

(cont'd)

REGION	DATA[a] P	E	IRON I STAGE[b] E	L	# KNOWN SITES	EST. POP.	CORR. FACTOR[c]
Jordan Valley	X		unknown		17–18	2,200	2
Lower Galilee[g]	X W,C	X E	X	X	20	2,000	1.5
Western Galilee[h]	X			X	25	2,500	1.25
Upper Galilee + north. Jordan Valley	X			X	23	2,300	1.5
			TOTAL		± 315	40,650	

NOTES TO TABLE

[a] In this column, P = data only partial, E = extensive data.

[b] In this column, E = early Iron I, L = late Iron I.

[c] The numbers in this column are correction factors which, in our opinion, are the maximum figures by which the population estimates can be multiplied to compensate for less-than-complete data.

[d] It is hard to determine whether the population of the Shephelah and the Sharon can be defined as "Israelite."

[e] Including sites in the vicinity of ʿIzbet Ṣarṭah.

[f] Calculation is based on the assumption that the large Iron I sites, located on the main tells of Manasseh, were inhabited mainly by indigenous sedentary population. We therefore have included only the 59 "villages," 13 "farms," and two "cultic sites" (Zertal 1986b:340–342) — altogether 12,500 people — and added 4000 to cover the possibility that some of the new groups settled alongside the Canaanite population in the major tells.

[g] In the DATA column, W, C, and E refer to western, central, and eastern Lower Galilee.

[h] Not including the coastal plain.

We have thus arrived at a total of about 40,650 sedentary inhabitants for the known sites west of the Jordan River. If we compensate for the fact that the data are, to varying degrees, incomplete by multiplying the population for each region by the correction factor in the far right-hand column, then the maximum number of Israelite inhabitants throughout the country would be nearly 55,000; this may even be a bit higher than the gaps in our information warrant. Moreover, this figure includes the population of the Shephelah and the Sharon, which were abandoned during the Iron I period; leaving them out our calculations, the number would drop to about 51,000. Other sites that existed for only part of Iron I include Giloh and Mt. Ebal; Shiloh, Raddana and Ai were destroyed or abandoned *ca.* 1050 BCE. The exclusion of such sites would reduce the figure even farther, since our population estimates reflect the number of Israelites at the end of the 11th century BCE, on the eve of the inauguration of the Monarchy.

No less important for appreciating the character of Israelite Settlement is the size of the population at the beginning of the process. In attempting to estimate this figure, we first eliminated those regions where settlement began only at a relatively late stage of Iron I. We used the results of our survey in the territory of Ephraim as a model for other regions where occupation was continuous throughout Iron I. According to our analysis of the pottery from Iron I sites in Ephraim, only about half of the sites were inhabited early in the period. These sites developed over the years and probably reached their zenith later in Iron I; in other words, they initially encompassed less surface area. For example, the size of the early Iron village at Ai was about 12 dunams, but initially it was undoubtedly considerably smaller.

Assuming that the early Israelite Settlement sites in Ephraim covered an area about half of that attained by the end of the Iron I period, we arrived at an estimate of 3,800 individuals, about 40% of the population size at the end of Iron I. If this proportion held true for the other regions that were inhabited early on (for the Sharon and Judean Shephelah, we calculated the entire population), we could multiply the resultant figures by our 'correction factors' to obtain a total of about 21,000 sedentary Israelites living west of the Jordan River around the mid-late 12th century BCE.

During this early stage of Israelite Settlement, pastoralists were probably still fairly numerous, but they were not included in our estimates (Chapter 11). However, even if our figures are doubled or tripled in order to overcompensate for this omission and for any other deficiencies in our data that we may have overlooked, the number of Israelite inhabitants west of the Jordan River was obviously lower by far than any of the estimates previously promoted.

The size of the population of Israelite settlers accords well with what is known about the number of inhabitants in the country during the Late Bronze period, on the eve of the time with which we are concerned (more on this in the next chapter). The fact that the number of inhabitants was not large explains why the new settlers did not initially constitute a direct threat to the Canaanite centers, which were still extant throughout the country, and why those groups did not cause a shortage of land, which could have led to tension and conflict. No threat to Egyptian interests in Canaan was perceived, of course, and by the time Israelite Settlement expanded and strengthened, the Egyptians had already vanished from the scene.

CHAPTER 11

THE NATURE OF ISRAELITE SETTLEMENT

The Origin of the Israelites

The question of the origin of the people who settled in the hill country during the iron I period lies at the heart of research on Israelite Settlement in Canaan. Sooner or later, every attempt to reconstruct the events of this period runs up against this pivotal issue. If we fail to provide a satisfactory answer, we will be unable to solve the riddle of Israelite Settlement.

Until the early 1960s, scholars were virtually unanimous in regarding the desert, or the desert fringe, as the source of the newcomers; their differences concerned the manner in which these people appeared on the scene, whether by military conquest (Albright and others) or by peaceful infiltration (Alt and his followers). The last two decades have witnessed the advent of the revolutionary theory promulgated by Mendenhall and Gottwald, who rejected any eastern origin for the settlers and viewed them, instead, as refugees from the lowest, exploited classes of urban Canaanite society in the Late Bronze period.[38] A slightly variant version of this theory sought the roots of Israel in an early rural framework in the hilly areas of the country. The sociological view influenced discussions of other periods as well, and stimulated scholars to seek answers to archaeo-historical problems *within* the society of the country, rather than to speculate about migrations of new elements from the outside (e.g. Dever 1980 for the end of the third millennium BCE).

During our detailed survey of the various schools of scholarly thought (Chapter 8), we stressed that despite our rejection of many of the central tenets of the Mendenhall-Gottwald approach, we do accept two of their important points: Before the camel was domesticated as a herd animal, which apparently happened only toward the end of the 2nd millennium BCE, sizeable groups of people could not have lived deep in the deserts of the ancient Near East.

---

38 These explanations are closely connected with the three main theories about the relations between the Desert and the Sown in the ancient Near East, theories reflecting the views current among scholars studying similar modern phenomena: waves of settlers flooding over the inhabited country (e.g., Moscati 1959:29,42,72–73); a steady infiltration of nomads from the desert fringe (Kupper 1957; Klengel 1972); and the creation of a dimorphic society in which the nomads originated among the sedentary population (Luke 1965; Matthews 1978).

Therefore, the nomads/pastoralists (who herded flocks, not camels) and the sedentary dwellers were two specialized parts of one dimorphic society. The two groups lived in proximity and established mutual economic and social relations. Their relationship was characterized by symbiosis rather than by confrontation (Luke 1965; Matthews 1978).

In order to trace the roots of a specific group, regardless of the time frame or geographic location involved, three avenues of inquiry must be pursued: historical sources, to the extent that they exist; the material culture of the group under discussion, including what it indicates about the socio-economic character of the population, and its relationship to the material culture of the preceding period; and the settlement pattern of the period in question compared to that of its predecessor (and sometimes its successor as well).

The principal historical source at our disposal for the period of Israelite Settlement is, of course, the Bible. Without denigrating its overwhelming importance for reconstructing the history of Israel, the fact remains that attempts to reconstruct the course of Israelite Settlement on the basis of the biblical accounts have not been successful. The main reason for their failure is that the biblical narratives were redacted centuries after the events they purport to describe actually took place. As a result, what they really reflect is the version that was current in Jerusalem at the end of the period of the Monarchy (Lemche 1985:357–385).

This leaves us with material culture and settlement patterns to consider. Both of these factors strongly suggest that the people settling in the hill country in the Iron I period, or at least most of them, came from a pastoralist background. As for the material culture, the only conclusive evidence comes from the layout of the Iron I sites: The elliptical site plan, where a series of broadrooms encompassed a large central courtyard, was adapted from the nomadic tent camp. The proliferation of silos at Israelite Settlement sites was characteristic of a formerly nomadic society in the process of sedentarization (Chapter 6). Looking at the pattern of settlement, it is quite clear that Israelite Settlement was densest in regions suitable for cereal crops and pasturage, and that it was relatively sparse in areas appropriate for horticulture and mixed agriculture (Chapters 4,10)

A very important question — a decisive one in our opinion — concerns the extent to which the material culture of Israelite Settlement sites was related to Canaanite material culture of the Late Bronze period and the potential significance of these connections. Scholarly opinion on this matter is divided. According to the most widely accepted view, there was a sharp contrast between the two cultures. More recently, however, points of contact and continuity have been highlighted, especially with respect to pottery (Franken 1975a:337; de Geus 1975:70; Miller 1977a:262; Ahlström 1984a, 1984b; 1986; Kempinski 1985:403; see also Chapters 7–8), and naturally given considerable weight by adherents of the sociological school of scholarship.

There are, however, several mitigating factors that must not be overlooked:

— No total cultural break should be expected. Even when new groups of people enter a given area, their material culture is soon influenced by the material culture prevailing in that area, and thus a seeming link to the previous period is forged.

— Human material culture is influenced first and foremost by the socioeconomic situation and by the environmental conditions. Thus it is possible for the material cultures of two contemporary and propinquous groups to be dissimilar, e.g., Israelite culture in the hill country versus Philistine culture in the southern coastal plain and the Shephelah. The same holds true when contrasting Late Bronze Canaanite culture, which was primarily urban and commercially interconnected, with the culture of the Iron I inhabitants of the hill country, which was the product of isolated groups occupying small sites and preoccupied with daily subsistence. In cases where Israelites and Canaanites lived in physical proximity and shared a common environment, certain similarities were bound to be perceptible in their ceramic assemblages, despite the differences dictated by their divergent socio-economic situations (e.g., ʿIzbet Ṣarṭah and Aphek).

— The degree of similarity between Israelite material culture and its predecessor should be evaluated at undisputably Israelite sites, and not at borderline or questionable sites such as Tel Masōs.

All of these considerations lead us to conclude that most of the people who settled in the hill country in the Iron I period came from a background of pastoralism, and not *directly* from the urban Canaanite polity of the Late Bronze period. These people, who tended flocks but apparently did not herd camels, did not originate deep in the desert, but had lived on the fringes of the settled areas, or perhaps even in the midst of the sedentary dwellers. The material culture of indubitably Israelite sites, those in the central hill country, is completely different from that of the Canaanite centers. The contrasting socio-economic characters of these two cultures, their disparate environmental settings, and the changes occurring all over the country at the end of the 13th and beginning of the 12th centuries BCE underlay these differences. Certain points of contact between the two cultures, notably in pottery types, attest to relations between the settlers and the nearby Canaanite centers; we have already noted that some of the latter continued to exist until at least the mid-12th century BCE and probably even later (Chapter 8).

The Hill Country as a Frontier Zone

Prior to the Iron I period, the Land of Israel could be divided into two zones of occupation: regions where permanent settlement was continuous, with few and relatively short crises in occupation, i.e., the fertile areas of the coastal plain, the Shephelah and the northern valleys; and marginal regions where sedentary activities waxed and waned in accordance with historical developments, i.e., the semi-arid areas of the Negev Highlands, the Beersheba Valley, and the Judean Desert. Other areas that can also be described as 'frontier zones,' (to use the term that has come into fashion of late, e.g., Lenski 1980), include considerable portions of the hilly regions, especially in Upper Galilee, Ephraim and the Judean Hills. This frontier was geo-ecological rather than climatological; the harsh topography, difficult rock formations, and dense coppice were all obstacles to settlement. Moreover, only limited lands were available for agriculture; travel from one place to another required great effort; and it was difficult to hew out cisterns.

As a result, during the earlier periods, before the hilly regions were rendered arable by generations of labor, settlers chose the coastal plain and the valleys. Penetration into the frontier zones of the hill country commenced only when the more favorable areas became overcrowded. Conversely, when there was a decline in occupation, these marginal areas of the hill country were depopulated first (Finkelstein forthcoming d). Because discontinuity of occupation was indeed felt more acutely in the frontier zones than in the northern valleys and the coastal plain, such areas were particularly sensitive barometers of historical change. These observations pertain to sedentary dwellers. However, the frontier zones of the hill country — which generally were only rather sparsely inhabited and partly covered with dense coppice — were highly suitable for the needs of groups of pastoralists, who exploited them primarily for summer pasturage.

Occupation of the Hill Country from MB II to Iron I

The patterns of settlement in the central hill country during Iron I and earlier periods make an important contribution to clarifying the course of Israelite Settlement and also shed light on the origins of the Israelite population. We will briefly survey the pendulum swings of settlement in the hilly regions during the critical interval from MB II to Iron I.

The entire country flourished in MB IIB (Na'aman 1982:166–169; Broshi and Gophna 1986). In contrast to earlier periods of prosperity, however, an unprecedented number of settlers inundated the central hill country as well. Hundreds of sites of every size — fortified cities, villages, and individual farms — were founded throughout the region, especially along the fertile intermontane valleys, but also in more remote and inhospitable areas.

Zertal has surveyed some 116 MB II sites in Manasseh (1986b:175–200), and we have examined about 60 such sites in Ephraim. Although comprehensive archaeological information from Benjamin and Judah is lacking, many more sites were founded there in MB II than in the preceding periods (although still many fewer than in the northern hilly regions). Altogether, some 200 MB IIB-C sites have been found in the central hill country; as surveying continues, many more are bound to be discovered.

Study of the ceramic material from these surveys is just getting underway, so the chronological subdivisions of the period have yet to be nailed down. However, a preliminary comparison of the finds from the Middle Bronze sites encountered in the survey of Ephraim with the finds from the excavations at Shiloh, in the heart of the region, produced the following tentative outline: The wave of settlement crested in MB IIB; at that time, the small village was the primary unit of settlement (but some of the sites may represent pastoralist groups). In MB IIC (*ca.* 1650–1550 BCE), the nature of activities in the region changed somewhat. A number of the unfortified sites were abandoned, while at a few locales, impressively fortified centers arose (Finkelstein, forthcoming d.) The fortified centers of the hill country, as well as many of the major cities of the lowlands, were destroyed at the end of the Middle Bronze II.

In contrast to the extraordinary prosperity of MB II, the Late Bronze period was characterized by a severe crisis in settlement throughout the country. Ironically, until not long ago, the Late Bronze period was thought by some to have marked the epitome of development in the Land of Israel in the 2nd millennium BCE. The relative abundance of historical documentation and the richness of the material culture (pottery, ivories and other objects) unearthed in excavations at the large tells created this false impression. Now, thanks to the extensive surveys, a more realistic assessment of the state of settlement can be made. For, despite certain achievements in the realm of material culture and despite close commercial links with other Mediterranean shores, the Land of Israel in the Late Bronze period was a mere shadow of its former glory (Gonen 1984).

The crisis was most grave in the hill country, where the reduction in the number of settlements was drastic. Only 31 Late Bronze sites have been found in Manasseh (Zertal 1986b:201–223. This number includes four cemetry-sites and five Late Bronze I sites. The number of Late Bronze II settlements is therefore 22. This number may further decrease with a different pottery interpretation, since Zertal identifies Late Bronze sites according to local pottery, which in some cases may be ascribed to the early Iron I as well — note his dating of the "Bull-Site"also to the Late Bronze — p.114). A mere five Late Bronze sites are known in Ephraim and just two or three in Benjamin and Judah. Altogether only 25–30 sites were occupied in the Late Bronze II between the Jezreel and Beersheba Valleys. Because human activity was mainly confined to the large central tells, the majority of which are already known, it is highly unlikely that many additional settlements will be discovered in the future. Other regions were also practically deserted during the Late Bronze period (Chapter 3): only two or three sites were found in Upper Galilee; five in Lower Galilee; none in the Beersheba Valley; and few in the Transjordanian plateau (Sauer 1986:7–8 mentions only five centers).

Moreover, those sites where occupation did continue frequently shrank in size. For example, the fortified Middle Bronze settlement at Shiloh was abandoned and replaced by only small-scale cultic activity in the Late Bronze period. The survey shows that the contraction of occupation was pronounced at other sites as well (Sheikh Abu Zarad, Kh. ᶜUrma). Only in the southern coastal plain, the Shephelah and the northern valleys was human activity lively during this period as well (Na'aman 1975; 1982:174–175,212).

It is possible that within the Late Bronze period itself there were minor oscillations in occupation (Na'aman 1981:185; Gonen 1984:68), but these were insignificant and do not affect the overall picture. The conflicts between the Canaanite city- states, Egyptian military campaigns, and economic exploitation of the country by Egyptian overlords would have impeded any meaningful revival of settlement (Gonen 1979:230).

The decline of occupation during the transition from the MB II to Late Bronze periods was also noted in recent studies on the size of the sedentary population. Broshi and Gophna (1986) estimated the number of inhabitants west of the Jordan at 140,000 in the MB II period. Based on the work of Gonen (1979; 1984), Broshi judged the size of the Late Bronze population to be less than half as large — about 60,000–70,000 souls (lecture at Bar- Ilan University, 1982).

The Iron I period again witnessed a dramatic swing in the population of the hill country, this time in the opposite direction. About 240 sites of the period are known in the area between the Jezreel and Beersheba Valleys: 96 surveyed by Zertal in Manasseh, 122 recorded in our survey of Ephraim (including the vicinity of ᶜIzbet Ṣarṭah to the west), and some 22 in Benjamin and Judah. In addition, 68 sites have been recognized in Galilee, 18 in the Jordan Valley, and dozens of others in the Transjordanian plateau. Because sites proliferated all over the region, no doubt more remain to be discovered in the future.

These three settlement maps — portraying the MB II, Late Bronze and Iron I periods — illuminate the problem of the origin of the early Israelites. They leave two critical questions for which satisfactory answers must be found: Why and to where did over half of the MB II population, i.e., virtually all the inhabitants of the hill country, 'vanish'? From where did the people who settled the hundreds of sites in Iron I 'materialize'?

The Late Bronze Period in the Hill Country

Exactly when the severe population crisis described above began is difficult to determine, although the finds from our survey of Ephraim suggest that the decline had already set in before the end of the Middle Bronze period. In any case, the process was apparently gradual, though rapid, and took place mainly during the 16th century BCE. The reasons behind the disintegration of permanent settlement are not sufficiently clear. At first glance, one might be inclined to blame it on Egyptian military conquests at the beginning of the New Kingdom, which would have dealt a massive blow to the country (e.g., Kenyon 1971:194; Wright 1962:91; Weinstein 1981). Serious archaeological (or even historical) evidence that many sites across the country were destroyed simultaneously is, however, wanting (on the Egyptian evidence see Redford 1979:273; Shea 1979:3).[39] But even such a campaign would fail to explain the wholesale abandonment of hundreds of small unfortified settlements.

As noted, our research in Ephraim suggests that the changes in settlement pattern began even before the "expulsion of the Hyksos" and the conquest of Sharuhen by Ahmose, the founder of the 18th Dynasty. Perhaps ecological factors led to the dissolution of settlements in the hill country (Zertal 1986b:53–55,222).

But the most probable explanation lies in stresses and strains within the Canaanite socio-political system itself (also Bienkowski 1986:127–128). These internal problems initially led both to the disbanding of some of the unwalled settlements throughout the hill country and to the strengthening of the central sites. Subsequently, they brought about the total abandonment of small sites and the contraction of fortified centers (see Bienkowski 1986:128). It is possible that Hurrians and other northern elements entering the Land of Israel at the end of the 17th century BCE should also be implicated in these changes (B. Mazar 1968:89–97; for relevant archaeological evidence, see Finkelstein and Brandl 1985). The frequent destructions of Shechem, the most important site in the central hill country, might reflect turbulence and unrest during the Middle Bronze period (Dever 1974:31).

What happened to the sizeable population if it was not decimated by war or pestilence? There is plenty of documentary evidence for the phenomenon of nomads settling down in our region in recent generations, as they did in antiquity. But there is little literature on the subject of this trend in reverse — the nomadization of sedentary peoples (Kupper 1957: XIII; Klengel 1972:40,219), although analogous situations from modern times are known. (Barth 1961:118; Spooner 1972:261; Khazanov 1978:121; Glatzer 1982:61–63 and bibliography. For a similar process at the end of the Early Bronze period, see Dever 1980:58; Esse 1982:367; Prag 1985:85–87; for Transjordan in later periods see LaBianca 1985).

The reversion to nomadization could have been caused by increasing population pressure on finite natural resources, natural disasters, confiscations by the authorities, heavy taxation, insecurity, etc. An excellent example comes from recent history of the region: Ottoman heavy taxation and misrule in the 18–19th centuries brought about the destruction of the rural framework of

---

39 Without a comparative statistical analysis of the ceramic assemblages from the destruction levels closing the Middle Bronze period at the various sites, no accurate chronological assessment can be made.

Palestine and southern Syria and apparently the nomadization of large parts of the sedentary population (e.g. Cohen 1973:324–327, and Hütteroth 1975, who describes the desertion of Palestinian villages, especially in the frontier regions; for the same process in Syria see Sweet 1974:43). It seems probable that this is what happened in the 'frontier zones,' including the hill country, toward the end of the Middle Bronze period. The network of permanent settlements fell apart, and many of the inhabitants became nomadic. This would explain their archaeological 'disappearance,' for we have yet to find a way to detect and identify the activities of non-sedentary groups, especially in non-desert regions.

This reconstruction of events brings us back to population estimates. During the transition from the Middle Bronze to Late Bronze periods, the number of people in the country did not actually shrink in half. Rather, there was a change in the proportion of sedentary dwellers to pastoralist groups, but only the reduced ranks of the former category are reflected in archaeological field work and, consequently, in population estimates. The demographic balance between the two sectors of this dimorphic society (or rather, "polymorphous society" — Lemche 1985:198) has far-reaching implications for understanding the history of the country during other periods as well, but that is beyond the scope of the present work.

The only available statistical data on the share of groups of pastoralists in the Land of Israel come from the beginning of the 20th century CE, when the Beduin are known to have constituted about 15 % of the population (Shmueli 1980:73). However, the ratio of sedentary dwellers to nomadic pastoralists could have varied widely, from an almost absolute sedentary majority at times when the polity was well organized, e.g., the Iron II and Roman-Byzantine periods, to a preponderance of non-sedentary inhabitants, as in the intermediate Bronze Age and perhaps in the Late Bronze and early Iron I periods as well.

But can we produce any archaeologcal evidence whatsoever — or even the slightest hint in historical sources — for the existence of a large population of pastoralists in the Land of Israel in the Late Bronze period?

Archaeologically, there are, perhaps, two intriguing clues. The first is the phenomenon of isolated sanctuaries, either unrelated to any settlement or else located close to permanent sites, but beyond the boundaries of their built-up areas. The former type includes the Amman airport temple (see Herr 1983 for a different interpretation); the sanctuary at Tell Deir ʿAlla, which the excavator described as a "shrine of wandering Beduins" (Franken 1975b:322); the Late Bronze cult place at Shiloh, where no permanent settlement was found (Chapter 5); and perhaps also the shrine at Tel Mevorakh, described by the excavator as a roadside sanctuary (Stern 1984:36). The latter type includes the building discovered at Tananir (Shechem) that is generally identified as a shrine (Boling 1969) and the Fosse Temple at Lachish (on the possibility that the Amman and Shechem temples served tribal groups, see Campbell and Wright 1969). Four points favor the interpretation of these isolated sanctuaries as archaeological evidence for non-sedentary groups in the Late Bronze period:

— This phenomenon is unknown in those periods of antiquity characterized by urban activity.

— Faunal analysis of the remains from Shiloh suggests that the Late Bronze cult place served a population of pastoralists (Chapter 5).

— At both Shechem and Lachish, there were temples within the bounds of the city. The necessity for extramural shrines is otherwise difficult to explain, especially since neither site was particularly large in size. (In Lachish the intramural shrine of Stratum VI was built after the Fosse Tempel went out of use — Ussishkin 1987:28, but it is logical to assume that there was a sanctuary on the mound at that time too).

— Most of the sites enumerated above were situated in typical 'frontier zones' — the central hill country, the Jordan Valley and the Transjordanian plateau.

The second archaeological indication of the existence of a significant population of pastoralists in the Late Bronze period is the relatively large number of cemeteries that were not situated adjacent to permanent settlements. These have been found in various places, especially in the hilly regions and in the Transjordanian plateau — once again, unequivocally marginal zones (Gonen 1979:229–230; Zertal 1986b: description of sites; Sauer 1986:8). This phenomenon, too, was not so widespread during times of permanent settlement; on the other hand, it was a feature of those periods, such as the Intermediate Bronze, when the proportion of nomads in the population was large.

The problematical question then arises of whether groups of pastoralists could have achieved a level of material culture as highly developed as that reflected in the finds of the Amman and Lachish temples and in the debris of the cult place at Shiloh. The answer appears to be affirmative. The finds from both of these sanctuaries and from the cemeteries are, above all, cultic in nature, and as such need not be representative of ordinary, everyday material culture, which was probably much simpler in character.

Because similar ritual objects were common at contemporary urban centers in Canaan, it is likely that they came into the possession of the nomadic pastoralists as a result of their close ties with the sedentary inhabitants. We cannot preclude the possibility that certain cult sites (Shechem and Lachish, for example) served some of the residents of the nearby cities as well. Furthermore, some members of the groups of shepherds and nomads could have established close relations with the urban dwellers, including sojourning in physical proximity to or even within their cities (e.g., Rowton 1974:14,22); in the process, they would have adopted some aspects of urban material culture.

As for historical evidence for the existence of significant groups of pastoralists, we cannot ignore the information from New Kingdom Egyptian sources concerning elements operating outside urban Canaanite society, but nonetheless alongside that framework. Specifically, we are referring to the Shosu =Sutu and other groups (summarized by Na'aman 1982:233–241). The possibility of a connection between the early Israelite population and the Shosu has been raised by Weippert (1979:32–35), Giveon (1971:269–271); Na'aman 1982:240) and Redford (1986:199–200). Interestingly enough, these groups were generally mentioned in conjunction with the 'frontier' regions of the country — Transjordan, the hill country, and the south.

Iron I — The Resedentarization of the Pastoralist Groups

At the end of the 13th century BCE, the socio-economic and political tides turned, and conditions became favorable for groups of pastoralists to settle down. It is extremely difficult to analyze the causes that brought about this change, for the simple reason that our ignorance about the period exceeds our knowledge.

The most important and useful method of analysis at our disposal is the comparative study of similar processes in modern cultures. Various studies undertaken in the Middle East in the last generation — as well as in more distant lands — have identified a number of stimuli that are likely to set the pocess of sedentarization in motion (Shmueli 1980; Salzman 1980:esp. 1–19; Khazanov 1984:200–201). These include improved security conditions, the influence of adjacent cultures, the existence of external economic alternatives to subsistence based on herding, military pressure exerted by a central authority, climatic changes, the difficulties of subsistence based on pastoralism, and the breakdown of the socio-political organization of the sedentary dwellers alongside whom the nomads lived.

The first four factors are not relevant for Iron I, a period characterized by the weakening of Egyptian and Canaanite authority, political instability, and worsening security conditions. There is, at present, no evidence of any climatic change at the time under discussion. The two remaining factors, which are essentially two sides of the same coin, are applicable. However, we should not expect to come up with a rigid and monocausal model for the process of sedentarization, and it is entirely likely that other factors, which have escaped our notice, were at work too.

For our purposes, the end of the Late Bronze period was singular in that this relatively short span of time marked the culmination of a series of trends and events, which together had far-reaching consequences for the history of the Land of Israel. Egyptian military campaigns, economic exploitation of Canaan by Egyptian overlords, conflicts among the Canaanite city-states, possible long-period droughts, and, finally, the pressure exerted by the Sea Peoples all

345

shook the foundations of the political and economic order of Canaan and weakened the fabric of urban and rural life to an unprecedented degree (on the destruction levels during the course of the Late Bronze period, see Kelm and A. Mazar 1982:3,13,32). These same factors ultimately led to the settlement of non-sedentary groups.

Bates and Lees (1977) have described a different model than the generally accepted one for the sedentarization of nomads. The major expression of the symbiotic relations between the two components of a dimorphic society is that the nomadic pastoralists supply the sedentary dwellers with animal products in exchange for surplus grain. According to Bates and Lees, the nomads in such a society could not afford to cause any major reversal in the fortunes of the sedentary inhabitants without settling down in their stead, for the destruction of agriculture would prevent their continued specialization in herding. In other words, the disintegration of permanent settlements (or, at a minimum, the inability of sedentary dwellers to produce a surplus of grain) would necessarily bring about a gradual transition from pastoralism to farming, especially cereal growing, and this would lead to sedentarization (see also Coote and Whitelam 1986:121).

Even if this model is not the only valid one, it does help explain the causes that led to the settlement of groups of pastoralists starting at the end of the 13th century BCE. The internal dissolution and collapse of the Canaanite city-states dealt a crushing blow to agriculture, thus destroying the fragile symbiotic balance between the nomadic pastoralists and the sedentary population and setting in motion the forces that led to sedentarization. The most crucial factor in this process may have been the Egyptian economic exploitation of the urban centers (including taxation to support the Egyptian administration in Canaan), which seemingly reached its peak in the 13th century BCE (Weinstein 1981:17–22; Bienkowski 1986:155; Lemche 1985:423). This could have eliminated the ability of the Canaanite sedentary population to produce agricultural surplus and thus could have forced the pastoralists/nomads to engage in seasonal grain-growing agriculture, leading to the beginning of sedentarization (see already Weippert 1979:33–34).[40] The process of Settlement was probably gradual and lengthy. As the proportion of sedentary

40 Ostensibly, this model contradicts our views on the nomadization of the population at the end of the Middle Bronze. But the background of each period was so completely different that absolute comparisons between the two inverse processes cannot be drawn, especially since urban centers continued to flourish in the lowlands of the country during the Late Bronze period. Moreover, it is definitely possible to suggest the following sequence of events: weakening of the urban/rural communities and nomadization of large groups at the end of the Middle Bronze; further deterioration of the sedentary system at the end of the 13th century forcing pastoral groups to settle down (see also note 41 below).

inhabitants increased, the number of nomads dwindled.[41] But only toward the end of the 11th century and beginning of the 10th would the majority of the population have become sedentary.

The material culture of Iron I sites in the hill country therefore reflects the character of the people who lived there prior to sedentarization. On the one hand, the influence of the previous pastoralist mode of existence is still evident, especially in architecture. On the other hand, a certain connection with the material culture of the Canaanite cities is perceptible, especially in pottery, and this is best understood as the result of the lengthy coexistence of nomadic and sedentary elements of the population. (Fritz had already made this last point [Chapter 8], but he claimed that the groups of settlers came from without, i.e. from the desert.) At the same time, the finds from Settlement sites reflect the first stage of sedentary life in the frontier zones, when the Israelites lived in small isolated groups and wrestled with less-than-ideal topographical and

41 Certain reservations notwithstanding, the situation in Syro-Palestine over three millennia later, in the twilight of the Ottoman Empire, illustrates some of the events that took place in our region at the end of the Late Bronze period and beginning of Iron I. While the situations are obviously not analogous in every detail, even a general comparison sheds light on the behavior of nomadic pastoralists at a time when sedentary society was enervated. One of the most obvious differences between the two periods — the fact that in the Ottoman times, occupation was relatively dense *in the hill country* — is a result of historical and demographic developments that occurred long after Iron I. Nonetheless, because certain processes that are relatively well documented for the 19th and early 20th centuries CE are very similar to those which took place at the close of the 13th century BCE, an examination of the background to the more modern events is bound to be highly instructive (see also Lemche 1985:154).

Toward the end of the Ottoman period, Syro-Palestine had declined to the point of virtual exhaustion. The weak and corrupt central authority had brought about the deterioration of agriculture, the destruction of whole rural sectors, the nomadization of large sedentary groups, the reversion of cultivated land to desert, and the expansion of swampy regions. At the same time nomads from marginal areas penetrated into the heart of the country — the Sharon, the Jezreel Valley, and Galilee. Internecine fighting among the sedentary inhabitants further diminished their capability to withstand the incursions of Beduin (Amiran and Ben-Arieh 1963:165–166; Ashkenazi 1938:7–8; Oppenheim 1943:15ff), who quickly underwent the transition to sedentarization in these areas.

No flood of nomads poured out of the desert to inundate the cultivated areas. Rather, there was a peaceful infiltration by Beduin who moved away from the wilderness because of droughts, other tribes crowding them out, and, of course, the absence of any force that could prevent their entry into settled territory (Shmueli 1980:88,95,129–130). Yet another important factor in the sedentarization of these nomads was the decline of the settled territory, which upset the symbiotic balance and forced the nomads to produce by themselves the basic agricultural products that they used to receive through barter from the villages and cities.

In the turmoil of the Ottoman period both nomadization and sedentarization processes can therefore be traced. It seems that initially, misrule lead to nomadization, but later, the final deterioration of the rural population forced large groups of pastoralists to settle down.

environmental conditions in order to eke out their daily sustenance. The absence of luxury goods (which certain elements may have obtained before their sedentarization) was undoubtedly connected both to their basic economic conditions and to the general decline in the economy and material culture of the inhabitants of the country in Iron I.

Along with most other scholars, we accept that there must be a kernel of historical veracity in the deeply-rooted biblical tradition concerning the origin of Israel in Egypt (e.g. Weisman 1984:15–16). Certain elements among the settlers may well have come from outside the country, perhaps from the south, and a portion of the new population might have even come from a desert background. At the same time, we cannot brush aside the possibility that certain groups who settled in the hill country in Iron I originated directly from the Canaanite society of the lowlands; it is just that the archaeological evidence to support this view is vague, if existant at all.

But the vast majority of the people who settled in the hill country and in Transjordan during the Iron I period, must have been indigenous, without, however, being *direct* dropouts from either the Canaanite cities of the lowlands or a non-existent rural network in the hilly regions. These people had dropped out of the framework of permanent settlement back in the 16th century BCE and lived in pastoralist groups during the Late Bronze period. While they might have been active all over the country, their presence would have been felt most keenly in the sparsely inhabited 'frontier zones' that were suitable for pasturage — the Transjordanian plateau, the Jordan Valley, the desert fringe and the hill country. They had traversed these areas as part of a seasonal pattern of transhumance and established economic relations with the sedentary inhabitants, especially those resident in the few centers existing in these marginal regions, e.g., Shechem and Bethel. Starting at the end of the 13th century BCE, these groups began to settle down. The process lasted about two centuries and culminated in the political consolidation of the national identity of Israel.[42]

THE MANNER OF ISRAELITE SETTLEMENT

Groups of pastoralists, who had been active in a transhumant routine in the frontier zones of the country during the Late Bronze period, began to settle down at the end of the 13th century or beginning of the 12th. The best areas open to settlement were in the hill country, because they met two basic

---

42 At the same time, groups in Transjordan were undergoing a similar process of consolidation. Our reconstruction of the origin of the Israelite population brings us back to Weippert's interesting theory (1979:32–33) that the biblical description of the age of the Patriarchs actually portrays the situation in the Late Bronze period, when groups of pastoralists lived alongside a few permanent centers.

requirements: They were essentially devoid of Canaanites, and they were conducive to a combination of cereal crops and pasturage, the preferred economic structure during the initial stages of sedentarization.

Within the mountainous regions, Samaria (the territories of Manasseh and Ephraim), central Lower Galilee and Transjordan were the most suitable areas, while formidable environmental obstacles impeded settlement in Judah, Upper Galilee, the Beersheba Valley and the western slopes of the central hills. Israelite Settlement thus began in the desert fringe, intermontane valleys and convenient highland areas of the central hill country, and also in certain parts of the foothills. While these areas were only sparsely inhabited by Canaanites, they were not vacant, for several Canaanite urban centers were located in or near them in the Late Bronze period. It may be that as a result of earlier and ongoing symbiotic relations with the Canaanite cities, sedentarization deliberately began close to these centers.

This matter of the relations with the Canaanite centers is not yet sufficiently clear. Because the chronological data are still fluid, some of the following remarks must be regarded as no more than hypotheses based on our interpretation of settlement patterns and on our study of the lifestyle of nomads in general. At the stage prior to sedentarization, groups of pastoralists used to graze their flocks in the areas covered by vegetation and in the stubble of the fields near the Canaanite cities during the summers (Noth 1958:69; Matthews 1978:27), and perhaps even grew cereals in the winter in the adjacent areas where the natural vegetation was sparse. With the passage of time, these groups began to settle down on the edges of the intermontane valleys and in other suitable locales; in the process, they became less dependent on herding and put more effort into agriculture, which required clearing the more densely forested areas.

As the number of settlers increased, the lands available for agriculture — which were not extensive to begin with — no longer sufficed. This brought the settlers into conflict with the Canaanite centers in the hill country over the control of the best lands. These local clashes, which were not necessarily simultaneous, resulted in the destruction of several cities, which were, in any case, isolated from the main Canaanite urban network of the lowlands. Bethel, for example, could have been devastated in such a conflict. Some of the Canaanite settlements might have been gradually abandoned, rather than destroyed, due to pressures exerted by the new settlers.

However, Shechem and other sites in the territory of Manasseh continued to coexist with the new settlers well into the Iron I period. There were also entire regions, especially in the vicinity of the Jezreel Valley and the coastal plain, where relations with the sedentary population were apparently harmonious during the early part of the process of Israelite Settlement, no doubt because the Canaanites there were still numerically strong (Weippert 1976:129).

On the surface, it would seem that an alternative reconstruction of these events was possible, viz., that the Israelite Settlement sites in the hill country were founded only after the destruction of the Canaanite cities. However, at least for the western and northern portions of the hill country and perhaps for the upper Shephelah as well, it is quite certain that Israelite Settlement commenced before the devastation of the proximal Canaanite cities. An excellent example is Israelite ʿIzbet Ṣarṭah facing Canaanite Aphek. Both biblical allusions and archaeological evidence attest that Israelites settled alongside a large sedentary population in Manasseh (Chapter 3). The very fact that the Canaanite cities of Jerusalem, Bethel and Shechem delimited the boundaries of the allotments of the hill tribes may indicate that these cities were still extant at the beginning of Israelite Settlement (Alt 1939:8–9).

Israelite Settlement was multifaceted and strongly regional in character, as is clear from the settlement patterns arising from surveys all over the country and from the material culture at Israelite Settlement sites in various regions. In each area, the course of Israelite Settlement was directly affected by geographical conditions, economic potential, the strength of the Canaanites in the vicinity, and the nature of the links forged with them. Every region, therefore, was practically unique (as realized already by Noth 1938:21–22).

In the upper Shephelah and in the vicinity of Jerusalem, there was sparse Israelite Settlement alongside the Canaanite centers. In Benjamin, the new settlers were concentrated in the desert fringe, and a non-Israelite entity — the Gibeonites — inhabited the central ridge. The process of Israelite Settlement in Ephraim began primarily in the intermontane valleys and the desert fringe and expanded to the rugged and isolated western slopes only later. In Manasseh, a strong Israelite presence made itself felt alongside a sizeable sedentary population. In western Galilee, the new elements entered the area intermediate between the hill country and the coastal plain. In Upper Galilee, the Israelites occupied a difficult, hilly and rugged region.

In like manner, no single economic model can be applied to every site at the beginning of Israelite Settlement. Flocks still comprised the subsistence base of Giloh and ʿIzbet Ṣarṭah at a time when the well-developed villages at Khirbet Raddana and Ai had already become economically dependent on farming. While Khirbet Raddana and Ai might have been slightly later in date, there is no reason why contemporary groups could not have been at different stages of development (a phenomenon well known among modern nomads in the process of sedentarization: Amiran and Ben- Arieh 1963:173; Muhsam 1959:545). Nor can we preclude the possibility that some of the settlers at sites where the economy and material culture were comparatively advanced came from an urban background.

The area along the western margins of the hill country, adjacent to the coastal plain and the Shephelah, offers a good example of the variety of settlement processes that can be found by examining sites with similar geographical settings located in various parts of the country. In Judah, for example, settlers may have attempted to descend into the upper Shephelah at an early date, but they were beaten back either by the Philistines or by the Canaanites inhabitants before the Philistines arrived. Israelites also failed to expand westward from Judah even at a later date, due to the dense occupation by Philistines and Canaanites. In Ephraim, on the other hand, Israelite sites crept down as far west as the edges of the coastal plain in the vicinity of Aphek, inaugurating a lengthy period of neighborly coexistence (though the Israelites were periodically forced to withdraw to the east). But Israelite Settlement did not reach the coastal plain itself until the early 10th century BCE. In Manasseh, too, Israelite Settlement sites were apparently established on the border of the coastal plain; perhaps there was even an early attempt to settle in the plain, an attempt that was repulsed by the people who occupied the area north of the Yarkon River in the 12th century (Kochavi 1968:129). In Western Galilee, Israelite Settlement sites edged toward the coastal plain, as in the Aphek region, but stopped some distance to the east, which probably speaks volumes about their relations with the coastal inhabitants.

The process of Israelite Settlement was lengthy, probably lasting until the end of the 11th century BCE (on the likelihood that the sedentarization of a nomadic group would take centuries, see Patai 1958:187). As time passed, settlements took root in even more difficult and isolated regions. The time factor found expression in material culture as well; at some sites, well-developed villages grew rapidly, while at contemporary sites, the pace was slower.

During the 12th and 11th centuries, the hilly regions of the Land of Israel were the scene of the gradual transition by groups of pastoralists to a sedentary mode of existence. Although the cumulative results of archaeological field work all over the country support the view of the Alt school regarding the *manner* in which Israelite Settlement came about, the *origin* of the new settlers must be sought within the cultivated areas and the desert fringe, rather than in the adjacent deserts. The process itself was complex, variegated and complicated. Initially, the chief foes were natural obstacles; later, the Israelites came into conflict with the Canaanites living nearby and in the lowlands.

As the Israelites became stronger and consolidated into tribal units, they also established inter-regional institutions, the most important being cultic centers such as Shiloh. The need to join forces in the face of common adversaries — especially to facilitate expansion into additional areas and to defend against other expanding entities, mainly the Philistines — gradually created a sense of national, religious and ethnic awareness among the Israelite population, culminating in the inauguration of the Monarchy and the unification of most of the regions of the Land of Israel into a single sovereign state — for the first time in history.

CHAPTER 12

SUMMARY

The archaeological evidence presently available deals a fatal blow to the theory of a unified military conquest advocated by Albright and his followers. More and more sites that can be identified unequivocally with those mentioned in the biblical conquest narratives lack any remains of the Late Bronze period. In regions densely populated by Canaanites, which were supposedly conquered, there is virtually no evidence of Israelite Settlement prior to the 10th century BCE. Conversely, in most of the areas of Israelite Settlement in the hill country, where a major demographic upheaval did take place in Iron I, Canaanite sites were few in number, and there is almost no evidence of immediate Israelite Settlement on the ruins of the destroyed Canaanite cities. Chronological evidence indicates, moreover, that the Canaanite centers were not devastated simultaneously, but over a long period of time. It is now certain that Canaanite cities such as Lachish still flourished at the time when Israelite Settlement in the hill country was already well underway.

Proponents of the sociological school, who hypothesized that the Israelites came *directly* from the socio-political organization of Canaan at the end of the Late Bronze period, suffer from a strictly superficial acquaintance with the natural setting of the country — especially with its frontier regions, including the hill country — and they consequently ignored the important demographic and ethnographic data concerning the Land of Israel in recent generations. Both the settlement patterns arising from archaeological surveys and the material culture of Israelite Settlement sites refute any theory that the Israelites were malcontents fleeing from the Canaanite polity. Instead, it turns out that the new settlers in the hill country in the Iron I period came from a pastoralist background. Comparing Canaanite material culture at the end of the Late Bronze period with the material culture of Iron I sites in the hill country demonstrates that a demographic socio-economic, and cultural revolution occurred. However, various facets of the relations between nomadic pastoralists and sedentary dwellers, which were noted by scholars of the sociological school have contributed greatly to research into the socio-economic framework of the Land of Israel in antiquity.

In the final analysis, Alt's view of Israelite Settlement as a peaceful settlement in the less inhabited regions of the country came closest to predicting the results of field studies conducted decades later. Some details of his theory, however, especially those concerning the origins of the settlers cannot be reconciled with current archaeological data.

The origins of the Israelite settlers must ultimately be sought at the end of the Middle Bronze period, when the network of villages in the hill country broke apart and groups of people dropped out of this sedentary rural framework. These groups then underwent a lengthy pastoralist stage. They were particularly active in marginal areas, including the hill country, and their existence is attested in documents from the Late Bronze period. A change in political and economic circumstances led to their resedentarization starting at the end of the 13th century BCE and continuing throughout the Iron I period.

There is almost no archaeological support for dating the beginning of Israelite Settlement earlier than the 12th century BCE. Had permanent Israelite sites enjoyed a long period of coexistence with the Canaanite cities, it would have been reflected in the material culture of both the Israelite and the Canaanite settlements. On the other hand, the course of Israelite Settlement need not have been uniform, and some groups might have settled down as late as the 11th century BCE.

Due to their location on the distant fringes of the regions where the process of sedentarization largely took place, Upper Galilee and the Beersheba Valley — both the focus of the most intense research on the period under discussion since the 1950s — are of only ancillary importance for understanding Israelite Settlement. The number of known Iron I sites in both regions is relatively small, and Israelites settled there only at an advanced stage of the Settlement process, at the end of the 12th century and mostly in the 11th century BCE. It follows that syntheses of the period should be based on the results of work in the central hill country instead.

Even within the central hill country, however, the magnitude of Israelite Settlement was not uniform. No more than 10 Iron I sites in Judah and only about 12 in Benjamin are presently known, while around 120 sites have been encountered in Ephraim and about 100 in Manasseh. Approximately 90% of the Iron I sites in the central hill country were found in the area between Ramallah and the Jezreel Valley — and these represent 70% of all Iron I sites in the entire Land of Israel west of the Jordan River. The data from Transjordan are apparently compatible, with the majority of the Iron I sites located in Gilead, facing Samaria on the other side of the Jordan Valley.

In discussing the principal regions of Israelite Settlement — Ephraim and Manasseh — the significant geographical, demographic and historical differences between them must be taken into account. Manasseh is topographically and lithologically moderate and was the scene of considerable human activity in the Late Bronze period. Both archaeological and biblical evidence indicate that Canaanite population continued to exist here in the Iron Age. In contrast, topographic conditions in Ephraim were much harsher, and sedentary activity in the Late Bronze period was almost nonexistent. Consequently, the Iron I population here was far more homogeneous. This is one of the reasons why the first cult center serving the population of the hill country was located at Shiloh, in the heart of Ephraim.

A reconstruction of the process of Israelite Settlement in the territory of Ephraim, based on the data from our survey, can serve as a model for other areas of the hill country (despite the regional character of the process in general). At first, most of the sites were concentrated in the desert fringe and along the intermontane valleys of the northern mountain ridge, i.e., in the areas best suited for cereal crops and pasturage. The settlement pattern in Ephraim (and also in Benjamin and Judah) thus shows that the subsistence base of the inhabitants at the beginning of the period of Israelite Settlement was similar to that of pastoralists, not villagers.

In order to expand farther west, onto the slopes, the Israelites had to adjust to greater distances from stable water sources; clear away dense forests; adapt to more difficult rock formations and topography; and make the transition to horticulture. Westward expansion took place only in the second phase of the settlement process, when the intermontane valleys and the desert fringe had become relatively overcrowded, but before the Israelites were strong enough to challenge the Canaanite domination of the lowlands. It was also at this time that the harsh and remote regions of southern Upper Galilee and the Beersheba Valley were settled.

To a great degree, Israelite Settlement was regional in character. In some areas, Manasseh for example, the Israelites settled among the sedentary population, while elsewhere they occupied areas that were only thinly inhabited. Sometimes, Israelites settled close to Canaanite cities, e.g. the founding of ᶜIzbet Ṣarṭah (and perhaps other sites in the vicinity) near Aphek, while in other places, e.g., western Galilee, they kept their distance from the Canaanite centers.

Although the regions in which the process of sedentarization commenced were only lightly inhabited by Canaanites, they were, nonetheless, not vacant. Initially, the new settlers may have deliberately located themselves in proximity to the few Canaanite cities on the ridge of the central hill country (and Transjordan?), continuing the symbiotic relationship which they, as nomads, had enjoyed with the sedentary population. It is difficult to be certain that Israelite Settlement began alongside the Canaanite cities rather than only after the destruction of these cities in local takeovers; at present, the evidence from the hill country and the western slopes (ᶜIzbet Ṣarṭah and Aphek) favors the first option. The settlers would have come into conflict with the Canaanite cities only once the nearby lands available for agriculture no longer sufficed for both populations. These clashes probably underlie those biblical conquest traditions that are not part of the description of the unified conquest of Canaan; most of these traditions concern the central hill country.

As for the magnitude and date of settlement activity, field data from all across the country enable us to reconstruct Israelite expansion in Canaan as follows: Initially, settlement was largely confined to the mountain ridge and desert fringe of the territories of Ephraim and Manasseh, and, to a lesser extent, of Benjamin and Judah as well. From this nucleus, the Israelites subsequently spread out to the western side of the hill country and into Judah and Galilee. It was during this stage that areas previously almost devoid of Canaanites were settled. While some of the newcomers to these regions came from the central hill country, others settled down here directly. Archaeological evidence, therefore, casts doubt on the theory that there were two influxes of Israelite Settlers and refutes the notion that the "House of Joseph" was not settled until the second stage of the settlement process.

The gradual southward expansion of Israelites in the central hill country, from a nucleus in Ephraim and Manasseh, accords well with the serial relocation of the central cult site from Shiloh, which flourished in the late 12th and early 11th centuries BCE, first to Benjamin at the end of the 11th century and finally to Judah in the early 10th century BCE. The Bible also indicates that Judah achieved its special place of importance in the history of Israel only in the 10th century BCE.

We have at our disposal sufficient data to estimate the size of the sedentary Israelite population in the Iron I period. This calculation — arrived at by multiplying the number and size of sites by population density estimates and by "correction factors" for each region — leads us to conclude that on the eve of the Monarchy, the Israelites numbered in the tens of thousands, many times fewer than any of the figures bandied about by scholars in the past. Our modest estimate, of course, has far-reaching consequences for the study of virtually every aspect of the period of Israelite Settlement.

The transition from the Late Bronze to Iron I periods marked a turning point not only in settlement patterns, but also with respect to material culture. The urban culture of the Canaanites in the Late Bronze period was replaced by the rural framework of the hill country in Iron I. Points of cultural continuity, which a few scholars have belabored recently, were evident primarily in the coastal plain and the valleys — areas outside the Settlement regions. The unmistakable signs of Israelite Settlement sites — such as pillared buildings and collared-rim store jars — must be evaluated quantitatively, geographically, and functionally, and not simply on the basis of presence or absence at a given site. Such analyses demonstrate that these cultural traits originated in the central hill country at the beginning of the Iron Age.

The development of early Israelite architecture was largely influenced by two factors: the pastoralist background of the settlers and the hilly topography of the primary region of settlement. Regarding the former, elliptical courtyard sites, such as ʿIzbet Ṣarṭah Stratum III, reflect the traditions of tent and tent camp, and the proliferation of small silos at sites with little permanent architecture is characteristic of societies in the initial stages of sedentarization. The influence of the hilly topography is manifest in the plans of sites such as Ai and Tell en-Naṣbeh and perhaps in the widespread use of pillars as well. We can now trace the development of site plans from the earliest stages of Israelite Settlement (Giloh and ʿIzbet Ṣarṭah Stratum III), through flourishing farming villages (Ai, Khirbet Raddana), and finally to the established centers of the Monarchy (Beersheba, Tell Beit Mirsim).

The pottery of the Iron I sites in the central hill country accurately reflects the socio-economic circumstances of the inhabitants. The paucity of types indicates a poor agricultural society, while the profusion of variants testifies to social frameworks that were isolated, local, and tribal in nature. The assemblages differ according to geographical location and chronological sequence.

The solutions to other questions concerning the process of Israelite Settlement must await the continuation of regional studies in the hill country, the primary focus of Israelite Settlement. Three avenues of research need to be pursued: First and foremost, the comprehensive field surveys must be completed. Excavations must be conducted with the aim of solving clearly defined problems. Finally — and this sphere has been sorely neglected — the ecology and economic potential of the regions of Israelite Settlement must be studied as keys to understanding the settlement patterns arising from the surveys.

List of Abbreviations

AASOR	The Annual of the American Schools of Oriental Research.
ADAJ	Annual of the Department of Antiquities of Jordan.
AJA	American Journal of Archaeology.
BA	The Biblical Archaeologist.
BAR	Biblical Archaeology Review.
B.A.R.	B.A.R. International Series.
BASOR	Bulletin of the American Schools of Oriental Research.
BIES	Bulletin of the Israel Exploration Society (Hebrew).
CAH	The Cambridge Ancient Hisotry.
Enc. Arch. Exc. I-IV	Avi Yonah, M. ed. 1975, 1976, 1977, 1978. *Encyclopaedia of Archaeological Excavations in the Holy Land I-IV*. Jerusalem.
Enc. Miqr.	Encyclopaedia Miqra'it (Encyclopaedia Biblica). Jerusalem (Hebrew).
Had. Arch.	Hadashot Archeologiot. (Archaeological News). Department of Antiquities, Jerusalem (Hebrew).
HUCA	Hebrew Union College Annual.
JEA	Journal of Egyptian Archaeology.
IEJ	Israel Exploration Journal.
JBL	Journal of Biblical Literature.
JNES	Journal of Near Eastern Studies.
JPOS	The Journal of the Palestine Oriental Society.
JSOT	Journal for the Study of the Old Testament.
PEFQSt	Palestine Exploration Fund, Quarterly Statement.
PEQ	Palestine Exploration Quarterly.
PJb	Palästinajahrbuch.
QDAP	The Quarterly of the Department of Antiquities in Palestine.
RB	Revue Biblique.
VT	Vetus Testamentum.
ZDPV	Zeitschrift des Deutschen Palästina-Vereins.
ZAW	Zeitschrift fur die alttestamentliche Wissenschaft.

REFERENCES

Aharoni, M. 1981. The Pottery of Strata 12–11 of the Iron Age Citadel at Arad. *Eretz-Israel* 15: 181–204 (Hebrew).

Aharoni, Y. 1957. *The Settlement of the Israelite Tribes in Upper Galilee*. Jerusalem (Hebrew).

Aharoni, Y. 1970. New Aspects of the Israelite Occupation in the North. In: Sanders, J.A. ed. *Near Eastern Archaeology in the Twentieth Century, Essays in Honor of Nelson Glueck*. New York: 254–265.

Aharoni, Y. 1971a. Kh. Raddana and its Inscription. *IEJ* 21:130–135.

Aharoni, Y. 1971b. The Settlement in Canaan. In: Mazar, B. ed. *The World History of the Jewish People, Vol. III — Judges*. Givatayim (Isr.): 94–128.

Aharoni, Y. 1973. The Ten Thousands of Ephraim and the Thousands of Manasseh. In: Aviram, J. administrative ed. *Eretz Shomrom*. Jerusalem: 38–46 (Hebrew).

Aharoni, Y. 1975. Arad. *Enc. Arch. Exc. I;* 82–89.

Aharoni, Y. 1976a. Nothing Early and Nothing Late. Re-writing Israel's Conquest. *BA* 39: 55–76.

Aharoni, Y. 1976b. The Settlement of the Tribes in the Negev — A New Picture. *Ariel* 41: 3–19.

Aharoni, Y. 1979a. The Negev during the Israelite Period. In: Shmueli, A. and Grados, Y. eds. *The Land of the Negev, Part I*. Tel Aviv: 209–225 (Hebrew).

Aharoni, Y. 1979b. *The Land of the Bible; A Historical Geography*. Philadelphia.

Aharoni, Y. 1982. *The Archaeology of the Land of Israel*. Philadelphia.

Aharoni, Y. *et al.* The Ancient Desert Agriculture of the Negev V: An Israelite Agricultural Settlement at Ramat Matred. *IEJ* 10: 23–36, 97–111.

Aharoni, Y. and Amiran, R. 1964. Excavations at Tel Arad: Preliminary Report on the First Season, 1962. *IEJ* 14: 131–147.

Aharoni, Y., Fritz, V. and Kempinski, A. 1975. Excavations at Tel Masos (Khirbet el-Meshâsh, Preliminary Report on the Second Season, 1974. *Tel Aviv* 2: 97–124.

Ahituv, S. 1976. Shiloh. *Enc. Miqr.* 7: 626–632.

Ahlström, G.W. 1982. Where Did the Israelites Live. *JNES* 41: 133–138.

Ahlström, G.W. 1984a. The Early Iron Age Settlers at Hirbet el-Mšáš (Tel Masos). *ZDPV* 100: 35–52.

Ahlström, G.W. 1984b. Giloh: A Judahite or Canaanite Settlement? *IEJ* 34: 170–172.

Ahlström, G.W. 1986. *Who Were the Israelites?* Winona Lake.

Ahlström, G.W. and Edelman, D. 1985. Merneptah's Israel. *JNES* 44:59–61.

Albright, W.F. 1923. The Danish Excavations at Shiloh. *BASOR* 9: 10–11.

Albright, W.F. 1924. Excavations and Results at Tell el-Ful (Gibeah of Saul). *AASOR* IV.

Albright, W.F. 1925. The Administrative Divisions of Israel and Judah. *JPOS* V: 17–54.

Albright, W.F. 1929. New Israelite and Pre-Israelite Sites: the Spring Trip of 1929. *BASOR* 35: 1–14.

Albright, W.F. 1932. The Excavation of Tell Beit Mirsim in Palestine I, The Pottery of the First Three Campaigns. *AASOR* 12.

358

Albright, W.F. 1933. The Excavation of Tell Beit Mirsim IA: The Bronze Age Pottery of the Fourth Campaign. *AASOR* 13: 55–127.

Albright, W.F. 1935. Archaeology and the Date of the Hebrew Conquest of Palestine. *BASOR* 58: 10–18.

Albright, W.F. 1937. Further Light on the History of Israel From Lachish and Megiddo. *BASOR* 68: 22–26.

Albright, W.F. 1939. The Israelite Conquest of Canaan in the Light of Archaeology. *BASOR* 74: 11–23.

Albright, W.F. 1940a. Book Reviews. *AJA* 44: 546–550.

Albright, W.F. 1940b. *BASOR* 78: 7–9.

Albright, W.F. 1942. *Archaeology and the Religion of Israel.* Baltimore.

Albright, W.F. 1943. The Excavation of Tell Beit Mirsim III, The Iron Age. *AASOR* 21–22.

Albright, W.F. 1948. Book Reviews. *JNES* 7: 202–205.

Albright, W.F. 1950. *The Biblical Period.* Pittsburgh.

Albright, W.F. 1966a. *Archaeology Historical Analogy and Early Biblical Tradition.* Baton Rouge.

Albright, W.F. 1966b. Some Recent Excavation Reports and Publications. *BASOR* 183: 32–34.

Albright, W.F. 1971. *The Archaeology of Palestine.* Gloucester

Alt, A. 1925. *die Landnahme der Israeliten in Palästina.* (trans. 1966. *Essays on Old Testament History and Religion.* Oxford: 135–169).

Alt, A. 1932. Die Reise. *PJb* 28: 18–46.

Alt, A. 1939. Erwägungen über die Landnahme der Israeliten in Palästina. *PJb* 35: 8–63 (repr. *Kleine Schriften zur Geschichte des Volkes Israel I.* München: 126–175).

Alt, A. 1953. Megiddo im Übergang vom Kanaanäischen zum israelitischen Zeitalter. *Kleine Schriften zur Geschichte des Volkes Israel I.* München: 256–273.

Alt, A. 1964 (1930). Die Staatenbildung der Israeliten in Palästina. *Kleine Schriften zur Geschichte des Volkes Israel II.* München: 1–65.

Alt, A. 1966. *Essays on Old Testament History and Religion.* Oxford.

Amiran, D.H.K. and Ben-Arieh, Y. 1963. Sedentarization of Bedouin in Israel. *IEJ* 13: 161–181.

Amiran, D.H.K. *et al.* 1979. Spontaneous Settlement of Bedouin in the Northern Negev. In: Shmueli, A. and Grados, Y. eds. *The Land of the Negev, Part II.* Tel Aviv: 652–665 (Hebrew).

Amiran, R. 1962. Review on *AASOR* 34–35. *Bibliotheca Orientalis* 19(6): 263–264.

Anbar, M. 1985a. *The Amorite Tribes in Mari and the Settlement of the Israelites in Canaan.* Tel Aviv (Hebrew).

Anbar, M. 1985b. "Then Joshua built an altar unto the Lord God of Israel in mount Ebal". *Beth Mikra* 101(2): 345–352 (Hebrew).

Arnon, C. and Amiran, R. 1981. Excavations at Tel Qishon — Preliminary Report on the 1977–1978 Seasons. *Eretz-Israel* 15: 205–212 (Hebrew).

Ashkenazi, T. 1938. *Tribus semi nomades de la Palestine du Nord.* Paris.

Ashkenazi, T. 1957. *The Bedouin.* Jerusalem (Hebrew).

Avigad, N. 1965. Jericho. *Enc. Miqr.* 3: 839–858.

Avi Yonah, M. 1972. Population. *Enc. Miqr.* 1: 145–146.

Avi Yonah, M. 1976. *Gazetteer of Roman Palestine* (Qedem 5). Jerusalem.

Baily, Y. 1969(?). Er-Rmeilat Alliance — The Bedouin of the Raphiaḥ Region. In: *Studies on the Bedouin.* Sede Boqer College: 150–158 (Hebrew).

Balensi, J. 1981. Tell Keisan, témoin original de l'apparition du "Mycénien III C1a" au Proche-Orient. *RB* 88: 399–401.

Bar Adon, P. 1972. The Judaean Desert and the Plain of Jericho. In: Kochavi, M. ed. *Judaea, Samaria and the Golan.* Jerusalem: 92–149 (Hebrew).

Baron, A. 1971. Population. *Encyclopaedia Judaica* Vol. 13: 866ff.

Barth, F. 1961. *Nomads of South Persia.* Oslo.

Bar-Zvi, S. 1979. Characteristics of the Bedouins' Life in the Negev prior to their Sedentarization. In: Shmueli, A. and Grados, Y. eds. *The Land of the Negev, Part II.* Tel Aviv: 621–630 (Hebrew).

Basters, A. 1965. Le sanctuaire central dans Jud XIX-XXI. *Ephemerides Theologicae Lovanienses* 41: 20–41.

Bates, D.G. and Lees, S.H. 1977. The Role of Exchange in Productive Specialization. *American Anthropologist* 79: 824–841.

Beck, P. and Kochavi, M. 1985. A Dated Assemblage of the Late 13th Century BCE from the Egyptian Residency at Aphek. *Tel Aviv* 12:29–42.

Begin, Z.B. 1974. *The Geological Map of Israel, Sheet 9–III;* Jericho. Jerusalem.

Beit Arieh, I. 1977. *South Sinai in the Early Bronze Age.* (Ph.D. thesis). Tel Aviv University (Hebrew with English abstract).

Beit Arieh, I. 1981. A Pattern of Settlement in Southern Sinai and Southern Canaan in the Third Millennium B.C. *BASOR* 243: 32–55.

Ben David, Y. 1978. *The Bedouin Tribes in Southern Sinai.* Jerusalem (Hebrew).

Ben-Tor, A. 1975. The First Season of Excavations at Tell-Yarmuth 1970. *Qedem* 1: 55–87.

Ben-Tor, A. 1979. Tell Qiri: A Look at Village Life. *BA* 42: 105–113.

Bienkowski, P. 1986. *Jericho in the Late Bronze Age.* Warminster.

Bikai, P.M. 1978. *The Pottery of Tyre.* Warminster.

Biran, A. 1980. Tell Dan — Five Years Later. *BA* 43: 168–182.

Biran, A. 1985. Notes and News, Tel Dan, 1984. *IEJ* 35: 186–189.

Biran, A. and Cohen, R. 1981. Aroer in the Negev. *Eretz-Israel* 15: 250–273 (Hebrew).

Boardman, J. 1977. The Olive in the Mediterranean: Its Culture and Use. In: Clark, J.G.G., Jope, E.M. and Riley, R. eds. *The Early History of Agriculture.* Oxford: 187–196.

Boling, R.G. 1969. Bronze Age Buildings at the Shechem High Place: ASOR Excavations at Tananir. *BA* 32: 82–103.

Boraas, R.S. 1986. Iron IA Ceramic at Tell Balatah: A Preliminary Examination. In: Geraty, L.T. and Herr, L.G. eds. *The Archaeology of Jordan and Other Studies Presented to Siegfried H. Horn.* Berrien Springs (Michigan):249–263.

Boraas, R.S. and Geraty, L.T. 1978. The Fifth Campaign at Tell Hesban. In: Heshbon 1976. *Andrews University Seminary Studies* 16(1): 1–17.

Borowski, O. 1982. Four Seasons of Excavations at Tel Halif/Lahav. *Qadmoniot* 15: 57–60 (Hebrew).

Braemer, F. 1982. *L'Architecture domestique du Levant a l'Age du Fer.* Paris.

Brandl, B. 1982. The Tel Masos Scarab: A Suggestion for a New Method for the Interpretation of Royal Scarabs. *Scripta Hierosolymitana* 28: 371–405.

Branigan, K. 1966. The Four-Room Buildings of Tell en-Nasbeh. *IEJ* 16: 206–208.

Brawer, M. 1984. Transformation in Pattern, dispersion and Population Density in Israel's Arab Villages. *Eretz-Israel* 17: 8–15 (Hebrew).

Briend, J. and Humbert, J-B. 1980. *Tell Keisan (1971–1976); Une cité phenicienne en Galilée.* Paris.

Bright, J. 1974. *A History of Israel.* Philadelphia.

Broshi, M. and Gophna, R. 1984. The Settlement and Population of Palestine in the Early Bronze Age II-III. *BASOR* 253: 41–53.

Broshi, M. and Gophan, R. 1986. Middle Bronze Age II Palestine: Settlements and Population. *BASOR* 261: 73–90.

Buhl, M.L. and Holm-Nielsen, S. 1969. *Shiloh.* Copenhagen.

Bulliet, R.W. 1975. *The Camel and the Wheel.* Cambridge (Mass.).

Burkhardt, J.D. 1831. *Notes on the Bedouins and Wahabys.* London.

Callaway, J.A. 1965. The 1964 Ai (et-Tell) Excavations. *BASOR* 178: 13–40.

Callaway, J.A. and Nicol, M.B. 1966. A Sounding at Khirbet Haiyan. *BASOR* 183: 12–19.

Callaway, J.A. 1968. New Evidence on the Conquest of Ai. *JBL* 87: 312–320.

Callaway, J.A. 1969a. The 1966 Ai (et-Tell) Excavations. *BASOR* 196: 2–16.

Callaway, J.A. 1969b. The Significance of the Iron Age Village at ʿAi (et-Tell). *Proceedings of the Fifth World Congress of Jewish Studies.* Jerusalem: 56–61.

Callaway, J.A. and Cooley, R.E. 1971. A Salvage Excavation at Raddana, in Bireh. *BASOR* 201: 9–19.

Callaway, J.A. 1975. Ai. *Enc. Arch. Exc.* I: 36–52.

Callaway, J.A. 1976. Excavating Ai (et-Tell): 1964–1972. *BA* 39: 18–30.

Callaway, J.A. 1984. Village Subsistence at Ai and Raddana in Iron Age I. In: Thompson, H.O. ed. *The Answers Lie Below, Essays in Honor of L.E. Toombs.* Lanham: 51–66.

Callaway, J.A. 1985. A New Perspective on the Hill Country Settlement of Canaan in Iron Age I. In: Tubb, J.N. ed. *Palestine in the Bronze and Iron Ages, Papers in Honour of Olga Tufnell.* London: 31–49.

Campbell, E.F. 1968. The Shechem Area Survey. *BASOR* 190: 19–41.

Campbell, E.F. and Wright, G.E. 1969. Tribal Leage Shrines in Amman and Shechem. *BA* 32: 104–116.

Chambon, A. 1984. *Tell el-Farʿah 1.* Paris.

Chaney, M.L. 1983. Ancient Palestinian Peasant Movements and the Formation of Premonarchic Israel. In: Freedman, D.N. and Graf, D.F. eds. *Palestine in Transition.* Sheffield: 39–90.

Cohen, A. 1973. *Palestine in the 18th Century.* Jerusalem.

Cohen, M.A. 1965. The Role of the Shilonite Priesthood in the United Monarchy of Ancient Israel. *HUCA* 36: 59–98.

Cohen, R. 1979. The Iron Age Fortresses in the Central Negev. *BASOR* 236: 61–79.

Conder, C.R. 1878. *Tent Works in Palestine.* London.

de Contenson, H. 1964. The 1953 Survey in the Yarmuk and Jordan Valleys. *ADAJ* 8–9: 30–46.

Cooley, R.E. 1975. Four Seasons of Excavation at Khirbet Raddana. *Near Eastern Archaeological Society Bulletin* N.S. No. 5: 5–20.

Coote, R.B. and Whitelam, K.W. 1986. The Emergence of Israel: Social Transformation and State Formation Following the Decline in Late Bronze Age Trade. In: Gottwald, N.K. ed. *Social Scientific Criticism of the Hebrew Bible and its Social World: The Israelite Monarchy* (SEMEIA 37): 107–147.

Cross, F.M. 1947. The Tabernacle. *BA* 10: 45–68.

Cross, F.M. and Freedman, D.N. 1971. An Inscribed Jar Handle From Raddana. *BASOR* 201: 19–22.

Cross, F.M. 1979. Early Alphabetic Scripts. In: Cross, F.M. ed. *Symposia Celebrating the Seventy-Fifth Anniversary of the Foundation of the American Schools of Oriental Research (1900–1975).* Cambridge: 97–123.

Cross, F.M. 1980. Newly Found Inscriptions in Old Canaanite and Early Phoenician Scripts. *BASOR* 238:1–20.

Cross, F.M. 1981. The Priestly Tabernacle in the Light of Recent Research. In: Biran, A. ed. *Temples and High Places in Biblical Times.* Jerusalem: 169–180.

Cunnison, I. 1970. Camp and Surra [Baggara Arabs]. In: Sweet, L.E. ed. *Peoples and Cultures of the Middle East. Vol. I.* Garden City, New York: 315–345.

Currid, J.D. 1986. *Archaeological Investigations into the Grain and Storage Practices of Iron Age Palestine* (Ph.D. thesis). The University of Chicago.

Dalman, G. 1939. *Arbeit und Sitte in Palästina. VI.* Gütersloh.

Day, J. 1979. The Destruction of the Shiloh Sanctuary and Jeremiah VII 12, 14. *Supplements to Vetus Testamentum* 30: 87–94.

Demsky, A. 1973. Geba Gibeah and Gibeon — An Historico-Geographic Riddle. *BASOR* 212: 26–31.

Demsky, A. 1977. A Proto-Canaanite Abecedary Dating from the Period of the Judges and its Implications for the History of the Alphabet. *Tel Aviv* 4: 14–27.

Dever, W.G. 1974. The MBIIc Stratification in the Northwest Gate Area at Shechem. *BASOR* 216: 31–52.

Dever, W.G. 1976. Gezer. *Enc. Arch. Exc. II;* 428–443.

Dever, W.G. *et al.* 1970. *Gezer I.* Jerusalem.

Dever, W.G. *et al.* 1974. *Gezer II.* Jerusalem.

Dever, W.G. 1980. New Vistas on EBIV ("MBI") Horizon in Syria-Palestine. *BASOR* 237:35–64.

Dickson, H.R.P. 1949. *The Arab of the Desert.* London.

Dimant, A. 1971. *The Geology of Beth-Horon Region and the Western Slopes of the Bethel Anticline.* (M.A. thesis). Jerusalem, The Hebrew University (Hebrew).

Dorenmann, R.H. 1982. The Beginning of the Iron Age in Transjordan. In: Hadidi, A. ed. *Studies in the History and Archaeology of Jordan I.* Amman.

Dothan, M. 1955. The Excavations at Afula. *Atiqot* 1: 19–70.

Dothan, T. 1982. *The Philistines and their Material Culture.* Jerusalem.

Dotan, A. 1981. New Light on the 'Izbet Ṣarṭah Ostracon. *Tel Aviv* 8: 160–172.

Dror, T. 1979. *Changes in the Arab Village in Judea and Samaria, 1967–1974.* (M.A. thesis). Tel Aviv University (Hebrew).

Drori, I. 1979. *Tell Lachish; Subsistence and Natural Environment during the Middle, Late Bronze and Iron Age Periods.* (M.A. thesis). Tel Aviv University (Hebrew).

Druks, A. 1966. A "Hittite" Burial near Kefar Yehoshua. *BIES* 30: 213–220 (Hebrew).

Dus, J. 1975. Moses or Joshua? On the Problem of the Founder of the Israelite Religion. *Radical Religion* 2: 26–41.

Dussaud, R. 1935. Note additionelle. *Syria* 16: 346–352.

Eissfeldt, O. 1957. Silo und Jerusalem. *Supplements to Vetus Testamentum* 4: 138–147.

Eissfeldt, O. 1975. The Hebrew Kingdom. *CAH* Vol. II, Part 2: 537–605.

Eitam, D. 1979. Olive Presses of the Israelite Period. *Tel Aviv* 6: 146–155.

Eitam, D. 1980a. *Oil and Wine Production in Mt. Ephraim in the Iron Age.* (M.A. thesis). Tel Aviv University (Hebrew).

Eitam, D. 1980b. The "fortresses" of the Negev Uplands — Settlement Sites. *Qadmoniot* 13: 56–57 (Hebrew).

Engberg, M.E. 1940. Historical Analysis of Archaeological Evidence: Megiddo and the Song of Deborah. *BASOR* 78: 4–7.

Epstein, E. 1933. *The Life and Customs of the Bedouin.* Tel Aviv (Hebrew).

Esse, D.L. 1982. *Beyond Subsistence: Beth Yerah and Northern Palestine in the Early Bronze Age* (Ph.D. thesis). The University of Chicago.

Faegre, T. 1979. *Tents; Architecture of the Nomads.* London.

Feilberg, C.G. 1944. *La tente noire.* Copenhagen.

Finkelstein, I. 1978. *Rustic Settlement in the Foothills of the Yarkon Basin in the Israelite, Persian and Hellenistic Periods.* (M.A. thesis). Tel Aviv University (Hebrew).

Finkelstein, I. 1984. The Iron Age "Fortresses" of the Negev Highlands: Sedentarization of the Nomads. *Tel Aviv* 11: 189–209.

Finkelstein, I. 1985. ed. Excavations at Shiloh 1981–1984, Preliminary Report. *Tel Aviv* 12: 123–180.

Finkelstein, I. 1986. *'Izbet Ṣarṭah An Early Iron Age Site near Rosh Ha'ayin, Israel (B.A.R. 299).*

Finkelstein, I. forthcoming a. The Arabian Trade and the Socio-Political Situation in the Negev in the 12th–11th Centuries BCE. *JNES.*

Finkelstein, I. forthcoming b. Kh. ed-Dawara — A Fortified Site from the Early Monarchic Period North-east of Jerusalem. *Qadmoniot* (Hebrew).

Finkelstein, I. forthcoming c. The Emergence of the Monarchy in Israel — The Environmental and Socio-economic Aspects. *Eretz-Israel* (Yadin volume).

Finkelstein, I. forthcoming d. The Land of Ephraim Survey 1980–1986: Preliminary Report.

Finkelstein, I. and Brandl, B. 1985. A Group of Metal Objects from Shiloh. *The Israel Museum Journal* IV: 17–26.

Fitzgerald, G.M. 1930. *The Four Canaanite Temples of Beth-Shan, Part II — The Pottery.* Philadelphia.

Franken, H.J. 1961a. Review on *AASOR* 34–35. *VT* 11: 471–474.

Franken, H.J. 1961b. The Excavations at Deir ʿAlla in Jordan. *VT* 11: 361–372.

Franken, H.J. 1969. *Excavations at Tell Deir ʿAlla I.* Leiden.

Franken, H.J. and Power, J.A. 1971. Reviews. *VT* 21: 119–123.

Franken, H.J. 1975a. Palestine in the Time of the Nineteenth Dynasty, (b) Archaeological Evidence. *CAH* Vol. II, Part 2: 331–337.

Franken, H.J. 1975b. Deir ʿAlla, Tell. *Enc. Arch. Exc. I:* 321–324.

Free, J.P. 1954. The Second Season at Dothan. *BASOR* 135: 14–20.

Fritz, V. 1973. Das Ende der spätbronzezeitlichen Stadt Hazor Stratum XIII und die biblische Überlieferung in Josua 11 und Richter 4. *Ugarit Forschungen* 5: 123–139.

Fritz, V. 1975. Erwägungen zur Siedlungsgeschichte des Negeb in der Eisen I Zeit (1200–1000 v. Chr.) im Lichte der Ausgrabungen auf der Hirbet el-Mšāš. *ZDPV* 91: 30–45.

Fritz, V. 1977a. Bestimmung und Herkunft des Pfeilerhauses in Israel. *ZDPV* 93: 30–45.

Fritz, V. 1977b. *Tempel und Zelt.* Neukirchen.

Fritz, V. 1980. Die Kulturhistorische Bedeutung der früheisenzeitlichen Siedlung auf der Hirbet el-Mšāš und das Problem der Landnahme. *ZDPV* 96: 121–135.

Fritz, V. 1981. The Israelite "conquest" in the Light of Recent Excavations at Khirbet el-Meshâsh. *BASOR* 241: 61–73.

Fritz, V. 1982. The Conquest in the Light of Archaeology. In: *Proceedings of the Eight World Congress of Jewish Studies.* Jerusalem: 15–21.

Fritz, V. und Kempinski, A. 1983. *Ergebnisse der Ausgrabungen auf der Hirbet el-Mšāš (Tel Masos) 1972–1975.* Wiesbaden.

Gal, Z. 1979. An Early Iron Site Near Tel Menorah in the Beth-Shan Valley. *Tel Aviv* 6: 138–145.

Gal, Z. 1980. *Ramat Issachar.* Tel Aviv (Hebrew).

Gal, Z. 1982a. The Settlement of Issachar Some New Observations. *Tel Aviv* 9: 79–86.

Gal, Z. 1982b. *The Lower Galilee in the Iron Age.* (Ph.D. thesis). Tel Aviv University (Hebrew with English abstract).

Garsiel, M. and Finkelstein, I. 1978. The Westward Expansion of the House of Joseph in the Light of the ʿIzbet Ṣarṭah Excavations. *Tel Aviv* 5: 192–198.

Geraty, L.T. 1976. The 1976 Season of Excavations at Tell Hesbân. *ADAJ* 21: 45–53.

Geraty, L.T. 1983. Heshbon: The First Casualty in the Israelite Quest for the Kingdom of God. In: Huffmon, H.B. a.o. eds. *The Quest for the Kingom of God; Studies in Honor of George E. Mendenhall.* Winona Lake: 239–248.

de Geus, C.H.J. 1975. The Importance of Archaeological Research into the Palestinian Agricultural Terraces, with an Excursus of the Hebrew word gbî. *PEQ* 107: 65–74.

de Geus, C.H.J. 1976. *The Tribes of Israel.* Amsterdam.

Geva, S. 1984. The Settlement Pattern of Hazor Stratum XII. *Eretz-Israel* 17: 158–161 (Hebrew).

Giveon, R. 1971. *Les Bédouins Shosou des documents égyptiens.* Leiden.

Giveon, R. 1974. A Monogram Scarab from Tel Masos. *Tel Aviv* 1: 75–76.

Glatzer, B. 1982. Processes of Nomadization in West Afghanistan. In: Salzman, Ph.C. ed. *Contemporary Nomadic and Pastoral Peoples; Asia and the North* (Studies in Third World Societies 18). Williamsberg:61–86.

Glueck, N. 1934. Explorations in Eastern Palestine, I. *AASOR* 14.

Glueck, N. 1939. Explorations in Eastern Palestine, III. *AASOR* 18–19.

Glueck, N. 1951. Explorations in Eastern Palestine, IV. *AASOR* 25–28.

Glueck, N. 1959. *Rivers in the Desert*. New York.

Gonen, R. 1979. *Burial in Canaan of the Late Bronze Age as a Basis for the Study of Population and Settlements*. (Ph.D. thesis). Jerusalem, The Hebrew University (Hebrew).

Gonen, R. 1984. Urban Canaan in the Late Bronze Period. *BASOR* 253: 61–73.

Gophna, R. and Kochavi, M. 1966. Notes and News: An Archaeological Survey of the Plain of Sharon. *IEJ* 16: 143–144.

Gophna, R. and Porat, Y. 1972. The Land of Ephraim and Manasseh. In: Kochavi, M. ed. *Judaea, Samaria and the Golan*. Jerusalem: 195–241 (Hebrew).

Gottwald, N.K. 1974. Were the Early Israelites Pastoral Nomads? In: Jackson, J.J. and Kessler, M. eds. *Rhetorical Criticism, Essays in Honor of James Muilenburg*. Pittsburgh: 223–255.

Gottwald, N.K. 1975. Domain Assumptions and Societal Models in the Study of Pre-Monarchic Israel. *Supplements to Vetus Testamentum* 28: 89–100.

Gottwald, N.K. 1978a. The Hypothesis of the Revolutionary Origins of Ancient Israel: A Response to Hauser and Thompson. *JSOT* 7: 37–52.

Gottwald, N.K. 1978b. Were the Early Israelites Pastoral Nomads? *BAR* 4 (2): 2–7.

Gottwald, N.K. 1979. *The Tribes of Yahweh*. New York.

Gottwald, N.K. 1983. Two Models for the Origins of Ancient Israel: Social Revolution and Frontier Development. In: Huffmon, H.B. a.o. eds. *The Quest for the Kingdom of God; Studies in Honor of George E. Mendenhall*. Winona Lake: 5–24.

Government of Palestine 1945. *Village Statistics*. Jerusalem.

Grant, E. and Wright, G.E. 1939. *Ain Shems Excavations Part V*. Haverford.

Greenberg, R. 1987. New Light on the Early Iron Age at Tell Beit Mirsim. *BASOR* 265: 55–80.

Halligan, J.M. 1983. The Role of the Peasant in the Amarna Period. In: Freedman, D.N. and Graf, D.F. eds. *Palestine in Transition*. Sheffield: 15–24.

Halpern, B. 1983. *The Emergence of Israel in Canaan*. Chico, California.

Hamilton, R.W. 1935. Excavations at Tell Abu Hawam. *QDAP* 4: 1–69.

Hammond, Ph. 1965. Hébron. Chronique archéologique. *RB* 72: 267–270.

Hankey, V. 1986. A Sherd in the Simple Style of Late Mycenaean IIIB. In: Finkelstein, I. *'Izbet Ṣarṭah An Early Iron Age Site near Rosh Ha'ayin, Israel* (B.A.R. 299): 99–103.

Haran, M. 1962. Shiloh and Jerusalem: The Origin of the Priestly Tradition in the Pentateuch. *JBL* 81: 14–24.

Harding, G.L. 1953. Four Tombs Groups from Jordan. *Annual of the Palestine Exploration Fund* 6.

Hauser, A.J. 1978. Israel's Conquest of Palestine: A Peasants' Rebellion? *JSOT* 7: 2–19.

Hellwing, S. and Sade, M. 1985. Animal Remains. In: Finkelstein, I. Excavations at Shiloh 1981–1984, Preliminary Report. *Tel Aviv* 12: 177–180.

Hellwing, S. and Adjeman, Y. 1986. Animal Bones. In: Finkelstein, I. *'Izbet Ṣarṭah An Early Iron Age Site near Rosh Ha'ayin, Israel* (B.A.R. 299): 141–152.

Herion, G.A. 1986. The Impact of Modern and Social Science Assumptions on the Reconstruction of Israelite History. *JSOT* 34: 3–33.

Herr, L.G. 1983. The Amman Airport Structure and the Geopolitics of Ancient Transjordan. *BA* 46: 223–229.

Herrmann, S. 1975. *A History of Israel in Old Testament Times*. London.

Herrmann, S. 1985. Basic Factors of Israelite Settlement in Canaan. In: *Biblical Archaeology Today. Proceedings of the International Congress on Biblical Archaeology Jerusalem, April 1984*. Jerusalem: 47–53.

Herzog, Z. 1978. Israelite City Planning. *Expedition* 20 (4): 38–43.

Herzog, Z. 1984. *Beer-Sheba II The Early Iron Age Settlements*. Tel Aviv.

Hopkins, D.C. 1985. *The Highlands of Canaan*. Sheffield.

Hütteroth, W. 1975. The Pattern of Settlement in Palestine in the Sixteenth Century. In: Ma'oz, M. ed. *Studies on Palestine during the Ottoman Period.* Jerusalem: 3–10.

Hütteroth, W.D. and Abdulfattah, K. 1977. *Historical Geography of Palestine, Transjordan and Southern Syria in the Late 16th Century.* Erlangen.

Hyde, M.B. a.o. 1973. *Air Tight Grain Storage.* F.A.O. Agriculture Service Bulletin. Rome.

Ibach, R. 1976. Archaeological Survey of the Hesban Region. In: Heshbon 1974. *Andrews University Seminary Studies* 14 (1): 119–126.

Ibach, R. 1978. Expanded Archaeological Survey of the Hesban Region. In: Heshbon 1976. *Andrews University Seminary Studies* 16(1): 201–213.

Ibrahim, M. 1972. Archaeological Excavations at Sahab, 1972. *ADAJ* 17: 23–36.

Ibrahim, M. 1974. Second Season of Excavation at Sahab, 1973. *ADAJ* 19: 55–62.

Ibrahim, M. 1975. Third Season of Excavations at Sahab, 1975. *ADAJ* 20: 69–82.

Ibrahim, M. 1978. The Collared-rim Jar of the Early Iron Age. In: Moorey, R. and Parr, P. eds. *Archaeology in the Levant.* Warminster: 116–126.

Ibrahim, M. 1983. Siegel und Siegelabdrücke aus Saḥāb. *ZDPV* 99: 43–53.

Ibrahim, M., Sauer, J.A. and Yassine, K. 1976. The East Jordan Valley Survey, 1975. *BASOR* 222: 41–66.

Ilan, S. 1974. *The Traditional Arab Agriculture, its Methods and its Relationship to the Palestinian Landscape during the End of the Ottoman Period.* (M.A. thesis). Jerusalem, The Hebrew University (Hebrew).

Irwin, H. 1965. Le sanctuaire central Israelite avant l'establissment de la monarchie. *RB* 72: 161–184.

Israel Defense Force Command 1967. *Census of the Western Bank, Gaza Strip and Northern Sinai and the Golan Heights.*

Isserlin, B.S.J. 1983. The Israelite Conquest of Canaan: A Comparative Review of the Arguments Applicable. *PEQ* 115: 85–94.

Kallai, Z. 1967. *the Tribes of Israel.* Jerusalem (Hebrew).

Kallai, Z. 1972. The Land of Benjamin and Mt. Ephraim. In: Kochavi, M. ed. *Judaea, Samaria and the Golan.* Jerusalem: 151–193 (Hebrew).

Katakura, M. 1977. *Bedouin Village.* Tokyo.

Kaufmann, Y. 1953. *The Biblical Account of the Conquest of Palestine.* Jerusalem.

Kaufmann, A.Z. 1981. The Shiloh Temple — its Location and Dimensions. A Lecture in a Conference of the Society for Biblical Studies in Israel, Jerusalem (Hebrew).

Kay, S. 1978. *The Bedouin.* New York, London.

Kelm, G.L. and Mazar, A. 1982. Three Seasons of Excavations at Tel Batash — Biblical Timnah. *BASOR* 248: 1–36.

Kelso, J.L. 1968. The Excavation of Bethel (1934–1960). *AASOR* 39.

Kempinski, A. 1976. Reviews: Gezer II. *IEJ* 26: 210–214.

Kempinski, A. 1978. Tel Masos. *Expedition* 20 (4): 29–37.

Kempinski, A. 1979. Hittites in the Bible — What Does Archaeology Say? *BAR* 5(4) 20–46.

Kempinski, A. 1981. Baal-Peraẓim and the Scholarly Controversy on the Israelite Settlement. *Qadmoniot* 14: 63–64 (Hebrew).

Kempinski, A. 1985. The Overlap of Cultures at the End of the Late Bronze Age and the Beginning of the Iron Age. *Eretz-Israel* 18: 399–407 (Hebrew).

Kempinski, A. 1986. Joshua's Altar — An Iron Age I Watchtower. *BAR* 12 (1): 42, 44–49.

Kempinski, A. and Fritz, V. 1977. Excavations at Tel Masos (Khirbet el Meshash), Preliminary Report on the Third Season, 1975. *Tel Aviv* 4: 136–158.

Kempinski, A. *et al.* 1981. Excavations at Tel Masos: 1972, 1974, 1975. *Eretz-Israel* 15: 154–180 (Hebrew).

Kenyon, K. M. 1957. *Digging up Jericho.* London.

Kenyon, K. 1971. *Archaeology in the Holy Land.* London.

Kenyon, K.M. and Holland, T.A. 1982. *Excavations at Jericho Vol. Four*. London.

Khazanov, A.M. 1978. Characteristic Features of Nomadic Communities in the Eurasian Steppes. In: Weissleder, W. ed. *The Nomadic Alternative*. The Hague and Paris: 119–126.

Khazanov, A.M. 1984. *Nomads and the Outside World*. Cambridge.

Kingsbury, E.C. 1967. He Set Ephraim before Manasseh. *HUCA* 38: 129–136.

Kjaer, H. 1927. The Danish Excavation of Shiloh. *PEFQSt;* 202–213.

Kjaer, H. 1930. The Excavation of Shiloh 1929. *JPOS* X: 87–174.

Kjaer, H. 1931. Shiloh. A Summary Report of the Second Danish Expedition, 1929. *PEFQSt;* 71–88.

Klengel, H. 1972. *Zwischen Zelt und Palast*. Wien.

Kochavi, M. 1967. *The Settlement of the Negev in the Middle Bronze (Canaanite) I Age*. (Ph.D. thesis). Jerusalem, The Hebrew University (Hebrew with English abstract).

Kochavi, M. 1968. The Excavations at Tel Zeror. *Qadmoniot* 1: 128–130 (Hebrew).

Kochavi, M. 1969. Excavations at Tel Esdar. *Atiqot* 5: 14–48 (Hebrew).

Kochavi, M. 1972a. ed. *Judaea, Samaria and the Golan Archaeological Survey 1967–1968*. Jerusalem (Hebrew).

Kochavi, M. 1972b. The Land of Judah. In: Kochavi, M. ed. *Judaea, Samaria and the Golan*. Jerusalem: 17–89 (Hebrew).

Kochavi, M. 1974. Khirbet Rabud = Debir. *Tel Aviv* 1: 2–33.

Kochavi, M. 1977. An Ostracon of the Period of the Judges from ʿIzbet Ṣarṭah. *Tel Aviv* 4: 1–13.

Kochavi, M. 1978. Zeror, Tel. *Enc. Arch. Exc. IV;* 1223–1225.

Kochavi, M. 1981. The History and Archaeology of Aphek-Antipatris: A Biblical City in the Sharon Plain. *BA* 44: 75–86.

Kochavi, M. 1982. The Conquest and the Settlement. *Et-mol* 7: 3–5 (Hebrew).

Kochavi, M. 1984. The Period of Israelite Settlement. In: Ephʿal, I. ed. *The History of Eretz Israel Vol. 2, Israel and Judah in the Biblical Period*. Jerusalem: 19–84 (Hebrew).

Kochavi, M. 1985. The Land of Israel in the 13th–12th Centuries BCE. — Historical Conclusions from Archaeological Data. *Eleventh Archaeological Conference in Israel* (abstracts of lectures). Jerusalem: 16 (Hebrew).

Kochavi, M. and Finkelstein, I. 1978. Notes and News: ʿIzbet Ṣarṭah. *IEJ* 28: 267–268.

Kraus, H.J. 1966. *Worship in Israel*. Oxford.

Kupper, J.R. 1957. *Les nomades en Mésopotamie au temps des rois de Mari*. Paris.

LaBianca, Ø.S. 1985. The Return of the Nomad: An Analysis of the Process of Nomadization in Jordan. *ADAJ* 29: 251–254.

Lamon, R.S. and Shipton, G.M. 1939. *Megiddo I*. Chicago.

Lapp, N.L. 1978. ed. The Third Campaign at Tell el-Fûl: The Excavations of 1964. *AASOR* 45.

Lapp, P. 1967. The Conquest of Palestine in the Light of Archaeology. *Concordia Theological Monthly* 38: 283–300.

Lapp, P. 1968. Book Reviews. *AJA* 72: 391–393.

Lapp, P.W. 1969. The 1968 Excavations at Tell Taʿannek. *BASOR* 195: 2–49.

Lemaire, A. 1973. Asriel šrʾl, Israel et l'origine de la confédération israélitic. *VT* 23: 239–243.

Lemaire, A. 1982. Recherches actuelles sur les origines de l'ancien Israël. *Journal Asiatique* 270: 5–24.

Lemche, N.P. 1985. *Early Israel* (Supplements to Vetus Testamentum 37). Leiden.

Lenski, G. 1980. Review on N.K. Gottwald, The Tribes of Yahweh. *Religious Studies Review* 6: 275–278.

Lenzen, C.J., Gordon, R.L. and McQuitty, A.M. 1985. Excavations at Tell Irbid and Beit Ras, 1985. *ADAJ* 29: 151–159.

Liver J. 1971. The Israelite Tribes. In: Mazar, B. ed. *The World History of the Jewish People, Vol. III — Judges*. Givatayim (Isr.): 183–211.

Livnat, A. 1971. *The Geology of the Northwestern Foothills of the Judea Hill Country ('Abud-Qibya--Rantis Region)*. (M.A. thesis). Jerusalem, The Hebrew University (Hebrew).

Loud, G. 1948. *Megiddo II, Plates and Text*. Chicago.

Lucas, A. 1944. The Number of Israelites at the Exodus. *PEQ*; 164–168.

Luke, J.T. 1965. *Pastoralism and Politics in the Mari Period*. Ann Arbor.

Luncz, A.M. 1897. Caftor va-Pherach par Estori ha-Parchi. Jerusalem (Hebrew).

Luther, B. 1901. Die Israelitischen Stämme. *ZAW* 21: 1–77.

MacDonald, B.1980. The Wadi el-Hasa Survey 1979: A Preliminary Report. *ADAJ* 24:169-183.

Malamat, A. 1976a. Origins and the Formative Period. In: Ben Sasson, H.H. ed. *A History of the Jewish People*. London: 1–87.

Malamat, A. 1976b. Conquest of Canaan: Israelite Conduct of War According to Biblical Tradition. In: *Encyclopedia Judaica Year Book 1975/6*; 166–182.

Malamat, A. 1983. *Israel in Biblical Times*. Jerusalem (Hebrew).

Marquet-Krause, J. 1949. *Les fouilles de 'Ay (et-Tell)*. Paris.

Marx, E. 1974. *Bedouin of the Negev*. Tel Aviv (Hebrew).

Matthews, V.H. 1978. *Pastoral Nomadism in the Mari Kingdom (ca.1850–1760* BC). Cambridge.

Mayes, A.D.H. 1974. *Israel in the Period of the Judges*. London.

Mazar, A. 1977. *The Temples of Tel Qasile*. (Ph.D. thesis). Jerusalem, The Hebrew University (Hebrew).

Mazar, A. 1980a. An Early Israelite site near Jerusalem. *Qadmoniot* 13: 34–39 (Hebrew).

Mazar, A. 1980b. *Excavations at Tel Qasile, Part One The Philistine Sanctuary; Architecture and Cult Objects* (Qedem 12). Jerusalem.

Mazar, A. 1981a. Giloh: An Early Israelite Settlement Site Near Jerusalem. *IEJ* 31: 1–36.

Mazar, A. 1981b. Book Reviews. *University of London Institute of Archaeology Bulletin* 18: 291.

Mazar, A. 1981c. A Response to the Remarks by A. Kempinski. *Qadmoniot* 14: 64 (Hebrew).

Mazar, A. 1982a. Three Israelite Sites in the Hills of Judah and Ephraim. *BA* 45: 167–178.

Mazar, A. 1982b. The "Bull Site" — An Iron Age I Open Cult Place. *BASOR* 247: 27–42.

Mazar, A. 1985a. The Israelite Settlement in Canaan in the Light of Archaeological Excavations. In: *Biblical Archaeology Today. Proceedings of the International Congress on Biblical Archaeology Jerusalem, April 1984*. Jerusalem: 61–71.

Mazar, A. 1985b. *Excavations at Tell Qasile Part Two, The Philistine Sanctuary; Various Finds, The Pottery, Conclusions, Appendixes* (Qedem 20). Jerusalem.

Mazar, B. 1954. Gibeah. *Enc. Miqr.* 2: 412–416.

Mazar, B. 1968. The Middle Bronze Age in Palestine. *IEJ* 18: 65–97.

Mazar, B. 1974. *Canaan and Israel*. Jerusalem (Hebrew).

Mazar, B. 1981. The Early Israelite Settlement in the Hill Country. *BASOR* 241: 75–85.

Mazar, B. 1984. The Valley of Succoth. In: Schiller, E. ed. *Zev Vilnay's Jubilee Volume*; 215–217 (Hebrew).

McClellan, T.L. 1984. Town Planning at Tell en-Nasbeh. *ZDPV* 100: 53–69.

McCown, C.C. 1947a. *Tell en-Nasbeh I, Archaeological and Historical Results*. Berkeley and New Haven.

McCown, C.C. 1947b. The Density of Population in Ancient Palestine. *JBL* 66: 425–436.

Meek, T.J. 1936. The Israelite Conquest of Ephraim. *BASOR* 61: 17–19.

Mendenhall, G.E. 1962. The Hebrew Conquest of Palestine. *BA* 25: 66–87.

Mendenahll, G.E. 1973. *The Tenth Generation*. Baltimore.

Mendenhall, G.E. 1976. "Change and Decay in all Around I See" Conquest, Covenant and the Tenth Generation. *BA* 39: 152–157.

Mendenhall, G.E. 1983. Ancient Israel's Hyphenated History. In: Freedman, D.N. and Graf, D.F. eds. *Palestine in Transition*. Sheffield: 91–103.

Meshel, Z. and Cohen, R. 1980. Refed and Ḥatira: Two Iron Age Fortresses in the Northern Negev. *Tel Aviv* 7: 70–81.

Meyer, E. 1906. *Die Israeliten und ihre Nachbarstämme.* Halle a.s.

Military Government of Judea and Samaria 1974. *Animal Census* (unpublished).

Miller, J.M. 1975. Gibeah of Benjamin. *VT* 25: 145–166.

Miller, J.M. 1977a. The Israelite Occupation of Canaan. In: Hayes, J.H. and Miller, J.M. eds. *Israelite and Judaean History.* London: 213–284.

Miller, J.M. 1977b. Archaeology and the Israelite Conquest of Canaan: Some Methodological Observation. *PEQ* 109: 87–93.

Miller, J.M. 1983. Site Identification: A Problem Area in Contemporary Biblical Scholarship. *ZDPV* 99: 119–129.

Miller, J.M. and Hayes, J.H. 1986. *A History of Ancient Israel and Judah.* Philadelphia.

Mills, E. 1933. *Census of Palestine 1931.* Alexandria.

Mittmann, S. 1970. *Beiträge zur Siedlungs und Territorialgeschichte des nördlichen Ostjordanlandes.* Wiesbaden.

Montagne, R. 1947. *La civilisation du désert.* Paris.

Moscati, S. 1959. *The Semites in Ancient History.* Cardiff.

Muhly, J.D. 1982. How Iron Technology Changed the Ancient World. *BAR* 8(6): 40–54.

Muhsam, H.V. 1959. Sedentarization of the Bedouin in Israel. *International Social Science Journal* XI: 539–549.

Muhsam, H.V. 1966. *Bedouin of the Negev.* Jerusalem.

Musil, A. 1908. *Arabia Petraea III.* Wien. .

Musil, A. 1928. *The Manners and Customs of the Rwala Bedouins.* New York.

Na'aman, N. 1975. *The Political Disposition and Historical Development of Eretz-Israel According to the Amarna* Letters. (Ph.D. thesis). Tel Aviv University (Hebrew with English abstract).

Na'aman, N. 1980. The Inheritance of the Sons of Simeon. *ZDPV* 96: 136–152.

Na'aman, N. 1981. Economic Aspects of the Egyptian Occupation of Canaan. *IEJ* 31: 172–185.

Na'aman, N. 1982. Eretz Israel in the Canaanite Period: The Middle and Late Bronze Ages. In: Eph'al, I. ed. *The History of Eretz Israel Vol. I, Introductions: Early Periods.* Jerusalem: 129–256 (Hebrew).

Na'aman, N. 1984. Ephraim, Ephrath and the Settlement in the Judean Hill Country. *Zion* 49: 325–331 (Hebrew).

Na'aman, N. 1985. Bethel and Beth-aven: An Investigation into the Location of the Early Israelite Cult Places. *Zion* 50: 15–25 (Hebrew).

Na'aman, N. 1986. Migdal-Shechem and the House of El-berith. *Zion* 51: 259–280 (Hebrew).

Naroll, R. 1962. Floor Area and Settlement Population. *American Antiquity* 27 (4): 587–589.

Naveh, J. 1978. Some Considerations on the Ostracon from 'Izbet Ṣarṭah. *IEJ* 28: 31–35.

Nielsen, H. *Shechem, A Traditio-Historical Investigation.* Copenhagen.

Nijst, A.L.M.T. a.o. 1973. *Living on the Edge of the Sahara.* The Hague.

Noth, M. 1935. Bethel und Ai. *PJb 34:* 7–29.

Noth, M. 1938. Grundsätzliches zur geschichtlichen Deutung archäologischer Befunde auf dem Boden Palästinas. *PJb* 37: 7–22.

Noth, M. 1953. *Das Buch Josua.* Tübingen.

Noth, M. 1957. Hat die Bibel doch recht? In: Schneemelcher, W. ed. *Festschrift für G. Dehn.* Neukirchen: 7–22.

Noth, M. 1958. *The History of Israel.* London.

Noth, M. 1960. Der Beitrag der Archäologie zur Geschichte Israels. *Supplements to Vetus Testamentum* VII: 262–282.

Oded, B. 1972. Zeredah. *Enc. Miqr.* 6: 765–768.

Ohata, K. 1966. *Tel Zeror I.* Tokyo.

Olavarri, E. 1965. Sondages a 'Arô'er sur l'Arnon. *RB* 72: 77–94.

von Oppenheim, M.F. 1943. *Die Beduinen, II.* Leipzig.

Oren, E.D. 1978. esh-Shar'ia Tell (Tel Sera'). *Enc. Arch. Exc. IV;* 1059–1069.

Oren, E.D. and Morrison, M.A. 1986. Land of Gerar Expedition: Preliminary Report for the Seasons of 1982 and 1983. *BASOR Supplement* No. 24: 57–75.

Orlinsky, H. 1962. *The Tribal System of Israel and Related Groups in the Period of the Judges, Studies and Essays in Honor of Abraham A. Newman.* Jerusalem.

Owen, D. 1981. An Akhadian Letter from Ugarit at Tel Aphek. *Tel Aviv* 8: 1–17.

Patai, R. 1958. *The Kingdom of Jordan.* Princeton.

Pearce, R.A. 1973. Shiloh and Jer. VII 12, 14 and 15. *VT* 23: 105–108.

Perevolotsky, A. and Perevolotsky, A. 1979. *Subsistence Patterns of the Jebeliya Bedouins in the High Mountain Region of Southern Sinai.* The Society for the Protection of Nature in Israel, Tel Aviv (Hebrew).

Petrie, F. 1906. *Researches in Sinai.* London.

Petrie, F. 1928. *Gerar.* London.

Porath, Y. 1968. *Inventory of Sites, Samaria Survey II.* (Unpublished report in files of the Department of Antiquities). Jerusalem (Hebrew).

Porath, Y., Dar, S. and Applebaum, S. 1985. *The History and Archaeology of Emek-Hefer.* Tel Aviv (Hebrew).

Prag, K. 1985. Ancient and Modern Pastoral Migration in the Levant. *Levant* 17: 81–88.

Pritchard, J.B. 1962. *Gibeon; Where the Sun Stood Still.* Philadelphia.

Pritchard, J.B. 1963. *The Bronze Age Cemetery at Gibeon.* Philadelhpia.

Pritchard, J.B. 1964. *Winery, Defences and Soundings at Gibeon.* Philadelphia.

Pritchard, J.B. 1980. *The Cemetery at Tell es-Saidiyeh.* Philadelphia.

Rast, W.E. 1978. *Taanach I, Studies in the Iron Age Pottery.* Cambridge.

Raswan, C.R. 1934. *Im Lande der schwarzen Zelte.* Berlin.

Redford, D.B. 1979. A Gate Inscription from Karnak and Egyptian Involvement in Western Asia during the Early 18th Dynasty. *Journal of the American Oriental Society* 99: 270–287.

Redford, D.B. 1986. The Ashkelon Relief at Karnak and the Israel Stela. *IEJ* §¡: 188–200.

Richardson, N.H. 1968. A Stamped Handle from Khirbet Yarmuk. *BASOR* 192: 12–16.

Ripinsky, M. 1985. The Camel in Dynastic Egypt. *JEA* 71: 134–141.

Robinson, E. 1891. *Biblical Researches in Palestine Vol. III.* London.

Rosen, B. 1986. Subsistence Economy of Stratum II. In: Finkelstein, I. *'Izbet Sartah An Early Iron Age Site Near Rosh Ha'ayin, Israel* (B.A.R. 299): 156–185.

Rosenan, N. 1978. A Note on the Water Storage and Size of Population. In: Armiran, R. *et al. Early Arad I.* Jerusalem: 14.

Ross, J.F. 1963. The Excavation of Shechem and the Biblical Tradition. *BA* 26: 2–27.

Rowton, M.B. 1965. The Topological Factor of the Hapiru Problem. *Anatolian Studies* 16: 375–387.

Rowton, M. 1967a. The Physical Environment and the Problem of the Nomads. In: Kupper, J.R. ed. *La Civilisation de Mari. XV⁰ Recontre Assyriologique Internationale.* Paris: 109–121.

Rowton, M.B. 1967b. The Woodlands of Ancient Western Asia. *JNES* 26: 261–277.

Rowton, M.B. 1973a. Urban Autonomy in a Nomadic Environment. *JNES* 32: 201–215.

Rowton, M.B. 1973b. Autonomy and Nomadism in Western Asia. *Orientalia* 42: 247–258.

Rowton, M. 1974. Enclosed Nomadism. *Journal of the Economy and Social History of the Orient* XVII: 1–30.

Rowton, M.B. 1976. Dimorphic Structure and Topology. *Oriens Antiquus* XV: 17–31.

Salzman, Ph.C. 1980. ed. *When Nomads Settle.* New York.

Sauer, J.A. 1982. Prospects for Archaeology in Jordan and Syria. *BA* 45: 73–84.

Sauer, J.A. 1986. Transjordan in the Bronze and Iron Ages: A Critique of Glueck's Synthesis. *BASOR* 263: 1–26.

Schmelz, U.O. 1977. Population Changes in Judea and Samaria: Analysis of their Demographic Determinants. In: Shmueli, A., Grossman, D. and Zeevy, R. eds. *Judea and Samaria;* 81–92 (Hebrew).

Schoors, A. 1985. The Israelite Conquest: Textual Evidence in the Archaeological Argument. In: Lipinski, E. ed. *The Land of Israel: Cross-roads of Civilizations:* 77–92.

Seger, J.D. 1983. Investigations at Tell Halif, Israel, 1976–1980. *BASOR* 252: 1–24.

Seligman, N. a.o. 1959. *Natural Pasture of Israel.* Tel Aviv (Hebrew).

Sellers, O.R. 1933. *The Citadel of Beth-Zur.* Philadelphia.

Sellers, O.R. and Albright, W.F. 1931. The First Campaign of Excavation of Beth-Zur. *BASOR* 43: 2–13.

Sellers, O.R. a.o. 1968. The 1957 Excavations at Beth-Zur. *AASOR* 38.

Sellin, E. 1904. *Tell Ta'anach I.* Wien.

Shalem, N. 1968. *The Desert of Juda.* Jerusalem (Hebrew).

Shea, W.H. 1979. The Conquest of Sharuhen and Megiddo Reconsidered. *IEJ* 29: 1–5.

Shiloh, Y. 1970. The Four Room House — Its Situation and Function in the Israelite City. *IEJ* 20: 180–190.

Shiloh, Y. 1971. Reviews: Buhl, M.L. and Holm-Nielsen, S. Shiloh. *IEJ* 21: 67–69.

Shiloh, Y. 1973. The Camp at Shiloh. In: Aviram, J. administrative ed. *Eretz Shomron.* Jerusalem: 10–18 (Hebrew).

Shiloh, Y. 1978. Elements in the Development of Town Planning in the Israelite City. *IEJ* 28: 36–51.

Shiloh, Y. 1980. The Population of Iron Age Palestine in the Light of a Sample Analysis of Urban Plans, Areas, and Population Density. *BASOR* 239: 25–35.

Shimeoni, Y. 1947. *The Arabs of Eretz Israel.* Tel Aviv (Hebrew).

Shmueli, A. 1973. *The Sedentarization of Nomads in the Vicinity of Jerusalem in the 20th Century.* (Ph.D. thesis). Jerusalem, The Hebrew University (Hebrew with English abstract).

Shmueli, A. 1980. *Nomadism about to Cease.* Tel Aviv (Hebrew).

Sinclair, L.A. 1960. An Archaeological Study of Gibeah (Tell el-Fûl). *AASOR* 34–35: 1–52.

Singer, I. 1983. Takuḫlinu and Ḥaya: Two Governors in the Ugarit Letter from Tel Aphek. *Tel Aviv* 10: 3–25.

Sochin, A. 1879. Alphabetisches Verzeichniss von Ortschaften des Paschalik Jerusalem. *ZDPV* 2: 135–163.

Soggin, J.A. 1975. *Old Testament and Oriental Studies.* Rome.

Spooner, B. 1972. The Iranian Deserts. In: Spooner, B. ed. *Population Growth; Anthropological Implications.* Cambridge Mass.: 245–268.

Stager, L. 1982. The Archaeology of the East Slope of Jerusalem and the Terraces of the Kidron. *JNES* 41: 111–121.

Stager, L.E. 1985a. Merenptah, Israel and Sea Peoples: New Light on an Old Relief. *Eretz-Israel.* 18: 56*–64*.

Stager, L.E. 1985b. The Archaeology of the Family in Ancient Israel. *BASOR* 260: 1–35.

Stern, E. 1978. *Excavations at Tel Mevorakh Part One; From the Iron Age to the Roman Period* (Qedem 9). Jerusalem.

Stern, E. 1984. *Excavations at Tel Mevorakh Part Two; The Bronze Age* (Qedem 18). Jerusalem.

Stern, E. and Beit Arieh, I. 1979. Excavations at Tel Kedesh (Tell Abu Qudeis). *Tel Aviv* 6: 1–25.

Sweet, L.E. 1974. *Tell Toqaan: A Syrian Village.* Ann Arbor.

Talbot Rice, T. 1961. *The Seljuks in Asia Minor.* New York.

Thompson, A.D. 1972. The 1972 Excavations of Khirbet el-Hajjar. *ADAJ* 17: 47–72.

Thompson, T.L. 1978. Historical Notes on "Israel's Conquest of Palestine: A Peasants' Rebellion?" *JSOT* 7: 20–27.

Thompson, T.L. 1979. *The Settlement of Palestine in the Bronze Age.* Wiesbaden.

Thomsen, P. 1907. *Loca Sancta.* Leipzig.

Toombs, L.E. 1979. Shechem: Problems of the Early Israelite Era. In: Cross, F.M. ed. *Symposia*

Celebrating the Seventy-Fifth Anniversary of the Foundation of the American Schools of Oriental Research (1900–1975). Cambridge: 69–83.

Tufnell, O. 1958. *Lachish IV, The Bronze Age.* London, New York, Toronto.

Tufnell, O. 1961. Reviews and Notices: Hazor II. *PEQ* 93: 154–158.

Tushingham, A.D. 1972. The Excavations at Dibon (Dhiban) in Moab. *AASOR* 40.

Ussishkin, D. 1975. Dothan. *Enc. Arch. Exc. I;* 337–339.

Ussishkin, D. 1983. Excavations at Tel Lachish 1978–1983: Second Preliminary Report. *Tel Aviv* 10: 97–175.

Ussishkin, D. 1985. Levels VII and VI at Tel Lachish and the End of the Late Bronze Age in Canaan. In: Tubb, J.N. ed. *Palestine in the Bronze and Iron Ages, Papers in Honour of Olga Tufnell.* London: 213–228.

Ussishkin, D. 1987. Lachish — Key to the Israelite Conquest of Canaan? *BAR* 13(1): 18–39.

de Vaux, R. 1955. Les fouilles de Tell el-Farʿah près Naplouse. *RB* 62: 541–589.

de Vaux, R. 1961. *Ancient Israel Its Life and Institutions.* London.

de Vaux, R. 1978. *The Early History of Israel.* Philadelphia.

Vikander-Edelman, D. 1986. *The Rise of the Israelite State under Saul* (Ph.D. thesis). The University of Chicago.

Waisel, Y. a.o. 1982. *The Ecology of Vegetation of Israel.* Tel Aviv (Hebrew).

Waldbaum, J.C. 1978. *From Bronze to Iron* (Studies in Mediterranean Archaeology 54). Göteborg.

Wampler, J.C. 1947. *Tell en-Nasbeh II, The Pottery.* Berkeley and New Haven.

Weinstein, J.M. 1981. The Egyptian Empire in Palestine: A Reassessment. *BASOR* 241: 1–28.

Weippert, M. 1971. *The Settlement of the Israelite Tribes in Palestine.* London.

Weippert, M. 1976. Canaan, Conquest and Settlement of. *The Interpreter's Dictionary of the Bible. Supp. Vol.* Nashville: 125–130.

Weippert, M. 1979. The Israelite "Conquest" and the Evidence from Transjordan. In: Cross, F.M. ed. *Symposia Celebrating the Seventy-Fifth Anniversary of the Foundation of the American Schools of Oriental Research (1900–1975).* Cambridge: 15–34.

Weippert, M. 1982. Remarks on the History of Settlement in Southern Jordan during the Early Iron Age. In: Hadidi, A. ed. *Studies in the History and Archaeology of Jordan I.* Amman.

Weippert, H. and Weippert, M. 1976. Jericho in der Eisenzeit. *ZDPV* 92: 105–148.

Weir, Sh. 1976. *The Bedouin.* London.

Weisman, Z. 1984. The Period of the Judges in Biblical Historiography.In: Ephʿal, I. ed. *The History of Eretz Israel Vol. 2, Israel and Judah in the Biblical Period.* Jerusalem: 85–97 (Hebrew).

Wente, E.F. and Van Siclen, C.C. 1976. A Chronology of the New Kingdom. In: Johnson, J.H. and Wente, E.F. eds. *Studies in Honor of George R. Hughes* (Studies in Ancient Oriental Civilization 39). Chicago: 217–261.

Wilson, C.W. 1873. Jerusalem. *PEFQSt;* 36–38.

Woudstra, M.H. 1965. *The Ark of the Covenant from Conquest to Kingship.* Philadelphia.

Wright, G.E. 1940. Epic of Conquest. *BA* 3: 25–40.

Wright, G.E. 1962. *Biblical Archaeology.* London.

Wright, G.E. 1965. *Shechem, The Biography of a Biblical City.* New York.

Wright, G.E. 1975. Beth-Shemesh. *Enc. Arch. Exc.* I: 248–253.

Wright, G.R.H. 1985. *Ancient Building in South Syria and Palestine.* Leiden — Köln.

Yadin, Y. *et al.* 1958. *Hazor I.* Jerusalem.

Yadin, Y. *et al.* 1961. *Hazor III-IV.* Jerusalem.

Yadin, Y. 1970. The Megiddo of the Kings of Israel. *Qadmoniot* 3: 38–56 (Hebrew).

Yadin, Y. 1972. *Hazor* (The Schweich Lectures of the British Academy 1970). London.

Yadin, Y. 1979. The Transition from a Semi-Nomadic to a Sedentary Society in the Twelfth Century BCE. In: Cross, F.M. ed. *Symposia Celebrating the Seventy-Fifth Anniversary of the*

Foundation of the American Schools of Oriental Research (1900–1975). Cambridge: 57–68.

Yadin, Y. 1982. Is the Biblical Account of the Israelite Conquest of Canaan Historically Reliable? *BAR* 7: 16–23.

Yeivin, S. 1971a. *The Israelite Conquest of Canaan*. Istanbul.

Yeivin, S. 1971b. The Benjaminite Settlement in the Western Part of their Territory. *IEJ* 21: 141–154.

Yeivin, S. 1971c. Ai. *Enc. Miqr.* 6: 169–182.

Zarins, J. 1978. The Camel in Ancient Arabia: a Future Note. *Antiquity* 52: 44–46.

Zertal, A. 1980. *Arubboth, Hepher and the Third Solomonic District*. (M.A. thesis). Tel Aviv University (Hebrew with English summary).

Zertal, A. 1985a. The Water-Supply Factor in the Israelite Settlement in Manasseh. In: *Settlements, Population and Economy in Ancient Israel — The Annual Memorial Day for Y. Aharoni, Abstracts of Lectures*. Tel Aviv: 5–6 (Hebrew).

Zertal, A. 1985b. The Cult Site on Mt. Ebal. *Bamaḥane* 23: 25–32 (Hebrew).

Zertal, A. 1985c. Has Joshua's Altar been Found on Mt. Ebal? *BAR* 11 (1): 26–43.

Zertal, A. 1986a. How Can Kempinski Be So Wrong? *BAR* 12 (1): 43, 49–53.

Zertal, A. 1986b. *The Israelite Settlement in the Hill Country of Manasseh* (Ph.D. thesis). Tel Aviv University (Hebrew with English abstract).

Zeuner, F.E. 1963. *A History of Domesticated Animals*. London.

Zevit, Z. 1983. Archaeological and Literary Stratigraphy in Joshua 7–8. *BASOR* 251: 23–35.

Zimhoni, O. 1985. The Iron Age Pottery of Tel ʿEton and its Relation to the Lachish, Tell Beit Mirsim and Arad Assemblages. *Tel Aviv* 12: 63–90.

Zohari, M. 1959. *Geobotany*. Tel Aviv (Hebrew).

Zori, N. 1962. An Archaeological Survey of the Beth-Shean Valley. In: *The Beth Shean Valley*. Israel Exploration Society. Jerusalem (Hebrew).

Zori, N. 1977. *The Land of Issachar Archaeological Survey*. Jerusalem (Hebrew).

INDEX